# SEAWATER AQUARIUMS

# SEAWATER AQUARIUMS
## *The Captive Environment*

**STEPHEN SPOTTE**

**Vice President, Sea Research Foundation, Inc.**
**Director, Mystic Marinelife Aquarium**
**Mystic, Connecticut**

**A WILEY-INTERSCIENCE PUBLICATION**

**JOHN WILEY & SONS**

New York • Chichester • Brisbane • Toronto

**Library of Congress Cataloging in Publication Data**

Spotte, Stephen
  Seawater aquariums.

  "A Wiley-Interscience publication."
  Bibliography: p.
  Includes index.
  1.  Marine aquariums.   I.   Title.

  SF457.1.S67      639'.34      79-11038
  ISBN 0-471-05665-0

Printed in the United States of America

10 9 8 7 6 5 4 3 2 1

To
Bill Kelley
teacher and friend

We shall not cease from exploration
And the end of all our exploring
Will be to arrive where we started
And know the place for the first time.

T. S. Eliot, *Four Quartets*

# *Preface*

The successful maintenance of a seawater aquarium is mostly witch-craft mixed with a little science. In this book I have attempted to describe the science, but with the realization that understanding the witchcraft might be more useful. The writing was often difficult be-cause of the shadowy nature of the subject: aquariology exists as a parasite on the main body of science and is not a science itself. Other more specialized disciplines comprise the buttresses and supporting structures that shore up what little we know about how aquatic animals and plants live in captive environments. Most notable of these fields are seawater chemistry, engineering, and physiology, and accomplished aquarists must have at least a primitive understanding of all of them.

Between aquarists and specialists in these other fields is a chasm that has never been spanned. The purpose of this book is to bring the findings of the specialists into the realm of aquariology. I consider the attempt to be a footbridge across the chasm and nothing more. My bridge is narrow, quakes in places, and is sometimes difficult to traverse, but it is a bridge nonetheless. To build it, I set out on a personal odyssey through the vast hinterlands of science in search of information that might benefit my colleagues. After assembling what I found, it was clear that much of what aquarists knew already would have to be taken for granted and not restated. I chose not to define many biological terms, assuming that competent aquarists would know what they meant or be able to find definitions easily. I also assumed that even expert aquarists may have only a tenuous grounding in the basics of chemistry, engineering, and physiology. To bridge the dichotomy between the practical and the theoretical, I chose to include some elementary background material as a prelude to the presentation of more complex information. In some cases, information pertinent to one chapter occurs elsewhere in the text. For example, the basic functions of ionic and osmotic regulation are presented in Chapter 3 in the discussion of water and salt balance. The same material is helpful in understanding how ammonia is transported across gills of aquatic animals, although the latter subject is not discussed until Chapter 11. The organization of the book and choice of subject matter will not appeal to scholars and other specialists, who may find some of the discussions too thin, disjointed, and incomplete for their liking, and too unbalanced overall. I offer no apologies, because scholars are not the intended audience.

My investigations into the subject matter are personal and certainly not the last word. Many authors have written on the same themes, and others will doubtless write more. The techniques offered are based on my own experience in the public aquarium profession; as such, they should be useful to other public aquarists and to researchers and technicians maintaining collections of animals and plants in marine laboratories. The book is not oriented to aquaculturists, although some of the information may be applicable in certain situations. Aquaculturists are confronted with environmental control problems that differ from those seen by aquarists. Animal and plant densities ordinarily are much higher in hatcheries and aquacultural grow-out facilities, and fewer species are maintained, which may exacerbate the spread of transmissible, host-specific diseases.

The maintenance of aquatic animals and plants involves three areas of interest: (1) control of water quality factors that affect the physiology of the organisms; (2) disease control; and (3) nutrition. I shall deal only with the first. My thesis will be that aquatic organisms alter the water in which they live, and their well-being is in turn reflected by the extent and nature of the changes. The subject also has been limited to closed-system aquariums, in which the water is filtered and otherwise treated, then reused. In semi-closed and open systems part or all of the water is replaced in a given period of time with new water that is supplied continuously. In semi-closed systems, the water ordinarily is filtered and recycled and the volume of replacement water is small. Open systems usually are not filtered, and all of the influent water is eventually flushed to waste and replaced on a continuous basis. Mastery of closed systems is the most difficult, because there is no dilution factor to lower the level of toxic metabolites, or to replenish trace elements that are essential for the growth of plants.

The lengthy treatment of some subjects may seem unwarranted to readers who are not aquarists. Bacteriological filtration was considered in detail, for example, because it may be the single most important biochemical process occurring in closed-system aquariums. To leave out many of the small nuances would not do justice to the subject. Considerable space also has been devoted to the workings of ultraviolet sterilizers and ozonators, in part because they are poorly understood by many aquarists, and also because a certain mythology has evolved concerning the efficacy of sterilization that needs to be put into perspective. Techniques for processing large volumes of influent seawater are discussed in detail only because there is so little practical information available on how to engineer large filter systems. Ammonia excretion is considered in depth because of its importance to aquarists and because it seems to be widely misunderstood.

STEPHEN SPOTTE

*Mystic, Connecticut*
*April 1979*

# Acknowledgments

The following people read parts of the manuscript and offered many valuable criticisms and suggestions: Gary Adams, Department of Mathematics and Physics, Thames Valley State Technical College, Norwich, CT; James W. Atz, Department of Ichthyology, American Museum of Natural History, New York City; Carol E. Bower, Institute for Aquarium Studies, Hartford, CT; James N. Cameron, Marine Science Institute, The University of Texas, Port Aransas, TX; Pierre Dejours, Laboratoire de Physiologie Respiratoire, Strasbourg, France; Lee C. Eagleton, Department of Chemical Engineering, The Pennsylvania State University, University Park, PA; Shaukat Farooq, Department of Environmental Engineering, University of Miami, Coral Gables, FL; Glenn L. Hoffman, U. S. Fish and Wildlife Service, Fish Farming Experimental Station, Stuttgart, AR; Barbara J. Howell, Department of Physiology, State University of New York at Buffalo, Buffalo, NY; William E. Kelley, Aquarium Systems, Inc., Mentor, OH; Charlotte P. Mangum, Department of Biology, College of William and Mary, Williamsburg, VA; David Miller, Skidaway Institute of Oceanography, Savannah, GA; and George Tchobanoglous, Department of Civil Engineering, University of California at Davis, Davis, CA. Laura E. Kezer of Mystic Marinelife Aquarium, Mystic, CT, assisted in organizing the bibliography, and Paul Gaj of the same institution prepared the majority of illustrations, either from the previously published work of others or from crude sketches supplied by me. The final draft of the manuscript was typed by Anne Barrière.

Others helped generously by correspondence, notably Tom Almgren, Oceanografiska Instituionen, Göteborg Universitet, Göteborg, Sweden; Walter E. Castro, College of Engineering, Clemson University, Clemson, SC; F. B. Eddy, The University of Dundee, Dundee, Scotland; and David Randall, Department of Zoology, The University of British Columbia, Vancouver, Canada. I am indebted to Robert A. Berner, Department of Geology and Geophysics, Yale University, New Haven, CT, G. L. Bullock, U. S. Fish and Wildlife Service, National Fisheries Center—Leetown, Kearneysville, WV, Susumu Kawamura, James M. Montgomery, Inc., Pasadena, CA, and Paul W. Johnson and John M. Sieburth, Graduate School of Oceanography, University of Rhode Island, Kingston, RI, for supplying illustrations from some of their own published work.

Richard J. Benoit, EcoScience Laboratory, Norwich, CT, provided me with many useful ideas. Hermann Rahn, R. Blake Reeves, and Barbara Howell, Department of Physiology, State University of New York at Buffalo, Buffalo, NY, allowed me to sit in on a round-table discussion on acid-base balance in aquatic ectothermic animals. Peter Weyl, Iver Duedall, William Reeburgh, Peter Woodhead, and Orville Terry, Marine Sciences Research Center, State University of New York at Stony Brook, Stony Brook, NY, allowed me to listen in on a round-table discussion on carbonate buffering in the sea, and provided many criticisms and suggestions on my proposed approach to this problem as it affects aquarium seawater.

Finally, I would like to acknowledge the assistance of the library staff of the Marine Biological Laboratory, Woods Hole, MA, for its diligence in tracking down several obscure references.

S.S

# Credits

*Epigraph:* From "Little Gidding" in *Four Quartets* by T. S. Eliot, copyright 1943 by T. S. Eliot, copyright 1971 by Esme Valerie Eliot. Reprinted by permission of Harcourt Brace Jovanovich, Inc. *Figs. 2-1, 2-3, 2-6:* From "Photosynthesis" by G. E. Fogg. Modified and reproduced with permission of Hodder & Stoughton, Ltd. *Figs. 2-2, 2-4:* From "Principles of Plant Physiology" by James Bonner and Arthur W. Galston. W. H. Freeman and Company. Copyright © 1952. *Table 2-3:* Instrumentation Specialties Company, Lincoln, NE. *Fig. 3-3:* William A. Anikouchine, Richard W. Sternberg, "The World Ocean: An Introduction to Oceanography," © 1973, p. 75. Reprinted by permission of Prentice-Hall, Inc. Englewood Cliffs, New Jersey. *Tables 3-2, 3-3; Fig. 4-1:* From P. G. Brewer, T. R. S. Wilson, and D. R. Kester in "Chemical Oceanography," 2nd edition, Vol. 1, J. P. Riley and G. Skirrow (eds.). Copyright by Academic Press Inc. (London) Ltd. *Figs. 3-1, 7-1:* Thomas D. Brock, "Biology of Microorganisms," © 1970. Adapted by permission of Prentice-Hall, Inc., Englewood Cliffs, New Jersey. *Figs. 3-6, 3-7, 4-3, 4-4, 4-6, 5-1, 5-4, 5-5, 5-6, 6-5, 7-8, 8-11, 8-14, 8-15, 8-16, 8-17, 8-19, 8-20, 9-7, 9-8, 9-9, 10-2, 10-3, 10-4; Tables 3-10, 4-1, 7-1, 7-4, 10-1, 11-1, 12-3:* Reproduced with permission of John Wiley & Sons. *Tables 3-4, 3-5:* From J. McLachlan in "Handbook of Phycological Methods," J. R. Stein (ed.). Copyright by Cambridge University Press. *Figs. 4-2, 4-7:* Modified and reproduced with permission of Biologische Anstalt from *Meersforch.* and *Helgoländer Wiss. Meeresunters. Figs. 5-7, 5-9, 6-3, 10-6, 10-8, 10-9; Table 5-3:* Modified and reproduced with permission of

# Contents

# SEAWATER AQUARIUMS

# CHAPTER 1

*Temperature Control*

Temperature control is a critical aspect of good aquarium management, as even slight temperature changes may have harmful effects on the animals being maintained (Section 11.4). Various aspects of temperature, as they affect specific biological, chemical, and physical processes, are covered in other chapters. The purpose here is to explain briefly the mechanics of heating and cooling aquarium seawater, and to offer a method for calculating the amount of heat or refrigeration required under given conditions.

The same equations can be used for calculating the amount of cooling or heating needed in an aquarium. When calculating refrigeration requirements, the factor determined is the capacity of the chilling unit in horsepower (hp). In heated aquariums, wattage of the heater is determined. In either case, heat flow in or out of the aquarium must be computed on the basis of overall heat-transfer coefficients. The heat-transfer coefficients ($U$) for some common construction materials, in addition to the value of $U$ at the water surface, are given in Table 1-1. Heat flow is calculated by multiplying each heat-transfer area ($A$) in cm² by its respective overall heat-transfer coefficient and summing the terms. This answer is multiplied by the overall temperature difference in degrees Centigrade ($\Delta T$). Heat flow ($Q$) in cal sec$^{-1}$ is given by

$$Q = [A_1U_1 + A_2U_2 + \ldots] \Delta T \qquad (1)$$

Convert to Btu hr$^{-1}$ by multiplying the result by 14.3. Dividing by 12,000 converts the answer to tons of refrigeration, which is a close

1

**Table 1-1   Overall Heat-Transfer Coefficients (*U*) for Common Construction Materials**[a]

| Material | Coefficient (cal sec$^{-1}$ cm$^{-2}$ °C$^{-1}$) |
|---|---|
| Single plate glass | $1.60 \times 10^{-4}$ |
| Double glass with air space | $0.70 \times 10^{-4}$ |
| 5 cm concrete (typical wall thickness) | $0.91 \times 10^{-4}$ |
| 15 cm concrete (typical wall thickness) | $0.52 \times 10^{-4}$ |
| 1 cm fiberglass-reinforced plastic | $0.52 \times 10^{-4}$ |
| 1 cm fiberglass-reinforced plastic plus 2 cm wet (soaked) plywood | $0.80 \times 10^{-4}$ |
| 2 cm dry plywood (epoxy coated) | $0.80 \times 10^{-4}$ |
| Water surface | $2.30 \times 10^{-4}$ |

[a] The values presented are reasonable for surfaces with gently moving water on one side and gently moving air on the other. They are higher than natural convection coefficients.

approximation of horsepower requirements. In the case of a heated aquarium, the heat flow in Btu hr$^{-1}$ is multiplied by 3.41 to obtain the continuous wattage needed to maintain the desired temperature.

## 1.1   COOLING

The essential features of a vapor compression refrigeration cycle are shown diagrammatically in Fig. 1-1. A typical refrigeration unit consists of a high-pressure side and a low-pressure side. A compressor driven by an electric motor cycles a refrigerant (usually freon, $CCl_2F_2$) throughout the system. The freon changes states from liquid to gas and back again under varying pressure. In doing so, heat is removed from the aquarium water at the evaporator and dissipated into the room at the condenser.

A typical vapor compression refrigeration cycle will now be traced starting at the expansion valve (Fig. 1-1). The expansion valve is the transition point between the high-pressure and the low-pressure sides of the system. As liquid refrigerant leaves the expansion valve and enters the evaporator coils immersed in the water, some of it changes instantly into gas, because of the reduced pressure. In the process it removes heat from the remaining liquid refrigerant. The liquid (now cold) absorbs heat from the aquarium water circulating past the outside

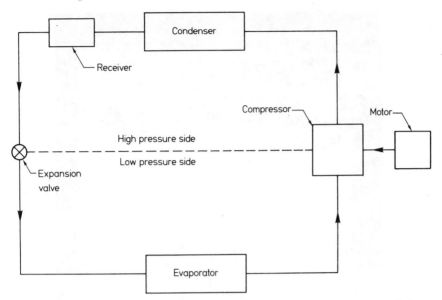

**Figure 1-1.**   Equipment diagram for a basic vapor compression refrigeration cycle (various sources).

of the evaporator coils. As the cold liquid refrigerant gains heat it changes to a cold gas.

The cold gas refrigerant flows from the evaporator coils to the compressor and enters the high-pressure side of the system. At the compressor, it is compressed to a high pressure and temperature. The temperature of the gas in the refrigeration system is now higher than the temperature of the room air. Hot gas leaves the compressor and enters the condenser, where its heat is absorbed by the cooler air in the room. As heat is lost, the gas condenses to a hot liquid and passes to the receiver. The receiver stores the hot liquid refrigerant until it can be cycled through the expansion valve and metered again into the evaporator coils to continue the cycle.

In seawater aquarium applications, the evaporator coils, which are copper, must be coated to protect the animals and plants from copper poisoning. Ordinarily they are coated with vinyl, polypropylene, neoprene, or epoxy. The evaporator coils can be placed in the water system anywhere adequate circulation is available to augment heat exchange. One method is to place the coils underneath the filter plate of the bacteriological filter so that all water is cooled as it leaves the filter and before it is returned to the surface of the aquarium by airlift pumping.

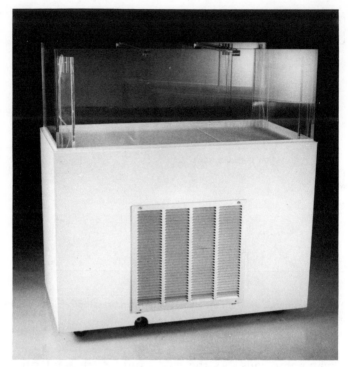

**Figure 1-2.** A refrigerated seawater aquarium with the evaporator coils installed under-neath the bacteriological filter (Aquarium Systems, Inc.).

The circular pattern inherent in such an arrangement provides stable temperatures throughout the water column. One commercially avail-able unit that utilizes this principle, manufactured by Aquarium Sys-tems, Inc.,* is shown in Fig. 1-2.

Another approach is to put the evaporator coils inside a box adjacent to the aquarium tank, as shown in Fig. 1-3. Heat exchange takes place inside the box and cooled water can be returned to the aquarium by airlift or mechanical pumping.

Still another way is simply to lower the evaporator coils into the aquarium and establish a flow pattern with airlift pumps or air diffus-ers. This technique works well in emergencies, or when it is not neces-sary to maintain cold-water organisms under display conditions. A unit designed to be portable is shown in Fig. 1-4.

Refrigeration requirements can be calculated by the following exam-

* Aquarium Systems, Inc., 8141 Tyler Blvd., Mentor, OH 44060.

**Figure 1-3.** Chiller boxes can be placed adjacent to individual aquariums. Water enters a chiller box by gravity, is refrigerated, and returned to the aquarium by airlift or mechanical pumping (Aquarium of Niagara Falls).

ple. An aquarium tank made of concrete with double glass (two panes of glass separated by an air space or vacuum) is shown in Fig. 1-5. It has an overall $\Delta T$ requirement of 11°C; that is, refrigeration temperature will be 11°C below ambient. The problem is to compute the horsepower needed to chill the water.

According to the dimensions given in the figure, heat transfer will occur at the places indicated in Table 1-1. The dimensions of each location, the material from which the aquarium is made, and values for $U$ and $AU$ are given in Table 1-2. Thus

$$Q = (\Sigma AU) \, \Delta T = 17.9 \times 11$$
$$= 197 \text{ cal sec}^{-1}$$

If the values for $AU$ were not known, to use equation 1,

$$Q = [1.8(0.52) + 3(0.52) + 1.9(0.52) + 5.4(0.52)$$
$$+ 4.7(2.3) + 1.13(0.70)] \, 11$$
$$= 197 \text{ cal sec}^{-1}$$

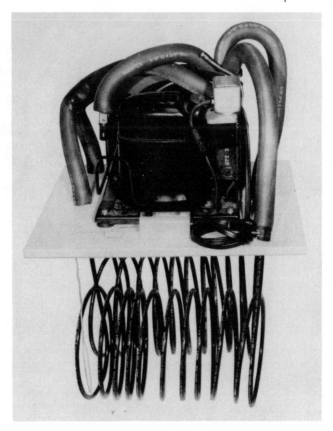

**Figure 1-4.**  Portable refrigeration unit (Aquarium Systems, Inc.).

To convert to Btu hr$^{-1}$,

$$197 \text{ cal sec}^{-1}\left(\frac{1 \text{ kg cal}^{-1}}{1000 \text{ cal}}\right)\left(\frac{3.97 \text{ Btu}}{1 \text{ kg cal}^{-1}}\right)\left(\frac{3600 \text{ sec}}{1 \text{ hr}}\right)$$

$$= 2813 \text{ Btu hr}^{-1} \text{ and}$$

$$\text{hp} = 2813 \text{ Btu hr}^{-1}\left(\frac{1 \text{ hp}}{12,000 \text{ Btu hr}^{-1}}\right)$$

$$= 0.23 \text{ hp}$$

Therefore a $\frac{1}{4}$-hp unit would suffice.

Various methods of refrigerating aquarium water were discussed by Gallagher (1967), McGregor (1973), Neyfert (1969), O'Neill (1968), and Robinson et al. (1978).

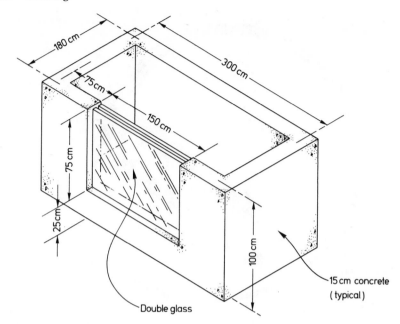

**Figure 1-5.** Aquarium tank made of concrete and containing double glass (see sample refrigeration and heating problems in text).

## 1.2 HEATING

Several writers have offered designs for heating large volumes of seawater (e.g., Barnabe 1974, Braren and Zahradnik 1974, Huguenin 1976, Tenore and Huguenin 1973). The work of Huguenin (1976) is particularly useful, because the author reviewed the different types of devices

**Table 1-2   Locations Where Heat Transfer Will Take Place in the Aquarium Tank Illustrated in Fig. 1-5**

| Location | $A$ (cm$^2$) | Material | $U$ (cal sec$^{-1}$ cm$^{-2}$ °C$^{-1}$) | $A \times U$ |
|---|---|---|---|---|
| Ends | $1.80 \times 10^4$ | 15 cm concrete | $0.52 \times 10^{-4}$ | 0.94 |
| Back | $3.00 \times 10^4$ | 15 cm concrete | $0.52 \times 10^{-4}$ | 1.56 |
| Front | $1.88 \times 10^4$ | 15 cm concrete | $0.52 \times 10^{-4}$ | 0.98 |
| Bottom | $5.40 \times 10^4$ | 15 cm concrete | $0.52 \times 10^{-4}$ | 2.80 |
| Glass | $1.13 \times 10^4$ | double glass with air space | $0.70 \times 10^{-4}$ | 0.79 |
| Water surface | $4.70 \times 10^4$ | — | $2.30 \times 10^{-4}$ | 10.81 |

**Figure 1-6.** Quartz heater manufactured by Glo-Quartz Electric Heater Company of California, Inc. (Mystic Marinelife Aquarium).

that are available. Nowak (1974) described a solid-state temperature controller for both heating and cooling water.

The subject here is limited to heating seawater with immersion heaters. The immersible portion of the unit can be made of any material that has reasonable heat-transfer properties and is inert in seawater. Common materials are quartz, impervious carbon, Teflon®, and the metals titanium and 316 stainless steel. Immersion heaters must be grounded properly or they are potential safety hazards, particularly the larger units that require more than 120 volts for normal operation. In addition, no immersion heater should be operated without a thermostat to control temperature.

The best designed and most reliable immersion heaters are those manufactured for the chemical industry. Glo-Quartz Electric Heater Company of California, Inc.* makes sturdy, safe, and reliable units that work well in seawater. An example is shown in Fig. 1-6. Glo-Quartz heaters are available in sizes up to 36,000 watts (480 volts) in stainless steel or titanium; smaller quartz heaters are also available from this company.

* Glow-Quartz Electric Heater Company of California, Inc., 98 N. San Gabriel Blvd., Pasadena, CA 91107.

If the aquarium used in the previous example is to be heated and maintained at 4°C above ambient, the wattage requirement can be found by

$$Q = [1.8(0.52) + 3(0.52) + 1.9(0.52) + 5.4(0.52)$$
$$+ 4.7(2.3) + 1.13(0.70)] \, 4$$
$$= 71.6 \text{ cal sec}^{-1}$$

$$71.6 \text{ cal sec}^{-1} \left( \frac{14.3 \text{ Btu hr}^{-1}}{1 \text{ cal sec}^{-1}} \right) = 1023 \text{ Btu hr}^{-1} \text{ heat flow}$$

$$1023 \text{ Btu hr}^{-1} \left( \frac{3.41 \text{ watts}}{1 \text{ Btu hr}^{-1}} \right) = 3490 \text{ watts}$$

# CHAPTER 2
## *Light and Algal Growth*

M any factors affect the photosynthesis and growth of aquatic plants, including spectral intensity and distribution of light, diel periodicity (photoperiod), $CO_2$ concentration, light penetration, and temperature. This chapter describes briefly the major groups of macroalgae in terms of their photosynthetic requirements. The term *macroalgae,* as used here, refers to the seaweeds, which are mostly multicellular and benthic (attached). *Microalgae* denotes the unicellular forms, which are usually planktonic (free-floating). Macroalgae often are cultured in aquariums to remove toxic metabolic products added by the animals (Sections 7-3 and 7-4). In addition, I present lighting specifications for the different classes of macroalgae, explain how to calculate the number of lamps needed to culture them, and offer some practical recommendations on the selection and use of lamps.

### 2.1  LIGHT PENETRATION

The extent to which light penetrates water depends partly on the amount of particulate and dissolved organic matter present in the water column. If these substances are uniformly distributed, light intensity decreases with increasing depth in exponential fashion, as illustrated in Fig. 2-1. Some of the light entering an aquarium is scattered or absorbed by the water molecules, but this effect is minor compared with the role played by organic solutes and particulate matter. Inorganic salts have little effect on light transmission in seawater (Morel 1966).

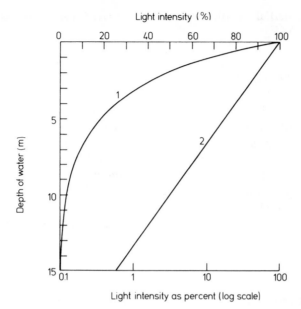

**Figure 2-1.** Change in light intensity with increasing depth of the water. Redrawn from Fogg (1968).

Dissolved organic carbon (DOC) is perhaps the most significant light-altering factor in seawater aquariums, provided that turbidity, and therefore particulate organic carbon (POC) is kept at low levels by mechanical filtration. Some of the "yellow" DOC fraction scatters incoming light, and in so doing imparts a yellowish or greenish cast to the water. In many aquariums, yellow compounds originate mainly from algal growth. More will be said about them in Chapter 6. Yellow compounds absorb some of the light not scattered. When heavily concentrated in the water column, yellow substances may absorb enough light to lower substantially the level of illumination near the bottom of the aquarium. This is particularly troublesome in deep tanks, because with reduced light photosynthesis by algae may be impaired.

The problem of low light penetration can be alleviated by: (1) physical adsorption methods, which remove DOC from the water (Chapter 9); (2) mechanical filtration, which reduces POC (Chapter 8); and (3) culturing macroalgae in shallow trays, preferably so that light has to penetrate only a thin film of water to reach the plants. Algal culture trays in which light must penetrate more than 30.5 cm are not recommended. An arrangement showing an aquarium with exhibit lighting and an attached algal culture tray for photosynthesis is depicted in Fig. 7-13 (p. 163).

## 2.2  THE ALGAE

With few exceptions, all the sea's flora can be placed in the primitive group of plants called algae. The algae are ancient and diverse, and their classification is still controversial. In aquarium work, nomenclature and morphology of the algae are secondary to understanding the nutrient, temperature, and light requirements of the groups being cultured. The taxonomic grouping given as a guide in Table 2-1 follows Chapman (1962). Dawson (1956) provided a concise phylogenetic list of the major genera of the green, brown, and red algae. His work is also an excellent field guide to the common seaweeds.

### Green Algae

The Class Chlorophyceae includes all the green algae. Only about 10% are marine forms. Nevertheless green algae in the sea are common,

**Table 2-1  Classification of the Algae**

|  | Class | Group Common Name | Size | Habitat |
|---|---|---|---|---|
| Euphycophyta | Charophyceae | stoneworts | macro | benthic (brackish) |
|  | Chlorophyceae | green algae | macro/micro | benthic/planktonic |
|  | Phaeophyceae | brown algae | macro | benthic |
|  | Rhodophyceae | red algae | macro | benthic |
| Myxophycophyta[a] | Myxophyceae | blue-green algae | micro | benthic |
| Chrysophycophyta | Chrysophyceae | yellow-brown algae | micro | planktonic |
|  | Xanthophyceae |  |  |  |
|  | Bacillariophyceae | diatoms | micro | planktonic |
| Pyrrophycophyta | Cryptophyceae |  |  |  |
|  | Dinophyceae | dinoflagellates | micro | planktonic |

Source:  Chapman (1962).
[a] Some authorities consider organisms in this group to be bacteria.

widespread, and diverse. The Chlorophyceae are green in color because their pigments are identical with those of higher plants and present in the same proportions. Structurally green algae range from simple unicellular forms to multicellular plants of moderate complexity (the brown and red algae are more complex morphologically). Common multicellular representatives from the temperate zone are *Enteromorpha, Ulva* (sea lettuce), and *Codium*. From the tropics are *Penicillus* (Neptune's shaving brush), *Acetabularia* (Venus cup), and *Caulerpa*. A particularly interesting genus is *Halimeda,* members of which secrete crystals of calcium carbonate.

### Brown Algae

The Class Phaeophyceae comprises the brown algae, so-called because their green chlorophyll is masked by a brown pigment, fucoxanthin. The brown algae are the common kelps and rockweeds of the seashore. Brown algae are almost exclusively marine, and nearly all species are confined to temperate and polar seas. Scarcely any brown macroalgae are tropical. Many of the rockweeds of the intertidal zone—*Fucus,* for example—are left dry at low tide and can tolerate prolonged periods of desiccation. Many rockweeds can also tolerate extreme fluctuations in salinity and temperature. The kelps are sublittoral and less adaptable to changes in their chemical and physical environment. Common rockweeds are members of the genera *Fucus, Pelvetia,* and *Ascophyllum.* The kelps belong mainly to the genera *Macrocystis* and *Laminaria.*

### Red Algae

The red macroalgae comprise the Class Rhodophyceae. Morphologically they are the most complex of all the macroalgae. Their reddish and bluish colors are produced by the pigments *r*-phycoerythrin and *r*-phycocyanin. Most species are marine.

## 2.3 PHOTOSYNTHESIS

Plants utilize only visible light (wavelength range 400–720 nm) for photosynthesis. Algae have evolved several pigments for the purpose of light absorption, and these can be combined into three major groups: (1) chlorophylls; (2) carotenoids; and (3) phycobilins (*r*-phycoerythrin and *r*-phycocyanin). The chlorophylls strongly absorb blue and red light. All algae have chlorophyll *a ;* chlorophyll *b* is present in the green algae only. The carotenoids absorb blue and green light. The pigment $\beta$-carotene is present in all algae, and fucoxanthin is the main pigment of the brown algal group. The phycobilins are the primary pigments of the red algae. They absorb green, yellow, and orange light. To use the metaphor of Govindjee and Braun (1974), all these pigments provide algae with the "antennae" with which to capture light.

### Light and Dark Reactions

Plants respire continuously, but in the presence of light, respiration is masked by photosynthesis, which is more intense. If a plant is kept in total darkness, it continues to respire but photosynthesis stops. If low-intensity light is added, photosynthesis starts again, resulting in $CO_2$ assimilation and the discharge of $O_2$. As the light increases, a point is reached at which the photosynthetic and respiratory gas exchange are equal. This is called the *compensation point* and is illustrated graphically in Fig. 2-2. Over a given range, photosynthetic gas exchange is almost proportional to light intensity, but at a certain light level the rate of gas exchange stops increasing. The plant is then *light saturated* and any additional light applied to its surface is wasted or even detrimental. In some phytoplankton, high light intensities cause membrane damage

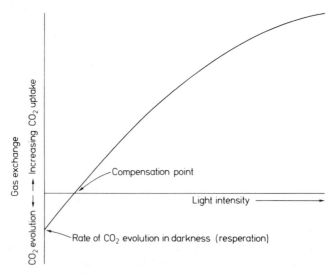

**Figure 2-2.** The rate of photosynthesis increases as light intensity is increased from 0 (darkness). At the compensation point photosynthesis just balances respiration. Redrawn and modified from Bonner and Galston (1952).

and the subsequent release of intracellular material produced during photosynthesis (Fogg et al. 1965, Hellebust 1965).

Efficient photosynthesis is contingent on a plant's photosynthetic pigments (mainly chlorophyll) becoming light saturated. Simply raising the ambient light level, however, is no guarantee of obtaining maximum photosynthesis. The photosynthetic rate is actually controlled by three factors acting in combination: (1) light intensity; (2) $CO_2$ concentration; and (3) temperature. Each may be rate limiting under certain conditions, thereby affecting light saturation and the efficiency of the light-absorbing pigments.

Light intensity and $CO_2$ can be considered together. With low $CO_2$ concentrations, maximum photosynthesis is achieved at relatively low light intensity. However higher light intensities do not result in greater photosynthetic rates, because $CO_2$ in this case is rate limiting. As the $CO_2$ concentration in the environment increases, a greater light intensity is necessary for plants to become light saturated, as illustrated in Fig. 2-3. If photosynthetic rate is considered as a function of $CO_2$ concentration at different light intensities, the result is the same. At relatively low $CO_2$ concentrations, the plants become light saturated at low light levels. As light intensity is increased, higher $CO_2$ concentrations become necessary to saturate the pigments. According to Fogg

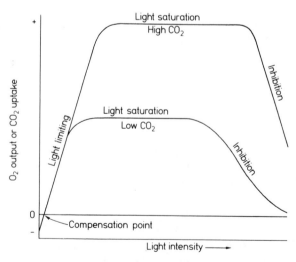

**Figure 2-3.**  The relationship of photosynthetic rate to light intensity as shown by a suspension of algal cells. The two curves are for different $CO_2$ concentrations. Redrawn and modified from Fogg (1968).

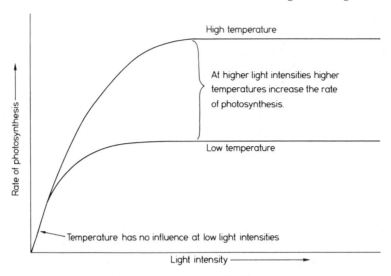

**Figure 2-4.** At low light intensities (light is rate limiting), photosynthetic rate is independent of temperature. At higher light intensities ($CO_2$ is rate limiting), photosynthetic rate is increased with increasing temperature. Redrawn and modified from Bonner and Galston (1952).

(1968), the $CO_2$ concentration in seawater is probably not adequate to saturate photosynthetic pigments at high light intensities. Excess light applied to macroalgae growing in a seawater aquarium would be wasted.

Photosynthesis consists of a *light reaction* (photochemical) and a *dark reaction* (chemical). The first is independent of temperature, whereas the rate of the second doubles or triples with each 10°C rise in temperature. Thus changes in temperature may or may not affect the rate of photosynthesis. It depends on whether the system is light or $CO_2$ limited at the time. As shown in Fig. 2-4, the photosynthetic rate does not increase significantly with increasing temperature under conditions of low light and high $CO_2$ concentration (light is rate limiting). However if light is intense and $CO_2$ is low ($CO_2$ is rate limiting), photosynthetic rate increases with an increase in temperature. In other words, photosynthesis consists of two steps, one requiring light and the other $CO_2$. The rate of the step that requires light is not affected by temperature, being a photochemical reaction. The $CO_2$ demanding step is temperature dependent because it is purely a chemical reaction.

### Photoperiod

Nearly all plants are affected by *diel periodicity* (photoperiodicity), or alternating cycles of light and dark. Photoperiod is expressed as the ratio of hours of light to dark; for a plant kept under 16 hr of daylight and 8 hr of darkness within a 24-hr period, this would be expressed as 16/8.

It is common for aquarists to culture algae under continuous light, (24/0). There is, however, evidence that such a practice is detrimental to the plants. Van den Driessche and Bonotto (1972) found that the photosynthetic rate in the tropical green macroalga *Acetabularia* decreased with time in continuous light. Harris and Lott (1973) demonstrated that continuous light had an adverse effect on photosynthesis in phytoplankton. The species studied showed a steady decrease in photosynthesis with time. A good rule of thumb for the routine culture of marine macroalgae is 12 to 16 hr of light in each 24-hr period.

## 2.4 APPLICATION

There are three basic types of lamps: (1) incandescent, (2) fluorescent, and (3) metallic vapor arc. All of them promote algal growth, but fluorescent lamps are preferred because they generate less heat than the others and still provide light of sufficient intensity and spectral distribution. Several interrelated factors concerning light must be considered before starting any program of algal culture: (1) the type of lamp, based mostly on spectral intensity; (2) the number of lamps and their distance from the plants; (3) the intensity of light required for the species to be cultured; and (4) potential trouble from heat generated by the lamps.

### Spectral Intensity

Wavelengths, or bands, of light are usually expressed two ways: in nanometers (nm) or in colors, as illustrated in Fig. 2-5. The spectral intensity curve for the Sylvania Standard Gro-lux® (Fig. 2-5b) shows maximum radiant power between 650 and 700 nm, meaning that it is strongest in the red portion of the wavelength scale. The percentages of spectral intensity for each wavelength in some common 40-watt fluorescent lamps are given in Table 2-2.

An illumination-level meter cannot be used to measure the energy

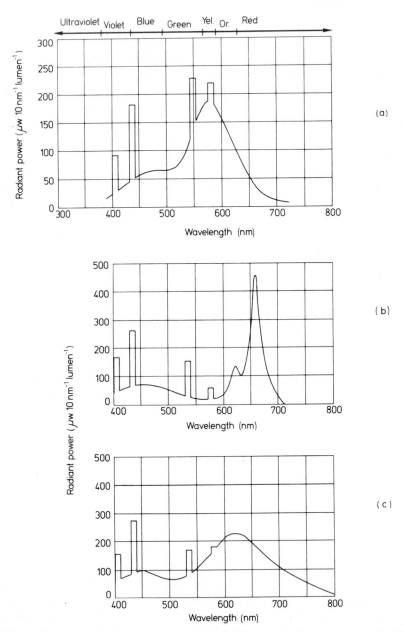

**Figure 2-5.** Spectral intensity curves for 40-w fluorescent lamps: (*a*) General Electric Cool White Panel Fluorescent, (*b*) Sylvania Standard Gro-Lux®; and (*c*) Sylvania Wide Spectrum Gro-Lux® (General Electric and Sylvania, Inc.).

**Table 2-2  Energy Emission in Arbitrary Color Bands of Some Common 40-w Fluorescent Lamps in Wattage and Percentage of Total Emission**

| Band | nm | Cool White watts | Cool White % | Warm White watts | Warm White % | Daylight watts | Daylight % | White watts | White % |
|---|---|---|---|---|---|---|---|---|---|
| Ultraviolet | <380 | 0.16 | 1.7 | 0.13 | 1.5 | 0.19 | 2.1 | 0.18 | 1.9 |
| Violet | 380–430 | 0.72 | 7.6 | 0.46 | 5.2 | 0.87 | 9.6 | 0.59 | 6.4 |
| Blue | 430–490 | 1.98 | 21.0 | 1.15 | 13.1 | 2.54 | 28.0 | 1.48 | 16.0 |
| Green | 490–560 | 2.35 | 24.8 | 1.80 | 20.6 | 2.49 | 27.4 | 2.14 | 23.2 |
| Yellow | 560–590 | 1.74 | 18.4 | 2.06 | 23.5 | 1.32 | 14.5 | 1.95 | 21.1 |
| Orange | 590–630 | 1.69 | 17.9 | 2.13 | 24.3 | 1.20 | 13.2 | 1.95 | 21.1 |
| Red | 630–700 | 0.81 | 8.6 | 1.03 | 11.8 | 0.47 | 5.2 | 0.96 | 10.3 |
| Total | | 9.45 | 100.0 | 8.76 | 100.0 | 9.08 | 100.0 | 9.25 | 100.0 |

| Band | nm | Cool White Deluxe watts | Cool White Deluxe % | Warm White Deluxe watts | Warm White Deluxe % | Natural watts | Natural % | Incandescent Fluorescent watts | Incandescent Fluorescent % | Gro-Lux® watts | Gro-Lux® % |
|---|---|---|---|---|---|---|---|---|---|---|---|
| Ultraviolet | <380 | 0.15 | 2.1 | 0.13 | 1.8 | 0.17 | 2.1 | 0.04 | 0.7 | 0.103 | 1.42 |
| Violet | 380–430 | 0.56 | 7.8 | 0.38 | 5.3 | 0.61 | 7.6 | 0.14 | 2.3 | 0.700 | 9.75 |
| Blue | 430–490 | 1.36 | 18.8 | 0.84 | 11.8 | 1.34 | 16.7 | 0.46 | 7.5 | 1.960 | 27.3 |
| Green | 490–560 | 1.73 | 24.0 | 1.68 | 23.8 | 1.68 | 20.9 | 1.24 | 20.1 | 1.015 | 14.1 |
| Yellow | 560–590 | 0.86 | 11.9 | 1.09 | 15.4 | 0.96 | 12.0 | 0.83 | 13.4 | 0.103 | 1.43 |
| Orange | 590–630 | 1.20 | 16.6 | 1.46 | 20.5 | 1.40 | 17.5 | 1.35 | 21.8 | 0.438 | 6.1 |
| Red | 630–700 | 1.36 | 18.8 | 1.52 | 21.4 | 1.87 | 23.2 | 2.11 | 34.2 | 2.864 | 39.9 |
| Total | | 7.22 | 100.0 | 7.10 | 100.0 | 8.03 | 100.0 | 6.17 | 100.0 | 7.183 | 100.0 |

Source:  Sylvania, Inc.

19

output for a given wavelength of light because the spectral distribution of each lamp is different. Other methods must be used instead, but the spectral intensity curves provided by manufacturers are accurate enough in most circumstances. Remember that the light, whatever its source, must pass through water before it reaches the plants. Turbidity, DOC, and the light-scattering and absorbing effects of water itself diminish or alter the light. Spectral distribution and intensity curves are approximations at best when lamps are suspended over water.

The absorption spectra for the common algal pigments chlorophyll *a* and chlorophyll *b*, extracted in ether, are shown in Fig. 2-6. For any given species, this sort of information reveals the types and amounts of pigments present. In addition, absorption spectra are necessary for photobiologists to calculate quantum yields of photosynthesis (number of $O_2$ molecules evolved per absorbed quantum of light), and of chlorophyll *a* fluorescence (number of quanta emitted per quanta absorbed). Quantum yields of chlorophyll *a* fluorescence and $O_2$ evolution as a function of wavelength (color) of light are facts required before the efficiency of the energy transfer between pigments can be determined.

It is tempting to think that the best algal growth can be achieved simply by matching the absorption spectrum of the species being cultured with the absorption spectrum of a lamp. It is known, for example, that fucoxanthin strongly absorbs blue light, but matching a brown alga

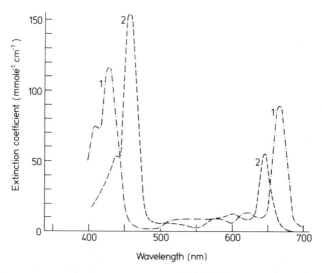

**Figure 2-6.** Absorption spectra of: (*1*) chlororphyll *a*; and (*2*) chlorophyll *b*, both in ether. Redrawn and modified from Fogg (1968).

with a lamp that is strong in the blue portion of the spectrum does not guarantee better growth than might be obtained with lamps of other spectral intensities. The reasons for this lack of congruence, according to Govindjee and Braun (1974), are as follows. The absorption spectrum of a given algal pigment can be used to get a rough idea of the photosynthetic spectral response of a green or brown alga under stated light spectrum conditions, but such data will be approximate only, because of the inefficiency of the carotenoids in light-gathering and also the existence of the "red drop phenomenon," in which there is a decline in the quantum yield of $O_2$ evolved and of chlorophyll *a* fluorescence at the red end of the light spectrum. In the case of red algae, absorption spectra are of no use at all, because the red drop starts long before the decline of the main absorption band of chlorophyll *a* and is accompanied by a "blue drop," or a drop in yield at the blue end of the spectrum.

### Number of Lamps

Once the lamps have been selected, the next thing is to calculate how many are needed. The light output of a lamp is most often measured in lumens, which is the sum of all the light leaving the lamp, and represents the total lux emanating from the lamp integrated over the entire area through which the light is passing.[*] The number of lumens is the lux output integrated over the surface of a sphere surrounding a point-source of light, the lamp. No allowance is made for any loss brought about by the lamp's reflector. Different lamps produce a different light output (in lumens) per electric power input (in watts). This ratio is the *efficacy* of the lamp and it depends on the conversion efficiency of electrical energy to radiant energy. The greater the percentage of radiant energy with a wavelength close to the maximum sensitivity of the human eye (555 nm), the higher the efficacy of the lamp. Efficacy values for some common lamps are given in Table 2-3. Efficacy can be used to provide a rough approximation of the illumination capability of a lamp expressed in lux. The lux output of a lamp with a reflector is given as

$$w = \frac{LA}{EU} \qquad (2)$$

where $w$ is in watts, $L$ is the light requirement in lux, $A$ is the area to be illuminated in $m^2$, $E$ is the efficacy of the lamp selected, and $U$ is the

[*] One ft-c = 1 lumn ft$^{-2}$, or 10.8 lumen m$^{-2}$. Thus 1 ft-c = 10.8 metre-candles, or lux.

**Table 2-3    Wattage and Efficacy of Lamps Commonly Used to Culture Algae**

|  | Wattage | Efficacy (lumen watt$^{-1}$) |
|---|---|---|
| Clear mercury | 400 | 45.0 |
| Color improved mercury | 400 | 50.0 |
| 100-watt tungsten incandescent | 100 | 17.5 |
| 25-watt tungsten incandescent | 25 | 10.5 |
| Wide Spectrum Gro-Lux® | 40 | 35.8 |
| Standard Gro-Lux® | 40 | 23.0 |
| Daylight fluorescent |  |  |
|    Standard | 40 | 63.8 |
|    High Output | 60 | 54.0 |
|    Power Groove® | 110 | 55.9 |
| Cool white fluorescent |  |  |
|    Standard | 40 | 79.0 |
|    High Output | 60 | 66.0 |
|    Power Groove® | 110 | 62.5 |
| Warm white fluorescent | 40 | 81.2 |

Source:    Newburn (1975).

utilization factor, or the effect of using a reflector. The utilization factor is actually the fraction of the light emitted by the source that falls on the area to be illuminated and can be considered a constant of 0.5.

Suppose macroalgae are to be cultured in a tank that is 1.6 m². The water flowing over the algae is very shallow and the lamps are to be suspended over the tank as closely as possible to the water. Assume that cool white fluorescent lamps will be used exclusively, and at an illumination level of 7560 lux. From Table 2-3, it can be seen that total lamp wattage for a standard cool white lamp is 40 watts and the efficacy is 79 lumen watt$^{-1}$. Therefore

$$w = \frac{(7560)(1.6)}{(79)(0.5)}$$

$$= 306$$

In this simple calculation, no allowance is made for places in the aquarium that may receive less light than others. The formula assumes that the lamps and reflectors will be suspended close enough together so that light loss is prevented and that 7560 lux will fall more or less evenly over the entire bottom where the plants are growing.

### Intensity of Light

Most microalgae can be cultured easily at light intensities that average 3789 lux of cool white fluorescent light. The microscopic stages of many macroalgae can also be grown under relatively low light levels (Chapman and Burrows 1970, Kain 1966). The saturation levels for larger (adult) plants, however, are likely to be much higher (Kain 1966).

Chapman (1973) noted that most marine algae do well under cool white fluorescent light. From an exhibit standpoint, this type of lighting most closely resembles subsurface illumination in the sea. As a general rule, photoperiod and light intensity are more important in algal culture than are the spectral intensity curves of the lamps used.

For the routine culture of adult macroalgae, the following light intensities are recommended. Keep in mind that considerable latitude exists

**Table 2-4   Representative Light Saturation Values for Macroalgae**

| Species | Intensity (lux) | Source |
|---|---|---|
| Green macroalgae | | |
| *Acetabularia sp.* | 16,200 | Colinvaux et al. (1965) |
| *Batophora sp.* | 16,200 | Colinvaux et al. (1965) |
| *Caulerpa sp.* | 16,200 | Colinvaux et al. (1965) |
| *Cymopolia sp.* | 16,200 | Colinvaux et al. (1965) |
| *Dictyosphaeria sp.* | 16,200 | Colinvaux et al. (1965) |
| *Halimeda sp.* | 16,200 | Colinvaux et al. (1965) |
| *Neomeris sp.* | 16,200 | Colinvaux et al. (1965) |
| *Penicillus sp.* | 16,200 | Colinvaux et al. (1965) |
| *Udotea sp.* | 16,200 | Colinvaux et al. (1965) |
| *Ulva fasciata* | 2,500 | Mohsen et al. (1973) |
| *Valonia sp.* | 16,200 | Colinvaux et al. (1965) |
| Brown macroalgae | | |
| *Laminaria hyperborea* | 3,400 | Lüning (1971) |
| Red macroalgae | | |
| *Chondrus crispus* | 10,800 | Burns and Mathiesen (1972) |
| *Eucheuma nudum* | 3,240 | Dawes et al. (1976) |
| *Gigartina exasperata* | 11,880 | Waaland (1973) |
| *Gigartina stellata* | 21,600 | Burns and Mathiesen (1972) |
| *Iridaea cordata* | 11,880 | Waaland (1973) |
| *Pilayella littoralis* | 1,620 | West (1967) |
| *Pleonosporium squarrulosum* | 1,620 | Murray and Dixon (1973, 1975) |
| *Rhodochorton purpureum* | 2,160 | West (1974) |

Table 2-5    General Lighting Specifications
for Marine Macroalgae Using Cool White
Fluorescent Lamps

| Algal Group | Intensity (lux) |
|---|---|
| Green (tropical) | 13,000–16,200 |
| Green (temperate) | 7560–10,800 |
| Brown | 7560–10,800 |
| Red | 2160–8640 |

for whatever values are chosen, and that some adjustment may be required before the best results are attained. Tropical green macroalgae should be cultured at 12,960 to 16,200 lux. Temperate species, such as *Ulva* and *Enteromorpha,* do not need this much light, and values of 7560 to 10,800 lux are suggested as a starting point. This same range is also suitable for the brown macroalgae. For the red species, levels of 2160 to 8640 lux are generally adequate, although individual species may require intensities of 10,800 lux or more (Burns and Mathieson 1972, Waaland 1973). This information is summarized in Tables 2-4 and 2-5.

Some species—green macroalgae particularly—absorb light heavily into the red end of the spectrum, and some incandescent lighting to supplement the fluorescent lamps often improves growth. Chapman (1973) recommended a ratio of 10 watts of incandescent per 100 watts of fluorescent.

### Heat

All lamps impart heat to the surrounding air. After burning for several hours, even low-intensity lamps may start to heat the water of an aquarium. Incandescent lamps burn hotter than fluorescent ones and should be used sparingly. Metallic vapor arc lamps probably should never be used. Starr (1973) reported that the temperature in an algal culture cold room was affected by heat from fluorescent lamps. The temperature near the shelves on which jars of microalgae were cultured rose 2 to 3°C when the lights were on, even with circulating room air. When high-intensity fluorescent lamps were used (General Electric Power Groove®), the temperature increased 8 to 9°C.

Starr (1973) suggested the use of single-pin fluorescent tubes of the type with two lamps per ballast. This reduced the heat output. In addition, the ballast could be mounted some distance away from the culture vessels where the heat generated could dissipate harmlessly. Starr also mentioned that fluorescent lamps become less efficient with time and should be replaced periodically. A good rule of thumb is to replace lamps when they have reached 80% of their "rated life," as specified by the manufacturer. The Sylvania Wide Spectrum Gro-Lux®, for example, has a rated life of 20,000 hr or approximately 2.9 years if operated at a photoperiod of 15/9. This is equivalent to an effective life of 16,000 hr (80% of 20,000 hr).

# CHAPTER 3
## Culture Media

$S$ eawater organisms are affected by the ionic strength of the culture medium, and by its composition. The first criterion can be met simply by maintaining the salinity near that of seawater. The second is more difficult to control with certainty—perhaps impossible—considering that the physiological need for individual elements varies greatly among species, and that many requirements have yet to be quantified. Moreover it is one thing to calculate the concentration of a given element in crystalline form, and quite another to predict its chemical state and concentration once it has been dissolved with other salts and DOC in an aqueous solution. Ordinarily the problem is not so serious as it first seems. The fact that many oceanic animals and plants have been cultured successfully in media of varied composition implies that most—perhaps all—of the elements essential for normal metabolic functions are being supplied, either by accident or design.

To emphasize that seawater organisms are fully in tune with the ionic composition of their environment, the chapter starts with a brief discussion of the mechanisms used by animals in normal water and salt balance. The next section covers elements that are essential to algae, a necessary prelude to formulating artificial media in which these plants are to be cultured. The rest of the chapter discusses the three types of "seawaters" that are commonly used: natural, enriched and artificial.

## 3.1 WATER AND SALT BALANCE

Aquatic organisms are solutions within a solution. One of their major tasks is to balance physiological water and salt while simultaneously taking in seawater. Most are stenohaline and can tolerate only limited changes in the ionic strength of their environment. Fluctuations in external salt concentration disturb normal water and salt regulation in the tissues, resulting in physiological stresses. The mechanisms controlling water and salt concentration are diffusion, osmosis, and active transport. Osmoregulation is the overall process by which water and salt balance is achieved.

### Diffusion, Osmosis, and Transport

*Diffusion* is the random distribution of substances throughout the space available to them. It occurs because molecules are in constant motion and the direction in which they move is random. Increases in temperature stimulate molecular activity. Thus diffusion rate increases with increasing temperature. *Osmosis* is the diffusion of water.

Many membranes of living organisms are *semipermeable,* meaning that certain molecules pass through them easily, others more slowly, and still others not at all. Often the effect of a semipermeable membrane is to override the forces of diffusion. All living membranes are essentially permeable to water, but their degree of permeability to solutes varies considerably.

When a solute causes a differential flow of water through a semipermeable membrane, it is said to exert *osmotic pressure.* The level of osmotic pressure applied to a membrane is directly proportional to the *number* of molecules or particles of solute, and not to the *kind* of solute. The distinction is important, because it allows some marine organisms to regulate water and salt balance by using their own metabolic products, as explained in the next section.

Diffusion and osmosis do not require an expenditure of energy on the part of living cells and are, in that sense, forms of *passive transport.* Some membranes can pump materials through themselves, often against a concentration gradient. This ability, called *active transport,* requires an expenditure of energy. The energy is provided by functioning cells. Many marine organisms concentrate certain solutes from seawater by active transport. These substances are sometimes necessary for carrying out metabolic activities. Active transport is also important in helping organisms with tissue solutes less concentrated than seawa-

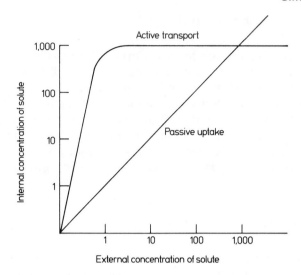

**Figure 3-1.** Relationship between external and internal solute concentrations in passive uptake and active transport. The external and internal concentrations are identical in passive uptake. In active transport the internal concentration is higher than the external concentration, but is saturated at high external concentrations. Redrawn from Brock (1970).

ter to eliminate excess salts. Active and passive transport are illustrated diagrammatically in Fig. 3-1.

### Osmoregulation

Most marine invertebrates have an osmotic pressure comparable to seawater; that is, they are *isosmotic* with seawater. If the seawater becomes more concentrated from evaporation, or more dilute from addition of freshwater, an invertebrate animal responds in one of two ways: (1) it maintains its osmotic pressure at the original level; or (2) it changes its osmotic pressure to match that of the culture medium and in so doing stays isosmotic. The former animal is an *osmoregulator*, because its osmotic pressure is now greater (*hyperosmotic*) or less than (*hyposmotic*) the culture medium. The latter animal is an *osmoconformer*, because its body fluids have conformed to the osmotic pressure of the new solution.

Most marine invertebrates are osmoconformers and their internal osmotic pressure varies with the osmotic pressure of the surrounding seawater. As Schmidt-Nielson (1975) noted, osmoconformers have rid themselves of a major physiological problem: they do not have to cope with the osmotic movement of water. However all animals regulate their internal solute composition to some extent, and even an osmoconformer does not have an internal salt makeup identical to seawater. Some invertebrates are good osmoregulators. Often they are inhabitants of estuaries, where fluctuations in the salt content of the water are routine. The osmoregulating ability of estuarine animals is accomplished in part because of structures that make them less permeable (e.g., the carapace of crustaceans).

In marine elasmobranchs (cartilaginous fishes), salt concentration of the blood and other body fluids is approximately one-third that of seawater, yet the animals are still isosmotic. This seeming anomaly can be explained as follows. Elasmobranchs secrete large quantities of organic molecules—mainly urea but also some trimethylamine oxide (TMAO)—into their body fluids until the osmotic pressure of the blood equals that of seawater. In other words, even though the salts *per se* in elasmobranchs are less concentrated than in seawater, the actual number of particules in the body fluids provides an osmotic pressure equal to that of the water. The advantage of being isosmotic is that no severe loss of tissue water can occur. Thus elasmobranchs do not drink copious quantities of seawater, as do the marine teleosts (bony fishes). Consequently they do not have a heavy sodium intake and the attendant problem of excreting it. The regulation of physiological water and salt in elasmobranchs living in seawater is illustrated in Fig. 3-2a.

Freshwater teleosts do not drink water because their tissue solutes are more concentrated than salts in the external environment. Freshwater fishes are thus hyperosmotic with the environment. Their problem is one of ridding the tissues of excess water, while preventing the loss of too much salt. The presence of surface membranes of reduced permeability is a partial solution, but even so, osmotic gain through the gills is substantial and there is the inevitable salt loss and water gain. The kidneys of freshwater teleosts help by retaining salts and eliminating water. The situation is summarized in Fig. 3-2b.

Marine teleosts have a different problem. Their internal salt concentration is less than that of the surrounding environment. Being hyposmotic, they tend to lose water by osmosis and gain salts by diffusion. Unfortunately the situation is exacerbated by surface membranes that are more permeable than the membranes of freshwater teleosts. Kidneys that retain salts and eliminate water present still another handicap. To gain on the water balance side, marine teleosts drink large quantities of seawater, ingesting salts in the process. Most of the divalent ions

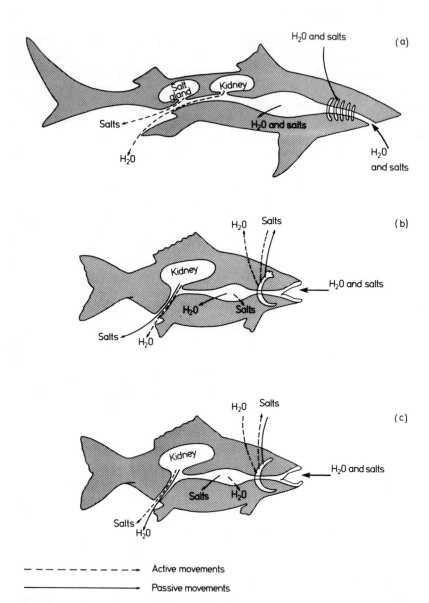

**Figure 3-2.** Regulation of physiological water and salt in: (*a*) a seawater elasmobranch, (*b*) a freshwater teleost, and (*c*) a seawater teleost. Redrawn and modified from McCauley (1971).

stay in the gut and are eliminated in the urine and feces. Monovalent ions are eliminated by active transport at the gills. Water and salt balance in seawater teleosts is illustrated in Fig. 3-2c.

## 3.2  ELEMENTS ESSENTIAL TO ALGAE

According to O'Kelley (1974), the following elements in inorganic form (plus C, H, and O) are essential to at least one species of algae: N, P, K, Mg, Ca, S, Fe, Cu, Mn, Zn, Mo, Na, Co, V, Si, Cl, B, and I. Of these, N, P, Mg, Fe, Cu, Mn, Zn, and Mo are required by all algae and are not replaceable even in part by other elements. However, Sr, K, and Ca can be replaced in certain circumstances by another ion of like chemical charge (e.g., strontium for calcium).

The *marginal elements* (those essential or stimulatory for only a few species) can be covered quickly. Cobalt is required by some algae in the form of vitamin $B_{12}$. In other species, cobalt acts as a growth stimulant but is not essential. Boron is essential only to the marine diatom *Cylindrotheca fusiformis,* insofar as is known (Lewin 1965, 1966). In the green macroalga *Ulva,* and the brown macroalga *Dictyota,* boron stimulates reproductive growth. Silicon (as silicic acid) is essential to diatoms and they cannot divide without it (Lewin 1955). Vanadium seems to be essential to the microalgae *Scenedesmus* and *Chlorella* (Arnon and Wessel 1953).

Considering the abundance of the major ions (Section 3.3) in all seawater culture media, there is never a problem of depletion. The functions of these and other elements in algal physiology are included in Table 3-1. Fluorine, a major constituent in seawater, usually is not added to artificial culture media. Fluorine is not essential to plants.

Many species of algae are *auxotrophic,* meaning that they require vitamins. Most higher plants do not. Auxotrophic algae are unable to synthesize the vitamins they need and must assimilate them from the water. Just three vitamins are required for auxotrophic species, and ordinarily only one or two per species. The vitamins are $B_{12}$, thiamine, and biotin. Adding other vitamins to aquarium water is useless if the purpose for doing so is to grow algae.

Provasoli and Carlucci (1974) reviewed the literature dealing with effects of water-borne vitamins on algal physiology and concluded that of the auxotrophic species, vitamin $B_{12}$ and thiamine are required alone or in combination by the majority, and that $B_{12}$ seemed to be essential more often than thiamine. Biotin was needed by only a few

Table 3-1    Functions of Some Elements Essential to Algae

| Element | Partial Replacement | Function |
|---|---|---|
| Sulfur | Selenium | Cell division |
| Potassium | Sodium, rubidium | Enzyme activation |
| Calcium | Strontium | Cell wall synthesis |
| Magnesium | None | Chlorophyll synthesis, phosphate transfer, nitrogen metabolism, RNA production |
| Iron | None | Biological oxidation-reduction, chlorophyll production |
| Manganese | None | Chlorophyll synthesis, $O_2$ and $CO_2$ utilization in photosynthesis |
| Copper | None | Photosynthesis |
| Zinc | None | RNA synthesis and structure |
| Molybdenum[a] | None | Nitrate assimilation and reduction |
| Phosphorus | None | Energy transfer |
| Nitrogen | None | Protein and chlorophyll synthesis |

Source:    Various sources.
[a]Also essential to the autotrophic nitrifying bacterium *Nitrobacter* (Finestein and Delwiche 1965).

chrysomonads and dinoflagellates, and by one euglenid. Biotin can be ignored in the routine culture of seaweeds in aquariums.

Of the major groups of algae commonly cultured (green, brown, and red), the green and brown groups have the fewest species needing vitamins. All the red seaweeds studied so far, with the exception of *Porphyridium*, a unicellular form, require only $B_{12}$. Auxotrophic green algae ordinarily need both $B_{12}$ and thiamine. Of the brown algal group, the growth of some species that do not require vitamins is still stimulated by them.

The growth of algae depends both on the concentration of trace elements (added as trace salts), and on their chemical states (Jackson and Morgan 1978). Trace element concentrations in seawater aquariums are depleted by physical adsorption and disinfection processes (Chapters 9 and 10), and by assimilation into the living tissues of animals, plants, and bacteria. A certain portion may also be lost by precipitation on gravel grains and bound up with detritus. Conversely an aquarium is a "sink" for many elements entering the system as food. In addition, major salts used to make artificial seawater always contain trace elements as contaminants, thus providing the finished solution with higher concentrations of individual elements than indicated by the formula of the culture medium. The benefits of adding trace salts to enriched and artificial seawaters are controversial at this time, and the fate of the important elements, once they enter solution, is largely unknown. It has yet to be demonstrated, for example, whether elements that accumulate with time are returned to the water in forms that are always biologically useful.

It is questionable whether addition of trace salts to enriched or artificial seawater benefits cultured marine animals. Algae are another matter. Marine algae depend directly on the composition of the culture medium, because they assimilate all nutrients directly from the water. Animals obtain many nutrients secondhand by eating plants or other animals. The position taken here is that addition of trace salts to culture media is done so entirely for the benefit of plants. Furthermore I see no reason why trace salts should be added in concentrations much beyond those found in natural seawater, unless there is a specific reason for doing it. Trace salts in enriched and artificial culture media often are concentrated many times beyond their strengths in nature. The rationale usually given is that many marine organisms accumulate specific elements in their tissues. This is often interpreted to mean: (1) the organism requires the element at the reflected tissue concentrations; and (2) the chore of assimilation is eased if the background strength of the element in the culture medium is magnified, often by several hundredfold. Such *a priori* assumptions may be faulty. Because the element is concentrated in tissues is not proof that it is needed in those amounts, or that it is needed at all. A few brown algae concentrate lead to 70,000 times the level in natural seawater, yet lead serves no known biological function. Perhaps as Bowen (1966) suggested, some of the heavier metals are concentrated by organisms simply because they can be more highly polarized. Moreover the fact that an organism can assimilate and concentrate a trace element speaks for an efficient active transport system, one that probably does not need assistance.

Few generalizations can be made correlating tissue concentration of a given trace element with phylogenetics. It is common to find closely related species accumulating the same element to different tissue levels. Riley and Roth (1971) studied 15 species of phytoplankton raised in culture media with orders of magnitude more Ag, Co, Cr, Cu, Fe, Mn, Pb, Sn, V, and Zn than seawater. All metals were chelated. Trace element analysis of the algal tissues revealed increased concentrations of each element with increasing levels in the media, but there were no trends that could be interpreted in phylogenetic terms.

It is sometimes beneficial to magnify the amount of a trace element in enriched or artificial seawater, but the practice ordinarily is limited to chemical species that are difficult to keep in solution. By adding more of an element than may be necessary, and carefully chelating it, enough may remain soluble during the interval between partial water changes to serve the needs of the plants. Nevertheless careful thought should be given to other possible effects. It is useless to concentrate substances that do not serve known biological functions. In other instances, raising the level of a trace element may be harmful and produce negative effects. Copper and zinc, for example, are toxic at levels only slightly higher than normally found in natural seawater. The toxicity of heavy metals can be reduced by chelating them with substances such as ethylenediaminetetraacetate (EDTA), as reported by Jackson and Morgan (1978). In still other situations, chelation increases the availability of elements in biologically active states (Jackson and Morgan 1978).

There are no general guidelines for estimating the amount of an element that should be in solution for proper growth of algae. A reasonable starting point is to supply essential and stimulatory elements in concentrations approximating their levels in seawater.

## 3.3  NATURAL SEAWATER

All the known elements probably are dissolved in the oceans. Thus natural seawater contains elements known to be essential to marine organisms, in addition to many others that do not serve a known biological function. The sum of these elements can be classified in two groups according to concentration: (1) major; and (2) trace. It is more convenient to think of seawater constituents as ions instead of individual elements. The ionic composition of seawater is shown in Table 3-2. Most species are present in trace amounts.

Culkin (1965) defined the *major ions* in seawater as those that make a significant contribution to the measured salinity. From an operational standpoint, this would encompass species with concentrations greater than 1 mg kg$^{-1}$. Major ions in seawater are given in Table 3-3.

The sum of the solutes in seawater of normal ionic composition can be determined by measuring the salinity, chlorinity, chlorosity, or density. *Salinity* traditionally is defined as the total amount of solid material dissolved in 1 kg of seawater when all the carbonate has been converted to oxide, all bromine and iodine replaced by chlorine, and all

Table 3-2  Ionic Composition of Seawater

| Element | Chemical Species | Molar | $\mu g \, l^{-1}$ |
|---|---|---|---|
| H | $H_2O$ | 55 | $1.1 \times 10^8$ |
| He | He (gas) | $1.7 \times 10^{-9}$ | $6.8 \times 10^{-3}$ |
| Li | $Li^+$ | $2.6 \times 10^{-5}$ | 180 |
| Be | $BeOH^+$ | $6.3 \times 10^{-10}$ | $5.6 \times 10^{-3}$ |
| B | $B(OH)_3$, $B(OH)_4^-$ | $4.1 \times 10^{-4}$ | 4440 |
| C | $HCO_3^-$, $CO_3^{2-}$, $CO_2$ | $2.3 \times 10^{-3}$ | $2.8 \times 10^4$ |
| N | $N_2$, $NO_3^-$, $NO_2^-$, $NH_4^+$ | $1.07 \times 10^{-2}$ | $1.5 \times 10^5$ |
| O | $H_2O$, $O_2$ | 55 | $8.8 \times 10^8$ |
| F | $F^-$, $MgF^+$ | $6.8 \times 10^{-5}$ | $1.3 \times 10^3$ |
| Ne | Ne (gas) | $7 \times 10^{-9}$ | $1.2 \times 10^{-1}$ |
| Na | $Na^+$ | $4.68 \times 10^{-1}$ | $10.77 \times 10^6$ |
| Mg | $Mg^{2+}$ | $5.32 \times 10^{-2}$ | $12.9 \times 10^5$ |
| Al | $Al(OH)_4^-$ | $7.4 \times 10^{-8}$ | 2 |
| Si | $Si(OH)_4$ | $7.1 \times 10^{-5}$ | $2 \times 10^6$ |
| P | $HPO_4^{2-}$, $PO_4^{3-}$, $H_2PO_4^-$ | $2 \times 10^{-6}$ | 60 |
| S | $SO_4^{2-}$, $NaSO_4^-$ | $2.82 \times 10^{-2}$ | $9.05 \times 10^5$ |
| Cl | $Cl^-$ | $5.46 \times 10^{-1}$ | $18.8 \times 10^6$ |
| Ar | Ar (gas) | $1.1 \times 10^{-7}$ | 4.3 |
| K | $K^+$ | $1.02 \times 10^{-2}$ | $3.8 \times 10^5$ |
| Ca | $Ca^{2+}$ | $1.02 \times 10^{-2}$ | $4.12 \times 10^5$ |
| Sc | $Sc(OH)_3$ | $1.3 \times 10^{-11}$ | $6 \times 10^{-4}$ |
| Ti | $Ti(OH)_4$ | $2 \times 10^{-8}$ | 1 |
| V | $H_2VO_4^-$, $HVO_4^{2-}$ | $5 \times 10^{-8}$ | 2.5 |
| Cr | $Cr(OH)_3$, $CrO_4^{2-}$ | $5.7 \times 10^{-9}$ | 0.3 |
| Mn | $Mn^{2+}$, $MnCl^+$ | $3.6 \times 10^{-9}$ | 0.2 |
| Fe | $Fe(OH)_2^+$, $Fe(OH)_4^-$ | $3.5 \times 10^{-8}$ | 2 |
| Co | $Co^{2+}$ | $8 \times 10^{-10}$ | 0.05 |
| Ni | $Ni^{2+}$ | $2.8 \times 10^{-8}$ | 1.7 |
| Cu | $CuCO_3$, $CuOH^+$ | $8 \times 10^{-9}$ | 0.5 |
| Zn | $ZnOH^+$, $Zn^{2+}$, $ZnCO_3$ | $7.6 \times 10^{-8}$ | 4.9 |
| Ga | $Ga(OH)_4^-$ | $4.3 \times 10^{-10}$ | 0.03 |
| Ge | $Ge(OH)_4$ | $6.9 \times 10^{-10}$ | 0.05 |
| As | $HAsO_4^{2-}$, $H_2AsO_4^-$ | $5 \times 10^{-8}$ | 3.7 |
| Se | $SeO_3^{2-}$ | $2.5 \times 10^{-9}$ | 0.2 |
| Br | $Br^-$ | $8.4 \times 10^{-4}$ | $6.7 \times 10^4$ |
| Kr | Kr (gas) | $2.4 \times 10^{-9}$ | 0.2 |
| Rb | $Rb^+$ | $1.4 \times 10^{-6}$ | 120 |
| Sr | $Sr^{2+}$ | $9.1 \times 10^{-5}$ | $8 \times 10^4$ |
| Y | $Y(OH)_3$ | $1.5 \times 10^{-11}$ | $1.3 \times 10^{-3}$ |
| Zr | $Zr(OH)_4$ | $3.3 \times 10^{-10}$ | $3 \times 10^{-2}$ |
| Nb | | $1 \times 10^{-10}$ | $1 \times 10^{-2}$ |

Table 3-2 (*continued*)

| Element | Chemical Species | Molar | $\mu g\ l^{-1}$ |
|---|---|---|---|
| Mo | $MoO_4^{2-}$ | $1 \times 10^{-7}$ | 10 |
| Tc | | | |
| Ru | | | |
| Rh | | | |
| Pd | | | |
| Ag | $AgCl_2^-$ | $4 \times 10^{-10}$ | 0.04 |
| Cd | $CdCl_2$ | $1 \times 10^{-9}$ | 0.1 |
| In | $In(OH)_2^+$ | $0.8 \times 10^{-12}$ | $1 \times 10^{-4}$ |
| Sn | $SnO(OH)_3^-$ | $8.4 \times 10^{-11}$ | $1 \times 10^{-2}$ |
| Sb | $Sb(OH)_6^-$ | $2 \times 10^{-9}$ | 0.24 |
| Te | $HTeO_3^-$ | | |
| I | $IO_3^-$, $I^-$ | $5 \times 10^{-7}$ | 60 |
| Xe | Xe (gas) | $3.8 \times 10^{-10}$ | $5 \times 10^{-2}$ |
| Cs | $Cs^+$ | $3 \times 10^{-9}$ | 0.4 |
| Ba | $Ba^{2+}$ | $1.5 \times 10^{-7}$ | 2 |
| La | $La(OH)_3$ | $2 \times 10^{-11}$ | $3 \times 10^{-3}$ |
| Ce | $Ce(OH)_3$ | $1 \times 10^{-10}$ | $1 \times 10^{-3}$ |
| Pr | $Pr(OH)_3$ | $4 \times 10^{-12}$ | $6 \times 10^{-4}$ |
| Nd | $Nd(OH)_3$ | $1.9 \times 10^{-11}$ | $3 \times 10^{-3}$ |
| Pm | $Pm(OH)_3$ | | |
| Sm | $Sm(OH)_3$ | $3 \times 10^{-12}$ | $0.5 \times 10^{-4}$ |
| Eu | $Eu(OH)_3$ | $9 \times 10^{-13}$ | $0.1 \times 10^{-4}$ |
| Gd | $Gd(OH)_3$ | $4 \times 10^{-12}$ | $7 \times 10^{-4}$ |
| Tb | $Tb(OH)_3$ | $9 \times 10^{-13}$ | $1 \times 10^{-4}$ |
| Dy | $Dy(OH)_3$ | $6 \times 10^{-12}$ | $9 \times 10^{-4}$ |
| Ho | $Ho(OH)_3$ | $1 \times 10^{-12}$ | $2 \times 10^{-4}$ |
| Er | $Er(OH)_3$ | $4 \times 10^{-12}$ | $8 \times 10^{-4}$ |
| Tm | $Tm(OH)_3$ | $8 \times 10^{-13}$ | $2 \times 10^{-4}$ |
| Yb | $Yb(OH)_3$ | $5 \times 10^{-12}$ | $8 \times 10^{-4}$ |
| Lu | $Lu(OH)_3$ | $9 \times 10^{-13}$ | $2 \times 10^{-4}$ |
| Hf | | $4 \times 10^{-11}$ | $7 \times 10^{-3}$ |
| Ta | | $1 \times 10^{-11}$ | $2 \times 10^{-3}$ |
| W | $WO_4^{2-}$ | $5 \times 10^{-10}$ | 0.1 |
| Re | $ReO_4^-$ | $2 \times 10^{-11}$ | $4 \times 10^{-3}$ |
| Os | | | |
| Ir | | | |
| Pt | | | |
| Au | $AuCl_2^-$ | $2 \times 10^{-11}$ | $4 \times 10^{-3}$ |
| Hg | $HgCl_4^{2-}$, $HgCl_2$ | $1.5 \times 10^{-10}$ | $3 \times 10^{-2}$ |
| Tl | $Tl^+$ | $5 \times 10^{-11}$ | $1 \times 10^{-2}$ |
| Pb | $PbCO_3$, $Pb(CO_3)_2^{2-}$ | $2 \times 10^{-10}$ | $3 \times 10^{-2}$ |

**Table 3-2**  (*continued*)

| Element | Chemical Species | Molar | $\mu g\ l^{-1}$ |
|---|---|---|---|
| Bi | $BiO^+$, $Bi(OH)_2^+$ | $1 \times 10^{-10}$ | $2 \times 10^{-2}$ |
| Po | $PoO_3^{2-}$ $PoO(OH)_2$ (?) | | |
| At | | | |
| Rn | Rn (gas) | $2.7 \times 10^{-21}$ | $6 \times 10^{-13}$ |
| Fr | | | |
| Ra | $Ra^{2+}$ | $3 \times 10^{-16}$ | $7 \times 10^{-8}$ |
| Ac | | | |
| Th | $Th(OH)_4$ | $4 \times 10^{-11}$ | $1 \times 10^{-2}$ |
| Pa | | $2 \times 10^{-16}$ | $5 \times 10^{-8}$ |
| U | $UO_2(CO_3)_2^{4-}$ | $1.4 \times 10^{-8}$ | 3.2 |

Source:   Brewer (1975).

organic matter completely oxidized. This amount of "solid material" is expressed in grams, and salinity is referred to in g $kg^{-1}$, or parts per thousand (ppt). The symbol for salinity is $S$; o/oo stands for ppt. Salinity includes both the inorganic ions in solution and the organic compounds. Thus a reading of 35 $S$ o/oo, the normal value for seawater, is an expression of all dissolved solids—ions such as sodium and chloride, and also organic phosphorus and nitrogen, plant pigments, vitamins, and so forth.

**Table 3-3   Major Ions in Seawater**

| Ion | $g\ kg^{-1}$ ($S = 35$ o/oo) |
|---|---|
| $Cl^-$ | 19.354 |
| $SO_4^{2-}$ | 2.712 |
| $Br^-$ | 0.0673 |
| $F^-$ | 0.0013 |
| B | 0.0045 |
| $Na^+$ | 10.77 |
| $Mg^{2+}$ | 1.290 |
| $Ca^{2+}$ | 0.4121 |
| $K^+$ | 0.399 |
| $Sr^{2+}$ | 0.0079 |

Source:   Wilson (1975).

Salinity is difficult to measure by direct chemical methods, as its definition implies, so it is usually defined in terms of another variable, chlorinity. The relationship, as demonstrated by Wooster et al. (1969), is

$$S \ o/oo = 1.80655 \ (Cl \ o/oo) \tag{3}$$

*Chlorinity* is a measure of the halogen concentration in a sample of seawater. Chlorinity is easier to measure chemically than salinity. The usual method is by titrating a sample of seawater with silver nitrate and using potassium dichromate as an indicator. By modern definition, chlorinity is the numerical value in g kg$^{-1}$ of a seawater sample identical to the number giving the mass in grams of atomic weight silver just necessary to precipitate the halogens in 0.3285233 kg of the sample. In the past, oceanographers considered chlorinity to be the total amount of chlorine, bromine, and iodine in grams contained in 1 kg of seawater, assuming that the bromine and iodine had been replaced by chlorine. The essential features of this definition still apply when defining chlorosity (see below). The symbol for chlorinity is $Cl$ and the expression used is $Cl \ o/oo$. It is usually not necessary to determine chlorinity in routine aquarium maintenance.

The halogen concentration of seawater is sometimes given as *chlorosity*, particularly by European chemists. Chlorosity means the same thing as chlorinity, but is given in g l$^{-1}$ instead of g kg$^{-1}$. Because volumetric measurements are affected by temperature, chlorosity is defined as the total amount of chlorine, bromine, and iodine in grams contained in 1 l of seawater *at 20°C*, assuming that the bromine and iodine have been replaced by chlorine. Chlorosity readings will be 2–3% greater than chlorinity determinations made on the same sample, because a litre of seawater has a greater mass than a litre of freshwater.

The terms density and specific gravity often are used interchangeably by aquarists, but they are not synonyms. The *density* of seawater refers to its mass per unit volume and is expressed as g ml$^{-1}$. *Specific gravity* is the ratio of a given volume of seawater and an equal volume of distilled water at 4°C. Because it is a ratio and nothing more, specific gravity cannot be stated in units; it is dimensionless. Distilled water must be defined as being at 4°C because pure water reaches maximum density at this temperature.

The density of seawater varies with changes in temperature and salinity. Pressure, a third factor, is inconsequential in aquarium operation. Even in oceanographic work, pressure is of minor importance, considering that seawater is nearly incompressible. Salinity affects density because when ions are added to water the mass of the water increases. Increasing the salinity by 1 o/oo, for example, increases the density by about 0.8 o/oo.

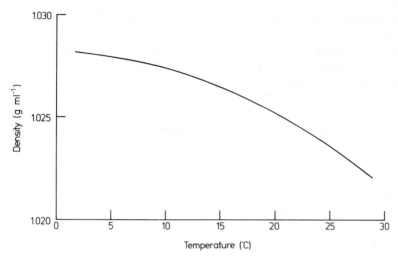

**Figure 3-3.**   Density of seawater versus temperature. Redrawn from Anikouchine and Sternberg (1973).

Temperature has a more pronounced effect on density than does salinity. The density of full-strength seawater ($S$ = 25 o/oo or more) decreases with increasing temperature, as illustrated in Fig. 3-3. In other words, cold seawater is more dense than warm seawater at the same salinity (salinity, being a weight per weight relationship, functions independently of temperature). As seawater is made brackish by dilution with freshwater, it starts to behave more like pure water and becomes less dense if cooled below the temperature at which it reached maximum density.

Density can be further defined by the relationship

$$\sigma_t = (p - 1)\ 1000 \qquad\qquad (4)$$

in which $p$ represents specific gravity and $\sigma_t$ is density at a specified temperature. For purposes here, the numerical values of specific gravity and density, as stated in the above equation, can be considered identical, although density will actually be a little smaller (Cox et al. 1968). In other words, a specific gravity value of 1.028 would equal a density of 1.028 g ml$^{-1}$, and $\sigma_t$ ("sigma-t" in an oceanographer's lexicon) would be expressed $\sigma_t$ = 28. At a temperature of 10°C, the expression would read $\sigma_{10}$ = 28. Density is not an easy concept to understand, nor is its measurement simple and direct. To make accurate density determinations, the effects of temperature and salinity must be considered both independently and in combination (Williams 1962).

## 3.4 ENRICHED SEAWATER

*Enriched seawater* is natural seawater to which nutrients have been added to promote the growth of algae. Formulas for enriched seawater media were reviewed by McLachlan (1973). I have chosen three from his paper for a quick summary. In most cases, the media are sterilized by autoclaving or microfiltration to eliminate contaminant microorganisms. This is particularly important when pure cultures of an alga are wanted.

The Erdschreiber Medium is one of the earliest enriched seawater media (Schreiber 1927). Its composition, along with the others described here, is presented in Table 3-4. The additives are sterilized separately and combined later under aseptic conditions. McLachlan (1973) suggested that iron, other trace metals, and vitamins could be used to replace soil extract. Some examples are shown in Table 3-5.

The *f* Medium of Guillard and Ryther (1962), and its later derivatives, such as *f*/2 (Guillard 1975), are some of the most widely used enriched seawater media for the culture of unicellular algae. Nutrients and seawater are autoclaved together and buffered with either 4.13 mmole tris [2-amino-2(hydroxymethyl)-1,3-propanediol] (*f*/2-t) or 3.8

**Table 3-4   Enriched Seawater Media**

| Additive (conc. l$^{-1}$) | Erdschreiber | *f*/2 | SWM |
|---|---|---|---|
| NaNO$_3$ | 1.18–2.35 mmole | 0.88 mmole | 0.5–2.0 mmole |
| Na$_2$HPO$_4$ | 56–140 $\mu$mole | — | — |
| NaH$_2$PO$_4$ | — | 36.3 $\mu$mole | 50–100 $\mu$mole |
| NaSiO$_3$ | — | 0.054–0.107 mmole | 0.2 mmole |
| Fe·EDTA | — | — | 2 $\mu$mole |
| Trace metal solution[a] | — | *f*/2 | TMS-I |
| Vitamin solution[a] | — | — | S-3 |
| Cyanocobalamin | — | 0.5 $\mu$g | — |
| Biotin | — | 0.5 $\mu$g | — |
| Thiamine·HCl | — | 100 $\mu$g | — |
| Tris | — | — | — |
| Glycylglycine | — | — | 5 mmole |
| Soil extract | 50 ml | — | 50 ml |
| Liver extract | — | — | 10 mg |

Source:   McLachlan (1973).
[a] Table 3.5.

**Table 3-5   Vitamins and Trace Metals for Enriched Seawater Media**

| Trace Metals ($\mu$mole l$^{-1}$) | $f/2^a$ | TMS-I$^b$ | Vitamins (conc. l$^{-1}$) | S-3$^c$ |
|---|---|---|---|---|
| Zinc | 0.08 | 35 | Thiamine·HCl | 0.05 mg |
| Manganese | 0.9 | 10 | Nicotinic acid | 0.1 mg |
| Molybdenum | 0.03 | 5 | Ca·pantothenate | 0.1 mg |
| Cobalt | 0.05 | 0.3 | $p$-Aminobenzoic acid | 10.0 $\mu$g |
| Copper | 0.04 | 0.3 | Biotin | 1.0 $\mu$g |
| Iron | 11.7 | 2 | $i$-Inositol | 5.0 mg |
| EDTA | 11.7 | 48 | Folic acid | 2.0 $\mu$g |
| Chelate:metal | 0.9:1 | 2:1 | Cyanocobalamin | 1.0 $\mu$g |
| Boron | — | 400 | Thymine | 3.0 mg |

Source:   [a] Guillard (unpublished 1968) in McLachlan (1973).
          [b] McLachlan (1973).
          [c] Provasoli (1964).

mmole glycylglycine ($f/2$-g) and the pH is adjusted to 7.4 (McLachlan 1973). According to McLachlan (1973), nitrogen and phosphorus can be lowered, even to values of 100 $\mu$mole and 5 $\mu$mole, respectively, without affecting growth.

The Sea Water Medium (SWM) of McLachlan (1964) has been used to culture many species of marine algae, both planktonic and benthic. The nutrients are added to seawater and autoclaved. Glycylglycine in some variations of the medium can be increased to 10 mmole for mass culture or when $CO_2$ gas is injected into the medium to enhance photosynthesis. The tris buffer added to other formulations of the SWM can be omitted because the rapid growth of the algae causes a quick increase in pH.

## 3.5   ARTIFICIAL SEAWATER

Artificial seawater mixes can be purchased from several manufacturers, or mixed on site from individual components. Many formulas have been published. McLachlan (1973) wryly noted that the number of formulas nearly equals the number of investigators. The result has been a bewildering array of recipes, some touted as the best available for culture of a particular animal or plant. But McLachlan further pointed out that such claims rarely are supported by sufficient data. The truth is that many formulations will maintain a variety of seawater organisms, although some obviously are more versatile than others.

A good artificial seawater is characterized by four factors: (1) it is simple but still contains, in reasonable concentrations, elements known to be essential to animals or plants; (2) it is relatively easy to measure and mix; (3) major ions are present in concentrations and ratios that approximate natural seawater; and (4) the components consist of salts that do not precipitate easily. It is critical that the desired amount of a salt dissolve promptly and stay in solution. Published recipes for artificial seawaters must be studied carefully before being reproduced. Those devised for algal culture frequently are low in salinity and pH and poorly suited for rearing animals. Conversely many formulas developed especially for animals lack vitamins essential to algae, or contain trace metals that are incompletely chelated.

### Prepackaged Mixes

Prepackaged artificial sea salt mixes are adequate in most situations, and eliminate the time, expense, and trouble of making small volumes of seawater from individual components. An example of one commercially available mix is shown in Fig. 3-4. Those brands that lack essen-

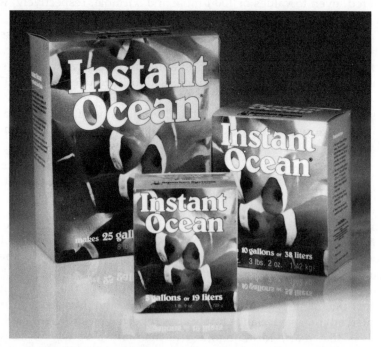

**Figure 3-4.** Artificial seawater mix (Aquarium Systems, Inc.).

tial trace elements in soluble form, or that contain major ions in abnormal ratios compared with natural seawater, should not be used to culture algae. No one has ever demonstrated that, when reconstituted, dehydrated sea salts can support the variety of life they once did (Atz 1964). Dehydrated sea salts are probably no better than prepackaged mixes made of technical and reagent grade components.

The most useful prepackaged mixes can be hydrated in a single step using tap water. Some need to be aerated for several hours before the pH equilibrates. In others, such as Instant Ocean® Synthetic Sea Salts,* the pH comes rapidly to equilibrium, allowing animals to be added immediately. When using most brands, check the pH hourly and do not add living organisms until it has equilibrated at 8.1–8.3. Of the commonly available prepackaged mixes, Instant Ocean® has proved satisfactory for culturing a great number of animals, both in the laboratory and in public aquariums. This medium also is used routinely in bioassay work. Other brands may be just as suitable, but my experience with them is limited.

Follow the instructions carefully when using any of the prepackaged mixes. Artificial sea salts can be hydrated in clean containers made from inert materials. Spare aquarium tanks, polyethylene cannisters or jerry cans, or plastic garbage cans with tight-fitting lids are adequate. The finished solution should be covered to prevent concentration of the salts from evaporation, and contamination by dust and airborne toxicants. Aquarium Systems, Inc.* manufactures a special polypropylene mixing container holding approximately 400 l (Fig. 3-5). The device is equipped with a mechanical pump for transferring the finished solution directly to aquarium tanks.

### Mixing Large Volumes

Large volumes of artificial seawater should be mixed in stages over a 3-day period, instead of in a single step. A good procedure is to dissolve the major salts one at a time. Dissolution is quicker if the container holding the salts is flooded continuously with tap water at approximately 30°C. Trace salts are mixed in two or three separate batches, depending on the formula, and added on the second and third days. Trace salts may precipitate if added before the major salts have dissolved completely and been diluted to volume. Heavy aeration can be used to disperse all elements evenly throughout the solution, and by the fourth day the medium should be suitable for use in culture.

* Aquarium Systems, Inc., 8141 Tyler Blvd., Mentor, OH 44060.

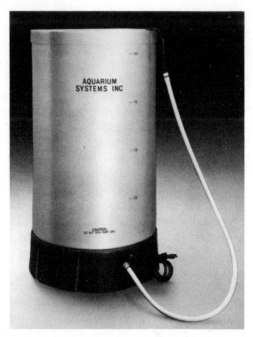

**Figure 3-5.** Mixing tank for 400 l of artificial seawater. The unit is equipped with a pump for transferring the finished solution to aquarium tanks (Aquarium Systems, Inc.).

A well-designed mixing arrangement for artificial seawater consists of a dissolving chamber for hydrating salts, and a storage vat underneath to hold the finished solution (Fig. 3-6). The dissolving chamber should be equipped with hot and cold tap water discharging through a common valve. An in-line thermometer placed after the mixing valve is useful for regulating the water temperature. An electric mixer (not shown) mounted on the side of the chamber aids in dissolving the salts. The storage vat should contain a large airlift pump for circulating the water. If an airlift is not used, a mechanical pump is required. A suitable airlift can be made from a straight length of PVC pipe (10 cm diameter or larger) with a hole drilled near one end. The size of the hole should be just large enough to make a tight fit for the airline (0.95 cm diameter flexible tubing works well). No dispersion device is necessary, because the primary purpose of the airlift is to circulate the water, rather than to aerate it. The airlift can be fixed permanently in place over the lowest part of the vat where salts accumulate, or anchored to the bottom with lead weights. It is not necessary for the top of the airlift to be above the surface of the water when the vat is full.

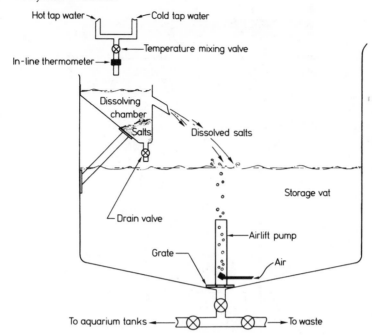

**Figure 3-6.** Dissolving chamber and storage vat for mixing and holding large volumes of artifical seawater. From Spotte (1979).

In large installations, it is convenient to add sodium chloride, the major constituent in seawater, as a concentrated brine instead of in crystalline form. This can be done with automatic dissolving equipment developed and sold by the International Salt Company* (Fig. 3-7). Bagged salt is awkward to handle in large quantities, and requires considerable storage space. Bulk salt is cheaper and takes less space to store. Concentrated brine can be pumped easily to artificial seawater storage vats, and its addition in this form is quicker and more accurate than the procedure of emptying large amounts of bagged NaCl into the dissolving chamber.

A diagrammatic illustration of a Sterling Brinomat® is shown in Fig. 3-7. Bulk salt is stored in the hopper. The hopper is refilled pneumatically through a connecting stainless steel pipe leading outside the plant to a truck loading ramp. Tap water entering the Brinomat® flows vertically through the salt bed and is regulated by a solenoid valve. As water moves downward, it forms a brine solution of increasing strength. Just above the bottom it reaches full saturation, provided that the hopper is

---

* International Salt Company, Clarks Summit, PA 18411.

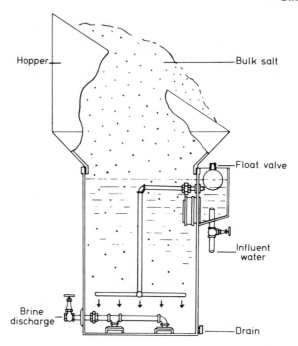

**Figure 3-7.** Automatic dissolving equipment, the Sterling Brinomat®, for making brine (International Salt Co.).

kept full. Dissolved salt is replaced automatically by dry salt from the hopper. It is important to note that the brine becomes saturated *before* it reaches the bottom of the Brinomat®. The lower portion of the salt bed never dissolves and acts as a mechanical filter, which removes insoluble impurities from the effluent brine. As brine is drawn from the Brinomat® and transferred to the mixing vat, a float valve opens the solenoid and brine making continues automatically. In seawater culture, a Brinomat® must be equipped with an accurate flow meter to measure the amount of solution passing into the storage vat. Brass or bronze meters are preferable, because they are corrosion resistant. The tiny amount of copper that may leach from the meter is insignificant from a toxicity standpoint. All-brass, bronze, plastic, or stainless steel pumps are recommended for pumping brine or seawater.

The two artificial seawater recipes that follow are suitable for culturing seawater organisms on either a large or small scale. The GP Medium formulation is new and has not been published before. It is a four-part mix, formulated for culturing both animals and plants (hence the name

GP, or General Purpose Medium). The formula is based mainly on elemental values as found in natural seawater. I also considered the best features of some published formulas. Among the most useful was that of Segedi and Kelley (1964), which led to the Instant Ocean® formulations (e.g., King and Spotte 1974). The recipes given by Segedi and Kelley, and by King and Spotte, proved suitable for the routine culture of marine animals, but largely neglected the needs of plants. To remedy that, I borrowed from the many excellent recipes used to grow marine algae (e.g., Guillard and Ryther 1962, McLachlan 1964). Other useful papers were the review by Droop (1969) on algal culture, the summary of the vitamin requirements of algae by Provasoli and Carlucci (1974), and the practical suggestions for making artificial seawater offered by McLachlan (1973). Kinne (1976) summarized the compositions of several of the more popular artificial seawater formulas.

The second recipe given in this chapter is a modified version of the Segedi-Kelley fomula published by Spotte (1979). It has been used for several years in at least two public aquariums (Aquarium of Niagara Falls and Mystic Marinelife Aquarium). The formula is a three-part mix.

**GP Medium**

The composition of the GP Medium is given in Tables 3-6 and 3-7. When mixed in large volumes, add Solution A the first day, Solution B the second day, and Solutions C and D the third day.

*Solution A*

1  Add some tap water to the empty mixing container.
2  Dissolve the salts separately and empty the clear solutions into the mixing container.
3  Dilute to approximately 75% of volume.
4  Cover the container to minimize evaporation, if mixed in small volumes, and provide aeration.

*Solution B*

1  Dissolve each component in distilled water (aluminum sulfate requires heat to dissolve).
2  Add to Solution A on the second day.

Table 3-6 Species Concentration for the GP Medium Formula (g $l^{-1}$)

| Species | Molar | $\mu g \ l^{-1}$ |
|---|---|---|
| $Cl^-$ | $5.40 \times 10^{-1}$ | $1.92 \times 10^7$ |
| $Na^+$ | $4.68 \times 10^{-1}$ | $1.08 \times 10^7$ |
| $SO_4^{2-}$ | $2.83 \times 10^{-2}$ | $2.71 \times 10^6$ |
| $Mg^{2+}$ | $5.31 \times 10^{-3}$ | $1.29 \times 10^6$ |
| $Ca^{2+}$ | $1.02 \times 10^{-2}$ | $4.08 \times 10^5$ |
| $K^+$ | $1.05 \times 10^{-2}$ | $3.99 \times 10^5$ |
| $HCO_3^-$ | $2.29 \times 10^{-3}$ | $1.40 \times 10^5$ |
| $Br^-$ | $8.38 \times 10^{-4}$ | $6.70 \times 10^4$ |
| $H_3BO_3$ | $4.11 \times 10^{-4}$ | $2.54 \times 10^4$ |
| $Na_2 EDTA$ | $2.95 \times 10^{-5}$ | $9.91 \times 10^3$ |
| $Sr^{2+}$ | $9.13 \times 10^{-5}$ | $8.00 \times 10^3$ |
| $HPO_4^2, PO_4^{3-a}$ | $1.63 \times 10^{-5}$ | $1.55 \times 10^3$ |
| $Li^+$ | $2.59 \times 10^{-5}$ | $1.80 \times 10^2$ |
| $Fe^{2+,3+b}$ | $1.20 \times 10^{-5}$ | $6.72 \times 10^2$ |
| $I^-$ | $4.96 \times 10^{-7}$ | $6.30 \times 10^1$ |
| $Mn^{2+}$ | $1.00 \times 10^{-6}$ | $5.50 \times 10^1$ |
| $Mo$ | $1.00 \times 10^{-7}$ | $9.60 \times 10^0$ |
| $Zn^{2+}$ | $7.96 \times 10^{-8}$ | $5.20 \times 10^0$ |
| $Co^{2+}$ | $5.00 \times 10^{-8}$ | $2.95 \times 10^0$ |
| $Cu^{2+c}$ | $4.00 \times 10^{-8}$ | $2.54 \times 10^0$ |
| $V$ | $4.00 \times 10^{-8}$ | $2.04 \times 10^0$ |
| $Al^{3+}$ | $7.40 \times 10^{-8}$ | $2.00 \times 10^0$ |

[a] Concentration factor compared to seawater = 8.
[b] Concentration factor compared to seawater = 300.
[c] Concentration factor compared to seawater = 5.

*Solution C*

1 Dissolve each salt in a little distilled water along with 2 molar equivalents of $Na_2EDTA$.
2 Boil for 5 to 10 min to hasten chelation.
3 Dilute to volume with distilled water. All chelates are stable at alkaline conditions.
4 Add the iron chelate if a combined solution is preferred.
5 Add to Solutions A and B on the third day.
NOTE: All components can be concentrated for 500- to 1000-fold dilution. Iron and boron require special attention to get them into

**Table 3-7   Salt Concentrations for the GP Medium Formula ($S$ = 33.1 o/oo Calculated from $Cl$)**

| Salt | Solution | Concentration |
|---|---|---|
| NaCl | A | 26.00 g $l^{-1}$ |
| $MgSO_4 \cdot 7H_2O$ | A | 6.58 |
| $MgCl_2 \cdot 6H_2O$ | A | 4.88 |
| $CaCl_2 \cdot 2H_2O$ | A | 1.46 |
| KCl | A | 0.675 |
| $NaHCO_3$ | A | 0.184 |
| KBr | B | 95.3 mg $l^{-1}$ |
| $SrCl_2 \cdot 6H_2O$ | B | 24.2 |
| $NaH_2PO_4 \cdot 7H_2O$ | B | 4.0 |
| LiCl | B | 1.04 |
| $Al_2(SO_4)_3 \cdot 18H_2O$ | B | 0.0235 |
| $H_3BO_3$ | C | 242000.0 $\mu g\ l^{-1}$ |
| $Na_2$ EDTA | C | 9440.0 |
| Fe·citrate·$H_2O$ | C | 3830.0 |
| $Na_2MoO_4 \cdot 2H_2O$ | C | 2220.0 |
| $MnSO_4 \cdot H_2O$ | C | 1610.0 |
| $ZnSO_4 \cdot 7H_2O$ | C | 1425.0 |
| $CuSO_4 \cdot 5H_2O$ | C | 97.7 |
| KI | C | 79.1 |
| $CoSO_4 \cdot 7H_2O$ | C | 13.4 |
| $Na_2VO_4 \cdot 4H_2O$ | C | 9.24 |
| Thiamine ·HCl | D | 1953.0 $\mu g\ l^{-1}$ |
| Cyanocobalamin | D | 0.977 |

solution. Iron is perhaps the most difficult trace metal to keep soluble at pH values above neutral. Duursma and Sevenhuysen (1966) and McLachlan (1973) mentioned some of the problems. Crystals of $FeSO_4 \cdot 7H_2O$ are easily hydrated and should not be used in the preparation of artificial seawaters. Iron in the forms $FeCl_3$ or $Fe_2(SO_4)_3$ and chelated with $Na_2$EDTA precipitates at pH values greater than 3. Iron-EDTA chelates prepared from ferric citrate are stable at pH values of 8 or more and should be used instead. Musani-Marazović and Pučar (1977) also discussed the chelation of iron with EDTA in seawater.

1   Dissolve the proper quantity of Fe·citrate in distilled water containing 2 molar equivalents of $Na_2$EDTA.

2  Boil for 5 to 10 min to hasten chelation. After boiling, the solution will have a pH of about 2. Adjust the pH to 7 with 1 $N$ NaOH.

3  Dilute to volume with distilled water and refrigerate until use.

NOTE: Boron is not essential to most marine organisms and its addition to artificial seawater is optional. However borate may account for 10 to 15% of the buffer capacity of seawater (Skirrow 1975), and its absence from artificial mixes affects how components of the carbon dioxide system are calculated if the medium is to be used in oceanographic work. For this reason, the concentration of boron in the GP Medium approximates that of natural seawater.

1  Dissolve the required amount of $H_3BO_3$ in distilled water.

2  Heat gently.

3  Add to the combined stock solution (Solution C) if desired. As McLachlan (1973) noted, $H_3BO_3$ is difficult to dissolve in cold water and stock solutions for 500- to 1000-fold dilution cannot be prepared.

*Solution D*

Solution D, consisting of cyanocobalamin ($B_{12}$) and thiamine·HCl, does not require special preparation. Simply dissolve the required amounts of each component in distilled water.

**Modified Segedi-Kelley Medium**

The composition of the Segedi-Kelley Medium, as modified by Spotte (1979), is given in Tables 3-8 and 3-9. It is a three-part mix when used in large volumes, with Solution A being added the first day, Solution B the second, and Solution C the third day. A procedure for mixing this formula in large volumes is given in the next section. The addition of $NaH_2PO_4·7H_2O$ is to initiate plant growth, and $Na_2S_2O_3·5H_2O$ is present to reduce free chlorine in the tap water.

*Solution A*

1  Add some tap water to the empty mixing container.

2  Dissolve the salts separately and empty the clear solutions into the mixing container.

3  Dilute to about 75% of volume.

4  Cover the container to minimize evaporation, if mixed in small volumes, and provide aeration.

**Table 3-8  Salt Concentrations for the Modified Segedi-Kelley Medium Formula ($S = 35.3$ o/oo Calculated from $Cl$)**

| Salt | Concentration |
|------|---------------|
| NaCl | 27.60 g l$^{-1}$ |
| MgSO$_4$·7H$_2$O | 6.89 |
| MgCl$_2$·6H$_2$O | 5.40 |
| CaCl$_2$·2H$_2$O | 1.38 |
| KCl | 0.60 |
| NaHCO$_3$ | 0.21 |
| KBr | 26.90 mg l$^{-1}$ |
| SrCl$_2$·6H$_2$O | 19.84 |
| MnSO$_4$·H$_2$O | 3.97 |
| NaH$_2$PO$_4$·7H$_2$O | 3.97 |
| LiCl | 0.99 |
| Na$_2$MoO$_4$·2H$_2$O | 0.99 |
| Na$_2$S$_2$O$_3$·5H$_2$O | 0.99 |
| Al$_2$(SO$_4$)$_3$·18H$_2$O | 0.85 |
| RbCl | 149.00 $\mu$g l$^{-1}$ |
| ZnSO$_4$·7H$_2$O | 95.90 |
| CoSO$_4$·7H$_2$O | 89.30 |
| KI | 89.30 |
| CuSO$_4$·5H$_2$O | 9.90 |

Source: Segedi and Kelley (1964) and Spotte (1979).

*Solution B*

1  Dissolve each component in distilled water (aluminum sulfate requires heat to dissolve).

2  Add to solution A on the second day.

*Solution C*

1  Dissolve each component in distilled water.

2  Add to Solutions A and B on the second day.

**Large Volumes of the Modified Segedi-Kelley Medium**

The procedure given here for mixing large volumes of the Modified Segedi-Kelley Medium is taken from Spotte (1979). It assumes that the

Table 3-9  Salt Concentrations for 30,240 l of
Modified Segedi-Kelley Medium

| Salt | Solution | Mass |
|------|----------|------|
| NaCl | A | 834.60 kg |
| $MgSO_4 \cdot 7H_2O$ | A | 208.65 |
| $MgCl_2 \cdot 6H_2O$ | A | 163.29 |
| $CaCl_2 \cdot 2H_2O$ | A | 41.73 |
| KCl | A | 18.14 |
| $NaHCO_3$ | A | 6.35 |
| $SrCl_2 \cdot 6H_2O$ | B | 600.00 g |
| $MnSO_4 \cdot H_2O$ | B | 120.00 |
| $NaH_2PO_4 \cdot 7H_2O$ | B | 120.00 |
| LiCl | B | 30.00 |
| $Na_2MoO_4 \cdot 2H_2O$ | B | 30.00 |
| $Na_2S_2O_3 \cdot 5H_2O$ | B | 30.00 |
| KBr | C | 812.70 g |
| $Al_2(SO_4)_3 \cdot 18H_2O$ | C | 26.00 |
| RbCl | C | 4.50 |
| $ZnSO_4 \cdot 7H_2O$ | C | 2.90 |
| $CoSO_4 \cdot 7H_2O$ | C | 2.70 |
| KI | C | 2.70 |
| $CuSO_4 \cdot 5H_2O$ | C | 0.30 |

Source:  Segedi and Kelley (1964) and Spotte (1979).

mixing apparatus is similar to the one shown in Fig. 3-6, and that a
Brinomat® is used.

*Solution A*

1  Be sure the storage vat is clean. If it is dirty, scrub the walls and
   floor with a stiff bristle brush and hose it out with tap water. Do
   not use prepared cleansers. Stained areas can be cleaned with a
   strong solution of sodium bicarbonate and warm water, then
   rinsed with tap water.
2  Turn on the airlift pump and close the drain valve from the vat.
3  Turn on the tap water to the dissolving chamber and adjust the
   temperature to 30°C. Wait until there are approximately 30 cm of
   water in the bottom of the vat before proceeding.
4  Check the salinity of the brine from the Brinomat® effluent and
   determine the amount needed from Table 3-10.

**Table 3-10 Volume of Brine at Different Specific Gravity Values Needed to Make 30,240 l of Modified Segedi-Kelley Medium**[a]

| Specific Gravity | Volume (l) |
|---|---|
| 1.151 | 3655 |
| 1.154 | 3599 |
| 1.156 | 3546 |
| 1.158 | 3497 |
| 1.160 | 3447 |
| 1.162 | 3398 |
| 1.164 | 3349 |
| 1.167 | 3304 |
| 1.169 | 3258 |
| 1.171 | 3209 |
| 1.173 | 3168 |
| 1.175 | 3126 |
| 1.177 | 3084 |
| 1.180 | 3047 |
| 1.182 | 3005 |
| 1.184 | 2967 |
| 1.186 | 2930 |
| 1.188 | 2895 |
| 1.190 | 2858 |
| 1.193 | 2824 |
| 1.195 | 2790 |
| 1.197 | 2756 |
| 1.199 | 2722 |
| 1.202 | 2688 |
| 1.203 99% saturated | 2669 |

Source: Spotte (1979).
[a]Calculations based on the properties of brine at 15.56°C.

5 Weigh out the correct amounts of the components for Solution A, as shown in Table 3-9.

6 Turn on the Brinomat® pump and add the correct amount of brine.

7 Add the rest of the salts individually to the dissolving chamber while the tap water is running. Wait until each batch dissolves before adding the next. Use this procedure:

   a Fill the dissolving chamber half-full with a component salt after turning on the electric mixer.

    b  Refill the chamber half-full and repeat step a until all the salts are dissolved.

    c  Count the empty bags and containers as a check to be sure that no salts have been forgotten.

8  Continue filling the storage vat with 30°C water until proper salinity is reached. (Once the correct level in the vat has been found the first time, the water level should be marked permanently with epoxy paint.)

*Solution B*

1  One day after mixing Solution A, weigh out the proper amount of each constituent of Solution B. Combine the salts in a large beaker. Do not add water.

2  Sprinkle the dry mixture on the surface of the water in the storage vat.

3  Use the components for Solution B immediately. If the salts remain in the beaker for longer than 2 hr, noticeable reactions take place that alter their chemical states.

*Solution C*

1  Fill a 19-l polypropylene bottle with 2 l of distilled water.

2  Weigh each salt and place in individual, labeled beakers. Add sufficient distilled water to dissolve.

3  Add each solution to the bottle. Rinse the beakers with distilled water and add this water to the bottle.

4  Add distilled water to make about 12 l. Place an air diffuser in the bottle and aerate the solution moderately until it is needed. Add Solution C to the storage vat on the third day.

# CHAPTER 4
## Aeration

When an organism respires, the oxygen taken up from the external environment is transported by the circulatory system to individual cells within the tissues. At the same time, the circulatory system picks up carbon dioxide, an end product of cellular metabolism, and carries it to be released into the environment. *Respiration* is a physiological term applicable either to the whole organism or to one of its cells. The mechanical process by which respiration is achieved is called *ventilation*, which in this discussion is synonymous with breathing.

Water contains much less oxygen than air at a given $Pw_{O_2}$ (partial pressure of oxygen in water), and aquatic animals must breathe a volume of water that is 10 to 30 times greater than the volume of air breathed by terrestrial animals to obtain the same amount of $O_2$ (Dejours et al. 1970, Rahn 1966). Ventilation rate in many aquatic animals depends directly on the quantity of oxygen in solution (Dejours et al. 1977). The effect of *hypoxia* (insufficient tissue oxygen) is increased ventilation rate in fishes (Dejours 1973, Dejours et al. 1977) and crustaceans (Dejours and Beekenkamp 1977, McMahon and Wilkens 1975, Taylor 1976). One of the first considerations in maintaining a seawater aquarium is to supply continuous amounts of oxygenated water by aeration.

The subjects discussed in this chapter are the theoretical basis of gas exchange in aquarium water, aeration methods, the operating principles and design of airlift pumps, and the possible formation of particulate matter by aeration.

**55**

## 4.1  GAS EXCHANGE

Gas exchange in a seawater aquarium takes place at two locations: (1) the air-water interface; and (2) through air bubbles rising in the eduction pipes of airlift pumps. Some of the theoretical models used here describe gas exchange in the oceans, but the process in aquariums is similar in many respects. The three important gases to consider are nitrogen, oxygen, and carbon dioxide.

### Air-Water Interface

Gas exchange between air and water is a function of the differences in partial pressure of a gas in the atmosphere versus the water, and thickness of a surface film located at the air-water interface. This film, formed by surface tension, is known to oceanographers as the *laminar layer*. To simplify matters, the laminar layer can be visualized as a thin skin that is permeable to gas molecules. Kanwisher (1963) determined that the thickness of the laminar layer in the oceans varies from 0.002 to 0.020 cm; the thinner spots result from stirring of the underlying water. A model showing gas exchange across an air-water boundary is given in Fig. 4.1. The model depicts three regions: a turbulent atmosphere with constant partial pressure of a given gas, $p_G$; a turbulent underlying layer of water, also with a uniform partial pressure, $P_G$; and the separating laminar layer. The difference between the two partial pressures is, in the words of Kanwisher (1963), ". . . the driving force of diffusion through the film." In aquariums, $p_G$ is less important because there is no wind to create air turbulence.

The movement, or *flux*, of a gas through the laminar layer depends on differences in partial pressure between air and water, and also on the *diffusivity*, or rate of diffusion of the gas in question, as shown by

$$\text{flux} = \frac{\text{concentration} \times \text{diffusivity}}{\text{thickness}} \tag{5}$$

where concentration is the partial pressure × solubility. Oxygen and nitrogen, the most common gases in the atmosphere, have similar diffusivities (about $2 \times 10^{-5}$ cm sec$^{-1}$ at 20°C). However the concentration of any gas equals the partial pressure it exerts times its solubility, and this latter factor varies considerably from one gas to another. If nitrogen, oxygen, and carbon dioxide are compared, the ratio is approximately 1:2:70. In other words, at a given partial pressure the flux of different gases varies as a function of their solubilities. The

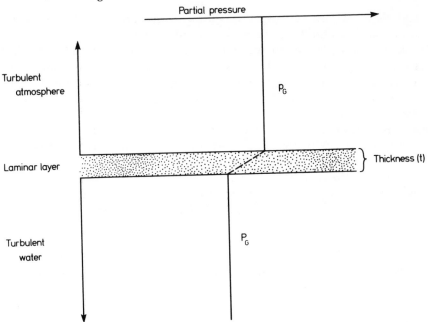

**Figure 4-1.** Diagrammatic illustration of the laminar layer model for gas exchange in the oceans. Redrawn and modified from Kester (1975).

concentration of a gas in solution at saturation varies according to solubility too, so even though the rate is faster for a more soluble gas, the quantity that must be transported to create a saturated state is also greater. In a series of laboratory experiments, Kanwisher (1963) altered the partial pressures of nitrogen, oxygen, and carbon dioxide in distilled water, then measured the time required for all three to re-equilibrate. The results were similar, indicating that when gases diffuse across an air-water interface, the presence of a laminar layer is the controlling factor.

Diffusion becomes easier if the laminar layer is made thinner. This can be accomplished by disrupting the water surface, which erodes away the underside of the laminar layer (Kanwisher 1963). Downing and Truesdale (1955) found that stirring water at different speeds in the laboratory caused gradual changes in the rate of oxygen solubility, until the surface became visibly disturbed. After that, the rate at which oxygen was dissolved increased markedly. Two factors accounted for this: (1) an increase in the surface area of water exposed to the atmosphere; and (2) decreased thickness of the laminar layer caused by turbulence. Until the surface was broken, the rate of oxygen exchange was less than could be attained with air bubbles.

In several studies of air-water gas exchange, an empirical factor called the *exit coefficient*, or exchange velocity, $f$, has been used. Ordinarily $f$ is treated as a measure of gas exchange through a stagnant laminar layer. However Higbie (1935) used it to account for the uptake of gas by water in which new surfaces are created too rapidly for steady-state, or stagnant diffusion, to be established. If "aeration" is considered to be the process by which water exchanges gases with the atmosphere, and not the mechanical means of agitating water, the aeration rate would depend on the amount of oxygen that can diffuse into newly formed surfaces during the split seconds they are exposed to the air. Under these conditions the exit coefficient can be expressed by

$$f = 2\sqrt{\frac{D}{\pi\theta}} \tag{6}$$

where $\theta$ is the time of exposure to the surface and $D$ is the diffusion coefficient of oxygen in water. If the surfaces are renewed randomly, then

$$f = \sqrt{D\,S} \tag{7}$$

where $S$ is the average rate of renewal.

The uptake of oxygen becomes highly temperature dependent once the surface of the water is agitated. Downing and Truesdale (1955) found that the exit coefficient of $O_2$ (the rate at which $O_2$ dissolved in water) increased linearly with increasing temperature, in effect doubling from 5 to 25°C.

### Rising Air Bubbles

Air bubbles driven beneath the surface of the sea by wave action are important in oceanic gas exchange (Kester 1975). Similarly bubbles rising in the eduction pipes of airlift pumps greatly augment gas exchange in seawater aquariums. Two of the controlling factors are the same as in gas exchange at the air-water interface: differences in partial pressure and the presence of laminar layers (in this case encompassing each air bubble). In air bubbles released beneath the surface of the water, hydrostatic pressure becomes still a third factor.

Kanwisher (1963) reported that small bubbles of 0.05 cm in diameter were rapid gas exchangers. Bubbles of this size, and with laminar layers 0.0010 to 0.0015 cm thick, were more than 90% equilibrated with $CO_2$ after rising through only 5 cm of water in 2.5 sec. Kanwisher noted that the relative amounts of the different gases that will be moved by a bubble are directly proportional to their differences in partial pressure between air and water. If it is assumed that a respiring aquatic organism consumes 1 ml $O_2$ $l^{-1}$ and produces 1 ml $CO_2 l^{-1}$, the $Pw_{CO_2}$ (partial pressure of $CO_2$ in water) will be roughly 0.04% of an atmosphere, compared with 0.03% in an air bubble injected beneath the surface in an aquarium. Air is 21% $O_2$, whereas the $Pw_{O_2}$ in seawater will be 17% (5 to 6 ml $O_2$ $l^{-1}$ in solution). Thus an air bubble can move 4% of its volume of $O_2$ and only 0.01% of $CO_2$. In other words, oxygen and nitrogen in air bubbles proceed toward equilibrium with seawater at a rate that is several hundred times faster than carbon dioxide.

Differences in equilibration rates of gases decrease if the laminar layer around a bubble is made thinner. Consequently forces that erode away the laminar layer are important in establishing rates of gas exchange. Liebermann (1957) found that freely ascending air bubbles showed a "diffusion coefficient" that was twice that of stationary bubbles. The turbulence surrounding a rising bubble probably exerts a shearing effect, causing the laminar layer to become thinner in places and increasing the rate of gas loss to the surrounding water.

Wyman et al. (1952) determined that air bubbles rising in seawater became depleted in oxygen and richer in nitrogen. This can also be explained in terms of solubility differences and hydrostatic pressure. If the pressure in an aquarium is considered to be 1 atm, and if the gases in an air bubble at the surface also are at one atmosphere, there can be no diffusion because no gradient exists. The system is at equilibrium. But if the hydrostatic pressure is increased by releasing a bubble near the bottom of the tank, a concentration gradient is immediately established, because the partial pressures of gases in the bubble have been increased. Because oxygen is approximately twice as soluble as nitrogen, it moves quickly across the laminar layer and into solution. Differences in solubility, and the fact that the diffusion constants for oxygen and nitrogen are nearly the same, cause the percentage loss of oxygen from the air bubbles to exceed the percentage of nitrogen lost and nitrogen is left behind to enrich the interior of the bubble.

**Aeration Methods**

Kils (1976/1977) tested three methods of aerating seawater, as determined by the dissolved oxygen concentration up to the saturation point. The equipment used consisted of: (1) a simple aerator, in which air bubbles were released at the bottom of the experimental tank; (2) a venturi, in which air was entrained into a stream of water discharged beneath the surface; and (3) a rotation aerator that utilized air bubbles pulled into the water by turbulence. The effectiveness of each method was calculated from the following exponential function

$$c_t = c_s(1 - e^{-kt}) \tag{8}$$

in which $c_t$ is the $O_2$ concentration at time $t$, $c_s$ is the $O_2$ saturation concentration, and $k$ is the effectiveness of the system. The higher the value of $k$, the more effective the system. The amount of air entrained in the venturi remained constant with increasing salinity. When the rotation aerator was used, the amount of air produced decreased with increasing salinity, being only half as much at 35 o/oo as at 0 o/oo. Salinity was increased from 0 o/oo to 40 in increments of 5 o/oo during the experiments. There was an increase in effectiveness with rising salinity in all three devises, as shown in Fig. 4-2. The simple aerator showed only moderate increases, whereas the venturi was twice as effective in seawater as in freshwater. The rotation aerator demon-

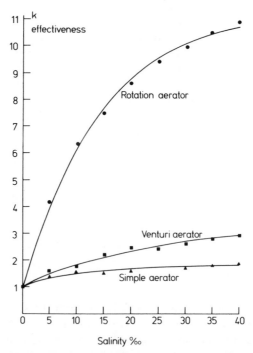

**Figure 4-2.**   The effect of salinity on oxygenation of seawater at 15°C. Redrawn from Kils (1976/1977).

strated the most significant increase in effectiveness, being approximately 10 times more effective in seawater than in freshwater.

Aeration was thought to be more effective in seawater because of the smaller bubbles that were produced when other factors remained constant. Moreover the effectiveness of aeration increased with increasing temperature. The conclusions were that seawater required less input of energy to aerate than freshwater, and that warm seawater was easier to aerate than cold seawater of the same salinity.

Simple aerators are preferable to venturis and rotary aerators in seawater, despite their reduced efficiency. Use of the other two devices increases the danger of the water becoming supersaturated with oxygen or nitrogen, which may result in gas-bubble disease in fishes and other aquatic animals. Ordinarily aeration *per se* is unnecessary if airlift pumps are installed to both circulate and aerate the water (see the next section).

## 4.2   AIRLIFT PUMPS

Gas exchange in aquariums is more efficient if the surface is disrupted, exposing a greater percentage of water to the atmosphere in a given period of time. This process is made even more efficient if air bubbles in a continuous stream are allowed to rise in the water column. Gases in the bubbles diffuse down a concentration gradient into the surrounding water.

Water in an aquarium can be circulated by mechanical pumps or airlift pumps, but only airlifts provide both surface agitation and an endless supply of rising bubbles. Spotte (1979) listed the other advantages that airlifts have over mechanical pumps as lower initial cost, lower maintenance (airlifts have no moving parts), easy installation, easily made portable, nonclogging, small space requirements, simplicity of design, easy to construct, greater efficiency than centrifugal pumps when operating at low head and high submergence, easily regulated flow rate, and highly versatile application.

Water in an aquarium flows in a vertical, circular pattern, as shown in Fig. 4-3. Processed water from the bacteriological filter is removed at the bottom of an aquarium and released near the top. This circular flow serves three purposes: (1) deoxygenated water from underneath the filter is removed before it can accumulate and create anoxic conditions; (2) the motion of the water disrupts the surface mechanically and facilitates gas exchange; and (3) deoxygenated water is continuously exposed at the air-water interface, an advantageous location for gas exchange,

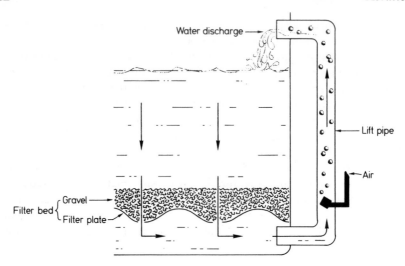

**Figure 4-3.** Airlift pumping arrangement showing the air inlet, eduction pipe, filter bed, and movement of water. From Spotte (1979).

considering that the partial pressure of oxygen in the air exceeds the partial pressure in solution.

### Operating Principles

The airlift pump concept was discovered in 1797 by Carl Loescher, a German mining engineer (Castro et al. 1975). The use of airlifts to circulate water is a well-established practice in modern aquarium management. Spotte (1973, 1974, 1979) described how airlift pumps operate. Basically when a pipe (called an *eduction pipe* or lift pipe) is submerged vertically in still water, the levels inside and outside the pipe equilibrate. At equilibrium there is no water movement. When air is injected into the pipe near the bottom, the equilibrium is upset. The air-water mixture, being lighter than water, rises in the eduction pipe; as it does, heavier water from outside enters the pipe at the bottom. So long as air is injected, equilibrium is never attained and the air-water mixture spills out the top. It should be noted that water is not actually lifted by air; rather the lighter mixture is displaced upward by water and the term "airlift" is, in that sense, a misnomer.

Német (1961) recognized three stages in the starting up of an airlift. First, air is injected into the eduction pipe and the level of the fluid rises. When water spills out the top, a flow is established. Second, as more air is introduced the fluid flow increases and reaches the optimum

mixing rate. Third, if the air flow is increased further the maximum
fluid flow rate is reached. Afterward continued increases in the flow
rate of injected air reduce the volume output of water until it becomes
nearly zero.

### Design

The efficiency, or "performance," of an airlift is determined by several
factors, including: (1) percent submergence of the eduction pipe; (2) the
distance the water must be lifted; (3) diameter of the eduction pipe; and
(4) volume of injected air. How these four factors affect each other is
summarized in Fig. 4-6. A method for use of the graph is given later in
this section.

*Percent submergence* means the percentage of the total length of the
eduction pipe between the air injection point and the surface of the
water. As the percent of submergence increases and more of the pipe is
beneath the water, efficiency also increases. The distance of the eduction pipe between the water surface and the location where water spills
out the top is the *total lift*. Percent submergence and total lift are
depicted diagrammatically in Fig. 4-4.

Airlift performance diminishes with increasing distance that the
water must be lifted. Fluid friction on the inside walls of the pipe
account for most of this loss of efficiency. In addition, the diameter of
the eduction pipe and the flow rate of injected air affect performance.
Castro et al. (1975) pointed out that airlift performance data given in
engineering handbooks are for high-lift airlift pumps (eduction pipes
sometimes 200 feet or more in length and used to move water or oil from
deep wells). The figures cannot be applied to the low-lift requirements
of an aquarium. Castro et al. (1975) found that in any airlift pump of
given dimensions, there is an optimum air flow rate that results in
maximum performance. The usual occurrence in aquarium operation is
to supply more air than the eduction pipe can handle. The gurgling
sound of escaping air is the first sign that performance is below
optimum. The situation is easily corrected by reducing the volume of
the air flow.

Turbulence is an important factor affecting the performance of low-
lift airlift pumps (Német 1961). The mechanism by which air is deliv-
ered to the eduction pipe is important. If the air is injected through an
open-ended tube, the bubbles will vary in diameter. Air bubbles in
water rise at different velocities, with smaller ones rising more slowly.
When bubbles of different sizes enter an eduction pipe and mix with
the water, there is increased turbulence and reduced performance.

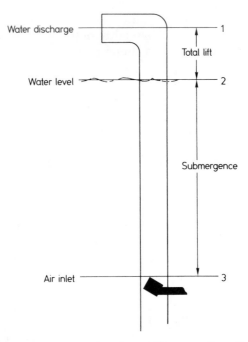

**Figure 4-4.** Operating principles of an airlift pump. From Spotte (1979).

More efficient mixing is attained if the air is dispersed in fine bubbles of uniform size, which rise in the pipe at the same speed. Moreover fine bubbles are more efficient gas exchangers than large bubbles. A standard carborundum airstone is adequate to reduce turbulence in small-diameter pipes. In larger airlifts, the air must be dispersed through a perforated polyvinyl chloride (PVC) nozzle inserted inside the eduction pipe. A design developed by Aquarium Systems, Inc.,* in which the perforated piece is an integral part of the eduction pipe, is shown in Fig. 4-5. Air enters a hollow jacket around a short length of perforated PVC pipe. As air fills the inside of the jacket, it is forced through the holes, all of which are the same diameter, and the bubbles that are produced are the same size.

There is still no widely accepted equation for the airlift pump design. Castro et al. (1975) gave a report on the performance of airlift pumps of short length and small diameter. Német (1961) developed a correlation based on a large number of airlifts of different lengths, diameters, and

* Aquarium Systems, Inc., 8141 Tyler Blvd., Mentor, OH 44060.

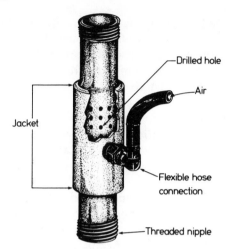

**Figure 4-5.**   Airlift pump with outer jacket (see text).

submergence values. When the Német correlation is adapted to airlifts used for pumping water, the result is equation 9

$$Q = [0.504 \ S^{3/2} L^{1/3} - 0.0752] \ D^{5/2} \tag{9}$$

where $Q$ is the maximum flow rate of water when air flow is optimum (l min$^{-1}$), $S$ is the submergence (pipe length below the water divided by total length), $L$ is the pipe length (cm), and $D$ is the pipe diameter (cm).

Castro (personal communication 1976) obtained approximately 140 sets of data over a range of $L$, $S$, and $D$ values appropriate for aquarium or aquaculture airlift design. Eagleton (personal communication 1978) fitted most applicable sets of data to an equation of the form developed by Német (1961). The flow rate dependence on diameter shown by the Castro data were fit more reliably by a 2.2 power on the diameter, rather than 2.5, as suggested by Német. Equation 10, which resulted from the linear regression, fits the Castro data well enough for design purposes, although possibly a better equation could be developed.

$$Q = [0.758 \ S^{3/2} L^{1/3} + 0.01196] \ D^{2.2} \tag{10}$$

The Castro data used by Eagleton to obtain equation 10 covered a range of diameters from 1.7 to 7.8 cm, lengths from 60 to 300 cm, and submergence values from 0.6 to 1 (60 to 100% submergence). However the minimum acceptable value for the operation of aquarium airlifts is $S = 0.8$ (Spotte 1979).

The Castro data (Castro personal communication 1976, Castro et al.

1975) were obtained for pumping water in a range of variables of likely interest to aquarists, whereas Német used data from many sources, including those reporting on oil flow from wells. As such, the Castro data and equation 10 are recommended here. Table 4-1 gives the flow rate obtained (assuming that air flow rate is optimum), for a number of different airlift configurations using equation 10. If the calculations presented in the tables were repeated using equation 9, it would be seen that the Német correlation gives lower flow rates than found by Castro for 1- to 2-cm diameter pipes, and larger flow rates for pipes of 6 to 8 cm in diameter. The equations give similar results for pipe diameters of 3 to 4 cm.

A safety factor of 25% is recommended when using equation 10 for airlift pump design (Eagleton, personal communication 1978). In other words, length, diameter, and submergence values should be selected that give a calculated flow rate that is 25% larger than needed. This factor guards against problems related to obtaining the optimum flow rate, and also provides a margin to cover minor restrictions to maximum flow, either at the bottom or the top of the pipe. A sample airlift design problem follows. It involves the use of Fig. 4-6, a graph of dimensionless ratios that depicts the volume of water that can be moved per volume of air at specified length to diameter ratios and percent submergence. For example, if an airlift pump consists of an eduction pipe that is 90 cm long and 2.5 cm in diameter, the length to diameter ratio would be 36. At 80% submergence ($S = 0.8$) this would yield a value of 0.5, or 1 l of water moved for every 2 l of air. The ratio becomes even more efficient at a submergence value of 0.9, with 0.75 l of water being moved for every 1 l of air. Maximum efficiency is reached at $S = 1$ when the air is moving more water than its own volume. Ordinarily less water is moved for the same amount of air as the length to diameter ratio becomes smaller, and from the data given by Castro et al. (1975), it looks as if the minimum acceptable ratio would be approximately 20:1.

The problem is to design an airlift pump for an aquarium tank 90 cm deep and with a surface area of 3 m².

1  Determine the water flow rate using the rule of thumb that each m² of surface area requires 40 l min⁻¹ of flow rate (equivalent to 0.7 × 10⁻³ m sec⁻¹ or 1 gal ft⁻² min⁻¹). Therefore

$$(3 \text{ m}^2) (40 \text{ l m}^{-2} \text{ min}^{-1}) = 120 \text{ l min}^{-1}$$
$$\text{plus } 25\% = 150 \text{ l min}^{-1}$$

2  Choose a submergence value (e.g., 0.9). From Table 4-1, find the pipe diameter needed for the flow rate determined in the first

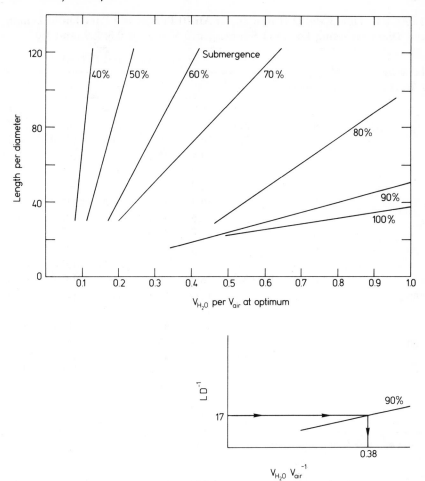

**Figure 4-6.**  Dimensionless graph showing length to diameter ratios of eduction pipes versus water flow to air flow volume ratios when air flow is optimum. From Spotte (1979); drawn from data in Castro et al. (1975).

step. Thus $S = 0.9$ and $L = $ depth/submergence $= 90/0.9 = 100$ cm, and $D = 6$ cm. Equation 10 can be solved for $D$ (equation 11), and $D$ can be calculated directly, but ordinarily this is not necessary.

$$D = \left[ \frac{150}{0.758 \ (0.9)^{1.5} \ (90)^{1/3} + 0.01196} \right]^{1/2.2} = 6 \text{ cm} \qquad (11)$$

Table 4-1    Flow Rate, $Q$ (1 min$^{-1}$), for Airlift Pumps as a Function of Length and Diameter Using Eq. 10 at Submergence Values of 0.8, 0.9, and 1.0

| Length, | | Lift pipe diameter, $D$ (cm) | | | | | |
|---|---|---|---|---|---|---|---|
| $L$ (cm) | Submergence | 1.0 | 2.0 | 3.0 | 4.0 | 6.0 | 8.0 |
| 30 | 0.8 | 1.7 | 7.7 | 18.7 | 35.3 | 86.1 | 162.1 |
|  | 0.9 | 2.0 | 9.2 | 22.4 | 42.2 | 102.9 | 193.7 |
|  | 1.0 | 2.4 | 10.9 | 26.5 | 50.0 | 122.0 | 230.0 |
| 50 | 0.8 | 2.0 | 9.1 | 22.2 | 41.9 | 102.2 | 192.4 |
|  | 0.9 | 2.4 | 10.9 | 26.6 | 50.0 | 122.1 | 229.8 |
|  | 1.0 | 2.8 | 12.9 | 31.4 | 59.2 | 144.0 | 272.0 |
| 75 | 0.8 | 2.3 | 10.4 | 25.5 | 48.0 | 117.0 | 220.4 |
|  | 0.9 | 2.7 | 12.5 | 30.4 | 57.3 | 139.8 | 263.2 |
|  | 1.0 | 3.2 | 14.7 | 36.0 | 67.7 | 165.0 | 311.0 |
| 100 | 0.8 | 2.5 | 11.5 | 28.1 | 52.8 | 128.9 | 242.7 |
|  | 0.9 | 3.0 | 13.7 | 33.5 | 63.1 | 153.9 | 289.8 |
|  | 1.0 | 3.5 | 16.2 | 39.6 | 74.5 | 182.0 | 342.0 |
| 150 | 0.8 | 2.9 | 13.2 | 32.1 | 60.5 | 147.6 | 277.9 |
|  | 0.9 | 3.4 | 15.7 | 38.4 | 72.2 | 176.2 | 331.9 |
|  | 1.0 | 4.0 | 18.6 | 45.3 | 85.3 | 208.0 | 392.0 |
| 200 | 0.8 | 3.2 | 14.5 | 35.4 | 66.6 | 162.5 | 306.0 |
|  | 0.9 | 3.8 | 17.3 | 42.2 | 79.5 | 194.0 | 365.0 |
|  | 1.0 | 4.4 | 20.4 | 49.8 | 93.8 | 229.0 | 431.0 |
| 300 | 0.8 | 3.6 | 16.6 | 40.5 | 76.3 | 186.1 | 350.4 |
|  | 0.9 | 4.3 | 19.8 | 48.4 | 91.0 | 222.2 | 418.3 |
|  | 1.0 | 5.1 | 23.4 | 57.0 | 107.4 | 262.0 | 493.0 |

Source:    Lee C. Eagleton and Gary Adams.

3    Calculate the length/diameter ratio (100/6 = 17). Using Fig. 4-6, read the volume ratio off the 90% submergence line, as shown by the inset in the figure.

4    Because the volume of water $V_{H_2O}$ equals 150 l, then $V_{air}$ = 150/0.38 = 400 l min$^{-1}$.

**The "Reverse Airlift"**

Sometimes a subsurface current of water through an aquarium is more beneficial than an air-water mixture entering at the top. Many creatures have evolved in the open ocean or in benthic habitats with strong currents and tidal action and do poorly when the aquarium water is circulated by conventional airlifts. A stream of subsurface water, when utilized properly, can help keep plankton in suspension for filter feeders, or prevent the floating larvae of many fishes and invertebrates from becoming trapped against the bottom. A mechanical pump is not necessary to maintain a bubble-free current beneath the surface of an aquarium; a modified airlift works just as well and is not subject to mechanical failure. I have termed this apparatus the *reverse airlift* to distinguish it from conventional airlifts.

The principle of the reverse airlift has been used many times by marine biologists. A typical arrangement, demonstrated by Greve (1970) to culture ctenophores, is shown in Fig. 4-7. It works like this. Air injected into a small-diameter eduction pipe removes water from underneath the bacteriological filter. The water is not returned to the surface, but is emptied into a pipe of larger diameter called the collection pipe. As explained previously, the water level in the eduction pipe is higher than it is in the aquarium tank because the equilibrium between the two has been upset. If water from the eduction pipe is emptied into the collection pipe, the level there will also be higher than the level in the aquarium, if only by a centimetre or so. That is enough to establish positive head pressure and cause water in the collection

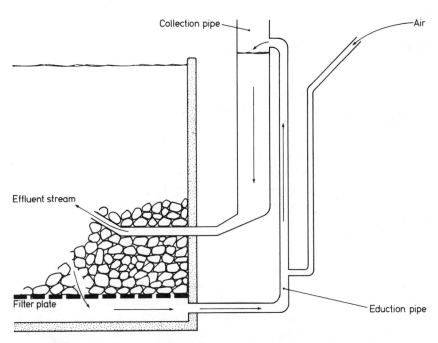

**Figure 4-7.** Reverse airlift. Redrawn and modified from Greve (1970).

pipe to sink. Water enters another pipe of narrow diameter at the bottom of the collection pipe. When the water enters the narrower pipe the pressure it exerts decreases, but its velocity increases, creating a strong stream at the effluent.

## 4.3  DETRITUS FORMATION

Aeration may be instrumental in the formation of particulate organic carbon (POC) in aquarium water (Spotte 1979). Included in the POC are particles, aggregates, and detritus. The terms are used loosely and often interchangeably by oceanographers, which has led to needless confusion when mechanisms of their formation are discussed. I shall consider particles as the smallest and first formed, followed by aggregates, which are composed of particles. Finally, detritus is the largest stage, being made up of clumps of aggregates.

In the oceans there are probably two mechanisms by which insoluble particles containing organic matter are formed. I shall assume, without direct evidence, that particle formation in seawater aquariums is analogous. According to Barber (1966) organic molecules come out of solution to form a skin about rising air bubbles. When a bubble reaches the surface, it is ejected out of the water, leaving behind its collapsed skin in the form of a monomolecular film. The film sinks, providing a seed onto which additional organics are scavenged from solution and aggregate. Alternatively small bubbles driven beneath the surface may lose their gases through dissolution to the surrounding water. In so doing, they leave behind a particle. This process was measured and even photographed by Johnson (1976).

Once formed, particles join together and grow larger. This activity is called *aggregation,* defined here as the physical process by which particulate matter clumps together in seawater. The term "organic aggregate," sometimes used as a synonym for aggregate, is a misnomer because the organic portion is seldom more than 30% (Wangersky and Gordon 1965).

Detritus forms from the clumping of aggregates. *Detritus* is the tan-colored floc, or "dust," common on the surface of aquarium filter beds. Unlike particles and aggregates, detritus is large and clearly visible.

Aggregate formation depends on three factors: (1) the presence of air bubbles and their size; (2) the concentration of dissolved organic carbon (DOC); and (3) the quantity of particles present at any given time. It should be pointed out that aggregates can form in stagnant water (e.g.,

Riley et al. 1965, Sheldon et al. 1967), but the rate of formation is much slower than in agitated water.

Baylor et al. (1962) and Sutcliffe et al. (1963) showed that organic particles could be produced by adsorption of organic material onto the surfaces of air bubbles. Menzel (1966), however, was unable to produce significant amounts of aggregate matter by bubbling, and Riley (1963) and Sheldon et al. (1967) were able to produce aggregates and particles, respectively, *in situ* in the absence of air bubbles. In a series of experiments to resolve the controversy, Batoosingh et al. (1969) discovered that small particles in the size range of 0.22 to 1.2 $\mu$m were important as seed matter, or nuclei, in the formation of aggregates from particles during bubbling. The discrepancies in the results of the earlier investigators were attributed to their having used different types of filters to remove particulate matter from seawater samples prior to starting the experiments.

Barber (1966) had postulated that bacteria were necessary in aggregate formation during bubbling, and Sheldon et al. (1967) suggested that bacteria played a part in the formation of particles *in situ*. Batoosingh and his fellow investigators were able to show that any particles, living or dead, accelerated aggregate formation, and they could not find any direct evidence that living bacteria were necessary to carry out the process.

Batoosingh et al. (1969) also determined that fine air bubbles were more effective producers of aggregates than large bubbles. This can probably be attributed to their larger surface areas available to adsorb surface-active organics from solution.

Sheldon et al. (1967) discovered that the quantity of particles formed in filtered seawater samples could be increased by raising the concentration of DOC. When the level was doubled to 4 mg l$^{-1}$ by addition of glycine, there was a 10-fold increase in particle formation.

When bubbling rates were varied, Batoosingh et al. (1969) noticed that the yield of aggregates was rapid at first, then tapered off so that a 24-hr experiment seldom produced more than twice as much material as one lasting only 3 to 6 hr. The presence of particles, either natural or artificially produced, seemed to inhibit further aggregate formation. Filtration on a continuous basis produced greater aggregate formation than intermittent filtration. Thus particles seemed to be necessary to initiate aggregate formation during bubbling, but too many were inhibitory.

Aggregates probably are the precursors of detritus in seawater aquariums, just as in the oceans. Aggregate formation in aquariums may occur at two locations: (1) inside the airlift pump; and (2) at the air-water interface near the effluent of the airlift. The mechanism would be similar in either case. Spotte (1979) suggested that aggregates could be formed on rising air bubbles in airlift pumps by the process described by Barber (1966). Adsorption of dissolved surface-active organics could take place on rising air bubbles. At the surface of the water, the ejected bubbles would fall back as collapsed monomolecular films, ready to adsorb other material.

Assuming these processes function in seawater aquariums, detritus formation in water high in dissolved organic carbon can be accelerated by: (1) the use of finer air bubbles in the airlift pumps; (2) increased intensity of bubbling; and (3) continuous removal of particles and aggregates by mechanical filtration, thus reducing inhibition of additional aggregate formation by the presence of too many particles. Accelerated detritus formation is a useful mechanism for indirectly reducing dissolved organic material in the water. Once formed from aggregates, the organics, along with detritus onto which they are adsorbed, are easily removed by mechanical means. In addition, adsorption of dissolved organics onto detritus is necessary before mineralization by heterotrophic bacteria can take place (Section 7.1). As a side benefit, intense bubbling removes orthophosphate from solution, as described in Section 6-2.

# CHAPTER 5
*Buffering*

The chemical interactions of free (dissolved) $CO_2$, water, and carbonate minerals constitute the carbon dioxide system, or buffer system in seawater. Atmospheric carbon dioxide dissolves in water when its partial pressure exceeds the partial pressure of $CO_2$ in solution. Having crossed the air-water boundary, free $CO_2$ becomes hydrated, first forming carbonic acid and then bicarbonate and carbonate ions, the principal buffers in water. The sequence is shown in the composite reaction

$$CO_{2(g)} \rightleftharpoons CO_{2(aq)} + H_2O \rightleftharpoons H_2CO_3 \rightleftharpoons H^+ + HCO_3^- \rightleftharpoons H^+ + CO_3^{2-} \quad (12)$$

Plants in the sea utilize carbon dioxide as a major source of carbon. During photosynthesis, inorganic $CO_2$ is reduced chemically to the organic state. Carbon accumulated in plant tissues is consumed by animals. When animals die, bacteria oxidize their remains and produce inorganic carbon ($CO_2$), which once again can be used in photosynthesis or released back into the atmosphere. Carbon dioxide in solution is precipitated as calcium carbonate and bound up in the shells of marine organisms. The shells eventually sink to the ocean floor, where many dissolve and replenish the subsurface layers with inorganic carbon. No single process dominates. In the vastness of the oceanic biosphere oxidation is tempered by reduction, and precipitation is counterbalanced by dissolution.

A seawater aquarium is, by comparison, eutrophic (high in plant nutrients) and unbalanced. Chemical species that affect the buffer system may accumulate or become depleted to a degree never encountered in the ocean. Typically, oxidation overrides reduction and acids are produced. Eventually, sources of bicarbonate and carbonate are reduced and equation 12 shifts to the left. The water then moves toward acidity, a trend considered to be harmful to most marine organisms.

This chapter defines the terms used to describe various aspects of the seawater buffer system. It also goes into the reasons why carbonate minerals fail to reach equilibrium with seawater and thus sustain the pH and alkalinity at their original values. Biological factors that contribute to the decline in buffer capacity are covered briefly in the third section. The last section deals with the practical aspects of maintaining buffer capacity in aquarium seawater.

## 5.1   THE SEAWATER BUFFER SYSTEM

Four terms are commonly used to describe various aspects of the seawater buffer system: (1) pH; (2) buffer capacity; (3) alkalinity; and (4) carbonate alkalinity.

### pH

The mathematical concept of $p$ means take the negative logarithm of the quantity following and multiply the result by minus one. Thus pH = $-\log_{10}H.^+$ The ionization of pure water results in formation of equal amounts of hydrogen and hydroxide ions. The concentration ion product of pure water, $k_w$, can be expressed

$$k_w = [H^+][OH^-] = (1 \times 10^{-7})(1 \times 10^{-7}) = 1 \times 10^{-14} \text{ at } 25°C \quad (13)$$

where brackets represent concentration in aqueous solutions at neutrality, the hydrogen ion concentration is $10^{-7}$, and the pH = $-\log 10^{-7}$. In a solution of pH less than 7 the hydrogen ion concentration will be greater than $10^{-7}$ and the solution will be acidic. A pH value of 3, for example, shows that the solution contains $10^{-3}$ mole $H^+ 1^{-1}$. In this case, the hydroxide ion concentration would be $10^{-11}$, because the product of the two concentrations ($10^{-3} \times 10^{-11}$) must always equal $k_w$, which is $10^{-14}$. To say it another way, pH + pOH = 14. Surface seawater is slightly basic with an average pH value of 8.2.

### Buffer Capacity

The *buffer capacity* of water refers to its ability to withstand changes in pH when acids or bases are added. Synonyms are buffer index and

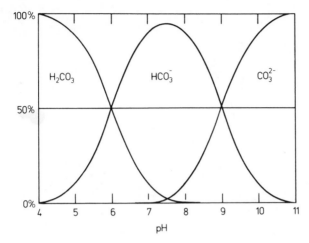

**Figure 5-1**   The relative concentrations of $H_2CO_3$, $HCO_3^-$, and $CO_3^{2-}$ in seawater as a function of pH. Redrawn from Weyl (1970).

buffer intensity. Aquarists often speak of alkali or alkaline reserve, but these terms are misleading because they reflect only the acid-neutralizing capacity of water and disregard the fact that buffering occurs in both directions along a pH scale. In seawater, for example, maximum buffer capacity appears at pH values near 6 and 9, and seawater is buffered very little, if at all, at its normal pH of 8.2 (Skirrow 1975).

Carbonate and bicarbonate ions are the primary buffers in water. They neutralize any addition or withdrawal of free carbon dioxide and maintain a constant pH by repressing fluctuations in hydrogen ion concentration. Bicarbonate ion is the dominant constituent in the buffer system within the natural pH range of seawater, as shown diagrammatically in Fig. 5-1.

The buffer capacity of seawater is inherent in the reaction

$$2HCO_3^- \rightleftharpoons CO_2 + H_2O + CO_3^{2-} \tag{14}$$

The shifting of equation 14 depends on two factors: ion pairing and the ionic strength of the medium at given temperature and pressure. It can be assumed that seawater has an ionic strength of 0.7 $m$ at $S = 35$ o/oo.

The original ion pairing model for seawater was presented by Garrels and Thompson (1962). Since then, the existence of ion pairs has been verified numerous times (e.g., Kester and Pytkowicz 1970, Pytkowicz and Atlas 1975, Pytkowicz and Hawley 1974). Ion pairing increases the buffer capacity of seawater approximately threefold (Morel et al. 1976). The influence is indirect, however, and ion pairs by themselves do not

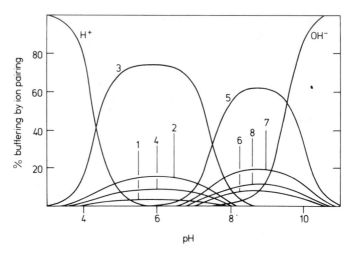

**Figure 5-2** Percentage contributions of the reactions listed in Table 5-1 to the buffer capacity of the $CO_2$ system in seawater, as calculated from an ion association model. Numbers on the curves refer to the reactions in Table 5-1. Redrawn from Whitfield (1974a).

buffer seawater (Pytkowicz 1972, Whitfield 1974a). Major cations involved in ion pairing and buffer capacity are $Na^+$, $Mg^{2+}$, and $Ca^{2+}$. The important anions are $HCO_3^-$ and $CO_3^{2-}$, although sulfate ion pairs also affect buffer capacity in a limited way. Of the anions, more than 90% of the carbonate is involved in ion pairing, 60% of the sulfate, and 20% of the bicarbonate.

Whitfield (1974a) calculated the buffer capacity of seawater at 25°C and 1 atm pressure. As seen in Fig. 5-2 and Table 5-1, reactions 5 to 7 affect buffer capacity significantly at pH values above 7.5 The formation of $MgCO_3$ contributes more than 50% of the total at pH 8.5. Whitfield also determined the effect of seawater composition on buffer capacity. This was done by making artificial seawaters of varied composition, then plotting acid-base titration curves and noting how changes in the medium affected pH. The $[Mg^{2+}]:[SO_4^{2-}]$ ratio was altered from a normal value of 1.9 through a range of 0.48 to 7.61. Titration curves showed little change in buffer capacity. When $Mg^{2+}$ was manipulated from a tenth to five times the normal value in seawater, the pH decreased by only 0.55 units from an initial value of 8. Under natural conditions, the removal of magnesium would probably be compensated by an increase in the concentration of sodium. Thus the portion of the buffer capacity affected by the pairing of a cation with carbonate would be only slightly affected, even if magnesium were to be depleted totally.

Table 5-1   Reactions Considered in Calculating the Buffer Capacity of the $CO_2$ in Seawater

| Reaction | | | $-\log_{10}K$ |
|---|---|---|---|
| 1  $Ca^{2+}$ | $+ H_2CO_3$ | $\rightleftharpoons CaHCO_3^+ + H^+$ | 5.450 |
| 2  $Mg^{2+}$ | $+ H_2CO_3$ | $\rightleftharpoons MgHCO_3^+ + H^+$ | 5.502 |
| 3  $H_2CO_3$ | | $\rightleftharpoons HCO_3^- + H^+$ | 6.124 |
| 4  $Na^+$ | $+ H_2CO_3$ | $\rightleftharpoons NaHCO_3^+ + H^+$ | 6.745 |
| 5  $Mg^{2+}$ | $+ HCO_3^-$ | $\rightleftharpoons MgCO_3 + H^+$ | 7.665 |
| 6  $Ca^{2+}$ | $+ HCO_3^-$ | $\rightleftharpoons CaCO_3 + H^+$ | 7.913 |
| 7  $Na^+$ | $+ HCO_3^-$ | $\rightleftharpoons NaCO_3^- + H^+$ | 9.186 |
| 8  $HCO_3^-$ | | $\rightleftharpoons CO_3^{2-} + H^+$ | 9.776 |
| 9  $H_2O$ | | $\rightleftharpoons OH^- + H^+$ | 13.791 |

Source: Whitfield (1974a).

In the case of sulfate ion, it was found that because of competition in the formation of $MgSO_4$, a decrease in $MgCO_3$ is balanced by an increase in the level of $NaCO_3^-$, which forms when carbonate ions are released in the dissociation of $MgCO_3$. The effect is much like a formal ball in which couples change partners but the total number of pairs on the dance floor stays the same. As Whitfield (1974a) noted, a decrease in magnesium and an increase in sulfate tends to increase the pH; however depleting the magnesium 10-fold and increasing the sulfate concentration by a factor of three results in a pH shift of only 0.25 units. Thus the buffer capacity is flexible within broad limits, even when contributing components are inflated or decreased several times their normal concentrations.

To summarize, ion pairs affect the concentrations of bicarbonate and carbonate ions, which in turn affect the pH directly and the buffer capacity indirectly. Again it should be stated that ion pairs do not buffer seawater. Buffering is accomplished through equation 14. Second, buffering in seawater is a function of the anions, not the cations. Third, at least half the buffer capacity of seawater at a pH value slightly higher than normal can be attributed to the presence of $MgCO_3$. Fourth, because the large buffer capacity of seawater is mainly a function of bicarbonate and carbonate ions, which are present in much smaller quantities than the major cations, alteration of the major cation concentrations has little effect on buffer capacity and pH. In other words, the major cation ratios can be changed drastically and still the buffer capacity will be affected only slightly. This helps to explain why even the most carelessly formulated artificial seawaters often contain sufficient buffer capacities to maintain temporarily stable pH values.

## Alkalinity

The buffer capacity of seawater can be described in terms of the anion concentration, as just mentioned. When considered separately, these anions are called the *alkalinity* (also known as titration alkalinity and total alkalinity), defined as the net negative charge of all ions that interact with hydrogen ion, expressed as meq $l^{-1}$. To say it another way, alkalinity is the sum of the analytical concentrations of the anions of carbonic and weaker acids. The only other weak acid of any significance is boric acid. Alkalinity can be expressed

$$A = [HCO_3^-] + 2[CO_3^{2-}] + [B(OH)_4] + [OH^- - H^+] \qquad (15)$$

In most seawaters, the last term can be eliminated, leaving

$$A = [HCO_3^-] + 2[CO_3^{2-}] + [B(OH)_4] \qquad (16)$$

The alkalinity of surface seawater varies between 2.1 and 2.5 meq $1^{-1}$.

Aquarists are often confused about how the addition or removal of a substance affects alkalinity. It is known, for example, that free $CO_2$ is being added to aquarium water continuously as the result of biological oxidation. It is a common practice for aquarists to maintain pH levels above 8 by addition of bicarbonate or carbonate salts. Then too, there is the dissolution of carbonate minerals, producing carbonate ions. Still other substances that are acidic or basic enter the water as by-products of metabolism.

Weyl (1970) provided four diagrams that show how different substances affect alkalinity. They are reproduced here as Figs. 5-3 through 5-6. Look at Fig. 5-3 and assume that point A represents the alkalinity of

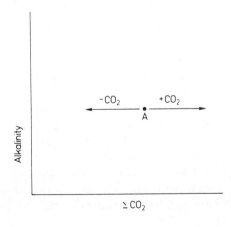

**Figure 5-3** Removal or addition of free $CO_2$. Redrawn and modified from Weyl (1970).

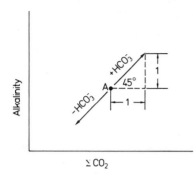

**Figure 5-4** Removal or addition of $HCO_3^-$. Redrawn and modified from Weyl (1970).

seawater. If carbon dioxide is added, the total inorganic carbon ($\Sigma$ $CO_2$), illustrated by equation 12, will increase by the amount of the addition. However $CO_2$ carries no electrical charge and so the alkalinity of the water does not change. From the diagram it is apparent that addition of $CO_2$ moves point A to the right; removal of $CO_2$ moves it to the left, but because the alkalinity neither increases nor decreases, the point never moves up or down.

If bicarbonate ions are added the situation is different (Fig. 5-4). If 1 meq of $HCO_3^-$ is added to a litre of seawater the total inorganic carbon is increased by 1 meq. Point A moves one unit to the right and one unit up, or upward at an angle of 45°. Removal of 1 meq has the opposite effect. As seen in the diagram, the alkalinity increases or decreases depending on whether $HCO_3^-$ is added or removed.

Consider next the effect of carbonate ion. If 1 meq of $CO_3^{2-}$ is added to a litre of seawater, the $\Sigma CO_2$ content is increased by 1 meq. Because the carbonate ion carries a double negative charge, however, the change in alkalinity will be 2 meq, as opposed to the single meq for bicarbonate. As seen in Fig. 5-5, point A is displaced one unit to the right and two upward, or upward at an angle of 63.4°. If carbonate ions are precipitated the effect is the opposite.

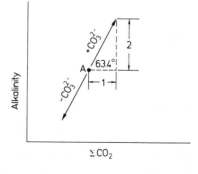

**Figure 5-5** Removal or addition of $CO_3^{2-}$. Redrawn and modified from Weyl (1970).

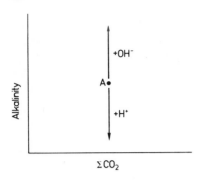

**Figure 5-6**  Addition of an acid or base. Redrawn and modified from Weyl (1970).

If a strong acid such as HC1 is added to a sample of seawater, the $H^+$ ions will combine with bicarbonate ions and form carbonic acid. The result is a decrease in alkalinity, although the $\Sigma CO_2$ content will stay the same (Fig. 5-6). Thus the alkalinity moves straight downward. Addition of a base, such as NaOH, increases the alkalinity but still has no effect on the $\Sigma CO_2$. The result is a shift of point A directly upward. In summary, addition of bicarbonate, carbonate, HCl, or NaOH to seawater affects the pH and alkalinity, but only bicarbonate and carbonate additions cause changes in both alkalinity and $\Sigma CO_2$. Addition of free $CO_2$ affects the pH but not the alkalinity.

### Carbonate Alkalinity

Carbonate alkalinity is a useful derivative of alkalinity, because it emphasizes the importance of carbonate and bicarbonate ions. Moreover this value is often needed before many of the constituents of the buffer system can be calculated (e.g., Park 1969). Carbonate alkalinity is obtained by subtracting the value for borate from the alkalinity (equation 16). Thus

$$CA = [HCO_3^-] + [CO_3^{2-}] \qquad (17)$$

Alkalinity is, of course, greater than carbonate alkalinity, but the difference between them decreases with declining pH.

### 5.2  SOLUBILITY OF MINERAL CARBONATES

Calcareous minerals, crushed and graded, ordinarily are used in seawater aquarium filter beds to buffer the water. Calcite, magnesian calcites, and dolomites are the common materials used for this purpose.

They invariably fail to maintain alkalinity at 2.1 meq l$^{-1}$ or more and the buffer capacity of the seawater diminishes gradually. Nitric acid from nitrification and organic acids excreted by algae and produced by bacteria cause the pH of the water to decline below a minimum acceptable value of 8. Why this should happen is not entirely clear. It is known, however, that the solution kinetics of carbonate minerals in seawater are slow because of the presence of magnesium and DOC. It is worthwhile to discuss the limitations of calcareous gravels because they are used so widely in seawater aquarium keeping.

Wattenberg and Timmerman (1936) first noted that surface seawater is supersaturated with calcium carbonate that fails to precipitate in predictable fashion. Weyl (1967) demonstrated that when surface seawater from the Gulf of Mexico was reduced to undersaturation by addition of 1 N HCl, pure calcite (Iceland spar) still had not reached equilibrium after 30 min. If the equilibration rate were determined solely by diffusion, equilibrium would have been attained in a few minutes. Thus in seawater there are inhibiting mechanisms that slow down the solution kinetics of carbonate minerals.

To understand clearly the behavior of carbonate minerals in seawater, the subject must be studied from opposite extremes: crystal growth (precipitation) and crystal breakdown (dissolution). The generally accepted explanation given in seawater aquarium guides that carbonate minerals simply go into solution when the pH declines and in so doing, "buffer" the water is a gross oversimplification of processes that really are very complex. Several factors bear on mineral carbonate precipitation and dissolution and recent evidence identifies substances inherent in seawater that inhibit both crystal growth and crystal breakdown under specific conditions. They are dissolved magnesium and DOC. There is no experimental evidence that the first process occurs in aquarium seawater, and little evidence to support the second, but it is probable that both are significant.

**Dissolved Magnesium**

It has been known for some time that the magnesium present in solution largely determines the form in which calcium carbonate will be precipitated. Aragonite and calcite have the same chemical formula ($CaCO_3$), yet aragonite precipitates before the more stable calcite in experimental solutions containing magnesium ions (Kitano 1962; Lippmann 1960, 1973; Simkiss 1964). Berner (1975) discovered that magnesium ions did not affect the rate of crystal growth of aragonite, but severely retarded the growth of calcite crystals. The precipitate that formed from seawater on pure calcite crystals contained 7 to 10 mole%

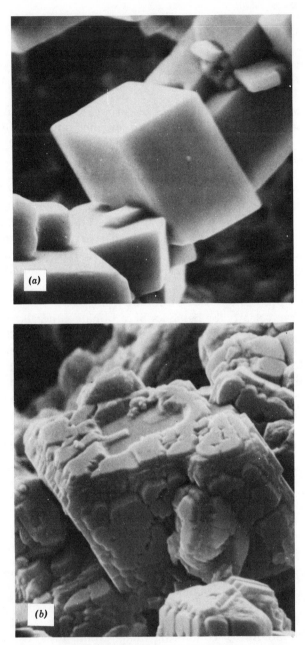

**Figure 5-7** Scanning electron photomicrographs of a magnesian calcite overgrowth on pure calcite seeds in artificial seawater: (a) initial seeds (×7,875); and (b) magnesian calcite precipitated on seeds (×8,250). From Berner (1975).

82

$MgCO_3$ (magnesian calcite) and it occurred as an overgrowth on the crystal surfaces, as shown by electron photomicrographs (Fig. 5-7). This confirmed the essential features of an earlier model by Weyl (1967).

The concentration of magnesium in solution is an important variable when considering calcite crystal growth. Berner (1975) found that when 95% of the magnesium was removed from artificial seawater, the remaining 5% did not significantly retard crystal growth of calcite. An explanation for this is that magnesium ions fit more easily into the crystal structure of calcite than in the crystal structure of aragonite. There is also the possibility that magnesium ions are adsorbed on the calcite surfaces to a greater extent than they are on aragonite surfaces (DeGroot and Duyvis 1966). Calcite surfaces are known to have a definite affinity for magnesium ions (Berner 1966, DeGroot and Duyvis 1966). Folk (1974) and Lippmann (1960) postulated that the inhibiting effect of magnesium on calcite crystal growth was the result of its acting as a "surface poison" and being adsorbed as hydrated ions at growth sites on the crystal surfaces. Another possibility is the incorporation of magnesium into the growing crystal to such an extent that its solubility is increased. The new surface of the crystal, being now composed of magnesian calcite instead of pure calcite, would reach equilibrium with the magnesium ions in seawater. The resulting overgrowth destabilizes the surface of the crystal and increases its solubility (solubility decreases as a substance becomes more stable). The basic elements of this concept were presented by Weyl (1967), and more recently by Berner (1975) and Plummer and Mackenzie (1974). Chave et al. (1962) found that the stability of carbonate minerals in seawater increased in the following order: high magnesian calcite, aragonite, low-magnesian calcite, pure calcite, and dolomite. Berner (1975) showed that calcites with 2 to 7 mole% $MgCO_3$ are thermodynamically stable in seawater.

The Mg:Ca ratio is a critical part of the picture. Lippmann (1973) reported that when this ratio was less than 1.0, only pure calcite was formed, whereas aragonite precipitated when the ratio exceeded 3.0. In normal seawater the ratio is 5.0. The work of Berner (1975) indicated that magnesium ions in seawater may act as a simple surface poison because they exceed dissolved calcium ions by such a large margin. However Berner considered this effect to be less important in retarding crystal growth than the uptake of magnesium and subsequent formation of magnesian calcite overgrowths.

While studying the solution kinetics of calcite in waters of different composition, Weyl (1967) found that calcium and magnesium ions retarded the equilibration of calcite, but that sodium had little effect. Weyl considered that the inhibiting mechanism involving calcium and magnesium could be ". . . either the formation of a barrier layer at the solid-liquid interface or a reaction in the solution itself that has slow kinetics." To check the second possibility he mixed $CaCl_2$ and $MgCl_2$ with water containing no solid carbonates but only $NaHCO_3$. The rapid kinetics indicated that the rate-inhibiting mechanism took place at the solid-liquid interface. This work, which has important implications in aquarium seawater buffering, will be considered in detail.

Based on a series of experiments, Weyl found that as seawater flowed through a laboratory apparatus containing carbonate minerals, the rate of magnesian calcite precipitation decreased significantly with time, suggesting that the precipitate formed on the mineral grains became less stable and therefore more soluble until the solubility of the overgrowth was nearly in equilibrium with seawater. This same phenomenon takes place in nature and accounts for the extreme differences in solution kinetics among carbonate minerals deposited only a few metres apart. Earlier studies (Deffeyes et al. 1964, 1965) had shown that in carbonate sand tested from the surf zone at Bonaire in the Netherlands Antilles, the water precipitated 3 mg $l^{-1}$ calcium carbonate in 3 min. Dry sand from higher on the same beach precipitated 13 mg $l^{-1}$; dry Bahama oolites (rock consisting of small grains of calcium carbonate cemented together) precipitated 24 mg $l^{-1}$. Thus the recent history of a given carbonate mineral largely determines its solution behavior at any point in time. The precipitation process on the surfaces of the carbonate minerals is rapid at first, slowing down as a soluble precipitate forms. In nature, oolites exposed to currents of seawater, then slowly buried in sediment out of contact with fresh seawater, experience recrystallization of an overgrowth in a less soluble (and hence more stable) form.

In still another experiment, Weyl (1967) arranged a double flow apparatus that could circulate seawater through packs of dolomite, or $CaMg(CO_3)_2$, and calcite set up in parallel. Once a steady state for each mineral was reached, the pH of the water was altered by adding an acid or a base. The study showed that a large range of carbonate concentration existed throughout which the dolomite neither dissolved nor precipitated significantly. Within this range, however, calcite quickly dissolved or precipitated. As Weyl noted, if seawater contains a mixture of calcite and dolomite and comes to equilibrium with calcite, then dolomite, because it falls outside this range, will not dissolve or precipitate readily.

Next a comparison was made between the solubility of carbonate minerals with new surfaces, because previous work had shown that the solubility of the precipitated layer differed from that of the substrate, or

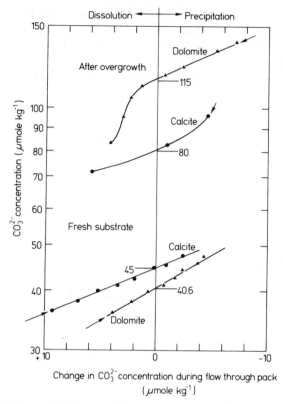

**Figure 5-8** Calcite and dolomite solubility in seawater. Redrawn from Weyl (1967).

underlying surface of the material. To use Weyl's metaphor, the experimental solution can only "see" the surface of the mineral and not what exists beneath it. The pH of the water was first acidified until the materials started to dissolve. This process was continued overnight and the mineral packs in the apparatus then were purged of the $CO_2$ gas formed in the dissolution reaction. Once the experiment commenced, the pH of the water was monitored as it flowed through the mineral packs. The degree of undersaturation, caused by the dissolution of each mineral, was noted by changes in pH; afterward, the water was made basic by addition of sodium hydroxide until both calcite and dolomite precipitated. Figure 5-8 shows the results. The factors measured at the point of precipitation were pH, magnesium, calcium, and total carbon dioxide ($\Sigma CO_2$). The pH was converted to the equivalent change in carbonate ion concentration and plotted on the $x$ axis; the $y$ axis shows the actual carbonate ion concentration plotted on a logarithmic scale. At concentrations of $40.6 \times 10^{-6}$ mole $kg^{-1}$ (dolomite) and $45 \times 10^{-6}$ mole $kg^{-1}$ (calcite), the minerals neither dissolved nor precipitated. Once the dissolution process had started (bottom of Fig. 5-8), the pH of the water was raised and precipitation was allowed to continue overnight. Later the pH of the water was lowered in stepwise fashion to find the carbonate concentration at which the precipitate of the magnesian calcite overgrowth would reach equilibrium with seawater. As shown in the upper part of Fig. 5-8, the solubility product of the overgrowth was about twice that of the substrate. The overgrowth of dolomite was more soluble than that of calcite, although in the uncontaminated state calcite had proved to be more soluble than dolomite.

This particular situation can be summarized as follows. If crystals of calcite and dolomite containing new surfaces are placed together in seawater, the dolomite will first grow at the expense of the calcite; that is, until its overgrowths of magnesian calcite reach the same solubility as the calcite. The minerals can coexist once their surfaces have come into equilibrium with the surrounding seawater. Dolomite cannot dissolve because in pure form it is less soluble than calcite when the two minerals are placed in the same solution. However it cannot grow either, because its magnesian calcite precipitate would become more soluble than either calcite or the overgrowth on the calcite.

In general, it can be said that the surface lattice of a carbonate mineral crystal acquires defects that lead to increased solubility. *Moreover the surface of any carbonate mineral comes into equilibrium with the seawater and not vice versa.* The mechanism is by acquiring an overgrowth. The work of Berner (1975), Katz (1973), and Plummer and Mackenzie (1974) indicated that in the case of calcite, the most stable form in Mg-Ca exchange with seawater contains 2 to 7 mole% $MgCO_3$.

The study of Weyl (1967) pointed out that solubility values determined in the presence of impurities can differ widely. Therefore measurements of solubility that consider only the equilibration point and fail to note points of dissolution and precipitation are of limited value and do not accurately describe carbonate mineral-seawater relationships.

### Dissolved Organic Carbon

Substances other than magnesium ions may affect the chemical states of carbonate minerals in seawater. Barcelona and Atwood (1978), Barcelona et al. (1976), Chave (1965), and Chave and Suess (1967, 1970) published data indicating that naturally occurring organic carbon compounds in solution inhibited the precipitation of carbonates from supersaturated natural and artificial seawaters. Meyers and Quinn (1971) and Suess (1970) described the adsorption of fatty acids and natural lipids onto calcite surfaces.

Chave and Suess (1970) added 0.1 mole $Na_2CO_3$ to seawater samples collected locally in the Hawaiian Islands, which brought the pH to 9.5. The change in pH with time after addition of the sodium carbonate was monitored (the pH drops suddenly with the rapid precipitation of $CaCO_3$), and the quantity of DOC was measured before and after precipitation. Natural seawater samples taken from laboratory aquariums were treated identically. The level of dissolved organics was much higher in the aquarium water because of the concentrated biomass. Precipitation was increasingly delayed as the level of DOC increased.

Chave and Suess (1970) measured 0.1 mg $kg^{-1}$ of organic carbon precipitated from freshly collected seawater and 0.25 mg $kg^{-1}$ from organically rich aquarium water. This represented approximately 10% of the organics present in both cases. Suess (1970) reported that from 10 to 14% of the DOC in seawater became associated with calcite surfaces when the mineral was ground to a fine powder before being added to seawater. Chave and Suess (1970) speculated that the nuclei that were being formed were rendered inactive at their reaction sites and that the interfering organics first had to be removed before calcium carbonate precipitation could take place. Removal by precipitation of the DOC probably happened because the high pH value decreased its solubility, or because the DOC became associated with early forming $CaCO_3$ nuclei. In either case, some organics had been removed from solution before the bulk of the calcium carbonate started to precipitate.

The inhibiting mechanism by which DOC delays the precipitation of calcium carbonate may occur when nuclei are inactivated by adsorption of DOC from solution onto the mineral surfaces. Chave and Suess (1967) had earlier suggested that the adsorption of DOC onto the surfaces of carbonate minerals occurred more rapidly than did the precipitation of $CaCO_3$ onto the same surfaces.

## 5.3  BIOLOGICAL FACTORS

Biological factors that affect buffer capacity are: (1) oxidation and reduction; and (2) photosynthesis and excretion of organic acids by algae. A summary is given in Table 5-2.

Table 5-2  **Biologically Mediated Reactions Affecting pH in Natural Waters**

| Process | Reaction | Effect on pH |
|---|---|---|
| Photosynthesis | $6\,CO_2 + 6\,H_2O \rightarrow C_6H_{12}O_6 + 6O_2$ | Increase |
| Respiration | $C_6H_{12}O_6 + 6O_2 \rightarrow 6CO_2 + 6H_2O$ | Decrease |
| Methane fermentation | $C_6H_{12}O_6 + 3CO_2 \rightarrow 3CH_4 + 6CO_2$ | Decrease |
| Nitrification | $NH_4^+ + 2O_2 \rightarrow NO_3^- + H_2O + 2H^+$ | Decrease |
| Denitrification | $5C_6H_{12}O_6 + 24NO_3^- + 24H^+ \rightarrow$ $30CO_2 + 12N_2 + 42H_2O$ | Increase |
| Sulfide oxidation | $HS^- + 2O_2 \rightarrow SO_4^{2-} + H^+$ | Decrease |
| Sulfate reduction | $C_6H_{12}O_6 + 3SO_4^{2-} + 3H^+ \rightarrow 6CO_2$ $+ HS^- + 6H_2O$ | Increase |

Source:  Weber and Stumm (1963).

## Oxidation and Reduction

The influx of free $CO_2$ from aerobic respiration by living organisms (an oxidation process) lowers the pH of seawater by causing equation 12 to shift to the left but does not affect alkalinity (Fig. 5-3). The high levels of nitrate and phosphate ordinarily found in aquarium water affect both pH and alkalinity. Nitrate is the end product of nitrification by autotrophic bacteria in the filter bed. Phosphate results from the lysis of dead cells during heterotrophic decomposition of organic matter. One result of these high nutrient levels is the declining alkalinity in old aquarium water, leading ultimately to reduced buffer capacity. The mechanisms are easily demonstrated with redox reactions and titration curves. Gundersen and Mountain (1973) showed how accumulating nitrate affected the alkalinity of surface seawater. If the reactions for nitrification are written to illustrate a gain or loss of electrons, the oxidation of ammonia is shown by

$$NH_4^+ + OH^- + 2H_2O \rightleftharpoons H^+ + NO_2^- + H_2O + 6\,[H^+ + e^-] \quad (18)$$

and the oxidation of nitrite by

$$NO_2^- + H^+ + H_2O \rightleftharpoons H^+ + NO_3^- + 2\,[H^+ + e^-] \quad (19)$$

The overall reaction is

$$NH_4^+ + OH^- + 3H_2O \rightleftharpoons H^+ + NO_3^- + H_2O + 8\,[H^+ + e^-] \quad (20)$$

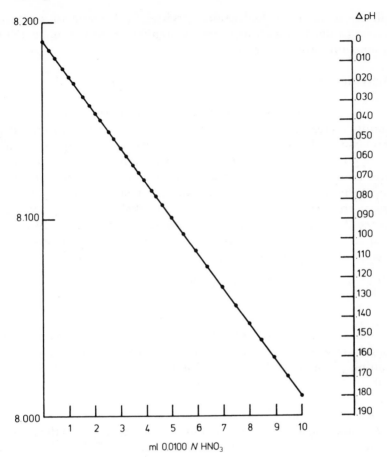

**Figure 5-9**   Change in pH of open ocean surface water titrated with 0.01 $N$ NHO$_3$. Redrawn and modified from Gundersen and Mountain (1973).

Equation 20 demonstrates that 1 mole each of hydrogen ion and nitrate ion are formed after the oxidation of 1 mole of ammonium ion. In other words, the end product of nitrification is, strictly speaking, *nitric acid,* and its effect is to reduce the buffer capacity of the water. Figure 5-9 illustrates how nitrate ion formation is accompanied by an equivalent amount of hydrogen ions. Seawater titrated using 0.01 $N$ HNO$_3$ with simultaneous pH monitoring produces a linear curve, indicating a drop in pH as nitrification proceeds.

Sulfide oxidation produces increases in pH and alkalinity, whereas sulfate reduction and dissimilation (Section 7.2) cause the pH and alkalinity to increase. Reduction activities by bacteria in a seawater aquarium filter bed are not normally significant insofar as overall pH and alkalinity are concerned.

### Activities of Algae

The culture of algae in seawater aquariums ordinarily results in pH and alkalinity increases, although many organic acids also are produced and the release of these substances into the water has the opposite effect. During photosynthesis, free $CO_2$ and nitrate ions are taken up from the environment, the latter after being reduced to ammonium ions before being assimilated across the cell wall. The result of $CO_2$ uptake is to increase the pH of the water, but not the alkalinity; uptake of nitrate increases both the pH and alkalinity. Brewer and Goldman (1976) studied uptake of nitrate by three species of marine phytoplankton and projected the overall effect of nitrate utilization, as shown by

$$106\ CO_2 + 138\ H_2O + 16\ NO_3^- \rightarrow (CH_2O)_{106}\,(NH_3)_{16} + 16\ OH^- + 138\ O_2 \tag{21}$$

In essence, one mole of amino-nitrogen results in one equivalent of strong base when nitrate is the energy source. Thus the trend toward declining pH and alkalinity in old aquarium water is reversed if the nitrate produced during nitrification by bacteria is assimilated by marine plants. Utilization of ammonium ions by plants results in a decrease in pH and alkalinity.

Plants are able to synthesize organic carbon from $CO_2$ in the presence of water and light, as shown by the first reaction in Table 5-2. Inorganic carbon is supplied from the atmosphere and the respiration of animals, algae, and bacteria. Algal respiration may be the most important, considering that old aquarium water is eutrophic.

When photosynthesis is intense, inorganic carbon is used faster than it can be replaced by diffusion from the atmosphere, or by respiration. In such cases, the pH rises and equation 12 shifts to the right. At pH 8.2, additional $CO_2$ is provided by the reactions

$$2\ HCO_3^- \rightleftharpoons CO_3^{2-} + H_2O + CO_2 \tag{22}$$

$$HCO_3^- + H_2O \rightleftharpoons H_2O + CO_2 + OH^- \tag{23}$$

with the first being dominant. As the pH increases from photosynthetic activity, carbonate ion becomes more prominent (Fig. 5–1). If the pH approaches 10 (a rare occurrence), carbonate ions are hydrolyzed to provide additional sources of carbon dioxide. The reaction is

$$CO_3^{2-} + H_2O \rightleftharpoons CO_2 + 2OH^- \qquad (24)$$

As Goldman et al. (1972) pointed out, only a portion of the total inorganic carbon can be utilized during photosynthesis. If all the bicarbonate and carbonate were to be converted to free $CO_2$ and hydroxide ions (equations 22 to 24), the pH would eventually reach 14.

Hellebust (1974) listed several organic acids that are excreted by algae during normal metabolic activities. Among the acids released into the environment are glycolate, formate, acetate, lactate, keto acids, mesotartrate, and isocitrate. Sieburth and Jensen (1969) noticed that in exudation experiments with the rockweed *Ascophyllum nodosum*, the pH dropped from 7.6 to below 5 in 48 hr. The rapid decrease was apparently caused by the release of a number of organic acids, in addition to the poor buffer capacity of seawater on the acidic side of neutral.

## 5.4 MAINTENANCE OF BUFFER CAPACITY

The maintenance of pH alone is a poor practice in managing seawater aquariums. The critical long-term factor is buffer capacity, which is, in effect, the alkalinity. Techniques that keep the pH value within acceptable limits but allow the alkalinity to decline are unsuitable. It is the buffer capacity that prevents sudden shifts in pH that may have deleterious consequences to important biological functions, such as ion exchange processes across membranes.

In some situations, it is possible to sustain consistently high pH values while the buffer capacity of the water declines unnoticed. Actively growing algae, for example, cause the pH to rise by removing $CO_2$ from solution, but alkalinity is increased only during algal utilization of nitrate ion. When the lights are turned off and photosynthesis stops, there can be a precipitous drop in pH caused by depleted alkalinity. It is therefore dangerous simply to monitor pH in aquariums with high levels of biological activity; alkalinity should also be measured regularly.

Ideal alkalinity levels in seawater aquariums fall within the range 2.1 to 2.5 meq $l^{-1}$. The ideal pH is 8.2 and the acceptable range is 8 to 8.3. The minimum acceptable limits for alkalinity and pH are, respectively, 2 meq $l^{-1}$ and 8.

Several techniques can be used to control alkalinity and pH: (1) the use of calcareous gravels as filtrants; (2) periodic addition of sodium hydroxide, sodium carbonate, or sodium bicarbonate; (3) the culture of algae; and (4) partial water changes. Some of these techniques work better than others, and some are suitable only when used in combination. Partial water changes alone, for example, may be inadequate to maintain correct pH and alkalinity levels, and the activities of a large culture of growing algae are difficult to control, often resulting in fluctuations in alkalinity and pH. The best combination is the use of calcareous gravels as filtrants, periodic addition of sodium bicarbonate in predetermined amounts, and regular partial water changes.

**Calcareous Gravels**

The use of calcareous gravels has long been advocated by aquarists as an aid in maintaining buffer capacity. The theory has been that a filter bed composed of carbonate-bearing minerals offsets a decline in the buffer capacity of the water. This is correct, but to a limited degree.

The dissolution of carbonate minerals in aquarium seawater is too slow to sustain alkalinity and pH at values found in the ocean. Solution kinetics are affected by the composition of the carbonate minerals themselves, and reflect a mineral's recent geological history. No two carbonate minerals are ever likely to dissolve at the same rate. Slow solution kinetics perhaps result from the presence of dissolved magnesium, and also from DOC, which inhibits ion exchange at the mineral surface. Dissolved organics may coat all or some of the exchange sites. A carbonate mineral placed in seawater may quickly acquire an overgrowth of magnesian calcite, the magnesium in the overgrowth being in equilibrium with magnesium in solution. The combination of DOC and magnesian calcite overgrowths would tend to even out the solubilities of different carbonate minerals and lessen the importance of their original composition with respect to buffer activity. Once exposed to seawater, it would not matter anymore that calcite is more soluble than dolomite in pure water, because the seawater ends up by "buffering" the surface of the overgrowth, or by not buffering the surface at all, if it is fouled by DOC. In practical terms, a naturally occurring carbonate mineral in seawater cannot retain its original buffering properties for long. Within hours, the alkalinity starts a slow, inevitable decline.

This is not to say that calcareous minerals should be disregarded as filtrants. Quite the contrary, although which one is best appears to be academic. Dolomite, magnesian calcites, and calcite seem to work equally well. Crushed oyster shell sold in feed stores for poultry grit is a good filtrant material; so is crushed coral rock (actually fossil coral), or crushed and graded dolomite and calcite. Without calcareous filtrants of some kind, the buffer capacity of captive seawater becomes dangerously depleted. Calcareous gravels prevent the alkalinity from dropping lower than about 1 meq $l^{-1}$ and the pH from falling below 7.5 (Hirayama 1970). Optimum alkalinity and pH values must be sustained by other methods.

### Culture of Algae

The fact that aquatic plants utilize $CO_2$ during photosynthesis points to their usefulness in controlling pH. Unfortunately the situation is complicated. Alderson and Howell (1973) demonstrated that dense cultures of the unicellular green alga *Dunaliella tertiolecta* raised the pH of captive seawater to unnaturally high values. Prince (1974) cultured *Enteromorpha linza* and *Fucus vesiculosus,* a green and brown macroalga, respectively, and noted that without harvesting some of the biomass every three days, the pH of the water rose to 9 or more. There is little doubt that living plants are capable of maintaining pH values in seawater at 8 or greater. The problem is controlling their growth.

The usual difficulties of quantifying and then engineering life processes enter into the design of aquarium systems in which plants are to play a major role in pH control. Even casual data are lacking at this time. In truth, it is far easier to maintain pH values by addition of bicarbonate or carbonate salts. When living plants are substituted, daily monitoring of pH and alkalinity is sometimes necessary.

Several factors bear on how efficiently plants regulate their physiological processes, and were discussed in Chapter 2. Basically the availability of nutrients and light—its duration, intensity, and spectral composition—are important, and factors controlling algal growth that seem to be perfectly balanced one day are hopelessly out of adjustment the next. The use of dense algal growths to maintain pH values of 8 to 8.3 is most worthwhile when the plants are cultured for a more important reason, such as removal of nitrogenous metabolites (Section 7.3).

### Chemical Buffers

Sodium hydroxide (NaOH), sodium bicarbonate ($NaHCO_3$), or sodium carbonate ($Na_2CO_3$) can be used to adjust the alkalinity and pH. Powdered limestone is not recommended because with time, the calcium in the lime may change the ratio of major cations (Breder and Smith

1932). Cooper (1932) reported that at the Plymouth Aquarium in England the addition of lime to maintain pH eventually increased the calcium concentration in the water to $0.62 \ g \ l^{-1}$, compared with $0.39 \ g \ l^{-1}$ in the seawater directly offshore.

Sodium, the predominant cation in seawater, can be added as carbonate or bicarbonate salts for longer periods before the cation balance is upset. Breder and Smith (1932) estimated that if all the bicarbonate ion in seawater at the New York Aquarium were to be replaced over a period of 2.5 yr with sodium bicarbonate, the sodium level would increase a mere 0.5%. If lime were used instead, the calcium level would increase by 10%, or 20 times the molar concentration of calcium in offshore seawater. As Breder and Smith pointed out, the danger associated with addition of lime is not immediate, but it is best to keep the possibility remote and not use it as a buffer material.

Sodium bicarbonate equilibrates slowly with seawater and is the safest material to use. The concentration of bicarbonate ion in seawater is affected by several factors, including the solubility of free $CO_2$ and the rate at which hydrated $CO_2$ (carbonic acid) dissociates. These will be discussed briefly before describing how to estimate the amount of $NaHCO_3$ that must be added to attain a pH value of 8.2 when the initial pH is below optimum. Full descriptions of the carbon dioxide system in seawater can be found in Riley and Chester (1971) and Skirrow (1975).

When carbon dioxide is dissolved in seawater, an equilibrium is established that coexists with the ionization equilibrium of water $(2H_2O \leftrightharpoons H_3O^+ + OH^-)$. Each reaction in equation 12 has an equilibrium constant that is determined by the thermodynamic activities (effective concentrations) of the species involved. The species shown in the composite reaction of equation 12 probably do not approach equilibirum in the open ocean, but the situation in seawater aquariums may be different, or at least I shall assume that it is. The assumption here is that when aquarium seawater is aerated there is greater opportunity for the mass transport of $CO_2$ from the water to the air and vice versa. The water tends to be near saturation with respect to the partial pressure of atmospheric $CO_2$, as demonstrated by

$$[CO_2] = \alpha p_{CO_2} \qquad (25)$$

where $[CO_2]$ = the concentration of $CO_2$, $\alpha$ = the solubility of free $CO_2$ in meq $l^{-1}$ atm$^{-1}$, and $p_{CO_2}$ = the partial pressure of free $CO_2$ in the atmosphere (the symbol $P$ stands for the partial pressure of a gas in solution). The solubility of gaseous $CO_2$ is depressed slightly by large amounts of chloride ion, and also by increases in temperature. Table 5-3 shows the solubility of $CO_2$ as a function of chlorinity and temperature.

**Table 5-3  Solubility of $CO_2$ in Pure Water and in Seawater (mole $l^{-1}$ atm$^{-1}$)**

| Cl (o/oo) | Temperature (°C) | | | | | | | | | | | | | |
|---|---|---|---|---|---|---|---|---|---|---|---|---|---|---|
| | 0 | 2 | 4 | 6 | 8 | 10 | 12 | 14 | 16 | 18 | 20 | 22 | 24 | 26 |
| 0 | 771 | 713 | 661 | 614 | 572 | 535 | 499 | 467 | 440 | 413 | 389 | 367 | 347 | $328 \times 10^{-4}$ |
| 15 | 670 | 620 | 576 | 536 | 500 | 468 | 437 | 409 | 385 | 364 | 344 | 325 | 308 | 291 |
| 16 | 664 | 615 | 571 | 531 | 496 | 464 | 433 | 406 | 382 | 360 | 341 | 322 | 305 | 289 |
| 17 | 658 | 609 | 565 | 526 | 491 | 460 | 429 | 402 | 378 | 357 | 338 | 319 | 303 | 287 |
| 18 | 652 | 603 | 559 | 521 | 486 | 455 | 425 | 398 | 374 | 354 | 335 | 316 | 300 | 284 |
| 19 | 645 | 597 | 554 | 515 | 481 | 450 | 421 | 394 | 371 | 350 | 332 | 313 | 297 | 281 |
| 20 | 638 | 591 | 548 | 510 | 476 | 445 | 416 | 390 | 367 | 347 | 328 | 310 | 294 | 278 |

Source:  Murray and Riley (1971).

Bicarbonate ion is the principal buffer in seawater. If the pH of a water sample is known, the concentration of $HCO_3^-$ in meq $l^{-1}$ at equilibrium is given by

$$[HCO_3^-] = \frac{k'_{L1}\, p_{CO_2}}{[H^+]} \tag{26}$$

where $k'_{L1}$ = the first apparent dissociation constant of carbonic acid and $\{H^+\}$ = the thermodynamic activity of hydrogen ion, expressed by

$$\{H^+\} = 10^{-pH} \tag{27}$$

where pH is based on the National Bureau of Standards (NBS) pH scale (Section 12.7). Note that $k'_{L1}$ is not the equilibrium constant as normally defined in terms of the activities of $H_2O$ and $CO_2$, expressed by

$$k'_1 = \frac{\{H^+\}\,[HCO_3^-]}{\{H_2O\}\,\{CO_2\}} \tag{28}$$

Rather $k'_{L1}$ is related to $k'_1$ by

$$k'_{L1} = k'_1\,(P_s/P_o)(\alpha_o/\alpha_s) \tag{29}$$

where $(P_s/P_o)$ is the ratio of the partial pressure of $CO_2$ in seawater to its partial pressure in pure water and $(\alpha_o/\alpha_s)$ is the ratio of the solubility coefficients of pure water and seawater.

The carbonate ion concentration can be calculated from

$$[CO_3^{2-}] = \frac{k'_{L1}\, k'_2\, p_{CO_2}}{\{H^+\}^2} \tag{30}$$

where $k'_2$ = the second apparent dissociation constant of $CO_2$. The $pk'_{L1}$ and $pk'_2$ values according to Lyman (1956) can be obtained from Tables 5-4 and 5-5. To derive $k'_{L1}$ and $k'_2$, use equations 31 and 32

$$k'_{L1} = 10^{-pk'_{L1}} \tag{31}$$

$$k'_2 = 10^{-pk'_2} \tag{32}$$

The calculations can be simplified by taking the $\log_{10}$ values of equations 26 and 30 to obtain equations 33 and 34

$$\log_{[HCO_3^-]} = pH - pk'_{L1} + \log\,(\alpha p_{CO_2}) \tag{33}$$

$$\log_{[CO_3^{2-}]} = 2pH - pk'_{L1} - pk'_2 + \log\,(\alpha p_{CO_2}) \tag{34}$$

The total inorganic carbon $(\Sigma CO_2) = [CO_2] + [HCO_3^-] + [CO_3^{2-}]$. To calculate the amount of total inorganic carbon that must be added to a

**Table 5-4   First Apparent Dissociation Constant of $H_2CO_3$ in Seawater, Expressed as $pk_{L1}'^a$**

| Cl (o/oo) | Temperature (°C) | | | | | | | |
|---|---|---|---|---|---|---|---|---|
| | 0 | 5 | 10 | 15 | 20 | 25 | 30 | 35 |
| 0 | 6.58 | 6.52 | 6.47 | 6.42 | 6.38 | 6.35 | 6.33 | 6.31 |
| 1 | 6.47 | 6.42 | 6.37 | 6.33 | 6.29 | 6.26 | 6.24 | 6.23 |
| 4 | 6.36 | 6.32 | 6.28 | 6.24 | 6.21 | 6.18 | 6.16 | 6.15 |
| 9 | 6.27 | 6.23 | 6.19 | 6.15 | 6.13 | 6.10 | 6.08 | 6.07 |
| 16 | 6.18 | 6.14 | 6.11 | 6.07 | 6.05 | 6.03 | 6.01 | 5.99 |
| 17 | 6.17 | 6.13 | 6.10 | 6.06 | 6.04 | 6.02 | 6.00 | 5.98 |
| 18 | 6.16 | 6.12 | 6.09 | 6.06 | 6.03 | 6.01 | 5.99 | 5.97 |
| 19 | 6.15 | 6.11 | 6.08 | 6.05 | 6.02 | 6.00 | 5.98 | 5.97 |
| 20 | 6.14 | 6.10 | 6.07 | 6.04 | 6.01 | 5.99 | 5.97 | 5.96 |
| 21 | 6.13 | 6.09 | 6.06 | 6.03 | 6.00 | 5.98 | 5.96 | 5.95 |
| 25 | 6.09 | 6.05 | 6.02 | 6.00 | 5.97 | 5.95 | 5.93 | 5.92 |
| 36 | 6.00 | 5.97 | 5.94 | 5.92 | 5.89 | 5.87 | 5.86 | 5.84 |
| 49 | 5.92 | 5.88 | 5.86 | 5.84 | 5.82 | 5.80 | 5.78 | 5.77 |
| 64 | 5.84 | 5.80 | 5.78 | 5.76 | 5.74 | 5.72 | 5.71 | 5.70 |

Source:   Lyman (1956).
[a] Values based on the NBS pH scale.

seawater aquarium to raise the pH to 8.2, use equations 33 and 34. For example, an aerated seawater aquarium has a chlorinity of 19%, temperature = 20°C, and pH = 7.9. Determine the total inorganic carbon present. From Tables 5-3, 5-4, and 5-5, $\alpha_{CO_2}$ is $332 \times 10^{-4}$ moles $l^{-1}$ atm$^{-1}$ = 33.2 meq $l^{-1}$ atm$^{-1}$, $pk_{L1}' = 6.02$, and $pk_2' = 9.17$. Because $p_{CO_2}$ is normally $3.31 \times 10^{-4}$ atm, $\log \alpha p_{CO_2} = \log (33.2 \times 3.31 \times 10^{-1}) = -1.96$. Applying equations 33 and 34,

$$\log [HCO_3^-] = 7.9 - 6.02 - 1.96 = -0.08$$

$$[HCO_3^-] = 10^{-0.08} = 0.832 \text{ meq } l^{-1}$$

and

$$\log [CO_3^{2-}] = 2(7.9) - 6.02 - 9.17 - 1.96 = -1.35$$

$$[CO_3^{2-}] = 0.047 \text{ meq } l^{-1}$$

$$[CO_3^{2-}] = \alpha P_{CO_2} = 0.011 \text{ meq } l^{-1}$$

The $\Sigma CO_2$ is

$$0.832 + 0.047 + 0.011 = 0.890 \text{ meq } l^{-1}.$$

To increase the pH of the aquarium, the $\Sigma CO_2$ must be adjusted upward until the pH reaches 8.2. This can be done by addition of

**Table 5-5  Second Apparent Dissociation Constant of $H_2CO_3$ in Seawater, Expressed as $pk_{L1}'$[a]**

| Cl (o/oo) | Temperature (°C) | | | | | | | |
|---|---|---|---|---|---|---|---|---|
| | 0 | 5 | 10 | 15 | 20 | 25 | 30 | 35 |
| 0 | 10.62 | 10.55 | 10.49 | 10.43 | 10.38 | 10.33 | 10.29 | 10.25 |
| 1 | 10.06 | 9.99 | 9.93 | 9.87 | 9.81 | 9.76 | 9.71 | 9.66 |
| 4 | 9.78 | 9.72 | 9.67 | 9.61 | 9.54 | 9.49 | 9.43 | 9.38 |
| 9 | 9.64 | 9.58 | 9.52 | 9.46 | 9.40 | 9.34 | 9.27 | 9.21 |
| 16 | 9.46 | 9.40 | 9.35 | 9.29 | 9.23 | 9.17 | 9.10 | 9.02 |
| 17 | 9.44 | 9.38 | 9.32 | 9.27 | 9.21 | 9.15 | 9.08 | 9.00 |
| 18 | 9.42 | 9.36 | 9.30 | 9.25 | 9.19 | 9.12 | 9.06 | 8.98 |
| 19 | 9.40 | 9.34 | 9.28 | 9.23 | 9.17 | 9.10 | 9.02 | 8.95 |
| 20 | 9.38 | 9.32 | 9.26 | 9.21 | 9.15 | 9.08 | 9.01 | 8.92 |
| 21 | 9.36 | 9.30 | 9.25 | 9.19 | 9.13 | 9.06 | 8.98 | 8.89 |
| 25 | 9.29 | 9.23 | 9.17 | 9.11 | 9.05 | 8.98 | 8.91 | 8.82 |
| 36 | 9.12 | 9.06 | 8.99 | 8.93 | 8.86 | 8.79 | 8.72 | 8.63 |
| 49 | 8.95 | 8.89 | 8.82 | 8.75 | 8.68 | 8.61 | 8.53 | 8.43 |
| 64 | 8.77 | 8.71 | 8.64 | 8.57 | 8.50 | 8.42 | 8.34 | 8.23 |

Source:   Lyman (1956).
[a] Values based on the NBS pH scale.

sodium bicarbonate, because nearly all of the total inorganic carbon exists as $HCO_3^-$. Table 5-6 and Fig. 5-10 show the required amount of $NaHCO_3$ needed to attain a pH of 8.2 for selected initial pH and temperature values. The values were obtained using the assumptions and equations above, after confirming their validity by determining the

**Table 5-6   Amount of $NaHCO_3$ (g $l^{-1}$) Needed to Raise the pH of Aquarium Seawater to 8.2 at Different Temperatures ($Cl$ = 19 o/oo)**

| Initial pH | Temperature (°C) | | | |
|---|---|---|---|---|
| | 10 | 15 | 20 | 25 |
| 7.5 | 0.144 | 0.133 | 0.127 | 0.117 |
| 7.6 | 0.135 | 0.125 | 0.119 | 0.110 |
| 7.7 | 0.124 | 0.115 | 0.110 | 0.101 |
| 7.8 | 0.110 | 0.102 | 0.0974 | 0.0896 |
| 7.9 | 0.0917 | 0.0854 | 0.0815 | 0.0751 |
| 8.0 | 0.0685 | 0.0640 | 0.0611 | 0.0562 |
| 8.1 | 0.0385 | 0.0363 | 0.0346 | 0.0317 |

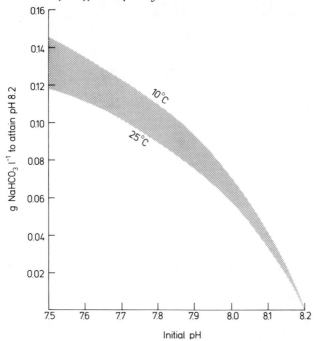

**Figure 5-10**   Amount of NaHCO$_3$ needed to raise the pH of aquarium seawater to 8.2. Curves were plotted from the same data used to prepare Table 5-6.

amount of NaHCO$_3$ needed to achieve a pH of 8.2 in acidified aquarium seawater. Spencer (1966) used a similar method of pH adjustment, and the values in the table are in close agreement with his conclusions, despite differences in approach. Spencer controlled the pH by injecting air-CO$_2$ mixtures into seawater of given alkalinity. In the technique described here, $p_{CO_2}$ was kept constant and the pH was manipulated by changing the alkalinity. The two studies agree, because

$$\Delta A = \Delta\Sigma CO_2 \qquad (35)$$

and the addition of CO$_2$ ($\Delta CO_2$) does not alter the alkalinity, but still results in a change in pH. A sample calculation on the use of Table 5-6 follows.

A 110 l aquarium tank of temperature 15°C and pH 7.9 must be adjusted to pH 8.2. How much NaHCO$_3$ is required? From Table 5-6 the right amount is 0.085 g l$^{-1}$, or (0.085)(110) = 9.35 g NaHCO$_3$. Several days may be required for equilibrium to be attained after the material has been added.

# CHAPTER 6
## *The Nutrient Elements*

A newly established aquarium can be considered oligotrophic (low in plant nutrients), because it is deficient in the nutrient elements carbon, phosphorus, and nitrogen. The ammonia level is many times higher than it will be days later, when sufficient numbers of nitrifying bacteria have become established in the filter bed. Nitrate is low because nitrification is concentrated initially on conversion of ammonia to nitrite. In the nitrification sequence, nitrite is the precursor to the formation of nitrate.

As the aquarium ages, its water becomes characterized by high levels of nitrate, inorganic phosphorus, and DOC, and it becomes eutrophic. Only nitrogen appears to accumulate indefinitely; carbon and phosphorus eventually reach equilibrium. Eutrophic conditions make aquarium management troublesome. Some of the forms that nutrient elements take are toxic. Others, such as DOC, increase the level of substrates available for oxidation by heterotrophic bacteria. Proliferation of these organisms increases the biomass of the aquarium environment. Overall, eutrophication in seawater aquariums reduces the carrying capacity of the water, interfering with its ability to support life.

This chapter concentrates on the origins of the nutrient elements, how they accumulate, and the means by which they are cycled. Techniques for their removal or conversion to less toxic forms are the subjects of Chapters 7 and 9.

## 6.1 CARBON

The buffer system of seawater is composed mainly of inorganic carbon compounds, as discussed in the last chapter. In aquarium seawater, inorganic carbon originates from the diffusion of $CO_2$ into the water from air bubbles or across the air-water interface, and from the respiration of animals, algae, and bacteria. The dissolution of carbonate minerals contributes to the buffer system through addition of carbonate ions. The subject here deals with dissolved organic compounds, all of which are composed in part of elemental carbon, although many contain phosphorus or nitrogen as well (e.g., urea). Besides the cycling of carbon, the main items of discussion will be the input of DOC by marine macroalgae, some fractions of which are chromophoric (pigmented) and contribute to the yellow color of old aquarium water.

### Carbon Cycling

The carbon cycle in seawater aquariums is shown in Fig. 6-1. Some of the organic carbon originates from the metabolism of food by animals. Animals assimilate organic carbon compounds, metabolize them, and excrete other organic carbon compounds into the environment in urine and feces. Still another portion of the organic carbon ingested by animals is oxidized and respired as $CO_2$. The part excreted in the urine and

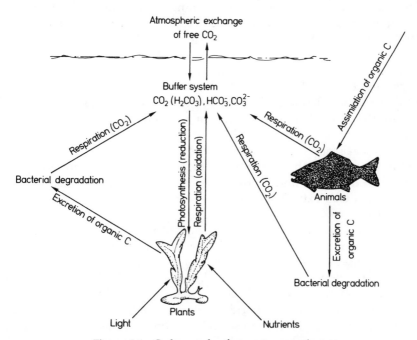

**Figure 6-1** Carbon cycle of seawater aquariums.

feces is mineralized by heterotrophic bacteria and respired by them as $CO_2$. All respired $CO_2$, regardless of its origin, is ultimately returned to the carbonate buffer system. Excess amounts diffuse into the atmosphere across the air-water interface.

Algae assimilate $CO_2$ during photosynthesis and reduce it to organic carbon, which is bound up in the tissues during growth. Plants also respire and give off $CO_2$. In certain cases, bicarbonate ions are perhaps utilized in photosynthesis in place of $CO_2$ and the carbon reduced to the organic state (Blinks 1963, Goldman et al. 1974, Jolliffe and Tregunna 1970).

Large portions of the extracellular products released by seaweeds into the environment may consist of cellular organic carbon (Kroes 1970). Simple and complex polysaccharides are liberated by many species, both macroscopic and unicellular. These substances are mineralized by heterotrophs, and the $CO_2$ is returned to the buffer system. The carbonate buffer system thus acts as a "sink," receiving $CO_2$ from many different sources.

### Eutrophic Effects

Ordinarily DOC in surface seawater ranges from 0.6 mg C $l^{-1}$ if the testing method is wet oxidation, to 1.5 to 2 mg C $l^{-1}$ by dry combustion (Williams 1975). Values of total organic carbon (TOC) at Mystic Marinelife Aquarium, measured by wet combustion, average 6 mg $Cl^{-1}$ or less, and the DOC is lower still. There is no convenient means of measuring DOC in seawater directly, and a value for TOC is likely to include a small fraction of the POC (particulate organic carbon) as well, despite the care taken to filter the sample beforehand.

The quantity of extracellular products released into the environment by macroalgae, and the rate at which they are liberated, depends mainly on three factors: (1) the species of plant; (2) whether the plant is kept in light or in darkness; and (3) the physical condition of the plant. Damaged plants leak extracellular products faster than specimens that are intact (Kroes 1970).

Sometimes the amounts of DOC released by algae represent a substantial portion of the carbon assimilated during photosynthesis. In the red microalga *Porphyridium purpureum,* for example, 15% of the carbon fixed during photosynthesis may be liberated as polysaccharides (Jones 1962). The green, brown, and red macroalgae may all release a considerable amount of polysaccharide materials under certain conditions (Sieburth 1969). Polysaccharides and heteropolysaccharides are released by the brown macroalgae *Ascophyllum, Fucus,* and *Laminaria* (Sieburth

1969), and by red algae of the genera *Porphyridium* and *Chondrus* (Jones 1962, Sieburth 1969). Generally the brown algae release larger amounts of extracellular materials than green and red species. For example, Sieburth (1969) found that about 40% of the net carbon fixed by the rockweed *Fucus vesiculosus* was released into the environment. However Craigie et al. (1966) and Majak et al. (1966) showed that some green and red seaweeds released carbon assimilated during photosynthesis at rates of only 0 to 4%. A summary of some of this information is presented in Table 6-1.

Sieburth and Jensen (1970) found that *F. vesiculosus* appeared not to exude organics in the dark (i.e., when not photosynthesizing). Some other brown algae were "leaky" in the dark, exuding their extracellular materials in heavy quantities despite the absence of photosynthesis. The kelps *Laminaria agardhii* and *L. digitata*, for example, lost extracellular products at a rate that equalled 60% of the total lost during photosynthesis.

About 10% of the DOC in the sea is strongly pigmented and imparts a yellow color to the water (Khailov and Finenko 1970). The appearance of this material is seasonal, being most prevalent during plankton blooms. The substance in question is not a distinct chemical entity but a complex blend of compounds. Some oceanographers refer to it as the uncharacterized fraction. Kalle (1937, 1966) popularized the term *gelbstoff.* Other synonyms are yellow fraction, yellow humus, and humic acid, but the last two are misleading. Like soil humus and humic materials indigenous to freshwaters, seawater gelbstoff absorbs light strongly into the ultraviolet region of the spectrum: Sieburth and Jensen (1968) noted a peak at 263 nm. Most of the humus of freshwater and soils, however, precipitates on contact with seawater (Khailov and Finenko 1970). Humic acids precipitate on being acidified, and not all seawater gelbstoff behaves in this way (Khailov and Finenko 1970).

A form of gelbstoff accumulates in seawater aquariums when eutrophic conditions prevail. Craigie and McLachlan (1964) stated that much of the seawater gelbstoff in nature is refractory and not biodegradable; the same holds true for yellow fractions in aquarium water. The raw materials of gelbstoff in seawater aquariums are the exudates of algae (primarily phenols and carbohydrates), and the excretory products of animals (mainly nitrogenous). Emphasis here will be on plant exudates that contribute to gelbstoff formation. The gelbstoff-forming exudates of marine algae must be soluble at the pH of seawater. This eliminates from consideration many insoluble products like lipids, pigments, cellulose, polysaccharides, and proteins (Mautner 1954). Thus the yellow substances in aquarium water containing viable algal

Table 6-1 Exudation of Dissolved Organic Carbon (DOC) for Marine Macroalgae under Normal Conditions of Photoperiod, Salinity, and Temperature (Values Are Rounded Off to Two Decimal Places)

| Classification | Exudation (mg C g$^{-1}$ hr$^{-1}$) | | Locale | Source |
|---|---|---|---|---|
| | Light | Dark | | |
| Green | | | | |
| Cladophora sp.[a] | 1.80 | — | Black Sea | Khailov and Burkalova (1969) |
| Cladophora utriculosa[a] | 1.25 | 0.00 | Black Sea | Khailov and Burkalova (1969) |
| Dictyota dichotoma | 0.04 | 0.01 | Caribbean | Brylinsky (1977) |
| Ulva lactuca | 0.21 | — | North Atlantic | Sieburth and Jensen (1970) |
| Brown | | | | |
| Ascophyllum nodosum[b] | 1.75 | — | Barents Sea | Khailov and Burkalova (1969) |
| A. nodosum | 0.31 | — | North Atlantic | Sieburth and Jensen (1970) |
| Fucus serratus[b] | 2.70 | — | Barents Sea | Khailov and Burkalova (1969) |
| F. vesiculosus | 2.55 | — | Barents Sea | Khailov and Burkalova (1969) |
| F. vesiculosus | 0.42 | — | North Atlantic | Sieburth and Jensen (1970) |

| | | | | |
|---|---|---|---|---|
| Laminaria saccharina[b] | 1.30 | — | Barents Sea | Khailov and Burkalova (1969) |
| L. agardhii | 0.38 | — | North Atlantic | Sieburth and Jensen (1970) |
| L. digitata | 0.45 | — | North Atlantic | Sieburth and Jensen (1970) |
| Padina pavonia | 2.05 | 0.00 | Black Sea | Khailov and Burkalova (1969) |
| Sargassum natans | 0.01 | 0.00 | Caribbean | Brylinsky (1977) |
| Red | | | | |
| Acanthophora specifera | 2.91 | 8.84 | Caribbean | Brylinsky (1977) |
| Callithamnion corymbosum[a] | 6.10 | 0.75 | Black Sea | Khailov and Burkalova (1969) |
| Chondria dasyphylla | 0.04 | 0.00 | Caribbean | Brylinsky (1977) |
| Chondrus crispus | 0.04 | — | North Atlantic | Sieburth and Jensen (1970) |
| Dasya elegans[a] | 1.55 | 0.25 | Black Sea | Khailov and Burkalova (1969) |
| Polysiphonia harveyii | 0.00 | — | North Atlantic | Sieburth and Jensen (1970) |
| P. sublifera | 2.85 | 1.85 | Black Sea | Khailov and Burkalova (1969) |
| Rhodimenia palmata[b] | 6.35 | — | Barents Sea | Khailov and Burkalova (1969) |

[a] Data from good growth periods.
[b] Values averaged for winter and summer.

growths are not necessarily plant pigments, but metabolic exudates that become yellow in quite another way.

Algae exude phenols into the water along with carbohydrates, other organics, and limited amounts of proteinaceous material. All seaweeds release large amounts of carbohydrates, but comparatively little nitrogen (Hellebust 1974). In some cases carbohydrates comprise more than 50% of all extracellular products (Sieburth and Jensen 1968). The sum of these fractions is colorless, or nearly so (Craigie and McLachlan 1964; Sieburth and Jensen 1969, 1970). Phenols become polyphenols under the mildly alkaline conditions of seawater. Polyphenols, in turn, react with materials containing carbohydrates and nitrogenous substances to form a large portion of the seawater gelbstoff in nature. The resulting compounds range from pale yellow to brown and are chemically indistinguishable from yellow fractions isolated from surface seawater (Sieburth and Jensen 1969, 1970).

As noted previously, brown algae exude organic substances in greater amounts than the green and red algae. Many brown algae release large quantities of phenols (Craigie and McLachlan 1964, Conover and Sieburth 1966, Khailov 1963, Sieburth and Jensen 1969). Little comparative work has been done with species of the green and red groups, but presumably they liberate phenols, too. In aquariums, some of the nitrogen that reacts with polyphenols may come from plants, but most is of animal origin.

## 6.2  PHOSPHORUS

Phosphorus exists in seawater in three states: dissolved inorganic phosphorus (DIP, also called phosphate, orthophosphate, and reactive phosphate), dissolved organic phosphorus (DOP), and particulate organic phosphorus (POP). This last form is associated with floating detritus particles and the cells of suspended microorganisms. Orthophosphate is the most important form in nature, and the same is probably true in seawater aquariums. In seawater of pH of 8, 1% of the orthophosphate is present as $H_2PO_4^-$, 87% as $HPO_4^{2-}$, and 12% as $PO_4^{3-}$ (Kester and Pytkowicz 1967).

### Phosphorus Cycling

In nature, the enormous mass of the primary producers (phytoplankton in particular) and primary and secondary consumers (herbivorous and carnivorous zooplankton) accounts for most of the phosphorus cycling.

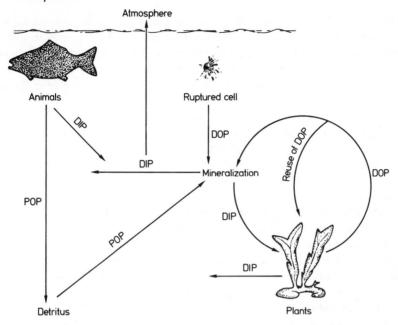

**Figure 6-2**   Phosphorus cycle of seawater aquariums illustrating the cycling of dissolved inorganic phosphorus (DIP), dissolved organic phosphorus (DOP), and particulate organic phosphorus (POP).

The onset of a phytoplankton bloom triggers a rise in all forms of phosphorus. The roles of planktonic organisms in the phosphorus cycling in seawater aquariums are insignificant. Phosphorus enters aquarium water in four ways: (1) excretion by macroalgae; (2) excretion by metazoan animals; (3) autolysis and release from damaged cells; and (4) lysis of dead cells and mineralization of dissolved and particulate organic matter by heterotrophic bacteria.

The phosphorus cycle in seawater aquariums is illustrated in Fig. 6-2. Macroalgae excrete DOP. A portion is reused during growth, whereas the rest is mineralized to the inorganic state (DIP) by heterotrophic bacteria. In addition, macroalgae excrete a certain amount of DIP. Both DOP and DIP are reassimilated by macroalgae. According to Owens and Esaias (1976), no evidence exists that algae can directly assimilate forms of phosphorus other than orthophosphate; however DOP can be hydrolyzed near the outer cell membranes and utilized indirectly.

Ruptured cells of animals, bacteria, and algae release DOP, some of which is mineralized by heterotrophic bacteria. Metazoan animals excrete some of their phosphorus in the inorganic state; the remainder appears in fecal material as POP. Some of the phosphorus in animal feces sinks to the bottom of the aquarium and is adsorbed onto detritus. When part of the detritus is mineralized, inorganic phosphorus is liberated. Excess inorganic phosphorus from the excretion of metazoan animals and macroalgae, and from mineralization of organic phosphorus by heterotrophic bacteria, appears collectively as reactive phosphate when measured in the laboratory.

Some of the excess phosphorus produced in a seawater aquarium may precipitate as inorganic salts on the surfaces of gravel grains in the filter bed, although the existence of such a pathway has never been demonstrated. Goldizen (1970) suggested that phosphorus precipitated as calcium salts; Saeki (1958, 1962) postulated that calcium and magnesium salts were formed in combination with phosphorus. However Saeki's work was carried out with water systems to which lime had been added to control alkalinity and pH. It seems logical that both magnesium and calcium would be involved in phosphorus precipitation. Kester and Pytkowicz (1967) demonstrated that 96% of the $PO_4^{3-}$ and 44% of the $HPO_4^{2-}$ exist in the sea as ion pairs, probably in association with the cations calcium and magnesium. Siddall (1974) could not find evidence of an inorganic phosphorus coating of old aquarium gravel by x-ray diffraction. However Malone and Towe (1970) showed that in cultures of aerated seawater, bacteria formed the mineral struvite ($NH_4MgPO_4 \cdot 6H_2O$) by a reaction between phosphorus and ammonium ions. The reaction occurred in the presence of magnesium and organic matter. The ammonia had been produced during the mineralization of DOC. Even if some of the orthophosphate is precipitated on gravel grains in the filter bed, it seems unlikely that much could be removed in this manner. Two other processes are more plausible, and aeration is the force that drives them.

Baylor et al. (1962) postulated that reactive phosphate was bound to organic molecules in solution and then adsorbed onto bubbles. In a series of experiments using seawater aerated by means of a standard home aquarium-type air compressor, they showed that the aeration process removed more than 90% of the reactive phosphate in 24 hr. The logarithm of the phosphate concentration remaining was a linear function of time, as illustrated in Fig. 6-3. The relationship was straightforward: orthophosphate was removed from aerated seawater at a rate proportional to its concentration. No biological process was involved. The disappearance of orthophosphate was purely a physicochemical phenomenon, described by

$$c_t = c_0 e^{-kt} \tag{36}$$

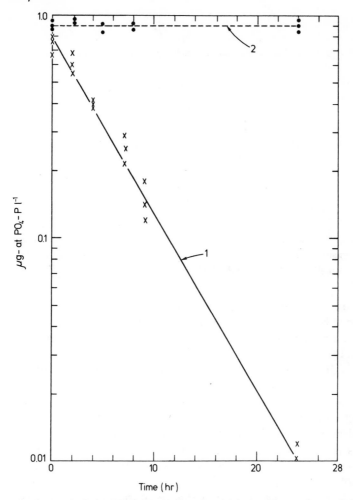

**Figure 6-3** Removal of phosphate by aeration from: (1) natural seawater, and (2) artificial seawater. Redrawn and modified from Baylor et al. (1962).

where $c_t$ is the concentration of reactive phosphate at time $t$; $c_0$ is the concentration of reactive phosphate at the beginning of the experiment; $e$ is the base of natural logarithms; and $k$ is a rate constant that, in this case, varied with the bubbling rate and was thought to be dependent on the total surface area produced by the bubbles. The value of $k$ for an aeration rate of 200 $cm^3$ $l^{-1}$ $min^{-1}$ of seawater was approximately 0.17 ± 0.03 (standard error of the mean for seven experiments).

During aeration, orthophosphate became bound to dissolved organic

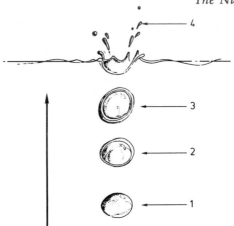

**Figure 6-4**  Possible mechanism for removal of phosphate from seawater by aeration (see text). Inorganic phosphorus is absorbed onto the surface of a rising air bubble (1 through 3) and dissipated as aerosol droplets when the bubble bursts at the surface.

compounds. These, in turn, were adsorbed onto the rising air bubbles produced by the air compressor. When the bubbles burst at the water surface, fine aerosol droplets were formed that included orthophosphate. In this way, much of the reactive phosphate was lost from solution directly to the atmosphere, and analysis of the aerosol showed higher total phosphorus levels than the seawater over which the aerosol was collected. The possible mechanism is illustrated in Fig. 6-4.

Reactive phosphate is probably lost from aerated seawater by still a second mechanism. Some of the organic molecules onto which phosphorus is adsorbed are highly surface-active. These substances collect on rising bubbles and produce monomolecular films that aggregate into insoluble organic particles (Section 9.2). According to Sutcliffe et al. (1963), total and reactive phosphate are bound to these particles as they are formed in surface foam produced by aeration. This was demonstrated by the disappearance of both forms of phosphorus from an experimental aeration chamber. The suggestion put forth was that during particle formation (Section 4.3) reactive phosphate is adsorbed onto insoluble organic particles and thus effectively removed from solution.

### Eutrophic Effects

Orthophosphate concentrations in the oceans are greater inshore than offshore. Latitude also makes a difference. Cold seas are richer in orthophosphate than warm seas, due mainly to the seasonal upwelling of nutrients from bottom sediments that occurs in the temperate and polar zones. Worldwide, orthophosphate in the oceans averages 0.5 to 1 $\mu$g-at $PO_4$-P $l^{-1}$ (Spencer 1975). The concentration of inorganic phosphorus in the North Pacific sometimes reaches 2 $\mu$g-at $PO_4$-P $l^{-1}$. Values in tropical seas often are no more than 0.1 to 0.2 $\mu$g-at $PO_4$-P $l^{-1}$.

When levels of orthophosphate are compared, even the richest polar sea pales before average aquarium water. At Mystic Marinelife Aquarium, the values in exhibits with stable animal populations fall within the range 1 to 3 mg $PO_4$-P $l^{-1}$. Converted to microunits, a value of 3 mg $PO_4$-P $l^{-1}$ equals 96.8 $\mu$g-at $PO_4$-P $l^{-1}$.

The orthophosphate level in seawater aquariums stabilizes as the water ages. Each exhibit at Mystic Marinelife Aquarium operates as a separate closed system and receives a 10% partial water change biweekly, yet reactive phosphate seldom exceeds 3 mg $PO_4$-P $l^{-1}$. This is in line with other published values. Saeki (1958) reported that orthophosphate levels in the seawater aquariums studied by him seldom exceeded 6 mg $PO_4$-P $l^{-1}$. Yoshida (1967) measured 90 $\mu$g-at $PO_4$-P $l^{-1}$ in a closed-system seawater aquarium 134 days after it had been set up.

During heavy plankton blooms, POP and DOP in the oceans may be many times greater than orthophosphate. DOP concentrations in the oceans average 0.05 to 0.2 $\mu$g-at P $l^{-1}$ (Williams 1975). The POP level reflects the quantity of detritus and plankton in suspension, whereas the concentration of DOP is an index of biological activity. Values for POP and DOP in aquarium seawater have not been published and it is not known whether, like orthophosphate, they are substantially greater than their counterparts in nature.

## 6.3  NITROGEN

Inorganic nitrogen in seawater occurs mainly as ammonia, nitrite, and nitrate. Urea is a common nitrogenous organic compound in seawater containing animals (McCarthy and Kamykowski 1972, Mohsen et al. 1974). Other organics containing nitrogen, such as amino acids and peptides, may also be present, but usually in small concentrations. Particulate substances with nitrogen are free-floating in the water column, either as nonliving entities or as protein-based compounds in living microorganisms. The term "ammonia," as used here, refers to the sum of free ammonia ($NH_3$) and ammonium ion ($NH_4^+$). Whitfield (1974b) discussed the hydrolysis of ammonia in seawater.

## Nitrogen Cycling

As in the case of phosphorus, planktonic organisms play no significant role in the cycling of nitrogen through seawater aquariums. There are four pathways by which nitrogen enters aquarium water: (1) diffusion from the atmosphere or from subsurface air bubbles; (2) excretion by macroalgae; (3) excretion by metazoan animals; and (4) oxidation processes of heterotrophic bacteria. The nitrogen cycle in seawater aquariums is shown in Fig. 6-5.

Some molecular nitrogen, $N_2$, may enter aquarium water from the atmosphere, diffusing either through the surface or from air bubbles injected into airlift pumps (Chapter 3). The amount of $N_2$ present at a given time depends on differences in the partial pressure of nitrogen gas in the air compared with the water. The presence of $N_2$ is largely of academic interest, due to a paucity of nitrogen-fixing organisms in marine aquariums. Little of the molecular nitrogen in solution is biologically useful.

The cycling of nitrogen starts with its release into aquarium water by animals and plants. Marine algae release amino acids and peptides, but as Hellebust (1974) pointed out, these substances represent only a small fraction of the total extracellular material liberated into the environment by a healthy population of algae. Of the macroscopic forms, brown algae of the genera *Ascophyllum, Ectocarpus, Fucus,* and *Laminaria* are known to liberate complex proteinaceous materials (Fogg and Boalch 1958, Sieburth 1969). Similar substances are present in the extracellular products of the red microalga *Porphyridium* and the red macroalgae *Chondrus* and *Polysiphonia* (Jones 1962, Sieburth 1969).

Most nitrogenous material in aquarium water originates from animals. Nitrogen, mostly as proteins and amino acids, is simplified into a variety of end products by animals during metabolism. The forms in which these are excreted vary according to species. In addition to $CO_2$ and water, the three main end products of nitrogen breakdown are ammonia, urea ($CH_4ON_2$), and uric acid ($C_5H_4O_3N_4$). The form in which ammonia is excreted by aquatic animals is covered in Section 11.1.

Animals can be grouped according to which form of nitrogen they excrete in the greatest quantity. Those that eliminate mainly ammonia are *ammonotelic*. Urea excreters are *ureotelic*. Animals with uric acid as the dominant nitrogenous excretory product are termed *uricotelic*. No species is limited to a single excretory product. Some ammonotelic animals excrete considerable amounts of other substances besides ammonia. Nearly all ammonotelic species, for example, excrete some urea;

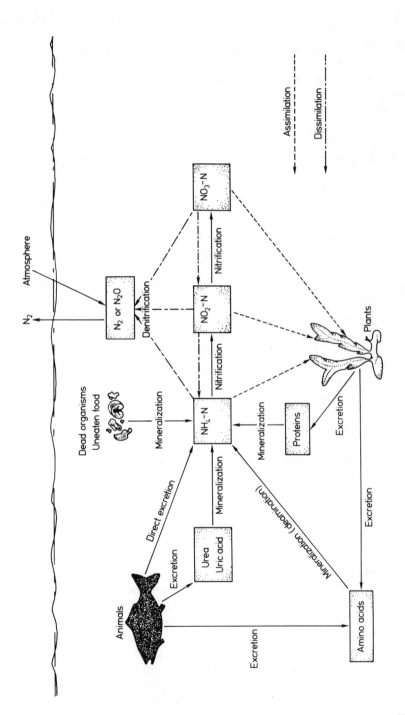

still others excrete uric acid. Echinoderms are ammonotelic, yet they lose amino acids to the environment in considerable quantity. So do crustaceans, which may release up to 10% of excreted nonprotein nitrogen as amino acids (Nichol 1967). Hoar (1975) noted that it was still uncertain whether the amino acids are actually excreted by echinoderms and crustaceans, or simply leaked into the water. Teleosts, although mainly ammonotelic, may also excrete large amounts of urea. Depending on the species, this often amounts to as much as 20% of the nitrogen released. Because animals excrete more than one form of nitrogen, the classification in which a species is placed is based on whichever end product totals more than 50% (Campbell 1973).

Most aquatic animals excrete ammonia, which is very soluble and eliminated easily to the surrounding water. Being hyperosmotic, freshwater fishes and invertebrates can perhaps lose ammonia by diffusion to the external environment. The situation with marine teleosts is more complicated. In those species that maintain hyposmotic body fluids and face possible desiccation, the problem is similar to that of terrestrial animals, in which the tissues can be considered physiologically "dry," and ammonia must be detoxified to prevent it from accumulating. This is accomplished by converting it to urea or another less toxic compound, such as trimethylamine oxide (TMAO). Hoar (1975) summarized the predicament by saying, ". . . excess ammonia arising in metabolism seems to require no further treatment if it can diffuse promptly into the surrounding water, but when water must be conserved, ammonia must be detoxified." The subject of ammonia excretion is complex. See Section 11.1 for a more detailed discussion.

No invertebrate group is ureotelic, although many species excrete small quantities of urea. Among vertebrates, only the marine elasmobranchs are ureotelic, excreting more than 80% of their nonprotein nitrogen as urea (Nichol 1967).

Uric acid is the only nitrogenous end product that can be excreted in solid form. Many marine invertebrates and fishes excrete small amounts of uric acid, but it is not a dominant means by which metabolic nitrogen is eliminated from the tissues.

The nitrogenous components of animal and plant excretory products are acted upon quickly by bacteria. The actual mechanisms and kinetics of the bacteriological breakdown of nitrogen-containing compounds are described in Chapter 7, as is the assimilation of nitrogen by algae. Urea, uric acid, and the nitrogenous extracellular products of algae are broken down by heterotrophic bacteria. The process, called *mineralization*, reduces nitrogenous organic compounds to their inorganic constituents, one of which is ammonia. Ammonia that is excreted directly by ammonotelic organisms is not mineralized, because it is already in an inorganic state.

The ammonia produced by mineralization, or excreted directly by animals, is oxidized to nitrate by nitrifying bacteria. These organisms are autotrophic and able to subsist on inorganic energy sources. The high level of nitrate produced as a result of nitrification is lowered somewhat by dissimilation processes carried out by anaerobic bacteria, assimilation by macroalgae, and through partial water changes. During dissimilation, anaerobic bacteria reduce nitrate, often to molecular nitrogen ($N_2$) or nitrous oxide ($N_2O$). Presumably excess molecular nitrogen is then lost to the atmosphere by diffusion. Nitrification, dissimilation, and assimilation are discussed in Chapter 7.

The assimilation of excess nitrate by plants is more important than dissimilation in seawater aquariums. Algae remove ammonia directly and incorporate it into their own tissues; nitrate and nitrite are reduced to ammonia and then assimilated. Many species of algae can also assimilate urea directly from solution (Section 7-3). The algal tissue produced during photosynthesis is a potential source of future nitrogen in the water, either by direct excretion from healthy plants, or through mineralization of dead tissue by heterotrophic bacteria.

The organic nitrogen in aquarium seawater has many other sources, but dead and dying organisms and bits of uneaten food are the most significant. Some of the organic nitrogen in solution is probably bound up in aggregates and detritus and removed when detritus is siphoned out. Techniques for lowering the total nitrogen level include periodic cropping of the algae, removal of dead organisms and uneaten food, and the use of physical adsorption methods (Chapter 9).

**Eutrophic Effects**

Inorganic nitrogen in the sea is distributed in much the same manner as orthophosphate. The greatest concentrations are found in the temperate and polar zones, where surface seawater is more biologically active than tropical ocean water. Like phosphorus, nitrogen in these regions is more abundant because of the seasonal upwelling of bottom sediments laden with nutrients. Nitrogenous organic compounds, just as organic phosphorus, are more prevalent inshore than offshore. Dissolved organic nitrogen in the open sea ranges from 2 to 20 $\mu$g-at N l$^{-1}$ (Williams 1975).

The total inorganic nitrogen concentration in seawater is the sum of ammonia, nitrite, and nitrate. The term is useful in oceanography because inorganic nitrogen concentrations are low. Spencer (1975) briefly reviewed typical values for surface seawaters worldwide. Total inorganic nitrogen levels in the Antarctic may be 40 $\mu$g-at N $l^{-1}$. The next highest values are found in temperate zones. The northeastern Pacific, for example, has a typical range of 8 to 15 $\mu$g-at N $l^{-1}$. Tropical seas have the lowest values, often no more than 1 to 2 $\mu$g-at N $l^{-1}$.

By comparison, inorganic nitrogen concentrations in aquarium water can be staggering, so large that it is impractical to add them together. Values for nitrate in the seawater at Mystic Marinelife Aquarium normally are less than 50 mg $NO_3$-N $l^{-1}$. Considerably higher values have been reported from other sources. In the public aquarium in Amsterdam, Honig (1934) measured levels of 165 mg $NO_3$-N $l^{-1}$. Oliver (1957) mentioned nitrate levels of 309 mg $NO_3$-N $l^{-1}$ in the seawater of the aquarium operated by the Zoological Society of London. Yoshida (1967) reported that nitrate values in the Misaki and Sakai aquariums in Japan averaged 70mg $NO_3$-N $l^{-1}$.

# CHAPTER 7
## Biological Filtration

It is inevitable that seawater aquariums will become eutrophic. The nutrients produced from the metabolism of animals, plants, and bacteria provide substrates for still more biological growth. Some of these nutrients—notably ammonia—are directly toxic to many species of marine organisms. Nitrogenous organic matter is indirectly toxic because it is all potentially ammonia, as illustrated by the aquarium nitrogen cycle in Fig. 6-5. The processes that occur when living organisms either remove nitrogen from solution or convert it to a less objectionable state are called mineralization, nitrification, dissimilation, and assimilation. The first three are functions carried out primarily by bacteria; the last is limited in this discussion to processes associated with marine algae. Both mineralization and nitrification alter the chemical forms of nitrogenous compounds but do not remove nitrogen from solution. This is accomplished through assimilation and dissimilation. *Biological filtration* results from the sum of the activities of bacteria (bacteriological filtration) and algae (algal filtration). It is defined here as a series of steps in which nitrogenous organic compounds are mineralized, converted to inorganic nitrogen of successively higher oxidation states, and finally removed from solution by complete biochemical reduction and subsequent loss to the atmosphere, or by incomplete reduction followed by assimilation into plant tissues.

The conversion of nitrogen requires energy. Photosynthetic organisms such as algae use light to fuel metabolic functions. Most bacteria are nonphotosynthetic and rely on other types of energy, primarily

**117**

chemical. Chemical energy is released from organic or inorganic compounds through chemical reactions. Organisms that utilize organic substances as energy sources are heterotrophic, whereas autotrophic organisms use mostly inorganic compounds. Whenever a chemical compound is used to supply energy, the process involves an oxidation-reduction or "redox" reaction. As the name suggests, many redox reactions include oxygen, but the true basis is a transfer of electrons. The substance that is oxidized is the energy source in any redox reaction, whereas the electron acceptor is not, although it is still necessary for the reaction to be completed. Once the electron donor has been oxidized, it is generally no longer a source of energy.

Oxygen is the most common electron acceptor in redox reactions. Aerobic respiration is one biochemical process in which oxygen becomes an electron acceptor. The bacteria responsible for mineralization and nitrification are aerobic, requiring oxygen for respiration. During mineralization, organic compounds are oxidized and used as energy sources. In autotrophic oxidation processes such as nitrification, the energy source and the electron donor are the same. Some organisms can carry out respiration in the absence of $O_2$ by the process of *anaerobic respiration*. Dissimilatory nitrate reduction is often accomplished by anaerobic means when one compound used in the reaction is inorganic and the other is organic.

The subject of this chapter is the conversion and ultimate removal of nitrogenous compounds from aquarium water by biological oxidation and reduction. The primary aim is the conversion of ammonia, which is toxic to aquatic animals. The different facets of biological filtration are discussed and practical suggestions are offered for the design and maintenance of bacteriological and algal filters.

## 7.1  MINERALIZATION AND NITRIFICATION

The bacteriological filter of a seawater aquarium consists of a submerged gravel layer supported by a perforated plate. The gravel and plate together comprise the filter bed, described briefly in Chapter 4. The plate is placed just above the bottom of the aquarium tank. Water circulating through the filter bed delivers oxygen to aerobic organisms attached to the gravel grains, as shown in Fig. 4-3 (page 62). Filtered water is drawn from beneath the filter bed and returned to the surface by airlift or mechanical pumps.

Heterotrophic and autotrophic bacteria are not attached as individual cells to gravel grains, but exist as colonies within self-secreted layers of slime that coat the surfaces of the grains. To some extent, the ultimate population of filter bed bacteria depends on the surface area available for attachment. Once attached, however, the viability of the organisms is a function of how efficiently dissolved gases and nutrients can penetrate the gelatinous matrix to the living cells inside. Viability is also affected by such factors as toxicants in the water, temperature, pH, and salinity.

**Mineralization**

In the open sea, the role of heterotrophic bacteria in the degradation of organic compounds far exceeds that of algae (Munro and Brock 1968). The same is true in captive seawater environments. In marine aquariums, organic compounds are the precursors of inorganic nitrogen—ammonia, nitrite, and nitrate. Moreover the gradual rise in the level of total organic carbon (TOC) to the equilibrium point is an important factor affecting the biomass of an aquarium: any rise in the concentration of organic matter leads potentially to an increase in the population or activities of heterotrophic bacteria. The added respiration and other metabolic activities of these organisms strain the limited resources of an isolated environment, resulting in accelerated eutrophication, which reduces the capacity of the water to support other forms of life. The breakdown of organics by bacteria—particularly nitrogen-containing compounds such as proteins and amino acids—is an important biochemical process in all seawater aquariums.

When amino acids are used as carbon sources by living organisms, the first step in their transformation is usually removal of the amino group to form an organic acid. A common method among microorganisms is *transamination,* in which the amino group is exchanged for a keto group of a keto acid, as shown in Fig. 7-1. A second method is *dehydrogenation,* in which the nitrogen in the amino acid is converted to ammonia instead of remaining bound up in another amino acid, as is the case during transamination. A third method is *decarboxylation,* in which a carboxyl group is converted to $CO_2$ and the amino acid to an amine. During *deamination,* the fourth method, the amino group is removed, leaving an organic acid plus ammonia. Each method requires a specific set of enzymes. Consequently different organisms may use one method in preference to the others, and many species are able to use two or more methods. Ultimately the breakdown of all organic compounds results in the formation of inorganic substances, a process called *mineralization.*

The origin of inorganic nitrogen was described in the last chapter.

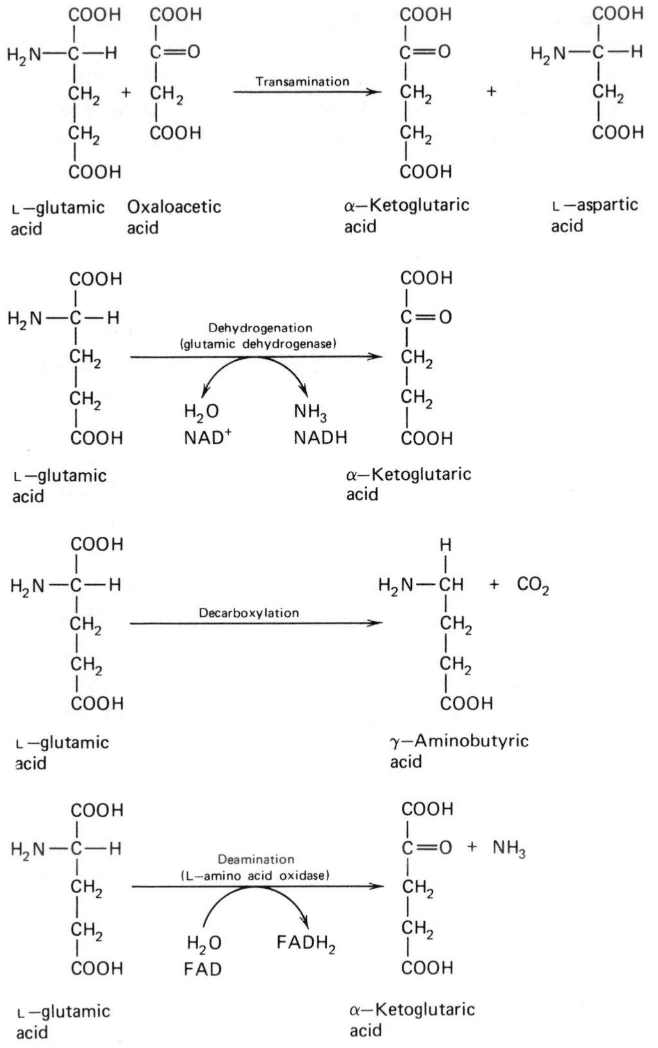

**Figure 7-1** Amino acid transformations. Redrawn from Brock (1970).

Some is excreted directly by animals and plants, and the rest originates from the heterotrophic decomposition of organic substances, mostly uneaten food and dead organisms. Thus mineralization is the first step in bacteriological filtration. A number of mineralization processes produce inorganic nitrogen, but I shall concentrate on deamination.

Painter (1970) listed three ways that ammonia could be produced from organic compounds by deamination: (1) from extracellular organic nitrogenous compounds, such as dead animal or plant tissue; (2) from living bacterial cells during respiration; and (3) from lysed or freshly dead cells. Ammonia produced by deamination is released during periods when the organic constituents of the nitrogenous substance are being oxidized and used as an energy source. Ordinarily the portions assimilated are hydroxy and keto acids (Painter 1970). Endogenous metabolism, the second mechanism, produces ammonia from internal precursors during respiration. The rate of degradation of organics under these conditions depends on such factors as concentration of the specific organics within the cell and the nutritional state of the organisms. As microbial cells respire and oxidize their own internal contents, they become smaller. Living cells have finite lifespans, which leads to the third mechanism. Eventually any cell becomes unthrifty and dies. The sequential process of lysis and death results in rupture of the cell membrane and release of the cellular contents into the external environment. One constituent is ammonia; others include nitrogenous organics, which provide energy sources for oxidation by heterotrophic bacteria.

Once mineralization has taken place, inorganic nitrogen ordinarily is converted to higher oxidation states by autotrophic bacteria. In some cases, heterotrophs also utilize inorganic nitrogen as an energy source. Johnson and Sieburth (1976) claimed that heterotrophic bacteria in aquarium water competed with nitrifiers for inorganic nitrogen. Culter and Crump (1933) reported that at least 104 species of soil heterotrophs could oxidize ammonia to nitrite. Tate (1977) found that cultures of the soil heterotroph *Anthrobacter* could oxidize ammonia directly to both nitrite and nitrate. In other instances, heterotrophic bacteria have been known to convert nitrogenous organic compounds directly to nitrite and nitrate without first forming ammonia (Doxtader and Alexander 1966, Jensen and Gundersen 1955, Quastel et al. 1950). Evidently the use of substrates by heterotrophic bacteria is less stereotyped than is commonly thought, and it would be wrong to think of these organisms only in terms of their ability to oxidize organic matter.

### Nitrification

Once nitrogenous organic matter has been mineralized, bacteriological filtration shifts to the second stage, which is nitrification. *Nitrification* is the biochemical oxidation of ammonia to nitrate and is carried out primarily by two groups of autotrophic bacteria. The principal genus of ammonia-oxidizers is *Nitrosomonas*, whereas nitrite oxidation is accomplished mainly by species of *Nitrobacter*. The reactions are shown below.

$$NH_4^+ + OH^- + 1\frac{1}{2}O_2 \rightarrow H^+ + NO_2^- + 2H_2O \qquad (37)$$

$$NO_2^- + \frac{1}{2}O_2 \rightarrow NO_3^- \qquad (38)$$

The significance of nitrification is the conversion of ammonia and nitrite to nitrate, which is less toxic. A review of nitrification was presented by Sharma and Ahlert (1977).

Nitrification is an important natural process, and its mechanisms have been studied in great detail. Nevertheless there is much confusion about the taxonomy of the bacteria involved. Some genera of ammonia-oxidizers are probably synonyms. The taxonomy of the nitrifying bacteria is of minor importance here except to demonstrate that perhaps fewer species exist than a quick perusal of the literature shows. Watson (1965) reviewed the status of ammonia-oxidizers. He concluded that the genera *Nitrosocystis*, *Nitrosogloea*, and *Nitrosococcus* are probably synonyms, and speculated that *Nitrosomonas* may be as important in the oceans as *Nitrosocystis*.

Nitrifying bacteria are not obligate autotrophs, as is commonly thought. By definition, such organisms are photoautotrophic or chemoautotrophic, and nitrifiers do not fit conveniently into either category. The former are unable to grow in the absence of light, whereas the latter cannot grow except in the presence of their specific nitrogen sources—ammonia or nitrite. Wallace et al. (1970) demonstrated that cultures of *Nitrosomonas europaea* and *Nitrobacter agilis* assimilated organic carbon compounds regardless of the inclusion or omission of their respective inorganic energy sources. Clark and Schmidt (1967b) showed that *N. europaea* could assimilate several amino acids, but the rate of uptake was enhanced by the presence of ammonia. Smith and Hoare (1968) found that cell suspensions of *N. agilis* took up acetate in the presence of nitrite, although more slowly than when nitrite was present.

The ability to assimilate organic compounds makes nitrifying bacteria *facultative autotrophs*. Under certain conditions, nitrifiers can use a significant amount of organic carbon in the environment, both as a source of cellular carbon and as an energy source during respiration (Smith and Hoare 1968). Delwiche and Finstein (1965) determined that labeled isotopes of acetate and glycine contributed significantly to cellular carbon. In the case of acetate, 42.2% of the amount supplied exogenously was incorporated into cellular carbon by resting suspensions of *N. agilis*. When glycine was used, 22.8% of the glycine-1-[14]C and 20% of the glycine-2-$^{14}$C were incorporated into cellular carbon. Smith and Hoare (1968) found that *N. agilis* could grow under heterotrophic conditions in the absence of nitrite. The organism assimilated acetate-1-$^{14}$C, and acetate-2-$^{14}$C and acetate carbon accounted for 33 to 39% of the newly synthesized cellular carbon. Moreover carbon from the acetate was utilized in the synthesis of all cellular materials, including most of the amino acids and cell proteins. Steinmüller and Bock (1977) reported that *N. agilis* could be grown autotrophically on nitrite, mixotrophically on nitrite together with either acetate or pyruvate, and heterotrophically on acetate and casamino acids, pyruvate and casamino acids, or pyruvate and nitrate.

Clark and Schmidt (1967a) reported that cultures of *N. europaea* incorporated $^{14}$C isotopes of several amino acids. Both protein synthesis and formation of nitrite were increased in the presence of *L*-glutamic acid, *L*-aspartic acid, *L*-serine, and *L*-glutamine. Other amino acids tested either were toxic or had no effect. However all were taken up and metabolized by growing cells when present in low concentrations, regardless of whether their effects at higher levels were stimulatory, inhibitory, or indifferent. Further evidence that low concentrations of $^{14}$C-amino acids (1 $\mu$g ml$^{-1}$ or less) added to the environment were taken up by *N. europaea* was presented in a later work (Clark and Schmidt 1967b). Wallace et al. (1970) incubated cell suspensions of *N. europaea* and *N. agilis* with $^{14}$C isotopes of $CO_2$, acetate, pyruvate, $\alpha$-ketoglutarate, succinate, glutamate, and asparate. After incubation periods of up to 1 hr, these tracer substances were found in proteins, soluble amino and organic acids, and neutral cell fractions.

### Factors Affecting Nitrification

The efficiency of the nitrification process is affected by factors that limit the proliferation of nitrifying bacteria, or inhibit their biochemical activities. The most significant factors are: (1) toxic substances in the water; (2) temperature; (3) pH; (4) the concentration of dissolved oxygen; (5) salinity; and (6) surface area available for microbial attachment.

#### Toxic Substances

Several published studies detail the effects of different chemical compounds on nitrification, but most of the information is of little value to aquarists. The majority of compounds mentioned in the literature as being inhibitory were tested using nitrifying bacteria isolated from soil or activated sludge. Even though the species may be the same, environmental conditions of aquariums are different and the data can seldom be applied directly. Furthermore most of the substances tested have been industrial wastes or other pollutants rarely encountered in aquarium water. Aquarists are concerned mainly with the effects of two groups of compounds on nitrification: (1) ammonia, sulfide, and other metabolites; and (2) medications.

It is difficult to evaluate much of the published data on the subject of toxic compounds, even when the information is pertinent to aquarium applications. Investigators have, in general, failed to distinguish whether the substances tested inhibited proliferation (growth) of nitrifying bacteria, or their activities (oxidation of substrates). The difference is important enough that the pointed reasoning of Lees (1952) is still valid: any compound that inhibits the oxidation of ammonia or nitrite by nitrifying bacteria must similarly inhibit their proliferation. The reverse is not always true, however, and compounds that inhibit the proliferation of nitrifiers do not always inhibit ammonia or nitrite oxidation. As Lees noted, care must be taken when interpreting data on the effects of various inhibiting substances, particularly when the experimental work was extended for days or weeks. The reason is that many compounds inhibit cell proliferation in culture, yet may not affect the ability of the remaining cells to oxidize the energy source. During prolonged experiments, the distinction becomes more nebulous if neither factor has been controlled. (For instance, by limiting the duration of the experiments to a few hours, cell proliferation as a variable can be eliminated.) If, for example, the suspected inhibitor $X$ is added to an experimental culture but not to the control, and if the nitrite or nitrate formed in the culture containing $X$ is less than in the control, there is still no indication of how $X$ behaved. If $X$ directly inhibited oxidation, less ammonia or nitrite would be formed in its presence. But if $X$ actually had no effect on oxidation and yet inhibited the proliferation of cells, the accumulation of ammonia-oxidizing enzymes would naturally be less than in the controls, and a smaller amount of nitrite or nitrate would appear in the experimental culture than in the control. The quantity of substance formed in each experimental culture might be the same, but the mechanisms of formation would be different. Thus to say that compound $X$ "inhibits the oxidation of ammonia" is not necessarily synonymous with the statement that $X$ "inhibits the growth of ammonia-oxidizing bacteria."

Nitrite sometimes persists in higher than normal concentrations long after the filter bed should have been conditioned. The cause may be dissimilatory activities by anaerobic bacteria (Section 7.2), or incomplete nitrification, a condition brought about by the inhibition of nitrite oxidation. Their own substrates are two of the substances most inhibitory to nitrifiers. The sequential rise and fall of ammonia and nitrite in aquarium water is due partly to this self-inhibition mechanism. Meiklejohn (1954) wrote: "The electrolytes to which the nitrifiers are sensitive include their own substrates, and in each case, the substrate of the other species was found to be much more toxic than the organisms' own substrate. Nitrite depressed both respiration and growth of *Nitrosomonas*. . . . *Nitrobacter* was sensitive to the ammonium ion, but even more so to free ammonia. . . . Nitrate . . . was only slightly toxic to both species."

In their investigation of the inhibition of nitrification by ammonia and nitrite, Anthonisen et al. (1976) postulated that the problem could be traced to the concentrations of free ammonia (FA = $NH_3$) and free nitrous acid (FNA = $HNO_2$). Their work was conducted in freshwater, but a similar process may also exist in saline environments. At high concentrations, free ammonia was believed to be inhibitory to both ammonia and nitrite oxidizers. As the concentration diminished, free ammonia became less inhibitory to ammonia oxidizers than to nitrite oxidizers. In addition, nitrification is an acid-forming process and nitrite exists in equilibrium with free nitrous acid, as shown by

$$H^+ + NO_2^- \rightleftharpoons HNO_2 \tag{39}$$

The reaction shifts to the left as the pH declines.

Ammonia inhibition is tempered by two factors. First, as the pH declines due to nitrification, the percentage of free ammonia relative to the concentration of total $NH_4$-N becomes smaller. Second, the total ammonia declines as some of it is oxidized to nitrite. Both processes lessen the severity of ammonia inhibition of nitrite oxidizers.

In some cases, low levels of nitrite persist, although the ammonia concentration is small. Anthonisen et al. (1976) attributed this to inhibition of nitrification by free nitrous acid. At certain concentrations, $HNO_2$ inhibits the activities of both ammonia and nitrite oxidizers. Anthonisen and his co-authors published a chart consisting of four successive zones to evaluate the effects of $NH_3$ and $HNO_2$ on nitrification. It is reproduced here as Fig. 7-2. In Zone 1, the concentration of $NH_3$ is great enough to inhibit activities of both ammonia and nitrite oxidizers. In Zone 2, the level of $NH_3$ is less. Ammonia oxidizers can function, but nitrite oxidizers are still inhibited. Zone 3 represents a situation in which the concentration of $NH_3$ is small enough to allow both nitrifiers to carry out normal physiological activities. If no $HNO_2$ is present, complete nitrification is represented by Zone 4. Boundaries of

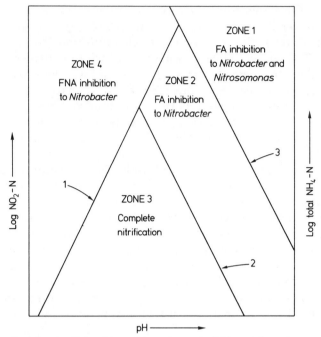

**Figure 7-2**  Postulated relationships of free ammonia (FA) and free nitrous acid (FNA) inhibition to nitrifying bacteria as described in the text. Redrawn and modified from Anthonisen et al. (1976).

the zones are noted at *1, 2,* and *3.* Delineations will not be sharp, as pointed out by the authors, because of such tempering factors as differences in the acclimation rate of the organisms to environmental conditions, numbers of organisms, and temperature effects on reaction rates.

Sulfide that is produced in anaerobic sections of a filter bed inhibits nitrification. Srna and Baggaley (1975) reported that sulfide ion at concentrations of 0.03 mg $l^{-1}$ severely inhibited the oxidation of ammonia in seawater aquariums at temperatures of 20 to 24°C. Inhibition continued until the sulfide ion concentration was reduced to 0.015 mg $l^{-1}$. Conversion of nitrite to nitrate was 14% slower when sulfide ion was present in concentrations of 0.1 mg $l^{-1}$. According to Yoshida (1967), nitrite formation in nearly pure cultures of marine ammonia oxidizers was not inhibited by the addition of $Na_2S$ until the level reached 3 mg $l^{-1}$; all activity stopped at concentrations of 30 mg $l^{-1}$.

It is sometimes thought that organic compounds, *per se* inhibit nitrification, but this is not true. Nitrifying bacteria show a wide range of responses to organics in the environment, including indifference and stimulation, in addition to repression of growth or activity. As Delwiche and Finstein (1965) observed, no general statement can be made about the effects that organic compounds have on nitrifying organisms. They attributed inconsistencies in the literature to differences in technique and to competition for nutrients in cultures of mixed organisms. Substrate concentration is still another factor to consider. In some instances the concentration of a particular substance dictates whether it is toxic. Gundersen (1955) reported that five amino acids tested— $L$-tryptophan, $L$-glutamic acid, $L$-histidine, $L$-tyrosine, and $L$-phenylalanine—inhibited the growth of *Nitrosomonas* in culture when added in concentrations of 100 mg $l^{-1}$. Clark and Schmidt (1967a), however, found that in the case of the first three compounds, only $L$-histidine inhibited the growth of *Nitrosomonas* at lower levels (4 mg $l^{-1}$).

Collins et al. (1975, 1976) and Levine and Meade (1976) reported that many common antibacterial agents and parasiticides used in treating fish diseases had no effect on nitrification in freshwater aquariums, but that others were toxic to various degrees. No parallel studies have been made using seawater, and the experimental results of these authors cannot be applied directly to saline environments. The data of Collins and his coinvestigators, and of Levine and Meade, are summarized in Table 7-1. Their results are not comparable in some respects because of differences in technique. Collins' group measured the effects of compounds they tested by taking water samples directly from aquarium tanks that contained fish and viable filter beds. Levine and Meade used inoculates of mixed bacteria and their measurements were done in culture. Levine and Meade acknowledged that their results possibly were more sensitive than would be the case under actual operating conditions. For example, their tests showed formalin, malachite green, and nifurpirinol (Furanace®) to be mildly toxic to nitrifying bacteria, whereas Collins et al. (1975, 1976) had shown the same compounds to be harmless. Levine and Meade suggested that the difference was attributable to the greater percentage of autotrophs in their inoculates, and that perhaps low inhibition thresholds for these substances do not exist in the presence of greater numbers of heterotrophs and higher concentrations of organic matter.

From the data in Table 7-1, there is little doubt that erythromycin, chlorotetracycline, methylene blue, and sulfanilamide inhibit nitrification in freshwater aquariums. Methylene blue was the most toxic of the substances tested. Mixed results were obtained with chloramphenicol

*Biological Filtration*

Table 7-1  Effects of Commonly Used Antibacterial Agents and Parasiticides on Nitrification in Freshwater Aquariums at Therapeutic Levels.

| Compound | Concentration (mg l$^{-1}$) | % Inhibition | Source |
|---|---|---|---|
| Chloramphenicol | 50 | 0 | Collins et al. (1976) |
|  | 50 | 84 | Levine and Meade (1976) |
| Oxytetracycline | 50 | 0 | Collins et al. (1976) |
| Sulfamerazine | 50 | 0 | Collins et al. (1976) |
| Sulfanilamide | 25 | 65 | Levine and Meade (1976) |
| Erythromycin | 50 | 100 | Collins et al (1976) |
| Nifurpirinol | 1 | 0 | Collins et al. (1976) |
|  | 0.1 | 20 | Levine and Meade (1976) |
|  | 4 | 44 | Levine and Meade (1976) |
| Chlorotetracycline | 10 | 76 | Levine and Meade (1976) |
| Formalin | 25[a] | 0 | Collins et al. (1975) |
|  | 15 | 27 | Levine and Meade (1976) |
| Malachite green | 0.1 | 0 | Collins et al. (1975) |
| Formalin + malachite green | 25 + 0.1 | 0 | Collins et al. (1975) |
| Methylene blue | 5 | 100 | Collins et al. (1975) |
|  | 1 | 92 | Levine and Meade (1976) |
| Copper sulfate | 1[b] | 0 | Collins et al. (1975) |
|  | 5 | 0 | Levine and Meade (1976) |
| Potassium permanganate | 4 | 0 | Collins et al. (1975) |
|  | 1 | 86 | Levine and Meade (1976) |

[a] Equivalent to 10 mg l$^{-1}$ formaldehyde.
[b] Hardness = 30 mg CaCO$_3$ l$^{-1}$.

and potassium permanganate. The data of Collins et al. (1975) showed copper to be nontoxic, but the concentration of organic matter present in solution was not stated. Tomlinson et al. (1966) determined that the heavy metals Cr, Cu, and Hg were more toxic to *Nitrosomonas* in pure culture than in activated sludge. They suggested that the results might have been due to the formation of chemical complexes between the metals and the organics. Long-term effects of heavy metals were more severe than short-term effects, possibly because adsorption sites on organic molecules were used up. In my opinion, future studies on the inhibitory effects that heavy metals have on nitrification in aquarium water should include an account of the total organic carbon (TOC). Aquariums are generally eutrophic and therefore more akin to activated sludge than to conditions that exist in pure culture.

*Temperature*

Watson (1965) found that pure cultures of *Nitrosocystis oceanus* grew best at 30°C. Carlucci and Strickland (1968), working with the same species, determined an optimum temperature of 28°C, with 20°C the next best temperature for activity (oxidation of ammonia). A second (unknown) ammonia oxidizer performed most efficiently at 37°C, as did an undetermined species of nitrite oxidizer. All three forms were isolated from seawater collected in the Pacific.

Kawai et al. (1965) found that nitrifying bacteria in seawater aquarium filter beds showed greatest activity at 30 to 35°C; activity diminished when the temperature was raised or lowered. This was different from the optimum temperature for freshwater nitrifiers, which was approximately 30°C. Below 20°C, the differences in activity between seawater and freshwater nitrifiers became more conspicuous. Yoshida (1967) noted an optimum temperature of 27 to 28°C for growth of marine nitrifiers. His organisms, however, had been isolated in culture at 25°C, so that an optimum growth rate near the acclimation temperature is not surprising. The highest level of activity for ammonia oxidizers occurred at 30 to 35°C. In another study (Yoshida et al. 1967), the optimum temperature of a marine ammonia oxidizer was determined to be 50 to 55°C.

Nitrification is most efficient at warm temperatures. None of the cultures tested by Carlucci and Strickland (1968) were able to carry out nitrification at 5°, even after 3 to 4 months of incubation. Temperatures of the seawater from which the organisms were taken varied from 9 to 26°C. Evidently nitrification is greatly inhibited at very cold temperatures. As to ideal temperatures above 30°C, Carlucci and Strickland (1968) pointed out that it is not uncommon for marine bacteria in culture to exhibit optimum temperatures that are much higher than temperatures found in their natural environments.

Carlucci and Strickland (1968) determined the rate constant, $k$, for several ammonia- and nitrite-oxidizing bacteria that were growing in a range of substrate concentrations. At substrate concentrations typical of those found in seawater, $k$ was approximately 0.05 da$^{-1}$ at 25°C, indicating slow oxidation. Buswell et al. (1954) found $k$ values in pure cultures of *Nitrosomonas* that increased from 0.5 da$^{-1}$ at 15°C to 2 da$^{-1}$ at 32°C. The calculated coefficient from these data is 8.2% °C$^{-1}$(Knowles et al. 1965). As shown in the review by Knowles et al. (1965), the $k$ values for nitrifying bacteria are highly variable.

## pH

Published reports on the ideal pH ranges for efficient nitrification in aquarium water differ considerably. Srna and Baggaley (1975) analyzed data from several sources, all but one of which dealt with freshwater. They suggested that the figures did not agree because of the varied conditions under which the test organisms were maintained. Evidently nitrifying bacteria can be conditioned to function throughout a fairly wide pH range, provided they are given time to adjust. Kawai et al. (1965) determined that the ideal pH for marine nitrifiers was 9. Saeki (1958) had earlier reported ideal pH values of 7.8 and 7.1 for ammonia and nitrite oxidation, respectively, in seawater aquariums. Srna and Baggaley (1975) determined that the marine nitrifiers used in their study operated best at pH 7.45, with an effective range of 7 to 8.2. Yoshida (1967) reported optimum values for four strains of unidentified marine ammonia oxidizers that varied from 7 to 9, and Yoshida et al. (1967) observed that the optimum pH range for a marine ammonia oxidizer identified as A6 was 8.5 to 8.7. Forster (1974) lowered the pH slowly in an experimental seawater aquarium; nitrification stopped completely at pH 5.5.

### Dissolved Oxygen

Reports dealing with the effects of oxygen on nitrification are conflicting. This is due in part to the adaptability of nitrifying bacteria, and future experimental work should note the partial pressure of oxygen to which the organisms were previously acclimated. The general statement can be made that nitrifying bacteria adapted to seawater are aerobic, although their oxygen requirements are lower than those of many other aerobic species.

Carlucci and McNally (1969) showed that nitrifying bacteria isolated from the open sea oxidized low concentrations of substrate (5 $\mu$g-at $NH_4$-N or 20 $\mu$g-at $NO_2$-N $l^{-1}$) in a liquid medium containing less than 0.14 mg $O_2$ $l^{-1}$ and in a solid medium when the level was less than 0.002 atm $O_2$. More carbon was assimilated per unit of substrate oxidized in low than in high oxygen concentrations. This was further confirmation of the earlier work of Gundersen (1966), who reported that nitrification took place under conditions of low $P_{O_2}$. *Nitrosocystis oceanus* grew more efficiently when the oxygen level was less than 0.05 atm than it did in

**Table 7-2   Inorganic Nitrogen Balance in Seawater Aquariums with Different Oxygen Tensions after 3 Months**

| Aquarium | 1 | 2 | 3 |
|---|---|---|---|
| Oxygen tension (% saturation) | 89 | 34 | 6 |
| Ammonia-N (mg $NH_4$-N $l^{-1}$) | 0.609 | 0.465 | 173.6 |
| Nitrite-N (mg $NO_2$-N $l^{-1}$) | 0.017 | 0.023 | 0.018 |
| Nitrate-N (mg $NO_3$-N $l^{-1}$) | 248.0 | 126.0 | 0.559 |

Source: Kawai et al. (1971).

air (0.2 atm $O_2$); that is, more carbon was assimilated per unit of nitrogen oxidized. In a liquid medium, the lowest oxygen concentration at which nitrification still occurred was about 0.05 mg $l^{-1}$.

Kimata et al. (1961) demonstrated that aeration seemed to have an adverse effect on cultures of nitrifying bacteria isolated from seawater, and Kawai et al. (1965) showed that high aeration rates actually decreased the activity of nitrifiers in seawater, although the effects were the opposite in freshwater. Kawai and his group noted that, although nitrifying activity was greatest at higher oxygen levels, some activity continued under virtually anaerobic conditions.

Kawai et al. (1971) evaluated the effects of oxygen on the balance of inorganic nitrogen compounds in freshwater and seawater aquariums at an unspecified temperature (presumably room temperature). The study lasted 3 months. No significant differences were noted with respect to shifts of inorganic nitrogen in the two environments. Oxidation of ammonia and nitrite was carried out most efficiently under aerobic conditions. In three experimental aquariums in which the oxygen tensions were maintained at $O_2$ saturations of 89, 34, and 6%, the aquarium with the lowest value showed the highest level of ammonia, as indicated in Table 7-2. Conversion of ammonia apparently was inhibited at very low oxygen tensions.

The effects of oxygen tension on the conversion of nitrite and nitrate were also measured. The values for nitrite after 3 months were similar at all three levels of oxygen saturation (Table 7-2). In the case of nitrate, the smallest value measured was in the experimental aquarium with the lowest oxygen saturation. This is not surprising, considering that dissimilatory nitrate reduction is predominantly an anaerobic process (Section 7.2). Forster (1974) found that ammonia conversion in aquarium seawater was inhibited at dissolved oxygen concentrations below 0.6 to 0.7 mg $O_2$ $l^{-1}$.

*Salinity*

Kawai et al. (1965) found that marine nitrifying bacteria performed best at salinities to which they had been acclimated. Their activity levels declined as salinity was raised or lowered. No activity was observed when the seawater was replaced with freshwater, but some remained even when the salinity of the normal-strength seawater was doubled. As might be expected, the nitrifying activity of freshwater filter sand was greatest before the addition of any seawater. Activity stopped entirely when the salinity reached the level of normal seawater.

The unknown marine nitrite formers cultured by Yoshida (1967) grew best in 50 to 60% seawater. Growth rates declined gradually as this saline water was either concentrated or diluted. Four strains of these organisms showed greatest activity in concentrations of seawater ranging from 40 to 100% of full strength.

*Surface Area*

Mineralization and nitrification are enhanced in the presence of particulate matter suspended in the water or trapped as detritus in the filter bed. The increased surface area offered by such material affects bacteriological growth, mainly by providing extra attachment sites. Saeki (1958) attributed 25% of the nitrifying capability of the filter bed of an experimental aquarium to accumulated detritus. In addition, the adsorption of nutrients onto detritus and suspended particles and aggregates encourages increased activity by concentrating energy sources at locations where microorganisms attach. Surface area is therefore a two-dimensional factor. The function at the first level is indirect and purely physical: more surfaces mean increased bacteriological conversion rates by allowing a larger population of organisms to exist. At the second level, chemical attraction of microorganisms to an attachment site increases activity directly because energy sources are concentrated. Surface area in mineralization is important at both levels; in nitrification, only the physical presence of added attachment sites is significant.

Khailov and Finenko (1970) concluded that DOC in the sea must be adsorbed onto solid substrates before it can be utilized by microorganisms. They saw the process as consisting of two steps: (1) physical (adsorption onto a substratum); and (2) biochemical (microbial conversion of the dissolved organic compounds once they have been adsorbed). The significant feature of this concept is the important role assigned to detritus in the conversion of organic carbon to inorganic substances. As Khailov and Finenko noted, it is untenable to think that heterotrophic organisms utilize DOC directly; rather the high surface activity demonstrated by many of these compounds suggests a mechanism by which they are adsorbed onto particulate material populated by bacteria. The authors went on to say, "The data give the impression that the traditional question: 'do micro-organisms populating detritus decompose organic matter dissolved in the surrounding water or organic matter of detritus itself?' was posed inexactly. Apparently the answer is that micro-organisms populating detrital particles decompose dissolved surfactants of sea water, but only after their adsorption on to the detritus surface."

Chemical attraction to the attachment site does not appear to be a factor in nitrification. Lees and Quastel (1946a, 1946b) thought that nitrification rates were increased in the presence of soil particles, supposedly because the nutrient ions available for utilization by nitrifiers were fixed at particle surfaces. According to this theory, ammonium ions are held in base exchange combinations and nutrient uptake occurs by ion exchange. Later work by Allison et al. (1951; 1953a, 1953b, 1953c) produced results that differed from those of Lees and Quastel: as more ammonium ions were adsorbed onto soil particles, fewer became available for nitrification. Kholdebarin and Oertli (1977) studied the effects of suspended solids from a freshwater river on nitrification in culture. They concluded that nitrification rates were indeed enhanced in the presence of particles, but not because of any chemical affinity of the organisms to their attachment sites. Rather the particles seemed to provide places for physical attachment and nothing more. The greater the number of particles in suspension, the more surface area there was for potential colonization.

Most of the bacteriological activity in seawater aquariums occurs inside living films attached to the walls, gravel, and other solid surfaces. Synonyms for this material are matrix and slime. Biological films are produced by the bacteria inhabiting them, and most consist of polysaccharides and gums. The thickness of biological films is limited by the nutrient load and dissolved oxygen concentration in the environment. The level of nutrients in the water at a given time is a function of animal density. Aquaculture installations, with their heavy animal loads, can be expected to contain thicker films than display aquariums. Johnson and Sieburth (1976) measured slime that varied from 1 to 5 mm thick on the surfaces of membrane filters submerged for 20 to 40 days in a freshwater salmon culture facility. By comparison, little slime was evident in the filtrant of a sparsely populated seawater aquarium. Electron photomicrographs showing nitrifying-like bacteria isolated from the aquarium are presented in Fig. 7-3.

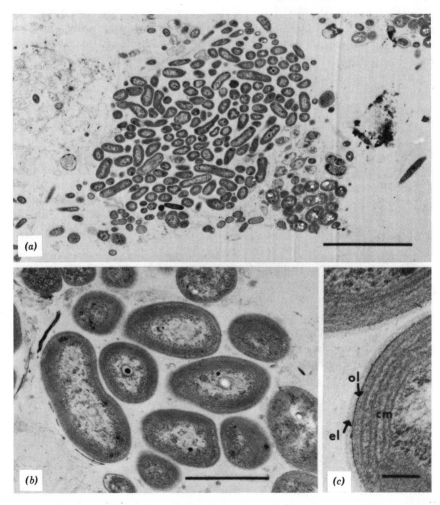

**Figure 7-3** Electron photomicrographs of marine nitrifying-like bacteria from a seawater aquarium containing striped bass (*Morone saxatilis*): (*a*) a zoogloeal-type colony from the slime on the wall of the tank (cells are not embedded in a polysaccharide-like matrix), bar = 5 μm; (*b*) typical rod-shaped marine bacterium with peripheral cytomembranes characteristic of a species of *Nitrosomonas*, bar = 1 μm; (*c*) higher magnification showing the cytomembranes (cm) and outer wall layers (ol), and also the extra cell wall layer (el) commonly found in most marine species of *Nitrosomonas*, bar = 0.1 μm. From Johnson and Sieburth (1976).

Heavy films have been reported from the surfaces of gravel grains in trickling filters (Hoehn and Ray 1973), in which wastewater (domestic or industrial waste suspended or dissolved in freshwater) is sprayed over a bed of gravel exposed to the atmosphere. Nutrients are oxidized by aerobic bacteria as the wastewater "trickles" through the gravel. Thick films are possible partly because wastewater contains high nutrient levels. In addition, exposure to the atmosphere allows a cross section of slime to remain aerobic to a greater depth because of the larger concentration of oxygen in air compared with water. Biological films rely on the diffusion of oxygen from the environment to sustain aerobic bacteria. In submerged filters, where dissolved oxygen concentrations are much lower than in the atmosphere, thick films often become oxygen-limited near the base.

Film formation is a common process in nature. Bacteriologists in the 1930s first discovered that solid surfaces submerged in freshwater or seawater promoted microbial activity. Clean glass slides suspended beneath the surface in lakes (Henrici and Johnson 1935, Smith and ZoBell 1937), or in the sea (ZoBell and Anderson 1936), were soon covered with an assortment of bacteria, in addition to other microorganisms and particulate matter. To explain this phenomenon, Stark et al. (1938) and Heukelekian and Heller (1940) proposed that solid surfaces enhanced the concentration of nutrients, thus promoting microbial activity indirectly.

Microorganisms that attach to solid surfaces are called *periphytes* (ZoBell 1970). Heterotrophic and autotrophic microbes attached to the walls or gravel grains in the filter beds of seawater aquariums are therefore periphytic. Once attached, periphytic bacteria form microcolonies. The microcolonies, in turn, produce a biological film composed of their own products (Corpe 1970). Many periphytic forms that live in biological films are stalked, budding, or filamentous and thus truly sessile (Corpe 1974). Others presumably move about within the matrix.

Gravel grains in the filter bed offer the greatest amount of surface area for slime formation. At first the direction of growth is lateral, but as all available surfaces become coated, further expansion is outward and the film thickens. Nutrients required by the filter bed bacteria diffuse from the water into the film, along with dissolved oxygen. Waste products diffuse outward. As the film thickens, diffusion of oxygen and nutrients toward the basal layer is impeded and the deeper portions of the film turn anaerobic. Without oxygen, aerobes near the base die. The cells lyse and give up their contents to heterotrophic anaerobes. As time passes and the matrix continues to thicken, the flow of nutrients to

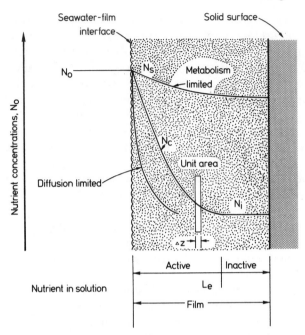

**Figure 7-4**   Possible substrate profile in a biological film. Redrawn and modified from Williamson and McCarty (1976).

deeper regions is restricted. Now the anaerobes die, lyse, and destroy the attachment point of the matrix to its surface. The film breaks apart and the original surface becomes available for colonization once again. Thus in the evolution and demise of a biological film, oxygen becomes limiting at first, then a nutrient supply (Hoehn and Ray 1973).

A conceptual view of nutrient utilization within a biological film was presented by Williamson and McCarty (1976). A simplified version is shown here as Fig. 7-4. Nutrient concentrations are represented by $N_0$ in the liquid outside the film, $N_s$ at the film surface, $N_c$ inside the matrix, and $N_i$ deep within the matrix as a constant limiting value. The gradient of $N_c$ at the water-film interface, where $z = O(\Delta N_c/\Delta z)$, is intermediate between low values (metabolism-limited) and high values (diffusion-limited). The nutrient concentration between the water and the surface of the film decreases as a result of incomplete mixing of water next to the film surface, and the mass transfer of nutrient material into the film.

In biological films that are not metabolism-limited, nutrient concentration inside the film will reach a minimum value of $N_i$, at which point metabolism stops. This is the case in the deep films common in trickling filters. In situations in which the slime is kept thin by the shearing force of water rushing past, or by frequent breaking apart as a result of biochemical activities, metabolism of the nutrient material may occur throughout the entire layer. The film depth at which $N_c = N_i$ is called the effective depth, $L_e$, and it contains those organisms that are actively metabolizing the nutrient substratum.

Biological film formation in wastewater treatment systems follows a predictable pattern, as reviewed by Hoehn and Ray (1973). The same features probably hold true in the filter beds of seawater aquariums. Where biological activity is concerned, a newly formed film is thin and not limited by lack of oxygen. Aerobic nutrient uptake is rapid and

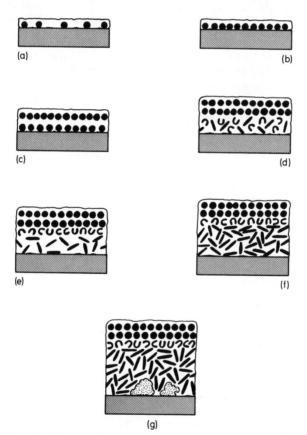

**Figure 7-5** Theoretical film development concept based on observed density changes. Growth changes are explained in the text. Redrawn and modified from Hoehn and Ray (1973).

efficient. At some point, nutrient removal declines abruptly. In the life of a film, this is the point of limiting thickness, at which outward growth has caused the underlying layers to become anaerobic. After a period of adjustment, activity rates increase again and become comparable with the initial rates.

The changes in the population of aerobic and anaerobic organisms within a maturing matrix are illustrated in Fig. 7-5. The population is low at first, as aerobes colonize the new surface (a). Abundant oxygen and nutrients result in rapid growth (b and c). As oxygen becomes limiting in the deeper regions, aerobes begin to die (d). Bacteria that are able to function anaerobically begin to appear. Lysing aerobes (open circles in d) furnish nutrients and the overall population of bacteria declines. At (e) the anaerobic organisms adjust to the change in conditions. They proliferate and the population density starts to stabilize. At (f) there is a steady state in the number of organisms. As shown in (g), steady-state conditions continue until nutrient supplies near the base are depleted, at which time the matrix breaks up. These postulated growth phases are illustrated graphically in Fig. 7-6.

The life of a biological film is short. It matures quickly, is sloughed off, and a new one forms in a matter of days. Heukelekian and Crosby

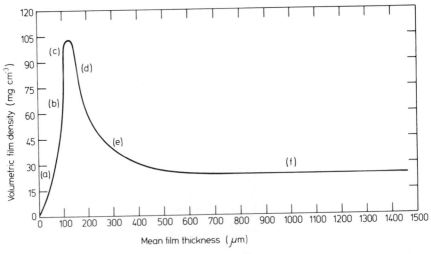

**Figure 7-6** Relationship of film density and thickness with the postulated film development stages (Fig. 7-5) shown in the appropriate regions. Redrawn and modified from Hoehn and Ray (1973).

(1956a, 1956b) estimated that most wastewater films broke apart regularly about every 14 days. Corpe (1974) found that microcolonies, consisting mainly of pseudomonads that became attached to glass slide suspended in seawater, turned over every 3 to 4 days.

## 7.2   DISSIMILATION

During dissimilation, or "nitrate respiration," nitrate ions ($NO_3^-$) act as alternate hydrogen acceptors to oxygen. Under anaerobic conditions, in other words, the primary removal mechanism for nitrate is through respiratory action, rather than by assimilation across the cell wall (Jeris and Owens 1975). In dissimilation, the actual nitrogenous end product depends on the species of microorganism and can be nitrite, ammonia, nitrous oxide ($N_2O$), or molecular nitrogen (Painter 1970). When the end product is $N_2O$ or $N_2$, the term used to describe this particular type of dissimilation is *denitrification*. Nitrogen as $N_2$ or $N_2O$ ultimately is removed from solution when its partial pressure in the water exceeds its partial pressure in the atmosphere. Many writers use the term denitrification to include bacteriological nitrate reduction processes of all kinds. This is incorrect. Bacteria that reduce nitrate to nitrite or ammonia and stop there are not denitrifiers. Denitrification, by definition, reduces inorganic nitrogen completely. Thus all dentrification is also dissimilation, but the reverse is not true, as shown in Fig. 6-5 (p. 113). In the discussion that follows I have substituted the term dissimilation for denitrification if the author of a cited work used denitrification to mean nitrate reduction. Denitrification is the most important dissimilation process, and specific reference will be made to it wherever possible. The subject of denitrification was reviewed by Delwiche and Bryan (1976).

There are many species of autotrophic and heterotrophic bacteria capable of dissimilation if conditions are right, but the heterotrophic forms are more important. Painter (1970) listed these organisms: *Achromobacter, Micrococcus, Pseudomonas, Denitrobacillus, Spirillum*, and *Bacillus*. Davies and Toerien (1971) isolated members of the first three genera from domestic sewage, in addition to *Alcaligenes, Aerobacter, Brevibacterium, Paracolobactrum, Enterobacter, Proteus, Serratia, Anthrobacter, Leptotricha*, and *Lactobacillus*. Ozretich (1977) reported on nitrate reduction by four species of bacteria isolated from seawater. Three of these belonged to the genus *Pseudomonas* and the fourth was *Vibrio anguillarum*.

## Factors Affecting Dissimilation

The factors affecting dissimilation and denitrification specifically are: (1) temperature; (2) pH; (3) oxygen; and (4) carbon source. Little work has been done on denitrification in saline waters. Salinity probably influences denitrification, but little information is available.

### Temperature

Despite scanty evidence, it is probably safe to conclude that dentrification functions effectively throughout the same temperature range as nitrification. The examples in this brief section were taken from studies conducted in freshwater. Virtually no information exists that describes the effects of temperature on denitrification in seawater.

St. Amant and McCarty (1969) found that denitrification was efficient in a pilot plant wastewater treatment column down to 12°C; below that, efficiency tapered off rapidly. In working with activated sludge, Dawson and Murphy (1972) noted that the denitrification rate declined by 80% when the temperature was lowered from 20 to 5°C. However once the organisms were acclimated to the lower temperature denitrification once again became efficient. Dawson and Murphy concluded that it was practical to carry on denitrification in water treatment between 5 and 27°C.

### pH

Little information is available on the effect that pH has on denitrification in either freshwater or seawater. Denitrifying bacteria apparently can function throughout a fairly wide range of pH values, and certainly within the narrow limits of seawater aquariums. Delwiche (1956) found evidence that the optimum pH value for denitrifiers depended on the concentration of nitrate ion, age of the culture, and the species of organisms. *Pseudomonas aeruginosa* was most active between 7 and 8.2, although denitrification took place within a much wider range (5.8 to 9.2). Delwiche also noted that pH affected both the rate of denitrification and the composition of the end products. Above pH 7.3, $N_2$ was the main end product; below this value, the percentage of $N_2O$ was greater. Wuhrmann and Mechsner (1965), working with denitrifying isolates from activated sludge, found that at pH values of 7 and higher, the inhibitory effects of oxygen increased. It thus seems that the synergistic effects of oxygen and increasing pH might be limiting factors at the alkaline pH of seawater, but experimental proof of this is lacking.

*Oxygen*

Dissimilatory bacteria are unusually sensitive to environmental factors, in part because there are alternate respiration pathways available (Dawson and Murphy 1972). Many bacteria that reduce nitrate ion are truly anaerobic; others use $O_2$ in preference to $NO_3^-$ and switch over only if the environment is made anoxic (Jeris and Owens 1975). These latter organisms are facultative because they opportunistically transfer electrons to whichever electron acceptor is available. Skerman and MacRae (1957), for example, provided evidence that when *Pseudomonas denitrificans* was exposed to oxygen levels as low as 0.2 mg $l^{-1}$, denitrification stopped and the organism shifted to aerobic oxidation of organic carbon. Ozretich (1977) found that *Pseudomonas sp., P. denitrificans, P. perfectomarinus,* and *Vibrio anguillarum* isolated from seawater could make the transition from aerobic to nitrate respiration.

In general, it can be said that oxygen inhibits dissimilation (Painter 1970). Bacteria grown anaerobically in the presence of $NO_3^-$ develop enzymes that chemically reduce nitrate ion. These substances are called nitrate and nitrite reductases. The addition of oxygen to an anaerobic system usually depresses the formation of more nitrate-reducing enzymes (Chang and Morris 1962). There are many examples of this phenomenon in the literature. Lam and Nicholas (1969), for instance, discovered that in *Micrococcus denitrificans*, $O_2$ had a repressing effect on nitrate and nitrite reductases when the enzymes had been induced to form by the presence of $NO_3^-$ as a hydrogen acceptor.

Because dissimilation is primarily an anaerobic process, optimum conditions for it to function are thermodynamically antagonistic with nitrification (Bishop et al. 1976). The presence of the more powerful electron acceptor, $O_2$, suppresses the use of $NO_3^-$ in the biological utilization of dissolved organic carbon. Moreover mineralization, which is also an oxidative process, removes DOC that could serve as a potential electron donor in dissimilation (Bishop et al. 1976).

Dissimilation probably takes place in seawater aquariums even though the environment is predominantly aerobic. Kawai et al. (1964) noticed that nitrate decreased after 3 months in seawater aquariums kept at 22°C, and they attributed this to dissimilation by filter bed bacteria. Aerobic bacteria in the filter sand numbered $10^7 \, g^{-1}$ after 3 months, and 10% of these organisms could reduce nitrate ion. The aerobes outnumbered the anaerobes 10:1, yet 50% of the anaerobic forms could reduce nitrate ion. Because dissimilation is mainly an anaerobic process, Kawai and his fellow investigators concluded that portions of an aquarium filter bed must be anaerobic, despite continuous aeration and circulation of the water. This is a perfectly logical yet seldom-considered characteristic of aquariums, particularly those with deep filter beds. Most of the oxygen is utilized in the first few centimetres of filtrant, and the remaining layers may become oxygen-deficient.

In working with cultures of mixed bacteria from activated sludge, Mulbarger (1971) reported that even when relatively high levels of oxygen were present (1 mg $O_2$ $l^{-1}$), denitrification was possible. The phenomenon was attributed to localized oxygen depletion in the sludge, which meant that denitrification still took place under anaerobic conditions. For aquarists, the implication is that a high dissolved oxygen level does not necessarily mean conditions are unsuited for denitrification everywhere in the aquarium. There may well be localized places of anoxia.

*Carbon Source*

Most dissimilatory bacteria are heterotrophic, and shifts in species composition of the population can be expected when the carbon source changes. Davies and Toerien (1971) monitored the rise and fall of denitrifying bacteria in a mixed-species population cultured from domestic sewage. When the carbon source was changed from glucose to malate, some species disappeared and the numbers of the others declined. New forms better able to utilize malate as a carbon source became dominant. There was time lag while the species better suited to the new carbon source proliferated and the activity and numbers of the rest gradually diminished.

Denitrification cannot be carried out unless a ready source of DOC is present (assuming heterotrophic forms to be more important). The amount of DOC that is normally found in wastewater and aquarium water is inadequate for dissimilation processes to be significant. The result is a steady increase in nitrate from nitrification. To remove nitrate from wastewater, a two-stage system is commonly used (e.g., Dodd and Bone 1975). Nitrification is carried out in the first stage under aerobic conditions. In the second stage, the system is made anaerobic and a source of organic carbon is added to stimulate denitrification. Methanol is the most commonly used organic, and the oxygen can be removed from a denitrification column by addition of more methanol than would be needed to complete denitrification (St. Amant and McCarty 1969). The reaction is

$$O_2 + \tfrac{2}{3} CH_3OH \rightarrow \tfrac{2}{3} CO_2 + \tfrac{4}{3} H_2O \qquad (40)$$

Meade (1974) mentioned that denitrifying bacteria could be supplied with other sources of organics, such as molasses, ethanol, or glucose. Still other sources have been used, including citrate (Dawson and Murphy 1972), acetate (Dodd and Bone 1975), and malate (Davies and Toerien 1971). Hasan and Hall (1977) reported that *Clostridium tertium* could reduce nitrate in the presence of glucose.

When methanol is used as the carbon source, denitrification is carried out according to reactions proposed by St. Amant and McCarty (1969):

$$NO_3^- + \tfrac{1}{3} CH_3OH \rightarrow NO_2^- + \tfrac{1}{3} CO_2 + \tfrac{2}{3} H_2O \qquad (41)$$

$$NO_2^- + \tfrac{1}{2} CH_3OH - \tfrac{1}{2} N_2 + \tfrac{1}{2} CO_2 + \tfrac{1}{2} H_2O + OH^- \qquad (42)$$

The overall reaction is

$$NO_3^- + \tfrac{5}{6} CH_3OH \rightarrow \tfrac{1}{2} N_2 + \tfrac{5}{6} CO_2 + \tfrac{7}{6} H_2O + OH \qquad (43)$$

As St. Amant and McCarty observed, denitrification is not a typical anaerobic reaction, but is similar to aerobic oxidation, except that nitrate ion is used instead of oxygen as the electron acceptor. In the process, nitrate is reduced. Methanol, as the electron donor, is oxidized and is the energy source. From the equations it can be seen that 1 mole of nitrate ion requires at least $\tfrac{5}{6}$ mole of methanol for total denitrification, or 1.90 mg $l^{-1}$ of methanol must be present for every mg $l^{-1}$ of nitrate. The shift of electrons is shown graphically in Fig. 7-7. Methanol, the electron donor, is oxidized and becomes the energy source. Nitrate ion, as an electron acceptor, is reduced to nitrite ion and subsequently cannot serve as a source of energy.

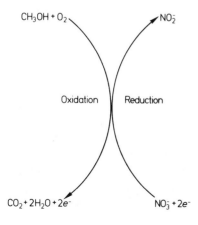

**Figure 7-7**   Nitrate reduction with methanol. Methanol (electron donor) is oxidized. Nitrate ion (electron acceptor) is reduced.

The water in a denitrification column must be isolated from the rest of the system, unlike the water in a nitrifying filter, which, being aerobic can be recycled past the organisms being cultured. Methanol is among the most efficient and inexpensive of organic additives, but it is toxic to fishes and aquatic invertebrates. Moreover the recycling process would only add oxygen to the water and inhibit denitrification. Consequently a denitrification column must rely on a lengthy contact time. Water entering the column must remain there until the nitrate has been reduced and the $N_2O$ or $N_2$ has dissipated into the atmosphere. According to available information, this may take several hours or even days.

Denitrification columns have other disadvantages. The methanol added in excess of denitrification may produce harmful substances such as hydrogen sulfide, unless it can be taken up by denitrifying bacteria (St. Amant and McCarty 1969). If too little methanol is added, the reactions given above will not go to completion and the result will be water that is high in nitrite.

Jeris and Owens (1975) found that the most difficult problem encountered in maintaining a denitrifying pilot plant for wastewater treatment was keeping a constant C:N ratio. Balderston and Sieburth (1976) called attention to the same problem in their study of a freshwater salmon hatchery. They maintained a C:N ratio of 1:0 by adding methanol. When the system was kept in a steady state at this ratio, 100% of the nitrate was removed in 5 days. Balderston and Sieburth (1976) emphasized that water quality in the effluent of a denitrification column was not necessarily improved even though the amount of nitrate had been reduced. When the C:N ratio was unbalanced, the effluent contained nitrite, ammonia, hydrogen sulfide, and DOC. Some of these substances are more harmful than nitrate. It seems that without careful monitoring of the C:N ratio, denitrification columns are impractical and potentially dangerous.

## 7.3 ASSIMILATION

Overall, living plants probably improve the quality of aquarium water. They add dissolved solids such as vitamins and amino acids, which may have beneficial effects, but mostly it is what plants remove from the water that makes their culture advantageous. Plants are able to assimilate animal metabolites, mainly nitrogen and phosphorus compounds, and incorporate them into their own tissues during growth.

Jones (1970) concluded that the presence of *Chlorella* improved the growth rate and survival of 40 species of marine fish larvae. Shelbourne (1964) utilized a marine macroalga (*Enteromorpha*) to improve water quality in a fish-rearing facility. The seaweed was grown attached to stones in a separate tank through which the culture water was circulated. Alderson and Howell (1973) reported that small Dover sole (*Solea solea*) grew faster in water containing the unicellular green alga *Dunaliella tertiolecta* than did fish grown in culture tanks without the alga. The efficient removal of $NH_4$-N by *Dunaliella* was thought to account for the improved growth rate.

Marine plants require nitrogen for protein synthesis and growth. Ordinarily this is supplied as ammonia or nitrate, although nitrite and urea are sometimes utilized. Factors affecting nitrogen assimilation are: (1) light; (2) the form and concentration of available nitrogen; and (3) the suppressing effects of ammonia.

## Light

In nature, the uptake of nutrients by marine algae is dependent on light and the concentration of nutrient elements. In eutrophic regions, nutrient levels are high and light becomes the limiting factor (MacIsaac and Dugdale 1972). The same is true in most aquariums. Light influences nitrate uptake by providing $H^+$ donors for chemical reduction to ammonia, either directly from photosynthesis or indirectly from respiration.

Photoperiod affects the rates at which nutrient elements are taken up by algae. The quantity of nitrogen present in the water is not a factor: for example, photoperiod influences nitrogen assimilation in environments that are both nitrate-rich and nitrate-poor (Malone et al. 1975). In general, phytoplankton assimilate nutrients more efficiently in light than in darkness. Eppley et al. (1971) found this to be the case with *Skeletonema costatum* and *Coccolithus huxleyi* during the uptake of ammonia and nitrate. Maximum assimilation rates for many species of phytoplankton occur during the first half of the light period, whereas minimum nutrient assimilation takes place in the first half of the dark period. This implies that on a photoperiod of 12/12, overall assimilation might equal assimilation during 24/0, but with slightly greater fluctuations in nutrient concentration in the water caused by the varying assimilation rates during alternation between light to dark.

## Form and Concentration of Nitrogen

Whatever its initial form, all external sources of nitrogen must be reduced chemically to ammonium ion before being incorporated into primary amino acids inside the cell. Several investigators (e.g., Lui and Roels 1972) reported that the assimilation of nitrate involves its step-wise reduction to $NH_4^+$, probably through the intermediates nitrite, hyponitrite, and hydroxylamine. Falkowski (1975) noted that to utilize nitrate as a substrate for growth, phytoplankton must transport the ion across the cell wall and membrane, reduce it to ammonium ion, and incorporate the $NH_4^+$ into primary amino acids.

Most seaweeds can efficiently remove either $NH_4^+$ or $NO_3^-$. Prince (1974) found that the rockweed *Fucus vesiculosus*, a brown alga, grew equally well on ammonia and nitrate. When the biomass of the plants in the culture container was high, 65–92% of the ammonia was removed and 40% of the phosphorus. Ammonia levels varied from 125 to 200 $\mu$g-at $NH_4$-N $l^{-1}$; phosphorus was 15 $\mu$g-at $PO_4$-P $l^{-1}$. In their study of another species of rockweed (*F. spiralis*), Topinka and Robbins (1976) found that greatest growth took place when ammonia and nitrate levels were raised from 1.7 $\mu$g-at $NH_4$-N $l^{-1}$ and 1.2 $\mu$g-at $NO_3$-N $l^{-1}$ to concentrations of 35 $\mu$g-at $l^{-1}$ for both nutrients. Waite and Mitchell (1972) measured increased photosynthetic activity in sea lettuce (*Ulva lactuca*), a green macroalga, when ammonia was added to the culture water. Greatest stimulation took place when the $NH_4$-N level was raised to approximately 43 $\mu$g-at $l^{-1}$.

Harvey (1940) was probably the first to demonstrate experimentally that some species of marine phytoplankton can utilize urea as a nitro-gen source. His evidence has since been confirmed many times (e.g., Dugdale and Goering 1967, McCarthy 1972b). The ability to assimilate and utilize urea is not universal among unicellular algae, however. Of 35 species of marine phytoplankton studied by McCarthy (1971), ap-proximately half could utilize urea as their sole nitrogen source. McCarthy (1972a) reported that some marine phytoplankton had the ability to take up urea from the surrounding water even though they could not utilize it for growth.

Some seaweeds may be even more adept at utilizing urea than single-celled species. Mohsen et al. (1974) tested the efficiency of amino acid synthesis in sea lettuce (*Ulva fasciata*) using three concentrations each of urea and nitrate supplied as $KNO_3$. They found that better growth occurred with urea. The optimum level of urea in the water for maximum amino acid synthesis was 0.5 g $l^{-1}$; a concentration of 0.125 g $l^{-1}$ resulted in significantly less amino acid synthesis. When $KNO_3$ was added to the water, 0.8 g $NO_3$-N $l^{-1}$ yielded maximum amino acid synthesis, followed by a concentration of 0.4 g $l^{-1}$. The third concentra-tion tested, 1.6 g $NO_3$-N $l^{-1}$, inhibited amino acid synthesis.

### Suppression by Ammonia

When both ammonia and nitrate are available, ammonia is assimilated preferentially by seawater algae (Strickland et al. 1969). The assimilation velocities of $NH_4$-N and $NO_3$-N are not independent of each other, as demonstrated by Dugdale and Goering (1967) and MacIsaac and Dugdale (1972). High levels of $NH_4$-N in nature may suppress the rate of $NO_3$-N uptake by phytoplankton. This ordinarily occurs when the ammonia level is greater than 0.5 $\mu$g-at $l^{-1}$ (MacIsaac and Dugdale 1972). In general, however, marine algae have no difficulty utilizing $NO_3$-N once the $NH_4$-N has been assimilated (Goldman 1976).

Ammonia suppression of nitrate uptake does not take place when the overall level of nitrogen is low enough to be a limiting factor for growth, nor is ammonia assimilated preferentially over nitrate at limiting nitrogen levels. Low environmental nitrogen results in the simultaneous and competitive uptake of both forms (Bienfang 1975). Bienfang pointed out that the preferential uptake of $NH_4$-N in a nonlimiting nitrogen environment is a shortcut to protein synthesis. Such a mechanism eliminates the expenditure of energy (77.4 kcal mole$^{-1}$ to reduce $NO_3$-N at 25°C).

Ammonia affects the uptake of other forms of nitrogen besides nitrate. Eppley and Rogers (1970) found that ammonia inhibited nitrite assimilation by the marine diatom *Ditylum brightwelli*. Urea uptake by marine algae also may be suppressed in the presence of ammonia (McCarthy and Eppley 1972).

## 7.4 CONDITIONING BACTERIOLOGICAL FILTERS

Kawai et al. (1964) considered a filter bed to be conditioned when it had acquired sufficient nitrifying capability. This required approximately 2 months under warm-water conditions. Their definition, while useful on a practical basis, is incomplete because nitrification is only one of the mechanisms by which nutrients in solution are utilized by microorganisms. Mineralization, for example, precedes nitrification in the initial sequence of events. Spotte (1979) thus defined a *conditioned* filter bed as one in which the bacteria in general are in equilibrium with the input of energy sources. Conditioning is not complete until *all* bacteria have acclimated to the aquarium environment. Nevertheless nitrification is a convenient measure of the status of a new filter bed, in part because it is frequently the bottleneck in the conditioning process:

nitrifying bacteria often are among the last groups of filter bed bacteria to become stabilized.

The three aspects of conditioning that are of interest to aquarists are: (1) the nature of the time lags that delay seawater aquariums from becoming suitable environments for animals; (2) how time lags can be reduced to some extent by accelerating the conditioning process; and (3) carrying capacity, or the animal load that a conditioned filter bed can support.

### Time Lags

Cultures of nitrifying bacteria grow slowly, and the number of cells per energy unit converted is low. Kimata et al. (1961) reported a time lag of 30 to 60 days before activity could be detected in cultures of marine nitrifiers maintained at 25°C. In an earlier study by Carey (1938), it took up to 90 days at room temperature before nitrification was evident. Yoshida (1967) mentioned 60 to 90 days of incubation at 25°C as having elapsed before nitrification could be detected with almost pure cultures of marine nitrifiers. Two months is more than twice the time required to enumerate soil nitrifiers using the Most Probable Number (MPN) method, according to Matulewich et al. (1975).

Similar lag phases are evident in filter beds of new seawater aquariums. Kawai et al. (1964) showed that the population of nitrifiers in a filter bed stabilized at approximately 60 days, and Srna and Baggaley (1975) found that 40 days were required to generate a significant population of nitrifiers in a new filter. Based on tests conducted at 26°C, Forster (1974) suggested that 30 days were necessary for a new filter bed to reach full nitrifying potential, but his study was based only on ammonia conversion; the remainder of the nitrification sequence was not monitored.

In the case of heterotrophs, the initial rise in numbers of cells is meteoric, but the different groups do not reach equilibrium until sometime later. Kawai et al. (1964) discovered that in a warm seawater aquarium, the numbers of bacteria increased by a factor of 10 within 2 weeks after addition of aquarium animals. Most of these organisms were heterotrophs. The level reached nearly $10^8 g^{-1}$ of filter sand. Afterward the total population was not much different at 134 days than at 90 days, indicating a leveling off of the different groups. A summary of this information is given in Fig. 7-8. The filter sand was 20 cm deep and small-grained (0.297 mm, or 50 mesh). Protein decomposers, or "gelatin liquefiers," increased markedly when the aquarium animals were given foods that were high in nitrogen, such as raw fish. From a beginning

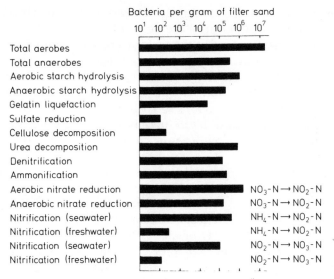

**Figure 7-8**   Population of filter bed bacteria in small freshwater and seawater aquariums after 134 days. Redrawn and modified from Kawai et al. (1964).

population of $10^3$ $g^{-1}$ of filter sand, protein decomposers increased to 100 times that level after a month. The population declined to approximately $10^4$ after 3 months and stabilized.

Starch decomposing bacteria were relatively few in number at the start, compared with protein decomposers. Their numbers declined still further after a month and were only 1/100th of the total bacterial population at the end of 3 months. As Kawai and his fellow investigators noted, the reduction in numbers of starch and protein hydrolyzers was probably caused by the selection of specific groups of bacteria and not to the diminished ability of organisms in the filter bed to decompose protein or starch.

Nitrifying bacteria, unlike the heterotrophs, are not present in large numbers at first. Their population builds gradually. Ammonia oxidizers reach maximum density after a month or so (Kawai et al. 1964) under warm-water conditions, whereas nitrite oxidizers require approximately 2 months. Kawai et al. (1964) determined that the numbers of each group seemed to stabilize after reaching maximum density. Populations were $10^5$ and $10^6$ for ammonia and nitrite oxidizers, respectively. However ammonia oxidizers showed much higher cell counts after the first 2 weeks, a fact that was apparent from the increased level of $NO_2$-N compared with $NO_3$-N. Kimata et al. (1961) found that the concentration

of ammonia oxidizers and nitrite oxidizers in the filter beds of conditioned seawater aquariums averaged $10^4$ and $10^5$ cells $g^{-1}$ of sand,
respectively. The numbers in the water were less, only $10^2$ and $10^3$ cells
$ml^{-1}$. Kimata and his co-workers reported that values in surface seawater were much lower: ammonia and nitrite oxidizers together averaged
0.3 cells $ml^{-1}$. Yoshida and Kimata (1967) found nitrifiers in surface
seawater to be $10^0$ to $10^2$ cells $l^{-1}$. Yoshida (1967) cultured marine nitrifiers at concentrations of $10^1$ to $10^3$ cells $ml^{-1}$ in the water and $10^4$ to $10^6$
$g^{-1}$ of filter sand at two public aquariums in Japan (Misaki Aquarium
and Sakai Aquarium).

Nitrification is a sequential process, and nitrite oxidation cannot
proceed until ammonia conversion is well established. This results in a
"peaking" of ammonia and nitrite concentrations as the populations
and activities of the different species of nitrifiers come into equilibrium
with their energy sources. Hirayama (1974) noted that in a newly established seawater aquarium at 20 to 21°C, ammonia built up rapidly until
the 10th day. Subsequently nitrite accumulated, reaching its highest
value at the 35th day; by the 50th day it had almost disappeared. Kawai
et al. (1964) reported nitrite values peaking at 30 days at 22°C. Yoshida
(1967), working with an experimental aquarium kept at 22°C, stated that
the nitrite peaked after 20 to 30 days. A conceptualized view of the
nitrification sequence is presented in Fig. 7-9.

In my opinion, much of the time lag in newly established filter beds

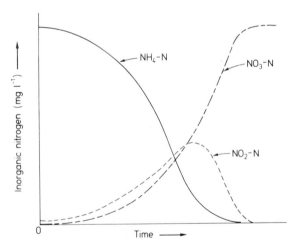

**Figure 7-9**  Stylized nitrification curves showing the sequential rise and fall of ammonia
and nitrite and the rise of nitrate in closed-system aquariums. Redrawn and modified
from Anthonisen et al. (1976).

is due as much to the need that nitrifiers have to acclimate to aquarium conditions as it is to the initial absence of organisms. Two facts support this argument: (1) pure cultures of nitrifiers show extended lag phases that obviously cannot be caused by an absence of organisms; and (2) time lags in filter beds can be reduced considerably by addition of bacteria already acclimated to aquarium conditions.

Heterotrophic and autotrophic bacteria capable of carrying out nitrification are ubiquitous, and a sterile filter bed established with artificial seawater many miles inland soon acquires bacteria that can function in a saline environment. Nevertheless environmental factors that affect nitrification—toxic substances, temperature, pH, dissolved oxygen, and salinity—are important considerations if conditioning is to be accelerated. Nitrifying organisms cultured in the laboratory are sometimes difficult to establish in new aquariums unless the new and old environments are similar. For example, it does little good to culture nitrifiers in low saline conditions and then add them to full-strength seawater. The same holds true for conditions of pH and dissolved oxygen. The most important factor is probably temperature. Bacteria cultured at 22°C cannot be expected to function at normal activity levels when added to aquarium water that is 10°C. The organisms will survive, but the time lag that ensues makes their addition no more efficient than to wait for nitrification to become established naturally.

Carlucci and Strickland (1968) noted that when cultures of *Nitrosocystis oceanus* acclimated to 20°C or 28°C were cultured at 37°C, there was a time lag of 40 to 60 days before significant amounts of nitrite were formed. In a like manner, a subarctic culture of nitrifying bacteria isolated from the Pacific showed evidence of nitrification when the temperature was raised to 12°C, but only after a time lag of 50 days. Warm-water cultures lowered to 12°C continued to produce nitrite, but also after long periods of time. Thus a time lag can be expected when the temperature of an aquarium is raised or lowered suddenly. In one 4000-l conditioned exhibit at Mystic Marinelife Aquarium, the warm-water animals were removed, cold-water animals added and the temperature lowered suddenly from 20°C to 12°C. The time it took for ammonia and nitrite to peak were 29 days and 62 days, respectively, despite the fact that the filter bed had been fully conditioned at the higher temperature.

### How to Accelerate Conditioning

New filter beds are characterized by insufficient numbers of bacteria to carry out bacteriological filtration effectively. Once the different groups of organisms become established, still more time is needed before their biochemical activities stabilize with energy source input. Conditioning can be accelerated by two methods: (1) adding an inoculant of filter bed bacteria; or (2) adding nutrients to the water to speed up stabilization of activity levels. It should be emphasized again that the distinction between heterotrophic and autotrophic bacteria is not always clear in terms of the utilization of energy sources. The initial inorganic nitrogen excreted by aquarium animals as ammonia may be oxidized to some extent by heterotrophic organisms. Conversely some organics are readily assimilated by autotrophic species—nitrifiers, for example. Once established, a population of filter bed bacteria probably does not fluctuate much with respect to the total number of cells, although its activity level will be geared to the input of energy sources. This was confirmed empirically for nitrifying bacteria by Srna and Baggaley (1975), who reported that when water in an experimental aquarium was "spiked" with ammonium chloride equal to twice the amount to which the filter had been conditioned, the conversion rate remained nearly the same, suggesting no net increase in population density.

Meade (1974) reported that addition of enriched cultures of nitrifiers decreased the conditioning time in brackish water and freshwater salmon culture systems. Scott and Gillespie (1972) added nitrifying bacteria to an unconditioned freshwater system designed for trout. The nitrifying organisms were isolated from soil. The authors did not state whether the procedure accelerated conditioning time.

There are easier methods of inoculating a new filter than culturing nitrifying bacteria in the laboratory. Saeki (1962) demonstrated that nitrification in new filters took 60 days to become established at 19°C. The time lag could be cut to 2 weeks when new sand was placed in an old (uncleaned) aquarium tank containing old seawater. Saeki attributed the shortened time lag to the populating of the new sand by organisms already present in the water and attached to the walls. The simplest way to accelerate conditioning is to add a handful of old gravel from a conditioned filter bed. This "dirty" method has the advantage of supplying heterotrophic bacteria along with the nitrifiers. Even the addition of detritus is useful. The dirty method works best when conditions in the new aquarium are similar to the old one in terms of temperature, salinity, and other factors.

Siddall (1974) and Srna and Baggaley (1975) reported that nitrification could be established and activity levels accelerated in new aquariums by the daily addition of measured amounts of ammonium chloride or ammonium sulfate. This procedure, called *preconditioning*, has a singular advantage: it enables the aquarist to wait until toxic ammonia and nitrite are oxidized before adding his animals. Preconditioning is especially effective if carried out after adding old aquarium gravel to the new filter.

Before preconditioning a new filter bed with inorganic nitrogen, the daily ammonia input by the animals that will be added later should be estimated. Unless this is done, the filter bed might be preconditioned to a nutrient level that is too low, resulting in sudden and fatal increases in ammonia. Meade (1974) gave the following formula for calculating the daily ammonia input by salmonids

$$R_F \times biomass \times N_L \times N_U \times N_E = \text{NH}_4\text{-N } 24 \text{ hr}^{-1} \qquad (44)$$

in which $R_F$ is the food added per 24 hr as a percentage of the total animal biomass, $N_L$ is the dietary protein-N level, $N_U$ is the protein utilization factor, and $N_E$ is the percentage of the total nitrogen excreted as $\text{NH}_4\text{-N}$. Salmonids have unusually high protein utilization rates: 2 to 4 times the conversion rates of birds and mammals, according to De-Long et al. (1958). As such, the formula given here should be considered conservative when applied to invertebrates and most fishes other than trout and salmon. In other words, by using the values for salmonids, the data derived will assure that the filter bed has been adequately spiked with inorganic nitrogen, probably more than will be excreted by the animals that will be added later.

In this sample problem, the filter to be preconditioned will later hold an animal population with the following nitrogen-related parameters: food input is 2% of the animal biomass, animal biomass is 10 kg, dietary protein level is 20% (3.2% nitrogen), protein utilization is 40%, and the amount of nitrogen excreted as total $\text{NH}_4\text{-N}$ is 90%. I have assumed that most proteins average 16% nitrogen. Thus

$$0.02 \times 10 \text{ kg} \times 0.032 \times 0.4 \times 0.9 = 0.115 \text{ kg NH}_4\text{-N } 24 \text{ hr}^{-1}$$

Based on this estimate the filter should receive additions of 0.439 kg $\text{NH}_4\text{Cl}$ or 1.084 kg $(\text{NH}_4)_2\text{SO}_4$ every 24 hr until the nitrite peaks and the animals can be added safely. The protein content of some common aquarium foods and food additives is presented in Table 7-3. Extensive information of this sort can be found in National Academy of Sciences (1973) and Sidwell et al. (1974).

### Carrying Capacity

Spotte (1979) defined *carrying capacity* as the animal load that an aquarium can support. Carrying capacity is usually considered in terms of nitrogen cycling and can be visualized as encompassing four steps:

**Table 7-3  Protein Content of Common Foods and Food Additives Fed to Aquarium Animals (Assume That Nitrogen Content is 16% of the Crude Protein)**

| Source | % Protein (wet) | % Protein (dry) |
|---|---|---|
| Alewife (*Alosa pseudoharengus*) | 19.4 | 75.0 |
| Anchovy (*Engraulis sp.*) | 16.1 | 70.9 |
| Atlantic herring (*Clupea harengus*) | 17.3 | 76.7 |
| Atlantic mackerel (*Scomber scombrus*) | 23.7 | — |
| Bluefin tuna (*Thunnus thynnus*) | — | 65.9 |
| Bluefish (*Pomatomus saltatrix*) | 22.5 | — |
| Butterfish (*Peprilus triacanthus*) | 16.7 | — |
| Capelin (*Mallotus villosus*) | 14.1 | — |
| White hake (*Urophycis tenuis*) | 18.4 | — |
| Daphnia (*Daphnia sp.*) | — | 61.0 |
| Common squid (*Loligo pealii*) | 15.3 | — |
| Crab meal (processed residue) | — | 33.4 |
| Fish meal (whole fish) | — | 68.7 |
| Shrimp meal (processed residue) | — | 52.7 |
| Soybean meal (mechanically extracted) | — | 48.7 |
| Casein | — | 90.9 |
| Beef heart | 14.8 | — |
| Beef liver | 20.2 | — |
| Beef muscle | 20.0 | — |
| Animal blood meal | — | 87.8 |
| Animal liver meal | — | 71.8 |
| Marine Zooplankton | 13.7 | 69.1 |
| Seaweed (Orders Fucales and Laminariales) | — | 10.7 |
| Poultry | — | 93.0 |

Source: Nat. Acad. Sci. (1973), Sidwell et al. (1974).

(*1*) nitrogen input into the water system; (2) the rate of nitrogen excretion by the animals; (3) the rate of nitrogen conversion by filter bed bacteria; and (4) the effects of important environmental variables (temperature, pH, dissolved oxygen, and salinity) on the first three steps.

The determination of carrying capacity is worthwhile when high densities of animals are maintained, such as in hatchery and aquaculture installations, because the ratio of animal biomass to volume of water often approaches a critical point. It is unimportant in the routine maintenance of laboratory holding facilities and public aquarium displays in which the animal biomass per volume of water is low. This book deals with low-density animal culture, and carrying capacity will be considered only in a cursory fashion, after first noting some of the problems that make its quantification difficult.

Most hatcheries culture only a single species of animal, which simplifies quantification of the four steps listed above. Meaningful values are difficult to obtain—perhaps impossible—in mixed-species aquariums, because the rate of nitrogen metabolism varies from one species to the next, and important variables in the environment may differ significantly among a group of aquariums. Furthermore the biology of a commercially cultured animal often has been studied extensively. The life cycles of most seawater animals displayed in public aquariums are unknown, to say nothing of their baseline propagation requirements and rates of nitrogen metabolism.

Even under the most simplified of experimental conditions the input, excretion, and conversion of nitrogen are difficult to follow. Hirayama (1966b, 1974) defined various elements of the carrying capacity of seawater aquariums. Spotte (1979), using Hirayama's equations, derived a series of values (Table 7-4) showing "pollution load" (Hirayama's expression, meaning essentially the amount of nitrogen excreted) as a function of the mass of a fish and its feeding rate. It should be noted that Hirayama's experiments, although the most comprehensive to date, used only a single species of marine fish maintained at one temperature. Presumably the values in Table 7-4 would be different if all the other factors were kept constant and just these two parameters were varied. The discussion that follows was taken from Spotte (1979). Remember that the equations and table are recommended to be used only as guidelines. No method exists presently for calculating the carrying capacity of a low-density seawater aquarium containing an animal population of mixed species.

Hirayama (1966b) derived the following formula for calculating the carrying capacity of seawater aquariums:

$$\sum_{i=1}^{p} \frac{10 W_i}{\dfrac{0.70}{V_i} + \dfrac{0.95 \times 10^3}{G_i D_i}} \geq \sum_{j=1}^{q}(B_j^{0.544} \times 10^{-2}) + 0.051F \qquad (45)$$

The lefthand expression represents the oxidizing capacity of the filter bed, or oxygen consumed during filtration (OCF), measured as milligrams of $O_2$ consumed per minute, where $W$ is the surface area of the filter bed ($m^2$), $V$ is the filtering rate or flow rate of water moving through the filter bed (cm $min^{-1}$), $D$ is the gravel depth (cm), and $p$ is the number of filters serving the aquarium. In the above formula (actually an inequality), $G$ represents the grain size coefficients of the gravel grains. This is determined by

$$\frac{1}{R_1}x_1 + \frac{1}{R_2}x_2 + \frac{1}{R_3}x_3 + \cdots + \frac{1}{R_n}x_n \tag{46}$$

where $R$ is the mean grain size of each fraction of gravel in the filter bed (if the gravel is graded) in millimetres, and $x$ is the percentage weight of each fraction.

The righthand expression of the inequality (equation 45) represents the rate of "pollution" by the animals. Like the lefthand expression, it is given in mg $O_2$ min$^{-1}$. In this expression, $B$ represents the body masses of the individual animals (g), $F$ is the amount of food (g) entering the aquarium daily, and $q$ is the number of animals being maintained.

As seen from the formula, the oxidizing capacity of the filter bed must be greater than or equal to the rate of "pollution" by the animals. It is also important to note that *as the masses of the individual animals decrease, the carrying capacity of the aquarium decreases.* In other words, carrying capacity is not simply a function of the total animal mass. An aquarium that can support a single 100-g fish cannot necessarily support 10 fishes each weighing 10 g. Assume, for example, that in a hypothetical aquarium $W = 0.35$ m$^2$, $V = 10.5$ cm min$^{-1}$, and $D = 36$ cm. If the gravel is all the same grade and $R = 4$ mm, then from equation 46, $G = \frac{1}{4} \times 100 = 25$. Substitution of these values into the lefthand expression of the original inequality (equation 45) gives the OCF value, which is equivalent to BOD min$^{-1}$.

$$\frac{10\,(0.36)}{\dfrac{0.70}{10.5} + \dfrac{0.95 \times 10^3}{25\,(36)}} = \frac{3.6}{0.067 \times \dfrac{950}{900}} =$$

$$\frac{3.6}{0.067 + 1.055} = \frac{3.6}{1.122} = 3.2 \text{ mg OCF min}^{-1}$$

Assume further that fishes of 200 g each are being maintained and that they are fed at 5% of their individual body masses per day. From the righthand expression of equation 45, $X$ represents OCF; therefore

$$X = \sum_{j=1}^{q} (B_j{}^{0.544} \times 10^{-2}) + 0.051F \tag{47}$$

Table 7-4 shows the value of $X$ for one fish as a function of mass in grams and feeding rate as a percentage of body mass per day. From the table, feeding a 200-g fish 5% of its body mass daily corresponds to a "pollution load" of 0.69 mg OCF min$^{-1}$. The value for $q = X/0.69 =$

**Table 7-4   "Pollution Load" as a Function of the Mass of a Fish and its Feeding Rate. Calculated from the Righthand Expression of Equation 45**

| Body Mass (g) | Feeding Rate (% of Body Mass da$^{-1}$) | | | | |
|---|---|---|---|---|---|
| | 0.0% | 2.5% | 5.0% | 7.5% | 10.0% |
| 30 | 0.06 | 0.10 | 0.14 | 0.18 | 0.22 |
| 40 | 0.07 | 0.13 | 0.18 | 0.23 | 0.28 |
| 50 | 0.08 | 0.15 | 0.21 | 0.28 | 0.34 |
| 60 | 0.09 | 0.17 | 0.25 | 0.32 | 0.40 |
| 80 | 0.11 | 0.21 | 0.31 | 0.41 | 0.52 |
| 100 | 0.12 | 0.25 | 0.38 | 0.50 | 0.63 |
| 150 | 0.15 | 0.34 | 0.54 | 0.73 | 0.92 |
| 200 | 0.18 | 0.43 | 0.69 | 0.94 | 1.20 |
| 250 | 0.20 | 0.52 | 0.84 | 1.16 | 1.48 |
| 300 | 0.22 | 0.61 | 0.99 | 1.37 | 1.75 |
| 400 | 0.26 | 0.77 | 1.28 | 1.79 | 2.30 |
| 500 | 0.29 | 0.93 | 1.57 | 2.21 | 2.84 |
| 600 | 0.32 | 1.09 | 1.85 | 2.62 | 3.38 |
| 800 | 0.38 | 1.40 | 2.42 | 3.44 | 4.46 |
| 1000 | 0.43 | 1.70 | 2.97 | 4.25 | 5.53 |
| 1500 | 0.53 | 2.45 | 4.36 | 6.27 | 8.18 |
| 2000 | 0.62 | 3.17 | 5.72 | 8.27 | 10.80 |
| 3000 | 0.78 | 4.60 | 8.43 | 12.30 | 16.10 |
| 4000 | 0.91 | 6.01 | 11.10 | 16.20 | 21.30 |
| 5000 | 1.03 | 7.40 | 13.80 | 20.20 | 26.50 |
| 6000 | 1.14 | 8.79 | 16.40 | 24.10 | 31.70 |
| 8000 | 1.33 | 11.50 | 21.70 | 31.90 | 42.10 |
| 10,000 | 1.50 | 14.20 | 27.00 | 39.70 | 52.50 |
| 20,000 | 2.19 | 27.70 | 53.20 | 78.70 | 104.10 |
| 30,000 | 2.72 | 40.90 | 79.20 | 117.50 | 155.70 |
| 40,000 | 3.19 | 54.20 | 105.20 | 156.19 | 207.20 |

Source:   Spotte (1979).

$3.2/0.69 = 4.6$ fishes, indicating that four fishes can be maintained in the aquarium. Care must be taken to be conservative when using this procedure. "Pollution load" increases as animals grow, and the carrying capacity of the filter bed may be exceeded suddenly when a fish dies or the water becomes oxygen-deficient.

As a second example, determine if the same aquarium could support 10 50-g fishes and one that weighs 600 g, all which are fed 5% of their individual body masses daily. As seen in Table 7-4, the "pollution load" is $10(0.21) + 1(1.85) = 3.95$ mg OCF min$^{-1}$. The answer is no, because the "pollution load" exceeds the carrying capacity, which is 3.2 mg OCF min$^{-1}$.

## 7.5  DESIGN AND MAINTENANCE

Design and maintenance techniques for bacteriological filters are well established. Little work has been done on the kinetics of nitrogen removal by marine macroalgae, making the design of algal filters vague.

### Bacteriological Filters

The four most important design criteria for bacteriological filters are as follows: (1) minimum depth of the gravel should be 7.6 cm, no matter how small the aquarium tank; (2) surface area of the filter bed should be equal to that of the aquarium tank; (3) gravel should be composed of calcareous material (e.g., oyster shell, fossil coral, calcite, or dolomite), and reasonably well graded with a grain size that falls within the range 2 to 5 mm; and (4) flow rate through the filter bed should be about 0.7 × 10$^{-3}$ m sec$^{-1}$. All are simply rules of thumb and perhaps other design criteria would work as well.

Spotte (1973, 1979) suggested that the minimum depth of filtrant in a bacteriological filter be 7.6 cm, and that the surface area of the filter bed equal that of the aquarium tank. Shallow filter beds with large surface areas seem to work better than deep beds with small surface areas. Perhaps this is because of the difference in the distribution of bacteria, which is a direct function of filter bed depth. The efficiency of nutrient conversion, however, is affected by depth only indirectly. Kawai et al. (1965) determined that heterotrophic bacteria were most numerous at the surface of filter beds (10$^8$ g$^{-1}$ of filter sand), and decreased by 90% at a depth of 10 cm. The same trend held true for autotrophic bacteria. The surface sand populations of ammonia and nitrite oxidizers, which were 10$^5$ and 10$^6$g$^{-1}$ of sand, respectively, fell by 90% at a depth of only 5 cm. Based on these findings, Kawai et al. (1965) recommended that filter beds be designed with large surface areas and shallow depths. Yoshida (1967) reported that maximum activity of nitrifiers occurred in the upper layer of filtrant (Fig. 7-10). Activity diminished rapidly with increasing depth of the filter bed. It should be kept in mind, however, that the changes in populations of bacteria through a vertical section of filtrant are not so dramatic when larger-grained filter media are used.

Hirayama (1966a) demonstrated that the effect of filter bed depth on nutrient conversion in aquarium water was indirect when OCF (BOD

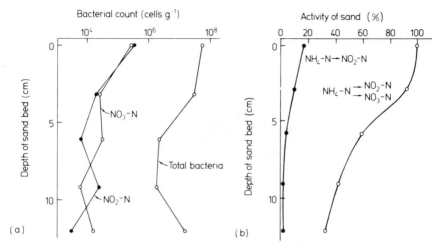

**Figure 7-10**   Populations (*a*) and activities (*b*) of nitrifying bacteria at different depths in the filter bed of a seawater aquarium. Redrawn and modified from Yoshida (1967).

min$^{-1}$) was used as an index. Conversely the time taken for the water to pass through the bed could be directly correlated with OCF. Hirayama's data showed that the apparent effects of depth were misleading, because the time required for water to pass through a filter bed of given depth was proportional to the depth. To prove the point, Hirayama designed an experiment in which aquarium water was passed through four filters that differed only in depth. The time required for water to move through each column of filtrant was made constant by adjusting the flow rate. It was shown that OCF values were the same in each column, even though the depths were different.

Filter plates of subgravel bacteriological filters should cover the entire bottom of the aquarium tank, as mentioned previously, and be sealed around the edges to keep gravel from accumulating underneath. Filter plates for large aquariums can be made of any material that is sturdy, porous, and inert in seawater. Fiberglass-reinforced plastic roofing panels and fiberglass-reinforced epoxy industrial grating are two materials used routinely at Aquarium of Niagara Falls and Mystic Marinelife Aquarium. Roofing panels are available at lumberyards and hardware stores. Industrial grating is manufactured by Joseph T. Ryerson & Son, Inc.*

When roofing panels are used, slits should be cut into them cross-

---

* Joseph T. Ryerson & Sons, Inc., Box 484, Jersey City, NJ 07303.

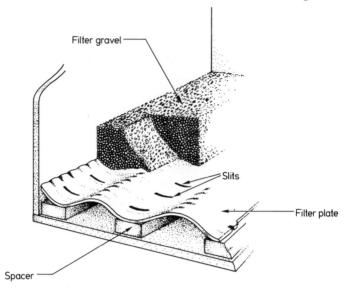

**Figure 7-11** Cutaway section of an aquarium tank showing a filter plate made of fiberglass-reinforced plastic roofing material. Redrawn and modified from Anon. (1971).

ways (at right angles to the ribs) using a table saw equipped with a blade for cutting plastic, as shown in Fig. 7-11. The slits should be about 1 mm wide, 2.5 cm long, and 5 cm apart. The panels are placed *slits down* in the aquarium tank and sealed where the edges meet the walls of the container. The best sealant is fiberglass tape (5 cm wide) embedded in clear silicone, such as Dow Corning† RTV 732 or equivalent. A rib or two on the leading edges of adjacent panels can be overlapped if necessary and sealed together with silicone. After the silicone hardens, gravel can be added to the desired depth and spread evenly over the filter plate.

With fiberglass-reinforced epoxy grating, saw the material to the required dimensions, then lay plastic flyscreen on top, as shown in Fig. 7-12. Tie the screen in place with monofilament fishing line or stainless steel wire. Afterward, seal the edges of the grate where it meets the walls of the aquarium tank. Both roofing and grating must be supported above the bottom of the aquarium tank with spacers. Any material can be used so long as it is inert and sturdy, including concrete bricks or semicircles of PVC pipe cut to the right length and stood on edge. The important criterion is that water must be able to circulate freely around

† Dow Chemical U.S.A., Midland City, MI 48640.

**Figure 7-12** Fiberglass-reinforced epoxy grating with overlying plastic flyscreen (Mystic Marinelife Aquarium).

the spacers. Concrete bricks should be sprayed with a prime coat of epoxy paint followed by two finish coats. It is not necessary to attach the spacers either to the bottom of the aquarium tank or to the filter plate.

Every 2 weeks, 10% of the water in the aquarium should be replaced. At the same time, some of the excess detritus that has accumulated since the last partial water change can be removed. Both processes are accomplished easily with a siphon consisting of a length of plastic hose. Once started, the discharge from the siphon can be directed to a floor drain, or to a bucket if the aquarium tank is small.

The removal of old aquarium water and detritus temporarily alters the biological and chemical balance of the system, mainly because large numbers of bacteria attached to detritus particles are subtracted from the filter bed biota. Moreover new water, if significantly different in temperature and salinity from water in the aquarium, will have an adverse effect on the remaining filter bed bacteria. If the biochemical processes of these organisms are interrupted for too long, the result can be sudden increases in the levels of $NH_4$-N and $NO_2$-N.

The surface gravel in a filter bed should be stirred just before every partial water change. Stirring accomplishes two things: (1) it breaks up impacted areas in the bed where water flow has become restricted from accumulated detritus; and (2) it puts detritus into suspension where some of it can be siphoned out with the old water.

Gravel should be stirred gently. Kawai et al. (1965) found that when filter sand in seawater aquariums was washed gently, 40% of the nitrifying activity was lost, and that still more was lost with subsequent washings. When the sand was washed vigorously, activity diminished by approximately two-thirds, and another 20% was lost with a second vigorous washing.

Like most living organisms, filter bed bacteria are able to adjust to gradual changes in the temperature of the external environment. Sudden and drastic fluctuations are detrimental to both activity and growth. During partial water changes, some of the filter bed bacteria are removed along with excess detritus. The bacterial population is reduced further when biological film that has broken loose is siphoned out with old water and detritus. In aquariums with low animal densities, the effect is seldom noticeable. If the aquarium supports an unusually large biomass, however, there is sometimes a detectable time lag in nutrient conversion immediately after a water change. The time lag continues until the filter bed bacteria reach their original population levels.

The growth of bacteria is affected to some extent by a change in any important environmental factor, but temperature may be the most critical. It is also the easiest to control. Time lags in the conversion of nutrients are sometimes prolonged if the temperature in the aquarium has been altered significantly by the makeup water. Srna and Baggaley (1975) studied the kinetics of nitrification in seawater aquariums. A 4°C increase in water temperature in conditioned aquariums increased ammonia and nitrite conversion rates by 50 and 12%, respectively, compared with calculated values. Lowering the temperature 1°C slowed down the oxidation rate of ammonia by 30%, and a 1.5°C decrease dropped the rate of nitrite conversion by 8%, compared with calculated values. The variation in replacement water should not exceed ±2°C.

Kawai et al. (1965) reported that nitrifying activities in a warm seawater aquarium were greatest at the salinity to which the filter bed bacteria had been acclimated, in this case normal-strength seawater. Nitrifying activity diminished as the water was made more dilute or concentrated, although some activity remained even after the salinity was doubled. No activity could be detected after the filter bed organisms were immersed in freshwater. Srna and Baggaley (1975) demonstrated that a decrease in salinity of 8 o/oo and an increase of 5 o/oo did not affect the rate of nitrification in aquarium seawater. Spotte (1979) recommended that the salinity of replacement seawater not vary more than ±0.2 o/oo.

### Algal Filters

It is not possible at this time to design filters using macroalgae with any degree of predictability. The only method is trial and error. A factor to keep in mind is that many seaweeds are "leaky" and exude organic acids, phenolic compounds, and other substances into the water. An active algal filter may thus accelerate eutrophication and increase demands on the physical adsorption system (Chapter 9). In addition, an actively growing culture of seaweed may raise the pH to dangerous levels unless this factor is monitored constantly, as discussed in Section 5.4. Algal filters thus have some negative aspects.

Basic design criteria include the following: (1) maximum depth of the tray in which macroalgae are cultured should not exceed 30.5 cm (Section 2.1); (2) the surface area of the tray should be as large as possible;

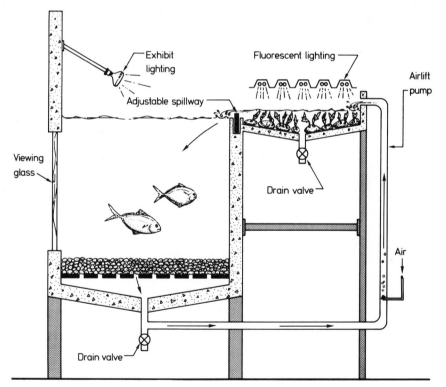

**Figure 7-13**  Algal culture tray illustrating the cycling of water between the tray and the aquarium tank.

(3) the photoperiod should be about 16/8; and (4) the light intensity should be estimated from Tables 2-4 and 2-5 (Section 2.4, pp. 23 and 24), then adjusted as the situation dictates. Many of the benthic macroalgae grow attached to objects on the bottom. Shelbourne (1964) described an algal culture tray in which *Enteromorpha*, a green macroalga, grew attached to cobbles that covered the bottom. The same technique is recommended here, with the added provision that the floor of the tray be sloped for easy draining, as shown in Fig. 7-13. The fronds of macroalgae should be wiped periodically to keep them free of epiphytic algae, and excess plants should be cropped when the biomass exceeds that needed to keep nitrate at minimum concentrations. This last factor can be determined empirically by estimating the biomass and monitoring the level of $NO_3$-N for a time after the bacteriological filter becomes conditioned and the animal population has stabilized. The best position for an algal filter is after the bacteriological filter but before physical adsorption and disinfection processes.

# CHAPTER 8
*Processing Seawater Supplies*

T wo stages are involved in the processing of large seawater supplies: (1) primary filtration by granular media filters; and (2) secondary filtration with diatomaceous earth (DE) filters. Not discussed are how these techniques can be adapted for filtering recirculated seawater, because they are not needed. Recirculation of seawater through subgravel filters using airlift pumps is adequate to sustain good clarity in individual aquariums, provided the bacteriological filters are correctly designed and maintained, and animal density is not excessive. Occasional increases in turbidity can be handled with small portable filters, either granular media or diatomaceous earth.

Mechanical filters can be classified by several criteria: (1) direction of water flow (e.g., downflow, upflow); (2) type of filter media (e.g., sand, dual or multimedia, diatomaceous earth); (3) flow rate (slow, rapid, high-rate); and (4) whether the water is moved by pressure or gravity. Gravity filters are usually rectangular, have open tops, and are made of concrete. Pressure filters ordinarily are cylindrical, sealed because they are pressurized, and fabricated from steel. Emphasis here will be on downflow gravity and pressure filters that use mainly dual media, multimedia, and diatomaceous earth. A *granular media filter* contains at least one of these constituents: sand, anthracite coal, gravel, ilmenite, or crushed garnet. A *diatomaceous earth filter* uses only DE as a filtrant.

The first three sections of this chapter describe mechanical filtration methods for removing turbidity from large volumes of influent natural seawater, or *seawater supplies.* Section 8.4 touches briefly on techniques used to process small volumes of seawater for laboratory aquariums.

**165**

## 8.1 SEAWATER SUPPLIES

Clark and Clark (1964) and Sprague (1966) summarized the methods used by several seaside laboratories and public aquariums to acquire continuous supplies of seawater. Both works give valuable insight into common problems associated with pumping and processing seawater in large volumes, although many of the suggested methods are out-dated. Lackey (1956) described some of the origins of turbidity in seaside public aquariums.

Seawater can be collected either from surface or groundwater supplies. There are pros and cons to both. Many devices are used that simply strain surface seawater to remove objects that would clog the intake pump, but do not actually filter it. Ordinarily such devices consist of a pipe jutting into the sea with a screen at the end, or a screened sump. Whatever the exact configuration, all are variations of a common technique that I shall call the *open-ended system.* The equipment is comparatively cheap to purchase and install and easy to maintain. However seawater obtained in this manner is plagued by localized and seasonal fluctuations in salinity and temperature. During stormy periods it may be laden with silt, which places a heavy burden on the filters and necessitates oversizing the mechanical system. The larvae of many fouling organisms, such as barnacles and mussels, are able to enter the water system. Once inside they attach, grow to maturity, and clog intake lines, severely restricting water flow. Red tide organisms and free-floating parasites are likely to be sucked into the water supply, causing mass fish kills, epizootic outbreaks of disease, or chronic low-level parasitism. Sprague (1966) recommended that an open-ended surface supply system be duplicated from start to finish. This allows the supply lines to be shut down alternately and "rested." Fouling organisms in the lines die when the flow of water is stopped and conditions inside the pipes become anoxic.

Groundwater pumped from deep wells produces a culture medium of stable salinity and temperature. Turbidity levels are lower than in surface supplies obtained from open-ended systems, and more predictable. There are fewer fouling and disease-producing organisms in groundwater because it has, in effect, been prefiltered through the surrounding substratum. On the negative side, deep-well groundwater often has a low pH and may be devoid of oxygen, necessitating heavy aeration before it is suitable for culturing marine organisms. The high concentrations of iron and manganese characteristic of many groundwaters may require aeration or settling before the water can be directed to the filters. If this is not done, black precipitates of oxide form on filter media grains, eventually cementing them together. This causes channeling in the filter beds and disrupts filtering efficiency. The result is an increased breakthrough of turbidity unless the filters are backwashed frequently. Many groundwaters also contain high concentrations of hydrogen sulfide, which, although toxic, is easily oxidized to harmless sulfate by aeration.

The ideal solution is a compromise. Well points sunk several metres below the low tide line on a stable, sandy beach with good tidal flow provide a supply of surface seawater that has been prefiltered (Fig. 8-1). Water trickling through sand to the collection point acts as a prefilter. This reduces both turbidity and the number of fouling and disease-

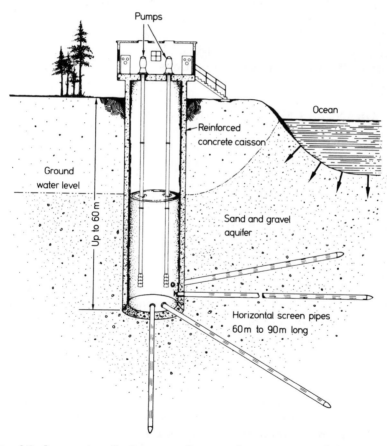

**Figure 8-1**   Large water collection system for processing seawater supplies (The Ranney Company).

producing organisms. Problems of low pH and dissolved oxygen are eliminated. So are the troubles associated with high concentrations of iron, manganese, and $H_2S$. Because the beach is swept daily by tides, the sand above the collection point stays porous and requires no maintenance. Surf is essential, because without it the well points eventually clog with silt.

In wastewater treatment, it is common to enhance turbidity removal by chemical flocculation. Drinking water is also pretreated in this way, but such practices are not advisable for treating seawater supplies in which delicate marine organisms are cultured. Just because humans drink flocculated and chemically clarified water does not mean that the same water would be a fit environment in which to culture aquatic organisms. There is no evidence that even low dosage levels of alum (aluminum sulfate), polyelectrolytes, and other additives are not toxic to marine fishes and invertebrates. Raw influent seawater must be processed by direct filtration, although settling and aeration can be used where dictated by local water conditions.

## 8.2 GRANULAR MEDIA FILTERS

When classified according to flow rate, there are three types of granular media filters: (1) slow; (2) rapid; and (3) high-rate. The first two use only sand with a supporting bed of gravel underneath. High-rate filters use anthracite and sand (*dual media*), or anthracite, sand, and either garnet or ilmenite (*multimedia*). *Mixed media* is a synonym for multimedia. Both dual and multimedia filtrants must be supported by a gravel bed, unless the underdrain system is designed to support the media directly. It should be noted that flow rate is not a rigid criterion with which to classify granular media filters. For example, high-rate filters can be operated at slower rates, and rapid sand filters are sometimes designed to accommodate flow rates that approach those of high-rate filters. Gravity and pressure filters that are suitable for rapid sand or multimedia filtration are shown in Figs. 8-2 and 8-3.

### Theory

Experts disagree on the exact mechanisms by which POC is removed from influent water passing through a granular media filtrant, although the term mechanical filtration is, in a sense, a misnomer because more is involved than simple straining. Among discussions that summarize the subject are those by Craft (1966), O'Melia and Stumm (1967), and

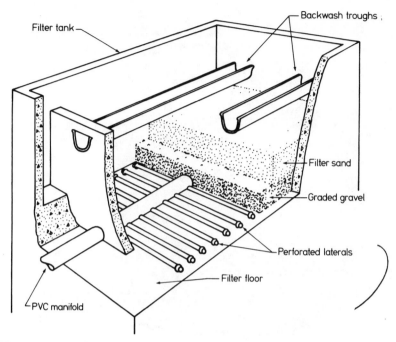

**Figure 8-2** Granular media gravity filter (American Water Works Association).

Tchobanoglous (1970). Some of the mechanisms thought to be important are: (1) straining; (2) sedimentation; (3) diffusion; and (4) strong chemical bonding (chemical adsorption). Weaker, more permanent bonds, such as the ones formed by van der Waals forces, probably are not significant. Figure 8-4 illustrates how three of the above mechanisms might work.

Straining involves the physical entrapment of POC in interstices formed by grains of filter media and detritus. The trapped material is held in place until the flow of water is restricted, at which point it is broken apart and driven deeper into the filter bed. During sedimentation, suspended POC settles out by gravity. As Selmeczi (1971) pointed out, however, sedimentation is unlikely to affect POC smaller than approximately 25 $\mu$m, considering that downward moving water has a velocity at least 100 times greater than the settling velocity of a smaller object. Small suspended bits of POC may be removed when they diffuse to places in the filter bed where there is virtually no movement of water. The formation of strong (and hence reversible) chemical bonds is probably significant even if the influent water is not treated with a

**Figure 8-3**  Granular media pressure filter (Cochrane Environmental Systems, Crane Co.).

flocculant. The surfaces of detritus particles and filter media are chemically charged, as is the coating of biological film that continuously sloughs off and reforms around grains of filter media (Section 7.1). It is likely that POC can attach to these fixed surfaces as it passes through the filter bed.

### Slow Sand Filters

Slow sand filters operate at flow rates of $0.7 \times 10^{-3}$ m sec$^{-1}$ (1 gpm ft$^{-2}$) or less. Bacteriological filters powered by airlift pumps are slow sand filters in terms of flow rate, but differ in other respects. Most are composed entirely of gravel instead of sand. Moreover bacteriological filters rely on bacteria to remove contaminants from solution in recirculated aquariums. The function of conventional slow sand filters is to concentrate POC from influent seawater on a single pass.

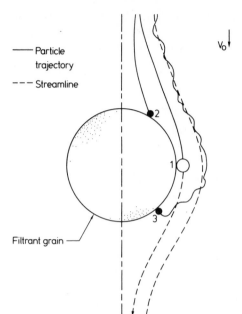

- Particle trajectory
- - - Streamline

Filtrant grain

Figure 8-4 Entrapment of POC against a gravel grain by (1) staining; (2) sedimentation; and (3) diffusion. Redrawn from Yao et al. (1971).

Slow sand filters used in wastewater treatment are 30 to 76 cm deep. They usually cannot be backwashed by reversing the flow of water through the underdrain system. Accumulated sludge is removed manually when head loss becomes excessive, and new sand is added to replenish the top layer that is lost during cleaning. Slow sand filters are not economical because they require lots of space and frequent maintenance.

**Rapid Sand Filters**

Rapid sand filters differ from slow sand filters in two important respects: (1) the flow rate of water through the filter bed is greater; and (2) they can be backwashed. The advantages are that more water can be filtered through a smaller surface area, and accumulated sludge can be removed mechanically, which reduces the amount of labor needed. The average flow rate is $1.4 \times 10^{-3}$ m sec$^{-1}$ (2 gpm ft$^{-2}$). Despite increased water flow, rapid sand filters are uneconomical because most of the particulate matter is taken out in the top few centimetres of sand, just as in slow sand filters. Little POC penetrates to the underlying layers. Tchobanoglous (1970) found, for example, that 75 to 90% of the head loss in a rapid sand filter occurred in the upper 2.5 cm. The situation was not changed appreciably by varying the flow rate. As described by Kawamura (1975a), heavy accumulations of POC can cause negative head pressure to develop in the upper portion of a filter bed if sand is the primary filtrant. This causes air pockets to form, resulting in air-binding of the filter. Thick layers of POC also cause the surface layer of sand to compact.

The inability to store large amounts of POC before suffering excessive head loss means that rapid sand filters require frequent backwash, with large volumes of water being lost in the process. This can be expensive if the backwash water comes from an already processed supply and has been filtered, heated or cooled, and disinfected.

### High-Rate Filters

The filtration rate of high-rate filters ordinarily is within the range $0.7 \times 10^{-3}$ to $5.4 \times 10^{-3}$ m sec$^{-1}$(1 to 8 gpm ft$^{-2}$). The usual rate is $3.4 \times 10^{-3}$ m sec$^{-1}$ (5 gpm ft$^{-2}$). The recommended rate for filtering seawater supplies used in the culture of marine organisms is $1.4 \times 10^{-3}$ to $2.7 \times 10^{-3}$ m sec$^{-1}$ (2 to 4 gpm ft$^{-2}$). The lower flow rate is necessary because no filter aids, such as alum or polyelectrolytes, can be used to augment turbidity removal.

By using more than one filter medium, high-rate filters provide additional voids throughout the vertical depth of the bed in which to collect POC. As a result, they can store more particulate matter than slow sand or rapid sand filters, and sustain longer filter runs. This is possible because the finest filtrant material is located at the bottom of the bed instead of the top, and more POC can be collected before significant head loss occurs. During filtration, larger particles are removed in the coarse anthracite and smaller particles are trapped farther down in the finer underlying filtrants.

High-rate filters are the first choice for filtering seawater supplies. Their advantages are: (1) greater surface area for POC removal; (2) high filtration rates, meaning that more water can be processed per unit time without loss of effluent quality; and (3) longer filter runs, which reduces labor costs and down time for backwash, and results in smaller volumes of water lost when averaged over an extended period of time.

### Selection and Placement of Media

Filtering efficiency depends on grain size and filter media depth; backwash flow rate is a function of grain size and specific gravity of the filter media. During a normal filtration cycle, the specific gravity of the media is unimportant because the filter media are not suspended. Thus even though very fine filter media give the best effluent clarity, such materials are not necessarily the most effective if they cause the filter bed to clog frequently. Selection of filter media should be based on how effectively they *fluidize*, or become uniformly suspended, during backwash.

Selection and placement of filter media involves three steps: (1) choosing the media for grain size and specific gravity for effective backwash; (2) deciding how deep each layer of filtrant should be; and (3) sizing the gravel that will support the filter media. Unless each step is planned carefully, a bed will not filter influent seawater efficiently, nor will it fluidize and backwash properly.

*Grain Size and Specific Gravity*

In civil engineering, filter media are often specified by effective size and uniformity coefficient. *Effective size* $(d_e)$ is the grain size in millimetres at which 10% of the grains by weight are smaller. Ten percent weight corresponds closely to the median size by actual count of grains in a random sample. The limits of effective size are defined by the *uniformity coefficient* (*uc*), which is the ratio of grain size that contains 60% finer material than itself to the size that has 10% finer than itself (effective size), or $d60:d10$, where $d$ is the grain size of the filtrant. This ratio covers the size range of half the grains of a single type of filter medium in a filter bed. Effective size and uniformity coefficient values for graded anthracite coal are given in Table 8-1.

Effective size is useful in determining hydraulic characteristics of a filter bed under nonfluidized conditions—during filtration, in other words—but does not hold true when chosen according to *representative size* $(d_e \times uc)$, which corresponds to 60% size by weight, or simply 60% size. Specific filter media should be selected according to guidelines established by Robinson (1972).

When rapid sand filters are used, fine sand should not be selected, even though it is a more efficient filtrant than coarse sand. Coarse sands give longer filter runs at nominal loss of effluent clarity. The best sand for rapid sand filters has a grain size (60% size) of approximately 0.7 mm. Sand for high-rate filters can be finer, and a grain size of 0.5 mm (60% size) works well.

As mentioned previously, specific gravity of the filter media is unimportant during the filtration cycle, but an improper combination of grain size and specific gravity causes: (1) inadequate backwash, which leaves the filters still dirty; (2) excessive intermixing of the filter media during

Table 8-1   Effective Size and Uniformity
Coefficient Values for Graded Anthracite
Coal

| Effective Size (mm) | Max. Uniformity Coefficient |
|---|---|
| 0.60–0.79 | 1.70 |
| 0.60–0.69 | 1.70 |
| 0.70–0.79 | 1.70 |
| 0.80–0.89 | 1.70 |
| 0.80–0.89 | 1.50 |
| 0.90–0.99 | 1.70 |
| 0.90–0.99 | 1.50 |
| 1.00–1.10 | 1.70 |
| 1.00–1.10 | 1.50 |
| 1.20–1.50 | 1.70 |

Source:   Reading Anthracite Coal Co., 200
Mahantongo Street, Pottsville, PA 17901.

backwash; and (3) loss of filter media during backwash. In high-rate filters, too much intermixing of the media can reduce filter runs by allowing mud balls to accumulate in the intermixed zone. The term "mud ball" is a vernacular expression used by engineers to denote the accumulation of DOC and POC around sand grains, causing the grains to stick together. Some intermixing in high-rate filters is inevitable (Cleasby and Woods 1975), but severe upsetting of the filter media leads ultimately to reduced filtering performance as mud balls accumulate. In rapid sand filters, mud ball formation takes place at the surface of the bed, instead of in the deep layers, as in high-rate filters.

In high-rate filters, differences in the specific gravity of the filtrants causes them to settle into their original layers after backwash, except in the intermixed zones. Specific gravity values for garnet, sand, and anthracite are shown on the curves of Fig. 8-5.

During backwash, the flow of water through the underdrain system is reversed and directed upward through the filter bed. At low upward velocities the grains of filter media are undisturbed and stay in contact with each other. As the velocity increases, grains of filter media are separated and the spaces between them enlarge, which increases the porosity of the bed and causes it to expand. Finally the velocity reaches a point at which most of the filter media grains move independently, no longer supported by grains around and beneath them. Now backwash

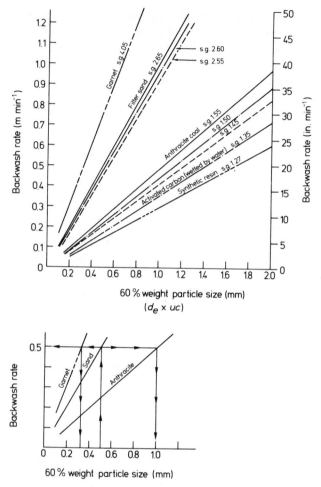

**Figure 8-5**   Backwash rate for granular media filters at 20°C. Redrawn and modified from Kawamura (1975a).

velocity is approximately equal to the terminal settling velocity of the filter media grains, and the bed is fluidized. In dual and multimedia filters, the grain size and specific gravity of the filter media must be carefully selected and the uniformity coefficients rigidly limited or fluidization will be incomplete.

The backwash rate is a function only of the terminal settling velocities of the different types of filter media, and is independent of filter media depth and the porosity of the filter bed. Backwash rate must be less than the terminal settling velocity of the filter media to avoid losing sand or anthracite during backwash. In addition, the backwash rate must be higher than the terminal settling velocity of POC trapped in the filter bed. Thus filter media should be chosen according to a single criterion: optimum backwash. There are three rules of thumb to follow, and they are so reliable that no further computations are needed:

1 The terminal settling velocities of all the media in a filter bed must be the same for the bed to fluidize properly.

2 To have equal terminal settling velocities, the ratios of grain size for garnet, sand, and anthracite should be $2:3:6$.

3 Based on rules one and two, backwash rate (in m min$^{-1}$) for garnet is 1.5 times particle size in mm (60% size). For sand, backwash rate numerically equals grain size. For anthracite, backwash rate is one-half grain size.

It is a simple matter to select filter media for optimum backwash characteristics. One medium must first be chosen arbitrarily before the appropriate grain size of the other two can be determined. This is most easily done with sand because sand is the filtrant common to nearly all granular media filters. As noted previously, proper size for sand in rapid sand filters is 0.7 mm (60% size); for high-rate filters, 0.5 mm (60% size).

The grain size and backwash rate for any of the three common filter media can be found from Fig. 8-5. Suppose, for example, that in a multimedia filter the grain size of the sand will be 0.5 mm. As the figure shows, the backwash rate for sand this size (in m min$^{-1}$) equals the grain size. The inset of Fig. 8-5 shows how to find the grain sizes of anthracite and garnet based on sand of 0.5 mm (this example) and a backwash rate of 0.5 m min$^{-1}$. The values are 1 mm (anthracite) and 0.32 mm (garnet).

The viscosity of water is influenced by temperature, which affects the fluidization of a filter bed. The backwash rate, as determined from Fig. 8-5, must be altered slightly for temperatures other than 20°C. This is done by using Fig. 8-6. For example, if the water temperature is 5°C, the multiplier is 0.87 and the corrected backwash rate in this case is 0.5 m min$^{-1}$ × 0.87 = 0.44 m min$^{-1}$. If the temperature is 27°C, the correction factor is 1.05 and the adjusted backwash rate should be 0.53 m min$^{-1}$. The procedure for using Fig. 8-6 is shown by the inset.

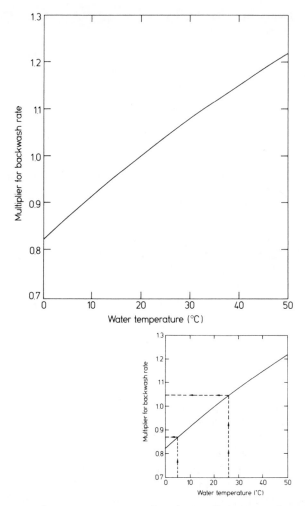

**Figure 8-6**  Backwash temperature correction factor. Redrawn and modified from Kawamura (1975b).

*Filter Media Depth*

Filtering efficiency—but not backwash—is mainly a function of the ratio of filter media depth to grain size ($d_e$). There are many combinations. As might be expected, filter media depth can be decreased when small grain sizes are used. This ratio is of theoretical interest, but of little practical value if filter media are selected on the basis of their

Table 8-2  Depth of Filter Media (cm) in High-rate Filters for Waters of Varying Turbidity

|  | Dual Media | | Multimedia | |
|---|---|---|---|---|
| Filter media | 76 cm bed (1–10 FTU)[a] | 91 cm bed (> 10 FTU)[a] | 76 cm bed (1–10 FTU)[a] | 91 cm bed (> 10 FTU)[a] |
| Anthracite | 51 | 64 | 42 | 63 |
| Sand | 25 | 27 | 23 | 20 |
| Garnet | — | — | 11 | 8 |

Source:  Culp (1977) for 76 cm values and Neptune Microfloc, Inc., P.O. Box 612, Corvallis, OR 97330 for 91 cm values.
[a] FTU = Formazin Turbidity Units.

backwash properties. A summary of filter bed depths that can be used in high-rate filters is given in Table 8-2. Deep filters (91 cm) should be used when influent water is highly turbid. In rapid sand filters, add 76 cm of 0.7 mm (60% size) sand to the top layer of support gravel (next section).

*Support Gravel*

The filter media must be supported above the underdrain system in most filter designs. Layers of graded gravel are commonly used for this purpose, and typical configurations for the three most popular underdrain systems are given in Tables 8-3 to 8-5.

Support gravel should be carefully washed, graded, and arranged evenly in layers in depths indicated by the tables. In addition, gravels should be round to facilitate even backwash, rather than angular and elongated. Culp et al. (1978) recommended that the specific gravity of any of the support media be not less than 2.5, and that not more than 8% by weight of the material in any layer be coarser or finer than the specified limit.

**Equipment**

The equipment to operate granular media filters consists largely of flow rate controllers, valves, turbidimeters, underdrains, and pumps. All piping should be PVC or fiberglass-reinforced plastic (for use of PVC, consult Mamrelli 1975).

Controllers

High-rate pressure filters should be equipped with flow rate controllers. A controller divides influent water evenly among a group of filter units, limits maximum flow, and prevents sudden surges in the lines of pressure vessels. This last factor can sometimes be severe enough to upset the filter bed and cause localized intermixing of the support gravel with the filter media.

Valves

Many filtration systems are designed with more valves than necessary. the number of valves should be minimized to prevent superfluous maintenance. Butterfly valves should be used wherever possible and actuated either manually by gears (Fig. 8-7), or pneumatically by air piped from a central compressor. Any pneumatic system should have manual overrides so that valves can still be opened or closed if the air compressor becomes inoperable. If pneumatic valves are used, the system can be operated from a central control panel.

Turbidimeters

Filter systems used to process seawater directly can be equipped with recording tubidimeters to monitor the quality of effluent water, if influent supplies are chronically turbid. When recording turbidimeters

**Figure 8-7**   Gear-actuated butterfly valve (Mystic Marinelife Aquarium).

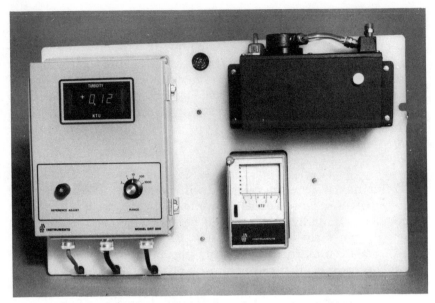

**Figure 8-8**   DRT-200 recording turbidimeter (HF Instruments Ltd.).

are used, they should be located at each of these places: (1) influent
water supply; (2) each filter effluent; and (3) combined filter effluent.
Recording turbidimeters become particularly important when seawater
is procured through an open-ended system. The HF Instruments DRT-
200* (Fig. 8-8) reliably monitors turbidity in the lower ranges. It is a
continuous flow nephelometer, relying on a strong beam of light passed
through a water sample, which is then scattered by particles of turbidity.

*Underdrains*

A filter underdrain has two functions: (1) to collect filtered seawater
evenly from all parts of the bed; and (2) to provide uniform backwash.
Designs are available in which the filter media are supported directly,
eliminating the need for an additional gravel bed. A brief description of
how these designs function was given by Culp et al. (1978). None has
been thoroughly tested in seawater, to my knowledge. I shall therefore
concentrate on three designs that have been used for many years in

* HF Instruments Ltd., 105 Healey Rd., Bolton, Ont. LOP 1AO, Canada (U.S. distributor
is Fisher Scientific Co., 711 Forbes Ave., Pittsburgh, PA 15219).

**Figure 8-9**   Leopold filter bottom (Sybron/Leopold)*.

wastewater treatment, and to a more limited extent to filter seawater supplies. They are: (1) the Leopold filter bottom; (2) the Wheeler filter bottom; and (3) the pipe lateral underdrain system. All require a supporting bed of gravel underneath the filter media. The first two designs can be used only in gravity filters; the last is suitable for either gravity or pressure filters.

The Leopold filter bottom, depicted in Fig. 8-9, consists of blocks of vitrified clay or plastic approximately 61 × 30 × 25 cm. The bottom half of a block contains two feed channels, each measuring 10 cm square and containing two 1.6 cm diameter orifices per 0.9 m². The channels feed water into the dispersion laterals (8.3 × 10 cm) located above. In the top of a typical block are 45 orifices (0.4 cm for each 0.9 m²) to further distribute backwash water and to dissipate the velocity head from the lower orifices. Grain sizes and depths of the filtrant and support gravel are given in Table 8-3. I have no personal experience with Leopold filter bottoms in seawater applications.

* Sybron/Leopold, 8227 S. Division St., Zelienople, PA 16063.

**Table 8-3   Depth and Grain Size (60% Size) of Filter Sand Plus Support Gravel for a Rapid Sand Gravity Filter Using a Leopold Bottom**

| Gravel (top to bottom) | Grain Size (mm) | Depth (cm) |
|---|---|---|
| Fine gravel | 3.2 × 6.4 | 12.6 |
| Medium gravel | 6.4 × 12.7 | 5.0 |
| Coarse gravel | 12.7 × 19.0 | 5.0 |

Source: Culp et al. (1978).

The Wheeler filter bottom (Fig. 8-10) consists of a series of conical depressions at 30.5 cm centers in each direction. A porcelain thimble with an orifice opening of 1.9 cm is located at the bottom of each depression. Within each cone are 14 porcelain spheres that range in diameter from 2.9 to 7.6 cm. The spheres are arranged to dissipate the velocity head from the orifice with minimum disturbance of the supporting gravel bed. I once examined a rapid sand gravity filter used for several years to process seawater originating from an open-ended sys-

**Figure 8-10**   Wheeler bottom (BIF, General Signal Corp., 1600 Division Rd., West Warwick, RI 02893).

**Table 8-4   Depth and Grain Size (60% Size) of Filter Sand Plus Support Gravel for a Rapid Sand Gravity Filter Using a Wheeler Bottom**

| Gravel (top to bottom) | Grain Size (mm) | Depth (cm) |
|---|---|---|
| Fine gravel | 4.8 × 9.5 | 15.2 |
| Medium gravel | 9.5 × 15.9 | 7.6 |
| Coarse gravel | 15.9 × 25.4 | 7.6 |
| Very coarse gravel | 25.4 × 31.8 | To cover underdrain |

Source:   Culp et al. (1978).

tem. The backwash had become uneven, as seen from the considerable amount of gravel mixed with the top layer of sand. The concentration of gravel was denser in some locations than in others. When the sand and gravel were shoveled out, the cause of the problem was obvious: many of the porcelain spheres were cemented to the walls of their conical depressions by a heavy precipitate. I do not know whether such problems are typical when Wheeler bottoms are used to filter seawater. Grain sizes and depths of the filtrant and support gravel for Wheeler bottoms are given in Table 8-4.

The most reliable underdrain system for seawater filtration consists of a PVC manifold with perforated PVC laterals, such as depicted in Figs. 8-2 and 8-3 for a pressure and gravity filter, respectively. Perforations should be located on the undersides of the laterals so that backwash water is dissipated against the bottom of the filter housing. Orifice diameters normally are 0.6 to 1.3 cm and spaced at distances of 7.6 to 20.3 cm. Fair and Geyer (1958) gave the following guide to designing a pipe lateral underdrain system:

1   Ratio of orifice area to bed served = 0.15:0.001.

2   Ratio of lateral area to area of orifices served = 2:1 to 4:1.

3   Ratio of manifold area to area of laterals served = 1.5:1 to 3:1.

4   Diameter of orifices = 0.6-1.9 cm.

5   Spacing of orifices = 7.6-30.5 cm on centers.

6   Spacing of laterals should be about the same as spacing of orifices.

Grain sizes and depths of the filtrant and support gravel for pipe lateral underdrain systems are given in Table 8-5.

*Pumps*

Pumps should be admiralty bronze. The next best choice is 316 stainless steel.

Table 8-5   Depth and Grain Size (60% Size) of Support Media for Pipe Lateral
Underdrain Systems

| Gravel (top to bottom) | Grain Size (mm) | Depth (cm) |
|---|---|---|
| Fine gravel | 3.2 × 6.4 | 17.8 |
| Medium gravel | 6.4 × 12.7 | 7.6 |
| Coarse gravel | 12.7 × 19.0 | 7.6 |
| Very coarse gravel | 19.0 × 25.4 | 10 cm above wash water outlet |

Source:   Culp et al. (1978).

### Design

The turbidity of the influent water and the amount of filtered water
required daily determine the type of filter media and size of the filter
units. Rapid sand filters are effective only so long as the influent water
does not exceed 3 FTU (Formazin Turbidity Units).* High-rate filters can
handle turbidity loads up to approximately 10 FTU without turbidity
breakthrough. If influent water exceeds this value, settling should precede filtration. Final clarity of effluent water that has passed through
both primary and secondary filters should equal that of drinking water
(0.1 FTU or less). Primary filtration alone should provide an effluent
turbidity value no greater than 0.3 FTU. These stringent requirements
can be met only with the right combination of seawater supply, method
of collection, and filtration. Decisions on filter configuration should
take into consideration these parameters: (1) method of collection
(open-ended surface supply, deep-well groundwater, or well-point
surface supply); (2) mean and maximum turbidity (monitored in surface
supplies only); (3) pretreatment requirements (aeration or settling); (4)
volume of filtered water needed daily; and (5) whether there are plans to
include secondary filtration with diatomaceous earth. Cost is an obvious factor. The use of dual media represents a cost savings at the time of
installation, compared with multimedia. Moreover, a number of available multimedia configurations for processing water are patented by
Neptune Microfloc, Inc.†

---

* Turbidity can be measured by several methods, including Jackson Turbidity Units
(JTU), Formazin Turbidity Units (FTU), and Nephelometric Turbidity Units (NTU). There
are no constants for converting measured values from one method to another, because the
measurements are based on different theoretical considerations (Vanous 1978).
† Neptune Microfloc, Inc., P.O. Box 612, Corvallis, OR 97330.

Water collected from surface supplies with open-ended systems will always be more turbid than groundwater or surface water pumped through well points, and multimedia filters are the best means of processing it. Dual media filters are suitable for filtering groundwater or water from well points.

The quality of deep-well groundwaters cannot be predicted, and test wells should be drilled. Clark and Eisler (1964) described some of the problems with test wells sunk for the Sandy Hook Marine Laboratory on the New Jersey shore. The presence of a freshwater lens made it difficult to secure a consistent supply of full-strength seawater. Ordinarily seawater from deep wells must be aerated to adjust dissolved oxygen and pH levels, and to precipitate iron and manganese if they are supersaturated in solution. Aeration also oxidizes hydrogen sulfide to sulfate.

The number and size of the filters depends in part on how much water is needed daily. If large amounts are needed, the best configuration is at least two concrete gravity filters with dual or multimedia and PVC lateral underdrain systems. The filters can be constructed with a common backwash trough to save space. For smaller volumes, the best choice is a bank of two or more pressure vessels that also are filled with dual or multimedia and equipped with PVC lateral underdrain systems. Both gravity and pressure filters should be plumbed with by-pass arrangements so that one unit can be drained for maintenance while the other continues to filter influent water. All other facets of the system must be duplicated in case a pump fails or a filter must be shut down and emptied for repair.

Direct filtering requirements are even more stringent if secondary filtration by DE is not provided. The use of DE "polishes" the water by removing most of the turbidity that remains after granular media filtration. As shown in Chapters 9 and 10, small concentrations of turbidity severely impair physical adsorption and disinfection processes, even rendering them ineffective. If no secondary filtration is provided, multimedia filters should be used in the direct filtration of seawater supplies, no matter how good the source.

### Gravity Filters

As noted by Culp and Culp (1971), gravity filters should be designed with walls to withstand hydrostatic pressure in two directions. They must also be watertight. Minimum wall thickness should be 22.5 to 30.5 cm. The design of gravity filters or concrete aquarium tanks and hatchery raceways cannot be left to contractors, architects, or engineers inexperienced in such matters. Mistakes in design and construction that result in leaks in the filter housing or deterioration of the concrete from exposure to seawater can be avoided if these recommendations are followed.

1   Do not use plastic waterstops between pours of concrete. Such joints encourage leaks as time passes, rather than prevent them.

2   Concrete filter housings should never be constructed as an integral part of a load-bearing wall of a room of another building. If the building shifts it will cause stress cracks in the filter housing.

3   There should be a minimum number of concrete pours during construction, and the material must be vibrated to assure uniform density. With careful preparation, it is possible to form all four walls in a single pour.

4   Use only salt-resistant concrete and work it to a steel-troweled finish. Pockmarks in untroweled concrete are difficult to fill with paint and are susceptible to deterioration by seawater. Broom finishes are rough, collect dirt, and are not recommended.

5   If PVC pipe is used, it must be rough-sanded where it is expected to bond with concrete. Even then, leaks often form around a pipe inserted through a new concrete wall unless the area around the pipe on each side of the wall is chipped out and filled with Bondex®* or equivalent.

The concrete of a filter housing, aquarium tank, or raceway must be protected from seawater, rather than the other way around. The small additions of inorganic ions to the seawater from leaching concrete are minor problems compared with the damage that seawater can inflict on new concrete surfaces. The best form of protection is to apply three coats (one prime and two finish) of high-quality epoxy paint. But unless the concrete has been properly aged and prepared, only superficial bonding will take place and the paint will eventually peel, leaving the concrete exposed. The following procedure has been used with success at Mystic Marinelife Aquarium.

1   Allow new concrete to age for a minimum of 30 days before painting.

2   Before painting, wash all surfaces with a dilute solution of trisodium phosphate, or Taskmaster®†#1 diluted 6:1. Afterward,

* Bondex International, Inc., Brunswick, OH 44212.
† Detroit Graphite, 200 Sayre Street, Rockford, IL 61101.

acid-etch all surfaces with dilute muriatic acid or Taskmaster®#4 diluted 3:1. Rinse with tap water.

3   When the concrete has dried, test for moisture with a moisture detector. Do not paint until the concrete has dried completely.

4   Touch up all exposed metal surfaces with one coat of zinc-rich epoxy primer.

5   Apply one coat of clear epoxy primer to all concrete surfaces by airless spray; overlap onto metal or PVC surfaces if necessary. There is no reason to mask them off.

6   Apply the first coat of finish epoxy paint, mixed and aged according to the manufacturer's specifications. Apply by airless spray. Rolling or brushing is not recommended. Epoxy is viscous and adheres easily to brushes or rollers, which makes filling pockmarks on vertical surfaces more difficult. It is imperative that all pockmarks be filled, no matter how small. Dry thickness of the first finish coat must be 2.5 mil.

7   After 6 hr but before 24 hr, apply the second finish coat of epoxy. Use airless spray and apply to a dry film thickness of 2.5 mil.

8   All finish coats should be high-gloss for easier cleaning. Never use epoxy paints when the air temperature is below 18°C.

*Pressure Filters*

The conventional steel pressure vessels used routinely in wastewater applications are unsuitable for filtering seawater without modification. This entails: (1) proper surface coating of any metal in contact with seawater; and (2) cathodic protection of the metal. Either measure alone is inadequate to quell the corrosive action of seawater. The way in which cathodic protection works is illustrated diagrammatically in Fig. 8-11. As shown, the use of a sacrificial metal reduces corrosion of the underlying surface metal. The use of sacrificial zinc blocks in steel filter

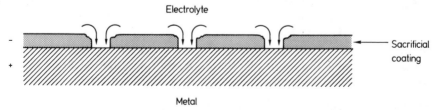

**Figure 8-11**   Diagrammatic illustration showing how steel is protected by sacrificial coatings. Redrawn from Uhlig (1971).

tanks protects the steel from seawater corrosion by the same mechanism. To minimize corrosion, these steps should be taken at the factory.

1  Sandblast all interior tank surfaces to near-white metal (Steel Structures Painting Council SP-10-63, or National Association of Corrosion Engineers No. 2 specification).

2  Apply one primer coat of coal-tar epoxy to a dry film thickness of 8 mil. Use Carboline* Carbomastic® No. 3 or equivalent, according to the manufacturer's specifications.

3  Apply a top coat of coal-tar epoxy to a dry film thickness of 8 mil (16 mil total). Use Carboline Carbomastic® No. 12 or equivalent.

4  Test the fully cured coating with a holiday detector suitable for locating pinholes and voids in thin film coatings. The Tinker and Rasor Model M1/AC Holiday Detector† is suitable. Repair any coating faults with coal-tar epoxy (Carbomastic® No. 12 or equivalent) and retest after curing.

5  Install a ring of zinc ribbon around the inside circumference of the filter housing. One ring should be near the bottom and the other near the top. In addition, there should be four vertical strips of zinc ribbon material spaced evenly apart and spanning the distance between the top and bottom rings. The material is installed by exposing approximately 7.6 cm of the steel core wire and spotwelding it to the walls of the housing. Use ASARCO Diamond Line® Zinc Anode Ribbon** (0.09 kg cm$^{-1}$) or equivalent.

6  Coat the exposed weld areas of the steel core wire at the ribbon connections with two coats of coal-tar epoxy (Carbomastic® No. 12 or equivalent). *Do not coat the zinc.*

7  Sandblast and coat each manhole cover and install a length of zinc ribbon on the seawater side.

8  Inspect the ribbons and coal-tar epoxy coating every 6 months.

All flanges, suction diffusers, blow-off nipples, and so forth must be nonmetallic or austenitic low-carbon stainless steel (e.g., 304L or 316L). If only steel parts and fittings can be obtained, they must be coated with coal-tar epoxy.

Steel filter tanks should be placed on concrete pads at least 20 cm thick to prevent spilled seawater from corroding the legs. Some manufac-

* Carboline, 350 Hanley Industrial Court, St. Louis, MO 63144.
† Tinker and Rasor, 417 Agostino Road, San Gabriel, CA 91778.
** ASARCO, Totowa, NJ 07511.

turers recommend that the interior bottom sections of steel filter tanks (the part below the underdrain assembly) be filled with concrete to eliminate anoxic conditions in the bottom layers of support gravel. This is a bad procedure, particularly where seawater is involved. The section of the tank covered by concrete is inaccessible for maintenance. Anoxic areas are far less serious than the corrosion that occurs on the walls of the filter tanks adjacent to the concrete. Only gravel or cobbles should be used in the bottoms of filter vessels.

Most conventional steel pressure vessels provide a small manhole at the top as the only means of entry. This makes changing the filter media or zinc ribbons difficult and prolongs the time that a filter is down for servicing. At Mystic Marinelife Aquarium, all steel pressure tanks have been modified to alleviate this shortcoming, as shown in Fig. 8-12. A circular opening 91.5 cm in diameter was cut into the side of each filter tank (183 cm diameter) and a hatch made of boiler plate 0.64 cm thick was welded over each hole. Steel face plates of 1.9-cm boiler plate with 0.64-cm rubber gaskets were bolted over the hatches. The parts of the hatch and face plate have a section of 0.64-cm-thick boiler plate welded to them at a right angle, each with a hole drilled in the center to hold a chainfall hook. The face plate itself is held in place against the hatch with 24 high-tension 1.27-cm steel bolts. When a filter tank needs to be serviced, it is drained, the face plate is unbolted and lifted out of the way with a chainfall, and the filtrant is shoveled quickly through the opening. Afterward the coal-tar epoxy coating is checked, zinc ribbons

**Figure 8-12**  Removable hatch installed the side of a conventional steel pressure filter vessel for easier removal of filtrant (Mystic Marinelife Aquarium).

are replaced and coated at the weld sites with coal-tar epoxy, and the unit is refilled with new filter media. Down time is short. The hatch and face plate assemblies were made to specifications at a local machine shop.

## 8.3  DIATOMACEOUS EARTH FILTERS

Technically diatomaceous earth is a granular substance, like anthracite, sand, and garnet, but in terms of function it must be considered separately from these other media. This is because DE is unsuited for filtering influent seawater directly; that is, until after the water has passed through sand, dual media, or multimedia. The role of DE filters in a water treatment scheme is therefore secondary, whereas that of the granular media filters is primary. Gravity and pressure DE filters are shown in Figs. 8-13 and 8-14.

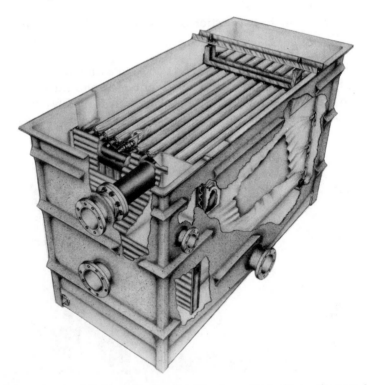

**Figure 8-13**  Gravity DE filter showing the filter bay with leaf-type elements (Keene Corp.).

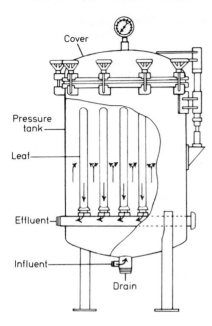

**Figure 8-14** Pressure DE filter showing the pressure vessel, gauge, filter elements, and direction of water flow (T. Shriver Co.).

## Theory

Diatomaceous earth filters remove suspended POC primarily by straining influent water through a dense layer of skeletal diatoms held against a porous substratum by pressure or vacuum. The small size, variation in form, and numerous ridges and depressions in a layer of diatoms means that a considerable surface area is available for entrapment of POC.

The septum of a DE filter consists of two parts: (1) a *central core;* and (2) a *filter sleeve.* Together they make up the *filter element.* The central core holds the sleeve in place and exposes it to the influent water. Central cores ordinarily are manufactured from porous, rigid poly-propylene. A series of cores is attached to a manifold. The sleeve is thin, tightly-woven polypropylene cloth that fits over the central core. Sleeves are removable. The sleeve supports a layer of diatomaceous earth called a *filter cake.*

## Factors Affecting Length of Filter Run

Diatomaceous earth filters are used only to "polish" seawater supplies that have been prefiltered by granular media, and the concentration of

**Table 8-6   Recommended Operating Parameters for Diatomaceous Earth Filters**

| | |
|---|---|
| Filtration rate | 0.05–0.15 cm sec$^{-1}$ |
| Precoat (dry wt of DE) | 1 kg m$^{-2}$ |
| Slurry feed (dry wt of DE) | 0.006 kg m$^{-2}$ hr$^{-1}$ |

POC in the influent to a DE filter is subsequently very low. The main concern is not how further POC removal can be effected, but rather to control factors that dictate the length of filter run. The filter medium of DE filters is not reusable and must be discarded at the end of each filter run. If runs are short, the cost of operation can be considerable on a yearly basis. The factors involved are: (1) thickness of the precoat; (2) slurry feed addition; (3) surface area of the filter sleeves available for filtration, and the filtration rate; and (4) grain size of the diatomaceous earth. Working values for these parameters are summarized in Table 8-6. They were derived empirically from personal experience and vary according to application.

*Precoat*

The initial layer of DE in a filter cake is called a *precoat,* and is illustrated diagrammatically in Fig. 8-15. Before precoating, the old filter cake is removed by backwash and flushed to waste, along with accumulated POC. A new cake must be started to protect the sleeves from becoming covered by DOC and POC, which would reduce their porosity. To precoat, water in the filter housing is isolated from the influent supply by opening and closing a series of valves. The water is then recycled within the housing. Diatomaceous earth is added and the filters recycled until the precoat forms. Filtration is resumed by diverting recycled water back to the effluent. The amount of precoat can vary, and should

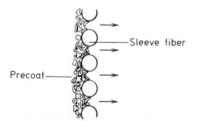

Sleeve fiber

Precoat

**Figure 8-15** Diagrammatic cross section showing the filter sleeve fibers and beginning of a filter cake, or precoat (Johns-Manville International Corp.).

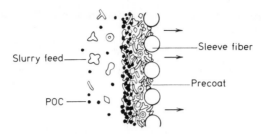

**Figure 8-16**   Diagrammatic cross section showing the filter sleeve fibers and filter cake porosity sustained with slurry feed (Johns-Manville International Corp.).

be thicker in waters containing high levels of influent POC. A useful rule of thumb is to use 1 kg (dry wt) of DE per square metre of filter sleeve surface area.

*Slurry Feed*

Slurry feed is perhaps the most critical factor affecting the length of a filter run. The precoat alone is insufficient to maintain the porosity of a filter cake. The accumulation of POC quickly clogs interstices in the DE and restricts water flow. The filtrate of most waters is compressible, diminishing the porosity of the filter cake as it builds up. Diatomaceous earth is less compressible, and cake porosity can be maintained by continuous addition of small amounts of DE, either dry or mixed with water, to the surfaces of the filter sleeves, as shown in Fig. 8-16. If added with water, the resultant mixture is a *slurry feed* (also called body feed).

The quantity of new DE that should be added in slurry or dry form is variable and increases with the concentration of POC in the influent water. There is no sure way of calculating the exact amount needed. Different concentrations should be tried at a constant feed rate until filter runs are extended to maximum. As a starting point, use 0.006 kg (dry wt) of DE per square metre of filter surface area per hour, then increase or decrease this amount as necessary.

*Surface Area and Filtration Rate*

Surface area of the filter sleeves and filtration rate affect the length of a filter run. Filtration rate is variable. A suitable range is 0.05 to 0.15 cm $sec^{-1}$.

Table 8-7  **Properties of Celite® Diatomaceous Earth**

| Grade | Color | Dry Wt (g $l^{-1}$ or kg m$^{-3}$) | Screen Analysis (% retained, 150 mesh) | Relative Flow Rate |
|---|---|---|---|---|
| Filter-Cel | Gray | 112 | 1 | 100 |
| 577 | Buff | 128 | 1 | 135 |
| Standard Super-Cel | Pink | 128 | 3 | 200 |
| 512 | Pink | 128 | 4 | 300 |
| Hyflo-Super-Cel | White | 144 | 5 | 500 |
| 501 | White | 152 | 8 | 750 |
| 503 | White | 152 | 9 | 900 |
| 535 | White | 192 | 9 | 1350 |
| 545 | White | 192 | 12 | 2160 |
| 550 | White | 290 | 20 | 2380 |
| 560 | White | 312 | 50 | 7500 |

Source:  Johns-Manville International Corp., Ken-Caryl Ranch, Denver, CO
80217.

*Grain Size of DE*

Length of a filter run is partly a function of grain size, or grade, of the DE
chosen as the filtrant. Grade selection is a trade-off between particle
size of POC removed from the influent water and length of filter run.
Smaller grain sizes naturally remove smaller bits of POC. Grain sizes of
DE available from two manufacturers are given in Tables 8-7 and 8-8.
In general, the finest and coarsest grades should be avoided when large
volumes of seawater must be processed. Several years ago, I tested
various grades of DE for efficiency of POC removal and cost effectiveness in the filtration system of a dolphin pool at Aquarium of Niagara
Falls. The pool holds $3.78 \times 10^5$ l and is filtered at a rate of 0.09 cm sec$^{-1}$.
Water in the pool is comparable to good-quality effluent from granular
media filters. It was found that Dicalite® 4200 or Celite® 545 gave best
results. Coarser grades resulted in longer filter runs and reduced
operating costs but poorer effluent clarity. Finer grades gave excellent
clarity but short filter runs and increased operating costs. The finest
grades of DE should be chosen when only a few litres of seawater must
be filtered for laboratory use.

**Table 8-8   Properties of Dicalite® Diatomaceous Earth**

| Grade | Color | Dry Wt (g l$^{-1}$ or kg m$^{-3}$) | Screen Analysis (% retained, 150 mesh) | Relative Flow Rate |
|---|---|---|---|---|
| 215 | Pink | 128 | — | 100 |
| Superaid | Pink | 128 | 1 | 120 |
| UF | Pink | 128 | — | 145 |
| Speedflow | Pink | 160 | 4 | 200 |
| 231 | Pink | 144 | 4 | 325 |
| Special Speedflow | White | 144 | 5 | 350 |
| Speedplus | White | 160 | 5 | 700 |
| Speedex | White | 224 | 8 | 1030 |
| 4200 | White | 256 | 12 | 1800 |
| 4500 | White | 256 | 13 | 1925 |
| 5000 | White | 304 | 20 | 2050 |
| 6000 | White | 320 | 35 | 2500 |

Source:   Grefco, Inc., 3450 Wilshire Blvd., Los Angeles, CA 90010.

### Design and Maintenance

Diatomaceous earth filters are available both as gravity (vacuum) and pressure units. In general design, they resemble the housings of granular media filters.

*Selection of DE Filters*

When large volumes of seawater must be processed daily, gravity units are clearly superior, although they cost more to install. Nearly any DE filter requires more maintenance than a granular media filter. The elements are fragile compared with a bed of sand or gravel, and the sleeves must be removed periodically and laundered or chemically treated to keep them porous. The working parts of a gravity filter can be inspected easily and are readily accessible. The parts of a pressure filter are concealed inside the filter tank where they cannot be seen without draining and opening the unit. Working space is sometimes cramped. Consequently a clogged or torn sleeve is less likely to be detected. During precoat, the water in a gravity filter can be recycled until it turns clear. With pressure vessels, precoating must be timed and there is no way of knowing for sure when the process is finished. The result is that some DE may be inadvertently pumped into the effluent once the filter cycle is resumed. This can increase turbidity downstream from the filter and interfere with physical adsorption and disinfection processes. Less equipment is needed to operate gravity filters because the precoat tank can be eliminated. The precoat tank is necessary in pressure systems because the initial layer of DE must be injected into the filter housing, as shown by the arrangement in Fig. 8-17. Diatomaceous earth for the precoat of a gravity filter can be sprinkled by hand evenly over the surface of the water while the filter is being recycled.

Both gravity and pressure DE filters can be purchased for immediate installation, and poured concrete housings for gravity filters often are unnecessary. Gravity units, such as the one shown in Fig. 8-13, ordinarily have housings made of fiberglass-reinforced plastic, which is inert and suitable for use in seawater. Pressure vessels can be purchased that also are made of fiberglass-reinforced plastic, but only small ones. Large vessels manufactured to withstand high working pressures would be prohibitively expensive. Large pressure units are made of steel and must be treated by the procedures described in Section 8.2 to protect them from corrosion.

The manifold and accessory plumbing should be entirely PVC. Some manufacturers use PVC manifolds and steel-threaded nipples into which the filter cores are inserted, but these are unacceptable. Only plastic nipples should be used, even is the plastics are different (polypropylene in the cores and PVC in the manifold). The reason to avoid steel is not so much the corrosion problem as the eventual stripping of the threads of the cores from contact with the much harder metal.

Filter elements are available in two basic configurations: (1) column; and (2) leaf. Examples of each are shown in Figs. 8-18 and 8-19. From my experience, column elements are superior.

In summary, the best DE filter is a gravity housing with PVC manifold and accessory plumbing and containing column filter elements.

### Cleaning

During backwash, the flow of water through a DE filter is reversed, just as in granular media filters, and the filter cake is flushed to waste, as illustrated diagrammatically in Fig. 8-20. Because there is no bed of dense grains to fluidize, backwash of a DE filter requires little pressure. All pressure filters and gravity filters with leaf elements are cleaned simply by stopping the flow of water, which causes DE held against the

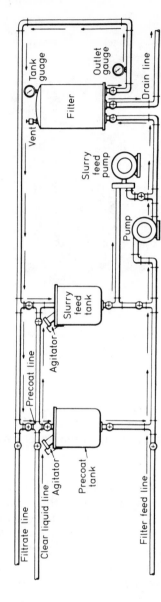

**Figure 8-17** A typical DE filter installation for large water systems showing the precoat pot, plumbing, pressure filter, and slurry feeder (Johns-Manville International Corp.).

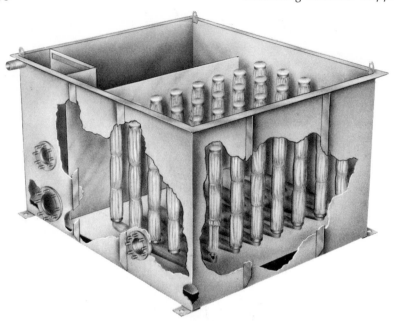

**Figure 8-18** A DE filter for large water systems showing the filter bay, manifold, and column-type elements (Keene Corp.).

sleeves by vacuum to drop off and fall to the bottom. The housing is then drained and the remaining DE adhering to the elements is washed off with a strong jet of water from a garden hose. Any gravity filter has the advantage of both methods: after backwash, the elements can be given a second cleaning with a hose.

The sleeves of any DE filter eventually become clogged by DOC. At this point, they should be removed from the central cores and laundered in a washing machine with a mild detergent and water softener. Polypropylene sleeves are heat-sensitive and should never be laundered in hot water. High temperature melts the material and closes interstices in the cloth. After the sleeves are laundered, they should be rinsed several times in clean tap water to eliminate any traces of detergent.

Sometimes sleeves can be cleaned in place after backwash. This is particularly convenient in large filters where down time of the filter and manpower to launder several dozen sleeves is costly. The signs that the filter sleeves have become clogged are: (1) shortened filter runs; (2) readings on the gauges that indicate a need to backwash immediately

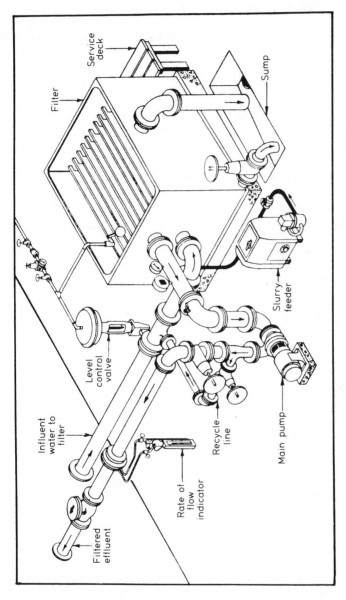

**Figure 8-19** A DE filter installation for large water systems showing the filter bay, plumbing, slurry feed unit, and leaf-type elements (BIF, General Signal Corp.).

199

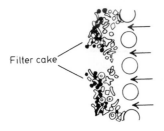

Filter cake

**Figure 8-20** Diagrammatic cross section of a filter sleeve showing the sleeve fibers and filter cake removal by backwash (Johns-Manville International Corp.).

after the filtration cycle has been resumed; and (3) bare spots on the sleeves after precoating.

A number of substances can clog filter sleeves, but the most common are DOC, iron, carbonate scale, algal growths, and manganese. The most prevalent is DOC accumulation. Spotte (1979) gave the following key to isolate specific fouling agents and take corrective measures.

1 Fill a pipette with orthotolidine or muriatic acid and squirt it on a clogged spot on an element. Let stand for 5 min, then rinse with tap water.

    a  The clogging substance does not change color, but the cloth turns white ......................... CA OR MG CARBONATE. Use *Treatment 1*

    b  The clogging substance turns red; after rinsing, the cloth is white ................................IRON OXIDE. Use *Treatment 1*

    c  The clogging substance turns dark gray or black .......... 2

    d  None of the above ..................................... 3

2 Dissolve several crystals of sodium sulfite in a few millilitres of orthotolidine or muriatic acid and squirt it on the gray spot. The gray disappears and the cloth turns white ....... MANGANESE. Use *Treatment 2*

3 a  The elements feel greasy ............................. 4

    b  The elements do not feel greasy. Squirt a few drops of 25% sulfuric acid on the spot. The spot is white after rinsing ........ ................................. LIGHT ORGANIC COATING. Use *Treatment 3*

4 If no positive results are attained at this point, the elements have a heavy organic coating, as indicated by the greasy quality of the cloth. This is most often caused by bacteriological decomposition of fatty components in fish flesh and oil (if fish flesh is used as food) and in animal excreta, although it is sometimes caused by algae. If the problem is recurrent, it can usually be traced to one of four conditions: improper

maintenance of the filters (e.g., careless backwashing which leaves the elements dirty, or failure to use *Treatment 3* routinely every 3 months), inadequate prefiltration, insufficient physical adsorption, or back-washing or precoating with old aquarium water ...................
............................................. Use *Treatment 4*

The following treatments should be used in conjunction with the above key. Before starting treatment, the filter should be drained and the elements cleaned thoroughly and inspected. Column elements should be backwashed twice. Both column and leaf elements should be hosed off with a strong jet of tap water from a garden hose (gravity filters). It is also necessary to know the exact volume of the filter. The chemical additives used in the various treatments are given per 115 l of water.

*Treatment 1*

1   Fill the filter with clean tap water. Do not precoat.
2   Be sure the return valve to the aquarium is closed.
3   Add 1 l of 34% muriatic acid per 115 l of water in the filter to make a 0.25% solution.
4   Recycle for 15 min, or until the cloth turns white. When a heavy concentration of iron oxide is present, the solution will turn brown.
5   Drain the filter and backwash the elements (or hose off leaf elements) three times in succession, letting the unit drain completely after each backwash or hosing.
6   Fill the filter with clean seawater. Precoat and resume normal filtration. The vacuum or pressure gauge should indicate zero after precoating. No bare spots should be visible on the elements.

*Treatment 2*

1   Fill the filter with clean tap water. Do not precoat.
2   Be sure the return valve to the aquarium is closed.
3   Add the same quantity of muriatic acid as in *Treatment 1*.
4   Gradually add 9.0 g of sodium bisulfite per 115 1 of water in the unit.
5   Recycle until the cloth turns white.
6   Drain the unit and backwash (or hose) the elements three times in succession, letting the filter drain completely after each cleaning.
7   Fill the filter with clean seawater. Precoat and resume normal filtration. The vacuum or pressure gauge should indicate zero after precoating. No bare spots should be visible on the elements.

*Caution:* Do not use this treatment without adequate ventilation.

### Treatment 3

1   Fill the filter with clean tap water. Do not precoat.
2   Be sure the return valve to the aquarium is closed.
3   Adjust the pH of the water to 5 with muriatic acid.
4   Add 0.38 l of 15% sodium hypochlorite per 115 l of water in the unit.
5   Recycle for 3 hr.
6   Reduce after 3 hr by adding 28 g of sodium thiosulfate per 115 l of water.
7   Continue to recycle until the total chlorine (see tests in American Public Health Association et al. 1976) is 0.0 mg l$^{-1}$ for three consecutive tests spaced 15 min apart.
8   Drain the unit and backwash (or hose) the elements three times in succession, letting the filter drain completely after each cleaning.
9   Fill the filter with clean seawater. Precoat and resume normal filtration. The vacuum or pressure gauge should indicate zero after precoating. No bare spots should be visible on the elements.
*Note:* It is particularly important that the elements be as clean as possible before starting this treatment. Otherwise the chlorine demand of the water may exceed the quantity of free chlorine in solution and result in incomplete oxidation of the organic film on the elements.

### Treatment 4

1   Fill the unit with clean tap water. Do not precoat.
2   Be sure the return valve to the aquarium is closed.
3   Add 225 g of Calgon® and 112 g of laundry detergent per 115 l of water in the filter.
4   Recycle for 1 hr.
5   Drain the filter and backwash (or hose) the elements three times in succession, letting the unit drain completely after each cleaning.
6   Fill the filter with clean tap water and recycle for 30 min, then drain and backwash (or hose) once more.
7   Fill the filter with clean seawater. Precoat and resume normal filtration. The vacuum or pressure gauge should indicate zero after precoating. No bare spots should be visible on the elements.
*Note:* Extra backwashing is necessary to remove all traces of residual detergent from the elements.

## 8.4  PROCESSING SMALL VOLUMES OF SEAWATER

Chemical and bacteriological changes occur within minutes in newly collected seawater, causing it to deteriorate and subsequently diminishing its ability to support life. The effect is more pronounced in small volumes because the magnitude of these changes varies as a direct function of surface area. Surface area takes into account the amount of suspended POC—including microorganisms—and not just the walls of the container. Consequently processing techniques must consider methods by which POC can be reduced at the start. Common practices are to filter small volumes of fresh seawater with a DE filter, microfilter, or both before storing it. Considered in this section are: (1) the nature of the changes that occur in stored seawater; (2) the methods of processing small volumes; and (3) storage practices.

### Nature of the Changes

From an aquarist's viewpoint, the most thoughtful and comprehensive summary of the changes that occur in stored seawater is the one by Atz (1964). Perhaps the most startling change takes place in the bacterial population. If temperature is eliminated as a variable, the growth of bacteria in stored seawater depends on two factors: (1) the surface area within the container, including POC; and (2) the nutrient level.

ZoBell and Anderson (1936) studied the populations of bacteria in stored seawater of different volumes and noted that growth rate was inversely proportional to the size of the container. The samples collected had an initial population of 932 organisms $ml^{-1}$. After storage, a 10 ml sample had 1,050,000 $ml^{-1}$. Further breakdowns were: 680,000 $ml^{-1}$ in a 100 ml sample; 251,000 $ml^{-1}$ in a 1000 ml sample; and 164,000 $ml^{-1}$ in a 10,000 ml sample. These results are summarized in Fig. 8-21. The seawater was filtered prior to storage, and the resulting bacterial population was obviously affected by the volume of the container. Simon and Oppenheimer (1968) found that in unfiltered seawater, the size of the container was not a factor in determining the growth of bacteria. By their own interpretation this did not contradict the findings of earlier investigators. Presumably the surface area provided by floating particles was enough to offset the surface area of the container, which in filtered seawater provides nearly the entire solid substratum.

Chemical changes that occur in stored seawater are the result of microbial activity, either directly or indirectly. Storage of seawater for 30 days "conditions" it in the same manner that a population of bacteria in a biological filter conditions aquarium water (Spotte 1974). Harvey

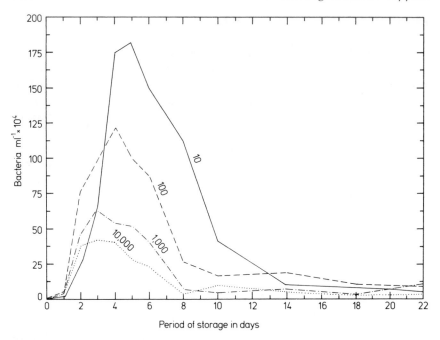

**Figure 8-21** Influence of water volume on the growth of bacteria in stored seawater. Different volumes tested (ml) are shown on the curves. Redrawn and modified from Zobell and Anderson (1936).

(1941) found that bacteria in stored seawater liberated ammonia, phosphate, and free $CO_2$. Autolysis of microorganisms provided substrates for oxidation by heterotrophic bacteria. Autotrophic species initiated nitrification by converting ammonia to nitrate. Thus the nutrients to sustain a population of bacteria in an isolated volume of seawater originate with plankton and other microorganisms present in the beginning.

Theoretically there are two reasons for storing seawater prior to using it in aquariums: (1) to minimize the chances of introducing parasites; and (2) to allow time for the bacterial population to stabilize. The first reason is valid, but the second is not.

Most free-floating parasites, such as pathogenic protozoans or fish lice, die eventually when no hosts are available. However there is evidence that storing seawater, even for months, does not stabilize the population of bacteria. Moebus (1972) noted that his seawater samples failed to attain stable populations after storage, even though some of them had been microfiltered and still others autoclaved. ZoBell and

Anderson (1936) discovered that although the total population of bacteria increased, the number of species in the storage containers declined. Some species disappeared entirely during storage. In a newly collected sample, ZoBell and Anderson cultured 25 to 35 species. After storage, only 4 to 5 remained. Storing seawater for long periods does not eliminate bacteria. These same investigators obtained a bacterial count of 209,000 ml$^{-1}$ in seawater that had been stored for 4 yr at 2 to 6°C.

## Processing

Seawater used in the routine maintenance of animals and plants does not have to be sterile, but neither should it contain unwanted plankton and other particulate matter. If these substances are removed immediately, the sources of energy available for bacteriological oxidation are reduced. Further deterioration of the medium is retarded because organic matter in any form is the precursor of ammonia and other toxic metabolic substances produced by microbial oxidation.

In small volumes, particulate matter is easily removed by filtering the water through diatomaceous earth, Whatman No. 1 filter paper, or a membrane filter. For removal of all but the smallest particles, McLachlan (1973) recommended a membrane filter of 0.45 $\mu$m pore size. Membrane filters and attendant apparatus can be purchased ready to use.* All components of the filter mechanism that come into contact with seawater should be plastic, glass, or stainless steel.

Microfiltration of seawater removes POC, but does not stop other particulate matter from forming afterward. Sheldon et al. (1967) demonstrated by Coulter Counter methods that soon after fresh seawater has been filtered there is a rapid increase in the number of small particles. This *in situ* phenomenon was thought to be physical in origin and not dependent on the presence of bacteria. Menzel (1966) and Batoosingh et al. (1969) showed that removal of the initial "seed" particles that might lead to the formation of other particulate matter could be accomplished, but required triple filtration through a membrane filter with a pore size of 0.8 $\mu$m.

For filtration of seawater at the collection site, McLachlan (1973) suggested that larger volumes could be pumped through a 193 mm diameter membrane filter contained in a plastic or stainless steel holder. A stainless steel or plastic pump should be used. Seawater can be collected, filtered, and bottled all in one operation.

* Millipore Corp., Bedford, MA 01730.

**Figure 8-22**   Diatomaceous earth filters for processing small volumes of seawater (Vortex Innerspace Products Corp.).

A useful piece of equipment for filtering small volumes of seawater with DE is shown in Fig. 8-22.* The unit consists of a 1 l mason jar with a small centrifugal pump mounted on top. Diatomaceous earth is trapped against a porous bag inside the jar. As seawater is pumped through the bag, particulate matter is removed by the filter cake and filtered seawater is returned to the storage container. When the filter cake becomes clogged, the pump is unplugged, the lid removed, and the bag washed out under a faucet before being recharged with new filtrant. The finer grades of DE are recommended for filtering small volumes of

* Vortex Innerspace Products, Inc., 3317 E. Bristol Road, Flint, MI 48507

seawater. Two readily available materials are Celite® Filter-Cel and Dicalite® 215 (Tables 8-7 and 8-8). They are comparable in grain size and both remove particles down to about 0.1 $\mu$m, but not consistently.

## Storage

Seawater can be stored at any temperature between 0 and 27°C, and no special effort must be made to keep it at one temperature in preference to another. Ideally stored seawater should be maintained at the same temperature as the water in the aquarium it will eventually replace, but this is not always convenient. Nevertheless if the aquarium tank is refrigerated, containers of seawater can often be kept in a nearby refrigerator or cold room.

The containers in which seawater is stored should be tightly covered to prevent contamination by dust, cigarette smoke, pesticides, and other airborne toxicants. The containers should be made of inert materials, such as polypropylene, PVC, or glass. Vinyls are sometimes toxic and containers made from these materials should be soaked in several changes of warm tap water (approximately 35°C) over a 3-day period. Concrete or wood containers painted with epoxy paint (Section 8-2) also are suitable after having been soaked in several changes of warm water for a week.

# CHAPTER 9
## Physical Adsorption

Some of the dissolved organic carbon (DOC) in aquarium seawater is *refractory*, meaning that it is neither biodegradable nor easily removed by conventional treatment methods. Refractory DOC thus accumulates as the water ages. Some refractory compounds may be chromophoric and contribute to the formation of the yellow color seen in old aquarium water. Biodegradable DOC also accumulates unless the activities of heterotrophic bacteria increase in parallel, in which case the biomass within the aquarium becomes greater. This results in more ammonia being produced, in addition to lowering the carrying capacity of the environment. Both refractory and biodegradable DOC provide seed material for detritus formation and may also be toxic under certain conditions. Some of the precursors of gelbstoff, for example, are known to be harmful to marine animals. Sieburth and Jensen (1970) reported that phenolic substances in the fresh exudates of the rockweed *Ascophyllum nodosum,* a brown macroalga, was initially nontoxic to plaice *(Pleuronectes platessa)* larvae. Under the alkaline conditions of seawater, polyphenol was converted to free polyphenol and had an $LC_{50}$ (lethal concentration at which 50% of the test animals died) value of 0.32 mg $l^{-1}$. Free polyphenol rapidly "tanned" proteinaceous and carbohydrate material to form gelbstoff, after which it again was nontoxic to plaice larvae.

The purpose here is to describe two methods of reducing the level of DOC in aquarium seawater. There are four reasons for keeping the DOC level low: (1) the concentration of toxic and potentially toxic

208

compounds is minimized; (2) less detritus is formed; (3) the unsightly yellow color in the water is reduced; and (4) the biomass of the aquarium is maintained at a lower level. Physical adsorption processes should follow biological and mechanical filtration and precede disinfection (Spotte 1979).

## 9.1  PHYSICAL ADSORPTION THEORY

*Adsorption* can be defined as the collection of DOC onto a suitable interface. The interface is the boundary between two phases, one being seawater. The other phase can be a gas or a solid. During adsorption, the substance collected (called the *adsorbate*) leaves the water and becomes bound to the surface of the gas or solid (called the *adsorbent*). If the chemical bond is strong, the adsorption process is irreversible and chemical adsorption is said to have occurred. If the bonds are weak, such as those formed by van der Waals forces, the process is one of *physical adsorption*. A weak bond means that the adsorption process is reversible, often as the result of a change in the adsorbate concentration. *Desorption* is the reverse process by which adsorbates that have been adsorbed pass back across the interface and reenter the water.

Physical adsorption is utilized in seawater aquariums when adsorbates are removed from solution by foam fraction or activated carbon. In the first technique, collection takes place on the surfaces of air bubbles (liquid-to-gas). When activated carbon is used, DOC is adsorbed onto a liquid-to-solid interface (water to activated carbon). Both methods lower the level of DOC, but are selective only in a broad sense. Much of the material taken out of solution may be refractory, but some biodegradable DOC is removed as well. In any case, the level of DOC is lowered. In the laboratory, this shows as a reduction in the total organic carbon (TOC) concentration, because there is no convenient way of measuring DOC. When used in series with a bacteriological filter, physical adsorption becomes an effective third stage, or tertiary treatment, in which organic compounds that are not biodegradable, or are too small to be filtered mechanically, can be removed from the water.

## 9.2  FOAM FRACTIONATION

Foam fractionation removes DOC from solution. The mechanism involves adsorption onto surfaces of air bubbles rising in a closed contact column. Accumulated organic matter is later discarded with the foam that is produced. The substances removed are call *surfactants* because they are *surface-active*, a characteristic of some organic compounds that will be discussed shortly. The term *foam fractionation* describes the removal of dissolved surface-active substances from solution. An accurate synonym is foam separation; less accurate ones are airstripping and protein skimming. *Froth flotation* refers to removal of surface-active particulate organics from water. To simplify the following discussion, this process is considered together with foam fractionation, with the idea that both are at work in aquarium water.

### Theory

When immersed in water, a surfactant molecule is polar at one end and nonpolar at the other. The polar end, if attracted to water molecules around it, becomes hydrophilic, whereas the nonpolar portion is not attracted to water molecules and is therefore hydrophobic. As the name suggests, surface-active molecules tend to congregate near the surface with their hydrophobic parts in contact with the air. This characteristic allows them to be concentrated at the air-water interface for rapid removal.

To be effective, the foam fractionation process requires a contact column in which air and water containing the surfactants can interact. Air-liquid interfaces are provided by supplying air bubbles to the contact column and allowing them to mix with water and flow to the top. The hydrophobic groups of dissolved and particulate surfactants migrate to the bubble-water interfaces, while the hydrophilic ends of the same molecules remain in the water (Fig. 9-1). The rising bubbles thus acquire "skins" of surface-active material. At the top of the contact column, the skins burst and form layers of foam. If the foam is stable, the surface-active portion accumulates, but the *residue* (water containing nonsurface-active substances) drains away. By removing the foam layer, surfactants—both dissolved and particulate—can be separated from seawater and discarded. Foam fractionation thus reduces the levels of DOC and turbidity in one step.

### Factors Affecting Foam Fractionation

Successful foam fractionation depends on the nature of the foam produced. Two important properties are drainability and stability. *Foam drainability* is the property that allows the residue to flow away from the newly formed foam by gravity. In foams that do not drain well, the pressure exerted by water flowing downward is enough to rupture the

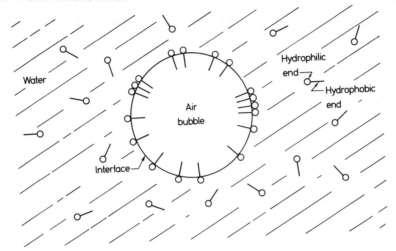

**Figure 9-1**   Diagrammatic illustration of an air bubble adsorbing the surface-active ends of DOC molecules. Redrawn from Ng and Mueller (1975).

bubbles of foam before they can be removed. Foam drainability is affected by foam bubble size, viscosity, and surface tension (Ng and Mueller 1975).

*Foam stability* is the property that enables foam bubbles to withstand drainage without rupturing. Unless a foam is somewhat stable, it will not last long enough to be removed. Foam stability requires that: (1) the film concentration of the surface layer be different from that of the water; and (2) the surface layer be of high viscosity. Other important factors that affect foam stability are the concentration of surface-active materials (also called bulk solute concentration), pH, temperature, and size of the air bubbles that are injected into the contact column. Small bubbles are more effective than larger ones because of their greater surface area for adsorption. Optimum values of all these factors provide a surface film concentration that is different from the bulk liquid (sea-water in this case), and which create a high viscosity in the surface layer (Ng and Muller 1975).

With one exception, all the factors listed in the preceding paragraphs are beyond the control of aquarists. The two primary factors that affect foam stability—differences in the composition and visocosity of the surface layer—are properties inherent in any liquid that contains surfactants. Temperature and pH must be adjusted to meet the immediate physiological needs of living animals and plants, rather than foam production. Surfactant concentration results from excretion of organic compounds by living organisms. The aquarist cannot control the rate at which these substances appear any more than he can control their composition. Only bubble size can be manipulated, and there are problems even with this.

The most critical factor affecting bubble size is the pressure drop across the air diffuser (Wallace and Wilson 1969). Pressure drop is a function of air flow rate and pore size of the diffuser. The first bubbles will emerge from the largest pores because less work is required than to force bubbles through small pores. Smaller bubbles appear as the pressure increases. Other factors affecting bubble size include such properties of the seawater as surface tension, viscosity, and density. In seawater that contains large amounts of surface-active material, the bubbles will be of smaller average size than in water with low concentrations of surfactants, because of the effect of surfactant concentration on the surface tension around bubbles. Smaller bubbles also are produced when either the viscosity or the density of the water increases.

Small bubbles have greater surface areas on which to adsorb surfactants than large bubbles. In addition, small bubbles are influenced more by fluid friction and rise more slowly. This increases their contact time with water in the contact column. Reducing the diameter of bubbles increases the efficiency of surfactant adsorption unless the bubbles become too small to break the surface tension at the air-water interface. Foam cannot be produced unless the surface of the water is broken.

Bubble diameter is a difficult parameter to gauge because the controlling factors are dynamic ones. The physical characteristics of rising bubbles change continuously from the moment they enter a contact column until they break at the surface. Furthermore uniform bubbles seldom are emitted in sequence from the same pore of an air diffuser. Often a stationary bubble is formed at a pore and remains attached there. New air enters and forces its way through the top of the original bubble. These secondary bubbles are smaller. If the pressure is increased, the stationary bubble is released and a new one forms. As any bubble rises it expands as a result of the drop in hydrostatic pressure. Moreover few bubbles remain spherical as they rise. Many become pear-shaped or elliptical from colliding with other bubbles or the walls of the contact column.

Bubbles sometimes join together between the release point and the surface of the water, especially when they are released in close proximity. Small bubbles gather gravitational energy when they coalesce and often gain enough during the ascent to break through the surface (Sebba 1962). Small bubbles tend to coalesce for the following reason. If two bubbles of radius $r$ meet and form a single bubble of radius $R$, the surface energy of the two separate bubbles will be $2\gamma \times 4\pi r^2$, where $\gamma = 80$ dyne cm$^{-1}$ in pure water. The surface energy of the single bubble will be $\gamma 4\pi R^2$. Total volume, however, will remain unchanged. Therefore

$$2 \times \tfrac{4}{3}\pi r^2 = \tfrac{4}{3}\pi R^3$$

and

$$R = r \times 2^{1/3}$$

The surface energy of the large bubble will be $\gamma \times \pi r^2 \times 2^{2/3}$, or less than the surface energy of the two small bubbles (Sebba 1962).

### Design and Operation

The design of effective foam fractionation devices is more art than science, mainly because the thermodynamics of the process are obscure (Lemlich 1972). From a chemical engineering standpoint, the important parameters to consider in the design of foam fractionation devices are the air-water ratio, bubble diameter, liquid height, foam height, and contact time between air bubbles and water in the contact column (Ng and Mueller 1975). Liquid height can be eliminated from consideration because the foam fractionation devices normally used in aquariums operate on the airlift principle. The liquid height in the contact column and in the aquarium tank are nearly the same. In such designs, foam drains away by gravity. The return of the residue to the water also is by gravity. Foam height depends on the nature and concentration of the surfactants, and on bubbling rate. Proper foam height and the methods of controlling it will be discussed shortly.

Bubble size and air flow rate are the most important design parameters, because they control the two processes that are potentially rate-limiting in foam fractionation: (1) transfer of the surfactant from the dissolved to the adsorbed state (mass transfer); and (2) transport of the adsorbed surfactant to the top of the contact column (solute throughput). The rate of mass transfer depends on three factors: the diffusion coefficient of the solute molecule, the degree of turbulence in the liquid column, and the amount of surface per unit volume to which the surfactant molecules can move (Wallace and Wilson 1969). *Solute throughput* is the amount of adsorbed surfactant transported per unit cross-sectional area of contact column per unit time.

Wace and Banfield (1966) determined that an ideal air-water ratio was obtained at a gas flow of 1.8 cm sec$^{-1}$ cm$^{-2}$ of contact column cross-sectional area. The ideal bubble size was 0.8 mm. Wallace and Wilson

(1969) studied the removal of surfactants from natural and artificial seawaters. They used bubble sizes that varied from 0.1 to 2 mm and a gas flow rate of 0.46 cm sec$^{-1}$ cm$^{-2}$ of contact column cross-sectional area. The extreme differences between these results and those of Wace and Banfield are attributable partly to variations in surface activity of the surfactants studied. Wallace and Wilson used highly proteinaceous substances such as bovine serum albumin, which were removed readily by foam fractionation. Consequently the design criteria of Wace and Banfield (1966) are recommended.

As noted earlier, small bubbles rise more slowly in a contact column because of the increased friction exerted on their surfaces by the water. Contact time can thus be increased by reducing the size of the bubbles. Another way is to design the contact column so that the bubbles must travel farther and be in contact with the water longer. One design technique is the *counter-current* method, in which the air and water move past each other in opposite directions. This increases friction and drag on the bubbles and reduces the rate at which they rise. In the *cocurrent*, or static method, water and bubbles rise together, just as in an airlift pump. The two methods are illustrated in Figs. 9-2 and 9-3.

In the cocurrent design (Fig. 9-2), air from a compressor is injected through a diffuser (2). As the bubbles rise (1) they mix, or "contact," with the water. The surface-active fraction of DOC is adsorbed onto the bubble surfaces, producing a foam at the air-water interface (3). As foam accumulates, it spills into a collection chamber (5). The collection chamber can be removed and cleaned. Treated water is returned to the aquarium at (4).

In the counter-current design (Fig. 9-3), water moves downward against a stream of rising air bubbles. In Fig. 9-3a, air moves from a compressor through a diffuser (4) and into the contact column (2). Untreated aquarium water enters the contact column near the top (3). In this design, the top of the column (2) also serves as a separation chamber, and excess foam passes into a collection chamber at (1), which can be removed for cleaning. Treated water is removed from below the surface instead of from above, as in the cocurrent design. Water passes from a connecting tube (6) near the bottom of the contact column and is airlifted back to the aquarium (5). In Fig. 9-3b, the mechanism is similar except that the contact column (2) is fitted with a larger outside column (3) that forms a sheath. The advantage is that untreated water in the contact column cannot be driven back to the aquarium by injected air, as it can be at (3) in the design shown in Fig. 9-3a. This makes the design of Fig. 9-3b slightly more efficient.

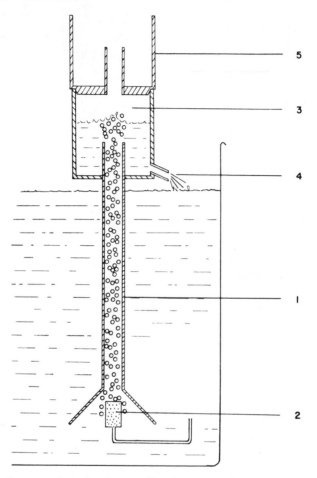

**Figure 9-2**  Cocurrent foam fractionator. Numbers are explained in the text. Redrawn and modified from Sander (1967).

Wallace and Wilson (1969) found that joints in their column created turbulence and resulted in reduced recovery rates of surfactants. Columns should be smooth inside, with no breaks or joints between the air injection point and the water surface. As mentioned previously, the air diffuser should be of known average pore size; it should also be made of stainless steel or fritted glass. The diameter of the column should be large enough to allow the bubble stream to rise without touching the walls of the contact column, as illustrated in Fig. 9-4. This eliminates

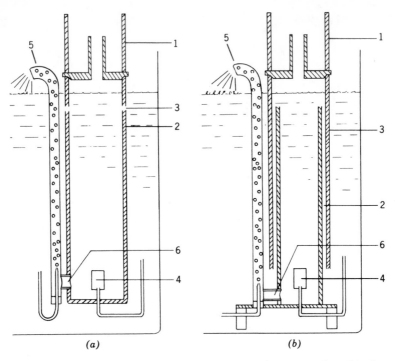

**Figure 9-3** Two counter-current foam fractionators. Numbers are explained in the text. Redrawn and modified from Sander (1967).

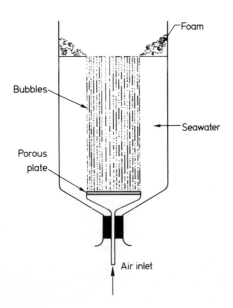

**Figure 9-4** Top of a contact column properly designed. The bubble stream rises without touching the walls of the column. Redrawn and modified from Sebba (1962).

216

turbulence caused when bubbles reflect off the inside walls of the column (Sebba 1962). This design also allows foam fractionation to take place at the center of a circle at the top of the contact column. The foam is forced to the edges where it can be collected and drained off. Nebel et al. (1973) noted that draining of the foam depended on the distance between the lip of the collection chamber and the effluent water level (point at which the residue is returned). They recommended that the distance not exceed 0.63 cm.

Foam height is controlled by the bubbling rate. If the bubbling rate is in perfect adjustment there is no excessive turbulence, the foam does not collapse before it can be removed, and surfactants do not reenter the water with the residue. The bubbling rate should be adjusted so that it barely exceeds the rate of foam collapse. If the bubbling rate is increased beyond this point, the removal rate of surfactants decreases rapidly (Sebba 1962). Foam stability diminishes with decreasing surfactant concentration in the water, making it necessary to adjust the bubbling rate upward.

## 9.3   ACTIVATED CARBON

Another means of removing DOC from aquarium water is to adsorb it onto activated carbon. Activated carbon is manufactured in two steps. The first is char formation, in which a carbonaceous material (e.g., coal, animal bone, wood, or nutshell) is heated to a red heat (approximately 600°C) to drive off hydrocarbons. Char formation must take place in the virtual absence of air to prevent combustion. The second step is activation. The char is reheated, this time to approximately 900°C in the presence of an oxidizing gas. The gas develops the porous internal structures of the carbon, which then become the surfaces onto which DOC is adsorbed. The size of the pores is not usually important in removal of adsorbates from a liquid phase (Tchobanoglous 1972).

It should be mentioned that the mechanisms by which activated carbon removes organic matter from water are unclear. Several processes may be at work and the overall effect may be additive or synergistic. Mechanical filtration in its many ramifications (straining, sedimentation, diffusion, chemical adsorption) influences the removal of organic matter at the surfaces and within the pores of activated carbon grains. Attached bacteria may also influence adsorption by altering the concentration and composition of organic molecules.

Activated carbon falls into either of two size categories: powdered or granular. Powdered varieties have more surface area, but they are more expensive and difficult to handle. I shall concentrate on granular forms. *Granular activated carbon* (GAC) can be defined as an activated carbon of particle diameter greater than 0.1 mm (Tchobanoglous 1972).

## Theory

The quantity of an adsorbate of species $i$ that can be taken up by an adsorbent such as GAC is a function of the concentration of the adsorbate and, to a lesser extent, the temperature. Ordinarily the amount of material adsorbed is determined as a function of adsorbate concentration at a constant temperature. The result is an *adsorption isotherm*. In mathematical terms, an adsorption isotherm is used to define the amount of adsorbate adsorbed per unit mass of adsorbent ($q_e$) as a function of the equilibrium concentration in solution ($c_e$) after adsorption at a constant temperature. A solution of known volume ($V$) and concentration of adsorbate ($c_i$) is shaken with a known quantity of adsorbent ($g$) for a period that exceeds the equilibration time. The adsorbent is filtered out, the equilibrium concentration ($c_e$) of the adsorbate in the solution is measured, and the adsorbed quantity is calculated as follows

$$q_e = \frac{(c_i - c_e) \times V}{g} \tag{48}$$

Actual adsorption data from batch tests can be evaluated by plotting on logarithmic paper the amount of TOC removed per unit of activated carbon dosage, or $(c_i - c_e)g^{-1}$ versus the TOC concentration in the residual, which is represented by $g$. The straight line of best fit through the plot is the adsorption isotherm.

When TOC is used as the adsorbate, adsorption isotherms in aquarium seawater with low densities of animals and plants are difficult to determine. The reason why is not clear, but it could be because TOC concentration in a heterogeneous solution such as seawater contains a high proportion of organics that are not adsorbed readily in the time period of conventional isotherm studies. Another reason could be the low values of TOC present in aquarium seawater to start with (usually less than 6 mg TOC $l^{-1}$).

## Factors Affecting Adsorption on GAC

The rate at which dissolved organic carbon is adsorbed from solution by GAC depends on several factors: (1) mass transfer of the adsorbate into the activated carbon; (2) contact time; (3) concentration and nature of the adsorbate; (4) particle size, pore surface area, and selectivity of the activated carbon; and (5) biological film on the surfaces of activated carbon granules. Temperature and pH cannot be considered significant factors because they must be controlled within narrow limits to keep animals and plants alive. Of the two, pH is probably more important. As Morris and Weber (1964) pointed out, adsorption equilibria generally are not affected much by temperature changes, particularly over the range encountered in natural waters.

As described by Tchobanoglous (1972), the adsorption process can be divided into three steps: transfer of the adsorbate through the film of water and biological film that surrounds the adsorbent; diffusion through the pores of activated carbon; and formation of chemical bonds between adsorbate molecules and GAC. Not all of these steps takes place at the same rate. The first two are rate-limiting; step three occurs instantaneously. Thus adsorption rate is, in effect, controlled by the rate at which solutes diffuse through the biological film and into the internal pores. Mass transfer becomes a function of steps one and two. The process is illustrated diagrammatically in Fig. 9-5.

The adsorptive capacity of a contact column filled with GAC can be increased by increasing the length of the column, or by decreasing the flow of water passing through it. Either measure increases contact time between seawater and granules of GAC. Dawson et al. (1976) found that the quantity of the fish toxicant TFM (3-trifluoromethyl-4-nitrophenol) changed from 7.1 mg removed per gram of activated carbon to 24.6 mg when the column depth was increased from 16 to 60 cm. When the flow rate was increased from 50 to 200 ml min$^{-1}$, adsorptive capacity decreased from 10.8 to 4.1 mg of TFM removed per gram of GAC.

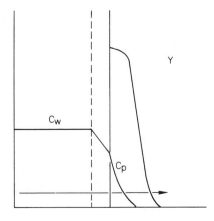

**Figure 9-5**  Combined film and pore diffusion model for adsorption of DOC by activated carbon: $c_w$ = DOC concentration in the water, $c_p$ = DOC concentration in the GAC, and $y$ = DOC concentration in the pore water. Redrawn from Sontheimer (1974).

According to Morris and Weber (1964), adsorption rate is partly a function of the square root of the concentration of adsorbate. In other words, a greater percentage of adsorbate is taken up per unit time in dilute solution and the process favors removal of trace concentrations of solutes. Nevertheless adsorption rate of a solute increases with increasing concentration, but the relationship is nonlinear. Morris and Weber also found that molecules of high molecular weight were taken up more slowly than smaller species. In addition, the configuration of a molecule was a factor that affected the rate at which it was adsorbed. Those species that were highly branched were removed more slowly than others of the same molecular weight but structurally more compact. These investigators suggested that adsorption rate could be enhanced by decreasing the hydrocarbon chains of larger chemical species. Chow and David (1977) also found that large molecules had a higher resistance to adsorption on activated carbon than small molecules.

Adsorption rate varies in part as the square of the diameter of individual carbon particles (Morris and Weber 1964). Once gathered at a water-carbon interface, diffusion of an organic molecule is rate-limited by its mass transfer into the activated carbon, as mentioned before. Particle size of the activated carbon also affects the rate of diffusion. Uptake is faster on smaller particles. This suggests that adsorption of DOC is faster on powdered activated carbon (PAC) than on GAC. However breaking up larger particles of GAC into smaller ones, although it may open additional pores, does not increase the adsorption rate appreciably (Morris and Weber 1964).

The pore surface area of GAC can be measured in general terms by its molasses, phenol, and iodine numbers. Each of these chemical compounds has a different molecular diameter and the extent to which it can be adsorbed is a function of how many activated carbon pores of that particular size are available. Iodine, as the smallest of the compounds, is used to estimate the total pore surface area in a brand of GAC. Molasses number gives an accounting of the largest pores. Pores that are intermediate in size between iodine and molasses numbers are identified by phenol number.

Activated carbons are manufactured by a variety of processes and from many different materials. Their adsorptive capacities for specific adsorbates vary considerably. Sontheimer (1974) found, for example, that a brand of GAC that was highly effective in removal of TOC from wastewater was ineffective in reducing the level of total organic chlorine (TOCl). The problems of selecting the right GAC for aquarium use will be discussed in a later section.

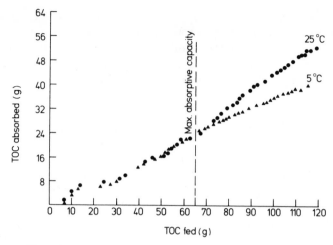

**Figure 9-6** Effect of temperature on the continued removal of TOC by bacteria from wastewater after the activity of the GAC became exhausted. Redrawn and modified from Maqsood and Benedek (1977).

The last of the factors that affect adsorption rates on GAC is the formation of biological film. GAC granules immersed in water soon acquire a biological film that is similar in all respects to those formed around gravel grains in a bacteriological filter (Section 7.1). The presence of slime has two effects on GAC: first, it interferes with mass transfer of DOC into the granules (McCreary and Snoeyink 1977); second, it accounts for continued removal of DOC after the physical adsorptive capacity of the GAC has been exhausted (Maqsood and Benedek 1977). Bacteria attached to activated carbon granules actively remove DOC from solution if it is biodegradable, causing a reduction in TOC. Maqsood and Benedek (1977) estimated that the number of cells was equal to $1 \times 10^9 \, g^{-1}$ of GAC in an experimental wastewater treatment column maintained at 25°C. The vertical dotted line in Fig. 9-6 indicates the approximate adsorption by the GAC to exhaustion. Continued removal of TOC, shown to the right of the dotted line, suggests that biological activity was responsible for removing DOC from solution from that point on. Greater removal rates occurred at 25°C than at 5°C, as would be expected when microorganisms are involved.

**Selection of GAC**

Ideally a brand of GAC should be selected based on the results of isotherm studies. Testing should be done with aquarium water, preferably using some measure of the DOC concentration as an index. Published isotherm studies done in single or bisolute solutions may give important insight into the mechanisms of physical adsorption on GAC, but the data cannot be applied to removal of complex organic compounds from natural waters. In my opinion, TOC is the most effective index for monitoring the organic carbon level in aquarium water, although the instrumentation needed to perform the test is delicate and expensive. The test for COD (chemical oxygen demand) gives a value for the fraction of the DOC that can be oxidized, but chloride interference in seawater makes any results of doubtful value.

Factors such as iodine, phenol, and molasses numbers are not reliable indicators of adsorptive capacity (Sylvia et al. 1977). Sontheimer (1974) found that in three brands of GAC tested for removal of TOC from wastewater, neither phenol number nor surface area had any relationship to adsorptive capacity. Johnson et al. (1964) summed up the problem of choosing a brand of GAC with this statement: "There are no valid theories that allow selection of the best active carbon in any single case without experimentation."

### Design

An activated carbon contactor should follow the bacteriological filter in series and precede any equipment used for disinfection (i.e., UV sterilizer or ozonator), as suggested by Spotte (1979). Some of the TOC will be mineralized by bacteria in the filter bed, which reduces the organic load passing into the activated carbon contractor and prolongs the life of the material. Disinfection is made more efficient if DOC and POC are reduced to minimum levels beforehand, as discussed in the next chapter. The recommended amount of activated carbon per treated volume of aquarium water is 1 g GAC $l^{-1}$. The material should be replaced a minimum of every 8 weeks, or when desorption starts to occur. The extent of desorption, or "breakthrough," of organic matter is determined by monitoring some aspect of the organic carbon (preferably TOC) in the water. The GAC should be changed before equilibrium is reached. Precise design criteria are not required as they are when foam fractionators are used.

GAC contactors for small aquariums (approximately 750 l) can be constructed from a length of PVC pipe, as illustrated in Fig. 9-7. Each end of the contactor should be threaded and fitted with removable caps for easier maintenance. The effluent end should have an inset perforated plate, a section of plastic flyscreen, or a plug of glass wool to prevent the activated carbon grains from being sucked into the airlift.

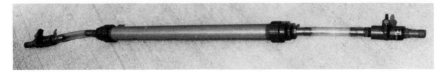

**Figure 9-7** GAC contactor made from a length of PVC pipe (Mystic Marinelife Aquarium).

The end caps are drilled, tapped, and fitted with threaded flexible hose nipples. The design should incorporate a by-pass arrangement that allows water to recirculate through the bacteriological filter when the contactor has to be removed for recharging, as seen in Fig. 9-8.

The GAC contactor shown in Figs. 9-7 and 9-8 is recharged by diverting the flow of water directly back to the aquarium, then unscrewing the influent and effluent caps. This step is easier if flexible hose is

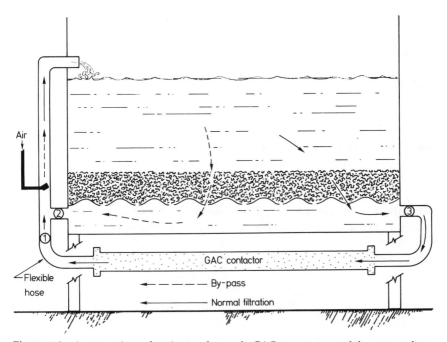

**Figure 9-8** An aquarium showing tank stand, GAC contactor, and by-pass valves. Valves 1 and 3 are open and 2 is closed for normal filtration. Valve 2 is opened and 1 and 3 are closed to recycle water through the bacteriological filter while the GAC is being changed. From Spotte (1979).

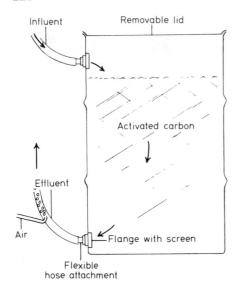

Influent

Removable lid

Activated carbon

Effluent

Air

Flange with screen

Flexible
hose attachment

**Figure 9-9.** Steel   drum   contactor
holding 100 l. From Spotte (1979).

used at the connection points instead of rigid PVC pipe. The exhausted
GAC can then be replaced with new material that has been washed in
clean tap water to remove the dust. The threaded male ends of the
fittings can be wrapped with one thickness of Teflon® tape to prevent
leaking.

A GAC contactor for still larger aquariums can be made from a 200-l
(55 U.S. gal) steel drum with a removable lid, as illustrated in Fig. 9-9.
The inside of the drum and lid should first be painted with two coats of
epoxy paint to retard rusting. Two 2.54 cm holes are drilled in the side
of the drum, one near the top and the other at the bottom. Threaded
PVC flanges (2.54 cm diameter) are sealed against each hole on the inside
with silicone sealant and stainless steel bolts, and PVC flexible hose
attachments are screwed into the threaded flanges from the outside. A
subgravel plate to suspend the GAC above the bottom is unnecessary if
a small section of plastic flyscreen is attached to the inside face of the
flange. This is adequate to keep the GAC from being carried into the
airlift returning to the aquarium. Influent water to the contactor should
come from a by-pass in the return line to the bacteriological filter. The
drum should be filled three-fourths full with washed GAC. One drum
should be used for every 4000 l of aquarium water.

Very large water systems require GAC contactors equipped with
mechanical pumps. Most granular media pressure vessels are suitable.
These units can be filled with GAC instead of sand and gravel. The best
designs include removable tops, or hatches in the side.

**Reactivation**

The adsorptive capacity of any activated carbon is exhausted eventually. At this point, the number of adsorption sites in the material is so reduced that DOC molecules are no longer removed from solution. The activated carbon in the contactor must be replaced or reactivated. Reactivation, or regeneration, is effective only when high heat and steam are used in combination to open up clogged pores and drive off volatile organic matter. Dry heat or steam alone is ineffective, as is the use of chemical oxidants. In any case, the degree of activity that can be restored declines steadily each time a batch of GAC is reactivated. No cost-effective technique yet devised restores the adsorptive capacity of exhausted GAC to its original level, and when small amounts are used it is cheaper and more convenient simply to throw away the old material and replace it.

Joyce and Sukenik (1964), studying the reactivation of ASB*-exhausted GAC with high heat and steam, found that only the larger pores were being opened. The molasses number of the reactivated material changed only slightly after 10 ERC (exhaustion regeneration cycles), from 195 to 188. The molasses number can be correlated with the surface area of activated carbon that corresponds to pores larger than about 18 Å in diameter. However there was a large decrease in the iodine number after 10 ERC (from 942 to 588). Iodine number, as explained previously, is identified more closely with total surface area. Joyce and Sukenik concluded that more of the fine pore structure of the activated carbon surface was being blocked with each exhaustion regeneration cycle. Parkhurst et al. (1967) used high heat and steam to study reactivation of GAC that had been used to treat wastewater. The iodine number dropped after each of the three ERC tests performed. The greatest decrease was after the first cycle (nearly 200 units from an initial value of 1100).

Joyce and Sukenik (1964) reactivated GAC that had become exhausted from treating a wastewater effluent. Reactivation was carried out in a rotary furnace that held approximately 3.78 l of GAC. The temperature was maintained at 926°C in an atmosphere consisting of 34% steam and 66% air, both percentages by volume. Reactivity was restored nearly to that of unused GAC after one ERC. No additional exhaustion regeneration cycles were attempted. Reactivation time was 14 min. In studies performed by Parkhurst's group, reactivation was carried out in a large-scale wastewater pilot plant. GAC was moved by conveyor

---

*Alkylbenzenesulfonate.

Table 9-1   Efficiency of Different Oxidant Regenerants on Activated Carbon
(Cliffs Dow 10 × 30 Mesh) Exhausted by Wastewater

| Oxidant | Oxidant Concentration (%) | Average Efficiency (%) | | |
|---|---|---|---|---|
| | | First ERC[a] | Second ERC | Third ERC |
| Chlorine water | 0.46 | 15 | 0 | |
| Bromine water | 3.50 | <10 | 0 | |
| $KMnO_4$ | 10.0 | 16 | 0 | |
| $Na_2Cr_2O_7$ | 10.0 | 61 | <20 | |
| $K_2S_2O_8$ | 0.75 | 49 | 20 | 0 |
| $Na_2S_2O_8$ | 0.75 | 55 | <20 | 0 |
| $O_3$ | 4.0 | 25 | 0 | |
| $Na_2O_2$ | 1.0 | 60 | <20 | 0 |
| $H_2O_2$ | 3.0 | 71 | 50 | <20 |

Source:   Johnson, et al. (1964).
[a] ERC stands for exhaustion regeneration cycle.

through a three-hearth furnace into which air and steam were alternately injected. Temperatures inside the furnace range from 926°C at the
bottom to 315°C at the top. Reactivation took 3 days.

Johnson et al. (1964) studied the ability of nine chemical oxidants to
reactivate exhausted GAC: chlorine, bromine, potassium permanganate, sodium dichromate, potassium persulfate, sodium persulfate,
ozone, sodium peroxide, and hydrogen peroxide. The adsorbate used
was ABS dissolved in wastewater. Some of the oxidizing agents were
able to partially restore activity through three ERC, but no activity was
evident on the fourth cycle. The effectiveness of the different oxidants is
summarized in Table 9-1. Additional studies were done using hydrogen peroxide, as it showed the most promise. Dilutions were made
from a stock solution of 30% $H_2O_2$. Different volumes of the $H_2O_2$
solutions were injected into a contact column holding 50 g of GAC. The
rate of flow was 100 ml min$^{-1}$. Best recovery (79% of the original
adsorptive capacity) took place when the oxidant concentration was
3%, oxidant solution volume 0.5 l, and the temperature 20°C. The
authors acknowledged that greater efficiency was attained at 20°C than
60°C, even though oxidation rates generally double for each 7% increase
in temperature. They attributed this to the increased deterioration of
$H_2O_2$ at the higher temperature.

## 9.4 EVALUATION

Physical adsorption processes should follow biological and mechanical filtration and precede disinfection, particularly when GAC is used. Mineralization by heterotrophic bacteria in the bacteriological filter helps to reduce the TOC load in the water before it reaches the activated carbon contactor, which prolongs the life of the material.

Foam fractionation is an effective method for removal of polar organic compounds, whereas GAC removes nonpolar substances more efficiently (Dawson et al. 1976). Adsorption of organics by GAC is preferred over foam fractionation if only one method can be used. Foam fractionators are more difficult to design and operate. Moreover adsorption of organic matter onto activated carbon is perhaps the most versatile means of lowering the level of DOC in water. Foam fractionation requires that the substances removed be surface-active. One of the dangers with activated carbon is desorption, and proper use of GAC requires continuous monitoring of the TOC level so that the material can be changed before equilibrium is reached.

Any physical adsorption method concentrates and removes trace ions from solution. Continuous use of foam fractionation results in severe depletion of trace metals in seawater. Wallace and Duce (1975) determined that trace metals associated with POC could be concentrated readily by foam fractionation. The species studied were Al, Cd, Cu, Cr, Fe, Mn, Ni, Pb, V, and Zn. Collected foam had more trace metal per unit of carbon than either the original seawater or the contactor effluent. Foam fractionation recovered more than 50% of all the trace metals that were bound up chemically with POC.

Activated carbon also concentrates trace metals and removes them from solution. Kerfoot and Vaccaro (1973) reported that just 10 mg of PAC was sufficient to concentrate complexed and ionic copper from seawater to 700 times its natural concentration. Both physical adsorption methods probably remove enough trace ions to interfere with the successful culture of algae.

# CHAPTER 10
## *Disinfection*

Disinfection is the destruction of pathogenic organisms by the application of physical or chemical agents. Disinfection of aquarium water ordinarily is accomplished by ultraviolet (UV) irradiation or ozonation. Either process reduces the numbers of free-floating microorganisms, but has little effect on infectious or parasitic organisms attached to host animals. It has yet to be shown that UV radiation or ozone produces any residual effect that is strong enough to kill pathogens after initial contact. Disinfection may be useful in preventing reinfection, but is not a substitute for antibiotics or other chemotherapeutic agents in the treatment of diseases (Spotte 1979).

Disinfection is affected adversely by the presence of dissolved and particulate organic carbon, and UV sterilizers or ozonators should be placed in series after the biological and mechanical filters and physical adsorption contactors. Ozonated water should be passed through another GAC contactor before being returned to the aquarium (Section 10.2).

This chapter attempts to describe the disinfection of aquarium seawater by the use of UV sterilizers and ozonators. But first a note of caution. Ozonation in particular is a difficult process to understand, and many of the proposed reaction mechanisms involving $O_3$ and water are controversial and incompletely known. Most of the work has been performed in pure water or wastewater, with comparatively few experimental studies having been done in saline water. The data derived from freshwaters are not applicable directly to seawater, because of differences in ozone demand. My discussion of ozonation is thus restricted in the number of valid conclusions that could be drawn on the basis of published work. Moreover descriptions about the efficacy of either UV irradiation or ozonation are plagued by much misinformation, particularly where disease prevention and treatment are concerned. Proponents of disinfection sometimes ignore unfavorable experimental evidence in preference of more palatable results observed in the absence of controls. In truth, the beneficial effects of disinfection often are not evident.

## 10.1   ULTRAVIOLET IRRADIATION

UV rays occupy the portion of the electromagnetic spectrum that falls between the visible light and the x-rays; in other words, the short wavelengths between 136 and 4000 angstroms (Å). The most active wavelengths biologically are those between 1900 and 3000 Å, and the most lethal rays are those at 2600 Å. UV lamps that are designed to sterilize have peak outputs at 2537 Å, because this is the most desirable wavelength for manufacturers to produce. As Herald et al. (1970) noted, 16% of a germicidal UV lamp output consists of wavelengths longer than 2537 Å. Ozone is generated in the 1000 to 2000 Å range and UV lamps designed to produce ozone operate at 1950 Å. From 2900 to 3100 Å is the antirachitic range, which stimulates vitamin D production. The portion of the UV spectrum that causes human skin to tan in sunlight falls in the range of 2800 to 3300 Å. A visual summary of this information is presented in Fig. 10-1.

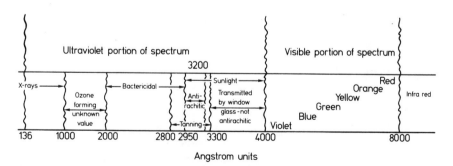

**Figure 10-1**   Ultraviolet and visible portions of the spectrum. Redrawn from Herald et al. (1970).

### Lethal Mechanisms

UV radiation can kill microorganisms directly by inactivating the deoxyribonucleic acid (DNA) within the cells, or indirectly by causing chemical changes in the water that produce toxicants. DNA absorbs UV light most strongly at 2600 Å (Deering 1962), or very close to the 2537 Å emitted by UV lamps. The lethal effects of this wavelength are shown in Fig. 10-2. Inactivation of DNA occurs when the molecules acquire lesions of pyrimidine dimers. The production of these compounds inhibits further DNA synthesis in the bacterium *Escherichia coli* (Poddar and Sinsheimer 1971, Swenson and Setlow 1966) and, to a lesser extent, ribonucleic acid (RNA) and protein synthesis (Swenson and Setlow 1966). Moderate doses of UV cause a marked lag in DNA synthesis in another bacterium, *Bacillus subtilis* (Billen et al. 1972). DNA inactivation causes cells to die or become nonviable in a number of ways. Swenson et al. (1974) found, for example, that UV irradiation interfered with a normal metabolic control system in *E. coli*. The formation of

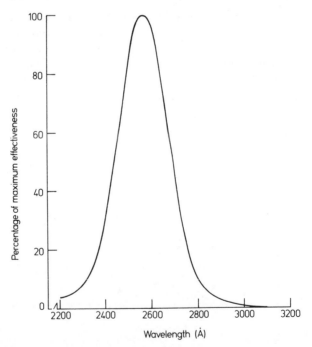

**Figure 10-2** Relative bactericidal effectiveness of ultraviolet light as a function of wavelength. Redrawn from Wheaton (1977).

excessive respiratory control proteins caused the organisms to stop respiring.

Resistance to UV radiation in bacteria varies not only with the species, but with the strain of a particular species. This implies that a "lethal" dose of UV is relative to a degree. Some organisms that are UV resistant can repair damaged DNA with only a temporary interruption in their viability. Repair is accomplished by excising the pyrimidine dimer, resynthesizing the damaged part, and rejoining the two ends of the polynucleotide chain. UV-sensitive organisms are unable to accomplish this. Setlow et al. (1963) noted that UV irradiation prevented colony formation in one strain of E. coli, but had relatively little effect on the colony-forming abilities of another strain. The authors correlated this to the different effects of UV radiation on DNA synthesis in the two strains. A strain that was sensitive to radiation showed inhibition of DNA synthesis at dosage levels that inhibited colony formation by 50%, whereas the synthesis of DNA in resistant cells was inhibited only temporarily by far higher doses that did not prevent colony formation.

The DNA repair process can lead to mutations. According to Witkin (1971), mutations caused by exposure to UV are brought about by errors in repair of the gaps left when pyrimidine dimers are excised. Strains of bacteria that lack the ability to excise pyrimidine dimers show increased mutability at low doses of UV (Hill 1965, Witkin 1966). Herald et al. (1970, 1962) anticipated that UV-resistant strains of microorganisms might develop in aquarium water that is irradiated continuously. This has not yet been demonstrated, but it remains a likely possibility. Feldhoff (1973) reported that a strain of *Neurospora crassa*, designated N51, showed a two- to sixfold increase in the number of colonies formed after treatment with UV rays. Wild strains were killed when exposed to the same dosage levels. Strain N51 had a low viability until irradiated. The authors suggested that a virus, perhaps present in the bacterial cells, was inactivated by exposure to UV, after which time the bacteria began to multiply.

### Factors Affecting Percent Kill

Three factors affect the percent kill of free-floating microorganisms by UV radiation: (1) size of the organisms; (2) radiation level; and (3) the extent to which UV rays are able to penetrate the water.

As a general rule, the larger the pathogen the more radiation required to kill it, although different species of the same size may show variations in their resistance (Hoffman 1974). Kimura et al. (1976) reported that 22,100 $\mu$w sec cm$^{-2}$ (microwatt seconds per square centimetre) of

UV reduced the numbers of five pathogenic fish bacteria and one strain of *E. coli* in pond water by 99.99%. The species monitored were *Aeromonas punctata* IAM 1646, *A. hydrophilia* IAM 1018, *A. salmonicida* ATCC 14174, *Pseudomonas fluorescens* EFDL, *Vibrio anguillarium* NCMB 6, and *E. coli* 0-26. The cell size of *A. salmonicida* is only $0.5 \times 2$ $\mu$m. Vlasenko (1969) found that the effective dosage needed to kill zoospores of the parasitic fungus *Saprolegnia thuretii* was 35,000 $\mu$w sec cm$^{-2}$ (LC$_{90}$) and 5000 $\mu$w sec cm$^{-2}$ (LC$_{50}$). The concentration of organisms was 60 zoospores ml$^{-1}$. Zoospores of this species are approximately 4 to 12 $\mu$m (Hoffman 1974). The myxosporidian *Ceratomyxa shasta*, which causes high mortalities in trout hatcheries, measures about $6 \times 14$ $\mu$m and Sanders et al. (1972) wrote that 215,000 $\mu$w sec cm$^{-2}$ was 100% effective in killing it, although lower doses might also have worked. The tomites, or "swarmers," of the freshwater parasitic ciliate *Ichthyophthirius* measures $20 \times 35$ $\mu$m and can be killed with a minimum lethal dose (MLD) of 336,000 $\mu$w sec cm$^{-2}$ (Vlasenko 1969) at organism concentrations of 265 ml$^{-1}$. The adult stage of this parasite is quite large (800 $\mu$m in diameter), and the MLD was determined by Vlasenko (1969) to be 1,717,200 $\mu$w sec cm$^{-2}$ at organism concentrations of 20 ml$^{-1}$. Hoffman (1974) reviewed the literature on MLD values in various microorganisms. Some of the data, acquired from other sources and summarized by Hoffman (1974), are given in Table 10-1.

**Table 10-1   Sizes and MLD of UV Radiation for Some Microorganisms Free-Living or Parasitic in Aquarium or Hatchery Water**

| Microorganism | Life Stage | Size ($\mu$m) | MLD ($\mu$w sec cm$^{-2}$) |
|---|---|---|---|
| *Trichodina sp.* | — | $16 \times 20$ | 35,000 |
| *Trichodina nigra* | — | $22 \times 70$ | 159,000 |
| *Saprolegnia sp.* | zoospore | $4 \times 12$ | 35,000 |
| *Saprolegnia sp.* | hypha | $8 \times 24$ | 10,000 |
| *Oodinium ocellatum*[a] | dinospore | $8 \times 12$ | — |
| *Sarcina lutea* | — | 1.5 | 26,400 |
| *Ichthyophthirius sp.* | tomite | $20 \times 35$ | 336,000 |
| *Ichthyophthirius sp.* | tomite | $20 \times 35$ | 100,000 |
| *Cryptocaryon irritans*[b] | tomite | $35 \times 56.5$ | — |
| *Chilodonella cyprini* | — | $35 \times 70$ | 1,008,400 |
| *Paramecium sp.* | — | $70 \times 80$ | 200,000 |

Source:   Hoffman (1974).
[a]Source: Nigrelli (1936).
[b]Source: Nigrelli and Ruggieri (1966).

Hoffman (1974) pointed out that the precise UV radiation levels necessary to kill fish pathogens have not been fully determined. Nevertheless some general guidelines can be established. Spotte (1973) recommended a minimum dosage level of 35,000 $\mu$w sec cm$^{-2}$ for the general disinfection of aquarium seawater. This amount of radiation is sufficient to reduce the numbers of free-floating viruses, bacteria, fungi, and small protozoans. Far higher dosage levels must be maintained to kill large protozoans. No information exists that describes the levels needed to kill still larger organisms, such as helminths and arthropods. It is likely that the amount of radiation that would have to be generated would make the control of these parasites by UV impractical.

A dosage level of 35,000 $\mu$w sec cm$^{-2}$ should be effective against the infectious stage of *Oodinium ocellatum*, a parasitic dinoflagellate that is often troublesome in seawater aquariums. This has not been confirmed experimentally, however. My assumption is based on the work of Hoffman (1975), which demonstrated that *Myxosoma cerebralis*, the freshwater sporozoan that causes whirling disease in salmonids, can be controlled effectively at this radiation level. The mature dinospores of *O. ocellatum* are 8 × 12 $\mu$m (Nigrelli 1936), or nearly the same size as the infectious stage of *M. cerebralis*, which measures 6 × 10 $\mu$m (Hoffman 1974).

Another common protozoan parasite in seawater aquariums is the ciliate *Cryptocaryon irritans*. The free-swimming tomites, which constitute the infectious state of the organism, measure approximately 35 × 56.5 $\mu$m (Nigrelli and Ruggieri 1966). They are considerably larger than the tomites of *Ichthyophthirius*, the freshwater analog of *Cryptocaryon*, for which Hoffman (1970) recommended a MLD of 100,000 $\mu$w sec cm$^{-2}$. The dosage level of 336,000 $\mu$w sec cm$^{-2}$, given by Vlasenko (1969), is perhaps more effective. The protozoan *Chilodonella cyprini*, which infects freshwater fishes, measures 35 × 70 $\mu$m, which makes it approximately the same size as the tomite stage of *C. irritans*. The MLD needed to kill *C. cyprini* was found by Vlasenko (1969) to be 1,008,400 $\mu$w sec cm$^{-2}$ at organism concentrations of 300 ml$^{-1}$. Because this organism is slightly larger than *C. irritans*, an empirical dosage level for the latter might be about 800,000 $\mu$w sec cm$^{-2}$, but this is only a guess.

The penetrating power of UV rays is affected adversely by such factors as turbidity, dissolved organic matter, and ions in solution (Nagy 1964, Huff et al. 1965). UV irradiation is slightly less effective in seawater than in freshwater because of differences in the concentrations of inorganic solutes. UV rays probably cannot penetrate water to a depth much greater than 5 cm under the best conditions. The control of dissolved organic matter, aggregates, and detritus particles is therefore of major importance if UV irradiation is to be effective.

Turbidity reduces the percent kill by shielding microorganisms from the lethal effects of UV rays. Sanders et al. (1972) reported that lowering the turbidity made the irradiation of water in a salmonid hatchery more effective. Hills et al. (1967) found that turbidity had a considerable influence on the percent kill of polio virus in seawater treated with UV radiation. At a turbidity of 70 mg $l^{-1}$, the survival values ranged from $1.9 \times 10^{-3}$ (a reduction of 99.81%) to $1.5 \times 10^{-4}$ (99.98% reduction) at flow rates of 15 to 25 l min$^{-1}$. When the turbidity was raised to 240 mg $l^{-1}$, the survival values ranged from $3.2 \times 10^{-2}$ (96.80% reduction) to $2.1 \times 10^{-4}$ (99.98% reduction) at flow rates of 5 to 25 l min$^{-1}$.

## Design and Operation

Wheaton (1977) described the types of UV lamps that are available and how they work. Lamps that produce significant amounts of UV radiation contain mercury vapor. An electrical current passed through the vapor excites the mercury atoms to different energy states. As the atoms return to their original lower states of energy, they give off radiation of defined wavelengths. All atoms have more than one excited state, and the particular wavelength emitted depends on the energy state at which the transition occurs. Phillips and Hanel (1960) reported that the probability for a particular energy state to occur can be improved by varying the mercury vapor pressure, the concentration and chemical form of mercury in the lamp, and the electrical conditions of the discharge.

### UV Lamps

There are high- and low-pressure UV lamps. Low-pressure lamps are used most often because of lower cost and the fact that approximately 95% of the radiation is given off within a narrow band centered around 2537 Å.

Low-pressure mercury vapor lamps can be divided into three types: hot cathode, cold cathode, and high-intensity. Hot cathode lamps operate on low voltage and are started with a ballast that is similar to the type used to start regular fluorescent lamps. Starting is made more efficient by argon gas, and also by a device to preheat the electrodes. The electrodes, which are located at the ends of the lamp tube, are made of tungsten filaments that have been coated with an oxide of barium, calcium, or strontium.

Cold cathode lamps can be started at low temperatures, mainly because they need high voltage. The nickel electrodes do not need preheating. Cold cathode lamps also operate at higher voltages. They contain argon and neon gases, in addition to mercury vapor.

High-intensity UV lamps have features of both the hot and cold cathode types. High voltage is needed to start them, but once in operation they function with hot cathodes. High-intensity lamps produce more UV radiation than either of the other types, and are superior from this standpoint.

Any of the three types of lamps can be used to disinfect aquarium seawater, although of the hot and cold cathode lamps the former probably works better in waters of high turbidity. According to Presnell and Cummins (1972), this is because hot cathode models generate more radiation (135 $\mu$w at 1 m) compared with 73 $\mu$w at 1 m for the cold cathode model in the lamps tested. Presnell and Cummins compared the effectiveness of both types of lamps in reducing the number of fecal coliform bacteria in turbid seawater. The hot cathode lamp was bactericidal when the flow rate was 16 l min$^{-1}$ and the turbidity 130 JTU (Jackson Turbidity Units). The cold cathode lamp failed to reduce the numbers of bacteria to levels equivalent to potable water at a flow rate of 18 l min$^{-1}$ at 90 JTU. It should be noted that in both cases, the turbidity level was far higher than would commonly be encountered in aquarium water equipped with conventional bacteriological filters. Most of the commercial UV sterilizers designed to disinfect water use high-intensity lamps.

*UV Sterilizers*

There are two types of UV irradiation systems, suspended and submerged. The submerged design is better because the units take less space and the engineering parameters can be controlled closely. Suspended systems consist of a battery of UV lamps and reflectors that hang over a shallow trough through which water flows, as depicted in Fig. 10-3. The lamps are usually placed 10 to 20 cm above the water (Wheaton 1977). If the lamps are too close to the water, radiation intensity may vary at different points in the system, and water splashing onto the fixtures causes a maintenance problem. This is magnified in seawater systems because the water is highly corrosive.

Reflectors are an integral part of the design of suspended UV sterilizers. Without reflectors there is considerable light loss: lamp intensity is proportional to the square of the distance from the lamp. Chief design parameters for suspended systems, as outlined by Wheaton (1977),

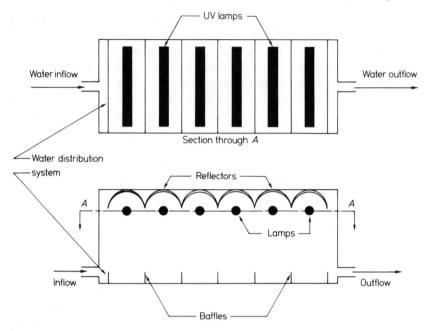

**Figure 10-3** Suspended UV sterilizer with reflectors. Redrawn and modified from Wheaton (1977).

include: water depth, quantity of dissolved and particulate organic matter in the water, lamp-to-water distance, spacing of the lamps, water flow rate, and design of the reflector.

One of the most copied suspended sterilizers is the Kelly-Purdy UV unit, described by Kelly (1961). It consists of 13 lamps suspended 14 cm above the water. The water flowing past must cross a series of baffles. The baffles reduce the depth of the water to 0.6 cm, enhancing the penetrating power of the UV rays. Presnell and Cummins (1972) found the critical turbidity level for the Kelly-Purdy unit to be between 43 and 82 JTU. This was based on the observation that at 145 l min$^{-1}$ and 43 JTU the water was sterilized effectively, whereas at the same rate of flow but at 82 JTU it was not.

Submerged UV sterilizers use a lamp immersed in the water, either directly or inside a quartz jacket. Quartz is superior to most other kinds of glass because of the higher percentage of UV rays that it transmits. The purpose of the jacket is twofold. First, it allows the lamp to function near its optimum temperature, maximizing UV light transmission. The effectiveness of UV radiation is related to temperature. Herald et al.

(1970) noted that a UV lamp in direct contact with water will operate at maximum efficiency only if the water is at least 40.5°C. At 21°C the lamp will function at only 50% efficiency. When a UV lamp is enclosed inside a jacket, the air space around the lamp provides insulation that allows it to operate at 40.5°C with the least effect from the temperature of the water outside. The second advantage of a jacket is that it makes changing a lamp easier. No seal is required around the lamp itself, as is the case when UV tubes are in direct contact with the water.

A typical design for a submerged UV sterilizer is shown in Fig. 10-4. Water enters the sterilizer at (1), flows past the UV lamp and jacket at a fixed rate (2), and returns to the aquarium through the outlet (9). As the figure shows, a submerged system, unlike a suspended one, allows light to be transmitted 360° around the lamp, eliminating the need to make reflector calculations. Moreover a submerged sterilizer purchased from a reliable manufacturer can be installed at any point in a water system. The same is not true of suspended systems, which require space in the design for troughs and batteries of overhead lamps and reflectors.

Any submerged sterilizing unit should be equipped with an intensity meter (Fig. 10-4), preferably with a narrow-band spectral response keyed to 2537 Å. An intensity meter is mandatory whether the purpose for irradiating the water is experimental or pragmatic. Without it, there is no way of computing dosage levels accurately, or knowing when the lamp has ceased to be effective. The housing and plumbing fixtures of

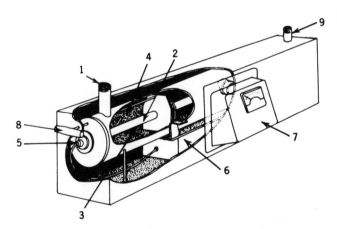

**Figure 10-4**  Submerged UV sterilizer illustrating the component parts: (1) inlet, (2) UV lamp, (3) jacket, (4) disinfection chamber, (5) lamp socket, (6) ballast, (7) intensity meter, (8) hand wiper, and (9) effluent. From Spotte (1973).

the sterilizer should be PVC or 316 stainless steel. Flow regulators and flow meters are two additional devices that make a UV sterilizer more effective. Dosage levels cannot be adjusted unless the flow rate is known. On larger units, ball valves should be used where the water flow must be adjusted with precision.

*Estimating MLD*

Dosage level is related inversely to flow rate. Before designing or purchasing a submerged UV sterilizer, this rule of thumb should be followed. Based on the volume of water to be treated, assume that a dosage level of $1 \times 10^6$ $\mu$w sec cm$^{-2}$ will be the maximum intensity required, and that at this level the entire volume of water in the aquarium should be passed through the sterilizer not less than once every 24 hr. A dosage level of this intensity is probably adequate to kill larger protozoans, such as the tomites of *Cryptocaryon irritans.*

Before an effective dosage level of UV radiation can be estimated, the flow rate of the sterilizer at a rated dosage level must be known, and the size of the infectious organisms estimated with reasonable accuracy. Specifications for submerged sterilizers manufactured by one company are given in Table 10-2, and the data will be used in the sample

**Table 10-2  Specifications of Some UV Sterilizers Used in Fish Culture**

| Model No. | Flow Rate ($1$ min$^{-1}$ cm$^{-1}$ lamp) | Dosage Level ($\mu$w sec cm$^{-2}$) |
|---|---|---|
| RM-2-1S | 7.57 | 36,000 |
| RM-2-1P | 7.57 | 35,942 |
| RS-5-1S | 18.93 | 39,409 |
| RS-5-1P | 18.93 | 39,409 |
| RL-10-1S | 37.85 | 45,203 |
| RL-10-1P | 37.85 | 45,203 |
| RS-20-4S | 75.70 | 39,345 |
| RL-50-4S | 189.27 | 36,192 |
| RS-50-9S | 189.27 | 35,503 |
| RL-100-9S | 378.53 | 40,697 |
| RL-150-12S | 567.80 | 36,253 |
| RL-200-16S | 757.06 | 36,246 |

Source:   REFCO Purification Systems, Inc., 2010 Farallon Drive, San Leandro, CA 94577.

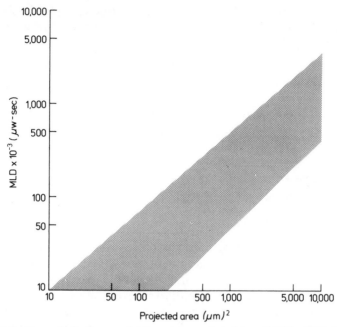

**Figure 10-5**   Zone of effectiveness for the minimum lethal dose (MLD) of UV of radiation at 2537 Å versus projected area of the microorganism. Use the upper portion of the shaded area for UV-resistant organisms. Drawn from data in Hoffman (1974).

calculation that follows. Size of the organism can be determined by using a microscope equipped with a measuring device calibrated in micrometres.

Once the size of the organism has been determined, the approximate MLD needed to kill it can be estimated from the graph in Fig. 10-5. Afterward the flow rate required to achieve the MLD can be calculated. Remember that the result will be an estimate only, because MLD data are not available for many species of infectious organisms, and data that are available do not always agree, as indicated by the width of the shaded area.

To take an example, suppose that an 800-l aquarium is infected with an unidentified microorganism that is 50 $\mu$m in diameter. The UV sterilizer to be used produces a radiation dosage of 36,000 $\mu$w sec cm$^{-2}$ at a flow rate ($F$) of 7.5 l min$^{-1}$ (Model No. RM-2-1S from Table 10-2). First estimate the size of the organism. Under the microscope it is seen that the cross-sectional area of a typical specimen is $(50/2^2)$ $(\mu$m$)^2 =$

1960 $\mu$m$^2$. According to Fig. 10-5, a conservative value for MLD would be about 100,000 $\mu$w sec cm$^{-2}$. Flow rate to achieve this dosage is found as follows:

$$F \times 100,000 = 7.5 \times 36,000$$

$$F = 2.7 \text{ l min}^{-1}$$

To compute the flow rate per 24 hr period,

$$2.7 \text{ l min}^{-1} \frac{1440 \text{ min}}{\text{da}} = 3900 \text{ l da}^{-1}$$

or five complete turnovers through the sterilizer per 24 hr.

*Maintenance*

The longevity of a UV lamp depends on electrode life, solarization, or both. Electrode life declines with the number of times it is switched on and off. *Solarization* is the slow darkening of the inside of the lamp glass with continued exposure to UV radiation. Some of the mercury that has been vaporized condenses on the glass, filtering out an increasingly greater percentage of the UV rays being generated. A UV lamp does not "burn out" in the conventional sense, nor does it dim or flicker with prolonged use. Hot cathode lamps are affected both by electrode life and solarization, with solarization taking place more quickly than in cold cathode or high-intensity lamps. The life of cold cathode lamps is primarily a function of solarization because the electrodes are operated in a "cold" state. High-intensity lamps, on the other hand, are affected mainly by electrode life. The effects of solarization can be measured on the intensity meter. When output has declined by 25%, the effective life of the lamp has been reached and it should be replaced. This ordinarily occurs after about a year of continuous use.

In submerged sterilizers, the formation of biological film on the sides of the quartz jacket exposed to the water reduces the intensity of UV radiation. In sterilizers that are properly designed, the jacket can be reached through a hatch and wiped off, or cleaned by pulling a hand wiper back and forth. A hand wiper is shown as (8) in Fig. 10-4. The lamps in suspended sterilizers can be cleaned of encrusted salt and dust by periodic wiping with a clean cloth. At such times, care should be taken not to look directly at the lamps because UV radiation can damage the eyes. A UV sterilizer should be shut down before cleaning or replacing lamps.

## 10.2 OZONE

Ozone is an allotrope of oxygen, meaning that $O_3$ and $O_2$ have different chemical properties but the same composition. Ozone in the gaseous phase is unstable, decomposing slowly to oxygen. The decomposition rate in air is slow at ordinary temperatures and low concentrations, but is greatly accelerated by heat. The unstable nature of $O_3$ results in rapid loss of the third oxygen atom through reactions 49 to 51 given below. Consequently ozone meant for the disinfection of water must be generated on site, because it cannot be stored. The salient properties of ozone are given in Table 10-3.

### Dissociation of Ozone in Water

In water, ozone may react with substrates either before or after dissociation. The work of Weiss (1935) and Stumm (1954) showed that the decomposition of $O_3$ in water is the result of a chain reaction in which hydroxyl ions ($OH^-$) serve as initiators. According to Peleg (1976), other free radicals formed by the dissociation of ozone include hydroperoxyl ($HO_2$), hydroxy ($OH$), oxide ($O^-$) and ozonide ($O_3^-$). Peroxide ($H_2O_2$) and molecular oxygen ($O_2$) also are formed. The most important dissociation product of ozone is hydroxyl. Baxendale (1964) found that the

**Table 10-3  Properties of Ozone**

| | |
|---|---|
| Symbol | $O_3$ |
| Molecular wt | 48 |
| Generation methods | Photochemical (UV) reaction |
| | Silent (electric) discharge |
| Specific gravity (air = 1.0) | 1.658 |
| Mass (0°C, 1 atm) | 2.144 g |
| Solubility in water | 1.09 g $l^{-1}$ (0°C) |
| | 0.57 g $l^{-1}$ (20°C) |
| Melting point | −251°C |
| Boiling point | −112°C |
| Oxidizing potential | −2.07 v |
| Absorption wavelength | 2537 Å |
| Color | None |
| Odor | Pungent, fresh (< 5 mg $l^{-1}$) |
| | Unpleasant, acrid (> 5 mg $l^{-1}$) |
| Toxic | Yes |

Source:  McCarthy and Smith (1974).

oxidation potential of this species was $-2.8$ v at $H^+ = 1\,M$. This is even higher than ozone itself, which has one of the highest oxidation potentials known ($-2.07$ v in acidic solutions and $-1.24$ v in basic solutions).

The free radicals produced when ozone dissociates become involved as *chain carriers*, in which one reaction is carried over into the succeeding one. Peleg (1976) suggested the following reactions for the different stages of ozone decomposition in water, with equation 54 becoming more important as the pH of the water increases

$$O_3 + H_2O \leftrightarrow O_2 + 2OH \tag{49}$$

$$O_3 + OH \leftrightarrow O_2 + HO_2 \tag{50}$$

$$O_3 + HO_2 \leftrightarrow 2O_2 + OH \tag{51}$$

$$OH + OH \leftrightarrow H_2O_2 \tag{52}$$

$$OH + OH_2 \leftrightarrow H_2O + O_2 \tag{53}$$

$$OH + OH^- \leftrightarrow O^- + H_2O \tag{54}$$

$$O^- + O_2 \leftrightarrow O_3^- \tag{55}$$

$$HO_2 + HO_2 \leftrightarrow H_2O_2 + O_2 \tag{56}$$

He noted, however, that knowledge of both the mechansisms and kinetics of ozone dissociation in water is incomplete.

## Lethal Mechanisms

Ozone acts as a protoplasmic oxidant on the cell membranes of microorganisms (Fetner and Ingols 1956). Farooq et al. (1977b) postulated that the disinfection process is limited by the chemical reaction rate of ozone at the cell surface, and not by mass transfer of $O_3$ through the cell membrane. The toxic mechanisms of ozone and UV radiation are quite different in that ozone ordinarily must penetrate the cell membrane before it is lethal. Once inside the cell, the effects that ozone has on intracellular DNA in microorganisms is similar to that produced by UV radiation (Section 10.1), although the nature of the ozone-induced lesion is unknown (Hamelin et al. 1977). Hamelin and Chung (1976) and Hamelin et al. (1977) demonstrated that at sublethal doses of ozone, bacteria can repair damaged DNA, just as they can after exposure to sublethal dosage levels of UV radiation.

Ozone at sublethal levels is known to affect the bacterium *E. coli* by producing mutations (Davis 1961), modifying the pyrimidine bases in the nucleic acids (Prat et al. 1968), and altering the genetic material within the cell, often before the cell membrane is destroyed (Hamelin and Chung 1974). These last authors postulated that at sublethal levels, increased permeability of the membrane promoted the diffusion of "active principles" into the cell, which altered the genetic material. Several investigators reported that sublethal doses of ozone selectively affect the nuclear material or nucleic activity of intact cells in some manner (Feder and Sullivan 1969; Fetner 1958, 1962; MacLean et al. 1973; Pace et al. 1969; Zelac et al. 1971). It is not known whether such effects are always indirect. Hamelin and Chung (1974) did not rule out the possibility that ozone itself was the "active principle."

It is commonly stated in the wastewater treatment literature that the effects of ozone on microorganisms are "all-or-none"; in other words, that contact of a microorganism with a lethal concentration of ozone results in immediate deactivation, provided that the organism is susceptible to oxidation (e.g., McCarthy and Smith 1974, Broadwater et al. 1973). The discovery is usually credited to Fetner and Ingols (1956), although an earlier discussion can be found in Giese and Christensen (1954).

The all-or-none effect is a phenomenon in which a threshold dosage level of a bactericide must be attained before any cells die. When that level is reached, all cells present are killed (Broadwater et al. 1973). This may be a valid concept in experimental situations involving only one species of organism, but it can scarely be applied in the case of wastewater or aquarium water, which contain many different species of microbes. These organisms apparently are not killed by ozone until their cell membranes have been penetrated. In a mixed-species population, the all-or-none theory implies that the membranes of all microorganisms present—regardless of species—do not vary appreciably in thickness, permeability to ozone, or chemical composition; in other words, organisms of all species present are killed at the same time when the $O_3$ concentration is brought to the threshold level. Such thinking is erroneous. Considerable variation is observed in the response of microorganisms to bactericides. As pointed out by Colberg and Lingg (1978), all-or-none data have been obtained in experiments using batch exposure of test organisms to different concentrations of ozone, and not from studies in which ozone was supplied continuously. Batch tests are less likely to delineate differences in ozone resistance among organisms. Colberg and Lingg demonstrated that no all-or-none effect was apparent in four species of bacteria subjected to ozone supplied continuously, even at low concentrations (0.05 mg $O_3$ $l^{-1}$). The all-or-none effect is useful only for comparing the activity of ozone with UV radiation, in which the lethal effects are graded instead of abrupt.

In the work of Giese and Christensen (1954), the dozen different organisms tested responded to ozonation in a startling variety of ways. Even when the dosage levels were lethal, the responses of the organisms were complex and varied. When the unfertilized eggs of a sea urchin (*Strongylocentrotus purpuratus*) were placed in ozonated seawater, the fertilization membrane rose quickly from the cell. The cell surface then erupted into the membrane. This was followed by cytolysis of the egg. The changes were much more dramatic when sea urchin eggs were placed in ozonated seawater 5 min after fertilization. As many as 15 granular buds appeared on the cortex. The buds separated gradually from the surface of the egg. Many coalesced and formed larger bodies that became wedged between the fertilization membrane and the intact egg cell. As this was happening, the egg itself remained intact, but there was no division. When sea urchin eggs undergoing incipient division (showing the beginning of furrows) were placed in ozonated seawater, some reverted to single cells and cytolyzed; the rest continued to divide but cytolyzed later. Much the same effects were observed in the fertilized and unfertilized eggs of the marine worm *Urechis caupo*, although some of the mechanisms observed were different.

Rotifers (*Philodina*) were more resistant to ozonation than protozoans, suggesting that multicellular organization confers greater ozone resistance, even when the organism is the same size as a protozoan. In the protozoans studied (*Amoeba, Blepharisma, Colpidium, Condylostoma, Didinium, Euglena, Fabrea, Paramecium,* and *Tillina*), all showed decreased activity when exposed to ozonated water. Injury to the motor organelles was common and some organisms developed vesicles on the pellicle, whereas others did not. When *Colpidium* cells were removed from ozonated water they started to divide at rates comparable to the controls, indicating that the nucleic acid components were not disturbed by sublethal doses of ozone. The color of stained *Paramecium* cells remained unchanged so long as the animals were intact. Once they had been badly injured by ozone, they were quickly decolorized, suggesting that ozone does not penetrate the cell membrane of this species at once, but produces its initial effects only on the cell surface.

When conditions are ideal (e.g., low levels of dissolved and particulate material, sufficient contact time, sufficiently high threshold levels of $O_3$), ozonation can kill up to 100% of the free-floating microorganisms. Numerous studies have been published describing the effects of ozonation on viruses and bacteria that are pathogenic in humans (e.g., Broadwater et al. 1973, Burleson 1975, Ingols and Fetner 1956, Nebel et al. 1973, Scott and Lesher 1963). By comparison, only a few studies have dealt with the effects that ozone has on microorganisms in aquarium or hatchery water. Conrad et al. (1975) found that ozonation reduced the numbers of the bacterium *Flexibacter columnaris* in water from a fresh-water salmonid hatchery, but did not draw any conclusions about threshold levels or contact time. Wedemeyer and Nelson (1977) described the effects of ozonated water on two bacterial fish pathogens, *Aeromonas salmonicida* and the enteric redmouth organisms (ERM). Both organisms are troublesome in salmonid hatcheries. In phosphate-buffered distilled water with no ozone demand (no significant amounts of dissolved or particulate organic carbon present), the ERM bacterium was eliminated by a residual of 0.01 mg $O_3$ $l^{-1}$ within 0.5 min, and *A. salmonicida* at 10 min. To match the 0.5 min contact time for a 100% kill, *A. salmonicida* required a dosage level of 0.04 mg $O_3$ $l^{-1}$. In soft and hard lake waters, a considerably higher dosage level (90 mg $l^{-1}$ $hr^{-1}$) was needed to effectively destroy both organisms within 10 min. Disinfection was more difficult in hard water, as might be expected, considering that raising the cation concentration of water may accelerate the dissociation rate of ozone. This, in turn, lessens the germicidal effectiveness, as will be discussed in another section. Schlesner and Rheinheimer (1974) applied ozone to aquarium seawater and observed a decrease in the number of microorganisms. However the dosage used was considered too small to be germicidal in such a high ozone demand environment, and the authors attributed their results to physical entrapment of microorganisms in the foam produced during ozonation. As Farooq et al. (1977a) pointed out, most of the studies that describe the percent kill of microorganisms with ozone have used single species in pure solutions. Such studies are of value because they deal with the mechanisms of disinfection under ideal conditions, but the data cannot be applied directly to wastewater or aquarium waters, which are high in inorganic and organic compounds that interfere with disinfection and contain microorganisms of many species.

### Factors Affecting Percent Kill

Factors that influence the dissociation rate of ozone in water also affect the percent kill of free-floating microorganisms. This is probably caused by the chemical state of ozone in solution, which affects its reactivity. Before following this line of reasoning, three assumptions must be made. First, dissociated ozone reacts with DOC in preference to POC. Included in the POC are free-floating microorganisms. Second, pH *per se* does not interfere with disinfection directly, but indirectly by controlling the rate at which $O_3$ dissociates, as shown by Farooq et al.

(1977a). Third, conditions that prolong contact time with undissociated $O_3$ probably result in increased percent kills of microorganisms. This was also demonstrated by Farooq et al. (1977a), but the subject is controversial. The same authors showed in another paper (Farooq et al. 1977b) that disinfection was more efficient at high temperature, because of the faster reaction rate with microorganisms, despite the increase in the decomposition rate of $O_3$. Evidently the increase in the disinfection reaction rate more than counterbalances the rapidly decreasing ozone concentration at higher temperatures.

There are two primary pathways by which susceptible species of DOC, POC, and inorganic ions are attacked by ozone. I shall call them Pathways 1 and 2. In water that is acidic or contains solutes that react quickly with $O_3$ molecules, the mechanism is one of direct reactivity. Typical organic compounds affected in this way are those that are unsaturated, chromophoric, or contain amino groups (Hoigné and Bader 1976). This is Pathway 1. Farooq et al. (1977b) and Giese and Christensen (1954) postulated that the disinfection process is limited by chemical reaction rates of ozone at cell surfaces, and not by the mass transfer of $O_3$ through the cell membrane, as mentioned previously. This indicates that: (1) longer contact times are required to kill microorganisms than to oxidize DOC or inorganic ions; and (2) disinfection is more effective with undissociated $O_3$. Disinfection is thus a function of Pathway 1, even though the "solutes" (microorganisms in this case) do not react quickly with oxidants. If no reaction occurs, either with a microorganism, DOC molecule, or inorganic ion, and the $O_3$ molecule dissociates, then free radicals (mainly OH) become the main oxidative species. This is Pathway 2, the means by which DOC and inorganic ions are oxidized.

The basis for Pathways 1 and 2 was proposed by Hoigné and Bader (1976) in the scheme illustrated in Fig. 10-6. As shown, $O_3$ reacts directly with the substrates ($S$) below a critical pH value (Pathway 1). Above that value, ozone decomposes prior to reacting with $S$. At this point, the dissociation products of ozone become the important oxidants and not $O_3$ itself (Pathway 2). The critical pH value at which the transition occurs depends on the rate at which undissociated ozone reacts with $S$, and also on the presence of any solutes ($S'$), including the dissociation products of ozone itself, that speed up or inhibit $O_3$ decomposition.

The factors that affect the dissociation rate of ozone in water are: (1) DOC concentration; (2) POC concentration, including microorganism cell density; (3) the concentration and species of inorganic ions in solution; (4) pH; and (5) temperature. The first four factors are some-

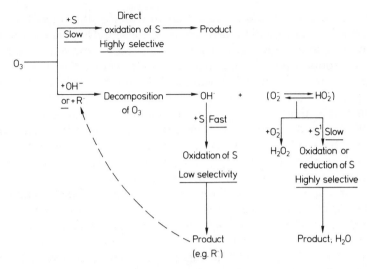

**Figure 10-6**  Schematic illustration showing the reactions of substrates (S) with $O_3$ and the competition for $O_3$ by ozone decomposition reaction products. Redrawn from Hoigné and Bader (1976).

times called the *ozone demand,* because an increase in any of them raises the threshold level of ozone needed for disinfection. Generally increases in DOC, POC, ionic strength of the water, or pH result in lower percent kills, whereas the kill rate increases with increasing temperature.

### DOC and POC

In chain carrier reactions involving the ozonation of water, conditions that accelerate prior $O_3$ decomposition often are favorable for the oxidation of DOC and inorganic ions by Pathway 2 (Huibers et al. 1969, Singer and Zilli 1975). This is not true when ozone is used as a disinfectant. Microorganisms must be considered particulate matter for ozonation purposes. In water that is high in DOC, free radicals formed by the dissociation of $O_3$, or $O_3$ itself, may be expended before encountering microorganisms, because the mean free path between DOC molecules is many orders of magnitude smaller than the mean free path between microorganisms. Such reasoning explains the results of Hoigné and Bader (1976), who reported that when microorganisms and DOC were present together, hydroxyl radicals reacted preferentially with DOC. Hoigné and Bader stated further that oxidation of particulate matter is a low-yield process under conditions in which the direct reactions of free radicals are relied on in water containing DOC. Thus the factors enhancing the reactivity of ozone with DOC often hinder its ability to oxidize POC, and vice versa. In some situations, the results can be pronounced. Gevaudan et al. (1971) showed that in distilled water containing 25 mg $l^{-1}$ of lactoalbumin and 50 mg $l^{-1}$ kaolin that 50 mg $O_3$ $l^{-1}$ were required to inactivate polio virus. With no organic matter and 50 mg $l^{-1}$ kaolin, only 0.16 mg $O_3$ $l^{-1}$ was needed. Farooq et al. (1977a) tested the effects that the initial density of microorganisms in clean freshwater had on disinfection. A yeast, *Candida parapsilosus*, was the test organism. The quantity of ozone used was 0.15 mg $l^{-1}$ and DOC was measured as TOC. In the first test solution there was a four-log reduction when the yeast cell density was $1.35 \times 10^5$ $ml^{-1}$, whereas no noticeable reduction occurred in the second solution in which the cell density was $1.55 \times 10^7$ $ml^{-1}$. When TOC values were compared, it was seen that the first test solution had a value of only 4 mg TOC $l^{-1}$, compared to 120 mg $TOC^{-1}$ in the second. These elevated TOC values were contributed primarily by the yeast cells. The authors concluded that a fraction of the DOC had been attacked preferentially by ozone, which resulted in reduced disinfection efficiency.

In the same study it was shown that the number of microorganisms per volume of water ozonated was an influential factor. The higher the cell density, the lower the disinfection rate. Microorganisms contribute to the POC, as stated previously, and POC in general reduces the effectiveness of ozonation, whether the fraction oxidized consists of particles, aggregates, detritus, or living microbes.

*pH and Temperature*

Temperature and pH affect the oxidation rate of DOC indirectly by controlling the rate of $O_3$ decomposition, assuming that DOC oxidation is accelerated by the presence of free radicals of ozone. As ozone dissociates with increases in either pH or temperature, oxidation is enhanced by chain reactions as the dissociation products themselves react with $O_3$ (see equations 50 and 51). Hewes and Davidson (1972) showed that the speed at which DOC was oxidized increased with increasing temperature and pH. In interpreting their results, Peleg (1976) pointed out that both factors affect the dissociation rate of $O_3$, indicating that the decomposition products are what control the oxidation process (Pathway 2) and not temperature or pH *per se*.

The percent kill of microorganisms is related inversely to increasing pH. Farooq et al. (1977a) found that the germicidal effectiveness of ozone in clean freshwater depended on the actual ozone residual (undissociated $O_3$) in the contact chamber. They noted that disinfection

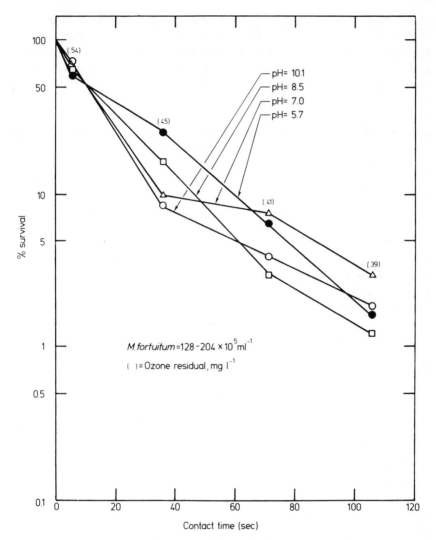

**Figure 10-7**   Effect of pH on the survival of *M. fortuitum*, a yeast, at a constant rate of applied ozone. Redrawn and modified from Farooq et al. (1977a).

was more effective at low pH values because a rise in pH resulted in accelerated decomposition of $O_3$ molecules. Some of the results are shown in Fig. 10-7. The data depict clearly how the kill rate of the yeast *Mycobacterium fortuitum* was similar at constant levels of ozone but four different pH values, indicating that pH had no direct effect on percent kill.

The relationship between temperature and disinfection is direct, and higher kill rates occur at elevated temperatures. Until the work of Farooq et al. (1977b), it had been assumed that changes in temperature had no effect on disinfection with ozone. Leiguarda et al. (1949) reported that the bactericidal activity of $O_3$ was unaffected by temperature. Kinman (1972) wrote that the germicidal strength of ozone at two temperatures (25 and 39°C) was the same. Using *Mycobacterium fortuitum* as the test organism, Farooq et al. (1977b) found that the degree of inactivation was affected significantly by temperature at constant dosage levels of ozone, with the degree of inactivation being less dependent on ozone residual. An increase in temperature caused a higher kill rate, even when the $O_3$ residual was considerably less (Fig. 10-8). In a second series of experiments, a constant ozone residual was maintained at a given contact time for four different temperatures (9, 20, 30, and 37°C). This was done by changing the partial pressure of ozone in the feed gas. The flow rate of ozonated air was kept constant at 0.5 l min$^{-1}$. As shown in Fig. 10-9, the degree of inactivation increased significantly with increasing temperature for a given ozone residual concentration.

*Inorganic Ions*

The presence of oxidizable inorganic ions in water accelerates the decomposition of ozone (Mangum and McIlhenny 1975), interfering with disinfection. Seawater contains greater concentrations of most inorganic species than freshwater and is more difficult to disinfect. Little has been written on how inorganic ions influence ozonation processes in seawater, and the subject is poorly understood at this time. The elements chlorine, bromine, iron, iodine, and manganese are particularly subject to oxidation in several chemical states in which they exist in seawater. Ozonation of seawater is known to oxidize iron and manganese to higher positive oxidation valences where each is less soluble (Mangum and McIlhenny 1975). The simplified reactions, according to Keenan and Hegemann (1978), are

$$Fe^{2+} + O_3 + H_2O \rightleftharpoons Fe(OH)_3 + O_2 + H_2O \qquad (57)$$

$$Mn^{2+} + O_3 + H_2O \rightleftharpoons MnO_2 + O_2 + H_2O \qquad (58)$$

Keenan and Hegemann (1978) also suggested that sulfur is oxidized by ozone, resulting in the formation of elemental sulfur or sulfate, as shown by

$$S^{2-} + O_3 + H_2O \rightleftharpoons S + 2OH^- + O_2 \qquad (59)$$

$$S^{2-} + 4O_3 \rightleftharpoons SO_4^{2-} + 4O_2 \qquad (60)$$

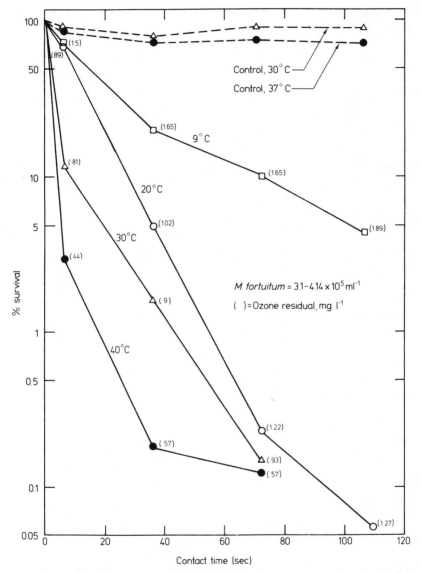

**Figure 10-8** Effect of temperature on the survival of *M. fortuitum* at a constant rate of applied ozone. Redrawn and modified from Farooq et al. (1977b).

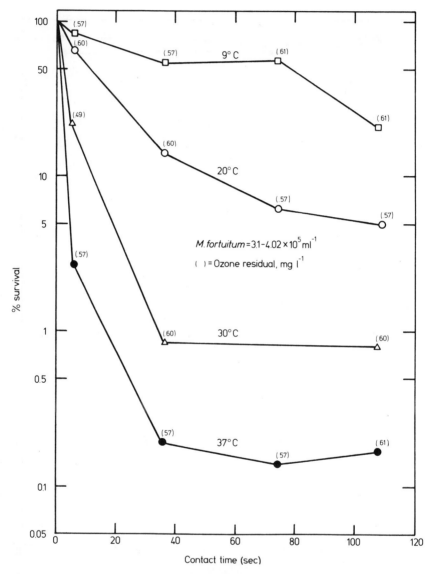

**Figure 10-9** Effect of temperature on the survival of *M. fortuitum* for a constant ozone residual at a given contact time. Redrawn and modified from Farooq et al. (1977b).

## Ozone Generation

Ozone can be produced either photochemically or by electrical discharge, and modern ozone generators, or ozonators, are of two general types: (1) UV and (2) silent (electrical) discharge. UV generators commonly are used where low ozone concentrations are required. The small ozonators designed for the home aquarium market are of this type. If oxygen is used as the feed gas, these generators produce approximately $1 \text{ g O}_3 \text{ hr}^{-1}$ at a concentration of 1 to $10 \text{ mg O}_3 \text{ l}^{-1}$ in the output gas. If an air feed is used, the output is at least 50% less. Depending on the design of the unit, feed gas flows either directly past the UV lamp or through an adjacent quartz jacket. In UV generators the output, or yield, of ozone is a function of the total effective radiation emitted in the range 1000 to 2000 Å. This, in turn, is dependent on design of the UV lamp and its total emission area, lamp current, feed gas composition (oxygen or air flow), feed gas pressure in the air space or *discharge gap*, and temperature of the feed gas.

Silent discharge generators are used where high yields of ozone are required, such as in public aquariums, fish hatcheries, and aquaculture installations. Silent discharge ozonators can produce up to 6% wt of ozone, but most efficient production occurs at 1 to 3% wt output. In simple terms, a silent discharge ozonator is an alternating voltage applied across two electrodes separated by an insulator, or *dielectric*, in a discharge gap (Fig. 10-10). The discharge gap must contain a dielectric

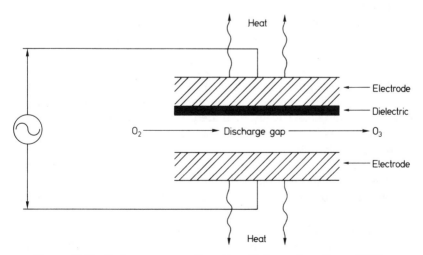

**Figure 10-10**   Basic ozonator configuration. Redrawn from Rosen (1973).

for ozone production to occur; otherwise there would be nothing but a spark or an arc. In addition, the current must alternate because none of it can pass through the dielectric. The insulating material collects charges of electrons on its surface during a half-cycle of the alternating current and releases them when the polarity reverses.

When the ozonator is working, the discharge gap is filled with a diffused glow called the *corona*. The electrodes are usually made of stainless steel and aluminum and the dielectric is borosilicate glass. One electrode is contiguous with the glass dielectric; the discharge gap is located between the dielectric and the second electrode, as seen in Fig. 10-10. The distance of the discharge gap at voltages less than 1500 v is commonly 1 to 3 mm. Silent discharge ozonators transform most of the input electrical energy into heat, and some form of cooling is necessary unless the gas flow entering the discharge gap is high in proportion to electrode area. Too high a gas flow, however, reduces the efficiency of ozone production.

Ozone output of a silent discharge generator is a function of the oxygen purity of the feed gas, feed gas temperature, feed gas flow, peak voltage, frequency, capacitance of the discharge gap, pressure of the feed gas in the discharge gap, and the capacitance of the dielectric. For a given ozonator configuration, ozone output is a function of current density when all other conditions are constant.

Most of the commercial ozonators of the silent discharge type are of three basic designs: (1) Otto plate; (2) tube; and (3) Lowther plate. The contemporary Otto plate ozonator, now largely obsolete, is based on an original design developed by M. P. Otto about 1905. The basic equipment is water cooled and operates with air as the feed gas. It consists of a number of sections arranged in this sequence: a cast aluminum or cast iron water-cooled block, a glass plate dielectric, a discharge gap, another glass dielectric, and a high-voltage stainless steel electrode. Alternate blocks are at ground potential and cooling water is passed directly through them. The rest of the blocks are at high potential and their cooling system is electrically insulated from ground by water sprays. In operation, air is blown into the ozonator and enters the discharge gap where ozone conversion takes place. Ozonated air is then drawn through a manifold formed by holes cut in the center of the electrodes and dielectrics. The largest Otto plate ozone generator manufactured consists of a housing holding 24 blocks with 96 plates and 48 discharge gaps.

The tube ozonator consists of several horizontal tubular elements. This design can operate either on dry air or oxygen and is water cooled. The outer electrodes are stainless steel tubes fastened into stainless steel spacers and surrounded by cooling water. Centered inside the stainless steel tubes are tubular Pyrex® glass dielectrics that are coated on the inside with graphite or aluminum. The coating serves as a second electrode. The stainless steel outer tubes are arranged in parallel and are sealed into a cooling water distribution system. The group of water cooled units is then enclosed as a gas-tight iron lung so that air or oxygen can be fed to the ozonator at one end and ozone collected at the other. The glass tube is sealed so that the feed gas passes only through the discharge gap. The discharge gap and glass thickness are each about 0.25 cm.

The Lowther plate ozonator (Fig. 10-11) differs considerably from the other two types. It is air cooled and operates with either air or oxygen as the feed gas. The basic unit is a gas-tight sandwich consisting of an aluminum heat dissipator, a steel electrode coated with a ceramic dielectric, a glass spacer to form the discharge gap, a second ceramic-coated steel electrode with an inlet for air or oxygen, and an ozone outlet that passes the newly-formed gas through a second aluminum heat dissipator.

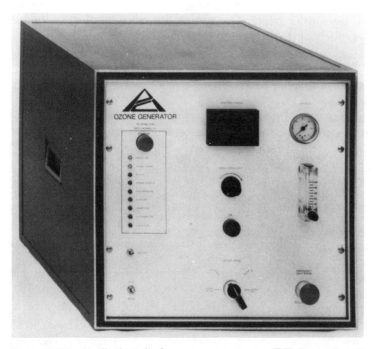

**Figure 10-11**   Small silent discharge ozone generator (PCI Ozone Corp.).

## Ozone Generator and Contactor Design

From an operational standpoint, engineering factors that affect the production of ozone are more important than chemical and physical phenomena that control its dissociation rate in water. The former are manageable, whereas the latter are not. Temperature, pH, and the ionic strength and composition of the seawater all affect the dissociation rate of ozone, but they cannot be manipulated without stressing the animals and plants. Only the DOC and POC concentrations can be controlled with any degree of effectiveness. Aquarists should concentrate on producing an optimum amount of ozone with the equipment available, then see that it is contacted with the water in ways that make it most effective. The efficiency with which these functions are accomplished depends largely on the capacity and operation of the ozone generator and contactor.

This section includes a short description of the general guidelines that can be used to size ozone generators, a discussion of mass-transfer principles that affect the movement of ozone from the gaseous phase into solution, a few words about commercial silent discharge ozonators, an outline of three basic methods for contacting ozone with water, and a note on personnel safety. The contacting equipment described is simple and much of it can be constructed easily and inexpensively. Moreover it can be adapted for use either on a large or small scale.

### Sizing an Ozone Generator

Few general guidelines exist for sizing ozonators to disinfect aquarium water. To further complicate matters, each application is different, varying with such factors as water volume, contactor design, and the ozone demand of the water. In the absence of data that can be applied directly, analogous figures from the wastewater literature can be used. In terms of the numbers of free-floating bacteria and TOC concentration, the water in aquariums compares favorably with good-quality groundwater if the animal density is low, and poor-quality surface water at high animal densities. If this comparison is used, the amount of $O_3$ residual needed for disinfection should be within the range 0.5 to 4 mg $l^{-1}$ (depending on the size of the microorganism) at contact times of 5 to 10 min (McCarthy and Smith 1974). Less ozone is needed when ozone demand is reduced by mechanical filtration and physical adsorption methods. Keep in mind, however, that little work has been done on ozone dosage levels that are required to kill free-floating pathogenic protozoans. It is likely that the swarming stages of parasitic dinoflagellates and ciliates are far more ozone-resistant because of their large size than bacteria and viruses.

The ozone generation rate controls the rate at which ozonated gas can be injected into a contactor (Nebel et al. 1973). For both economic and practical reasons, ozonators should be sized for the peak flow rate of water entering and leaving the contactor, and maximum dosage levels. Pilot studies can often be used to determine these factors in advance, eliminating the need to purchase equipment that is oversized.

*Mass Transfer of Ozone into Water*

As shown in Chapters 4 and 9, the effectiveness of aeration and foam fractionation depends largely on mass (molecular) transfer of gases from rising bubbles into the surrounding seawater. This is based on the two-film theory of gas transfer. The same principles apply to mass transfer of ozone from ozonated gas into water (Fig. 10-12). The method by which ozonated gas is injected into a contactor determines the configurations of bubble size, turbulence to which the bubbles are subjected, and the difference in concentration of ozone between the gas and liquid phases. Small bubbles increase the ratio of bubble area to gas volume and provide maximum surface area for diffusion. Meddows-

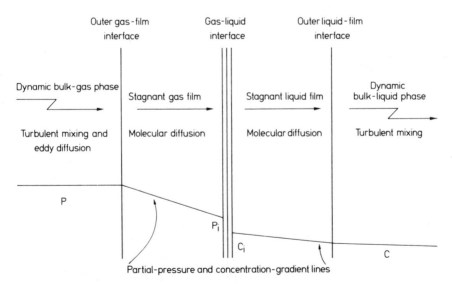

**Figure 10-12**   Film theory of gas transfer and the mechanisms by which ozonated gas enters water. Redrawn from McCarthy and Smith (1974).

**Table 10-4 "Contact Value" of Ozone Bubbles as a Function of Bubble Diameter**

| Bubble Diameter (cm) | Contact Value |
|---|---|
| 1.0 | 1.0 |
| 0.5 | 2.8 |
| 0.25 | 8.0 |
| 0.1 | 31.6 |

Source:   O'Donovan (1965) after Meddows-Taylor (1947).

Taylor (1947) introduced the concept of "contact value" with respect to bubble size of ozonated gas. He defined *contact value* as the product of total area multiplied by the time required to rise unit distance. As shown in Table 10-4, a bubble 0.1 cm in diameter has nearly 32 times the contact value of a bubble with a diameter ten times larger. Turbulence is desirable to a degree because shearing forces reduce the liquid film thickness at the surface of the bubble and facilitate mass transfer of ozone into the water. If turbulence is excessive, however, the dissociation rate of $O_3$ is accelerated. This causes rapid formation of free radicals and decreases the effectiveness of ozone as a disinfectant. The mass transfer rate through the gas-liquid interface increases with increasing $O_3$ concentration in the bubbles. Under normal conditions, the use of oxygen as the feed gas doubles ozone production. Oxygen, however, is expensive and air is free. McCarthy and Smith (1974) pointed out that no engineering design can make the most of all variables that affect mass transfer rates. The design of an ozonation system always involves trade-offs.

*Commercial Silent Discharge Ozonators.*

As summarized by Rosen (1973), to optimize ozone yield of silent discharge generators, the following conditions must be met. The pressure-discharge gap combination should be constructed so that the voltage can be kept relatively low while practical operating pressures are maintained. Low voltage protects the dielectric and electrode surfaces from high-voltage failure. Operating pressures from 0.703 to 1.055 kg cm$^{-2}$ gauge help if the ozonated gas is injected at the bottom of large contactors. Pressure from the ozone as it is injected supplies energy needed to bring the water and gas into contact.

Material for the dielectric should be thin with a high dielectric constant. Both properties allow for high ozone yield efficiency. On a practical basis, glass is the only suitable dielectric material. It is strong enough to resist puncture and also keeps the thickness of the dielectric at a minimum. A thin dielectric optimizes ozone yield and improves heat removal from the surface of the electrodes.

High-frequency alternating current should be used. This is less damaging to the dielectric surfaces than high voltage, resulting in lower maintenance and increasing both the life of the machine and ozone yield. There is a trade-off between voltage and frequency. To quote Rosen (1973): "Voltage is appealing. . . . However, this advantage can be deceiving in view of dielectric failures at high voltages. The idea is to maintain a dielectric as thin as possible while minimizing the practical problems involved in using thin material to construct an ozone generator and in preventing dielectric puncture at reasonable operating voltages."

Heat removal at the electrodes is critical. Gas flow through the discharge gap removes only enough heat to allow for the production of ozone. Ozonation is basically an inefficient process. Most of the electrical energy applied to ozone production is given off as waste heat, and the decomposition of $O_3$ in the discharge gap accelerates with rising temperature. For ozone to be produced efficiently, the discharge gap must be cooled. The feed gas also must pass through the discharge gap in a continuous stream to sweep the area of ozone. An increasing ozone concentration results in accelerated decomposition of $O_3$ as the molecules collide and fly apart. The ozone must be removed as fast as it forms.

If an ozonator is undersized for a particular application, the yield of $O_3$ can be increased by raising the electrical input, but the gain will be less than proportional unless the gas flow is also increased in such a way that the ozone concentration is held constant. The yield of ozone per unit of electrical energy consumed is the most useful measure of an ozonator's operating efficiency. In the best commercial generators this is approximately 70 g kw-hr$^{-1}$ when air is the feed gas, and 136 g kw-hr$^{-1}$ when oxygen is used.

With these factors in mind, the Lowther plate ozonator has obvious advantages over the Otto plate and tube generators. As outlined by Rosen (1973) these are: ability to operate on air or oxygen as a feed gas with less stringent drying requirements; the use of air cooling; low operating voltages, which extend dielectric life and lower overall maintenance requirements; a small discharge gap that allows high operating pressures without the need to function at high voltages; thin dielectrics that provide greater ozone output while exerting minimum interference with heat removal; high-frequency operation that produces large quantities of ozone without requiring high voltage (the high frequency is provided by a solid-state device that assures minimal energy-conversion losses); dielectric coating of both electrode surfaces, which lessens the possibility of electrode failure; heat removal from both electrode surfaces, which is more efficient and allows a greater quantity of ozone to be produced from a small electrode surface area; smaller floor space requirements as the result of the high output efficiency; and power requirements that are less than the other two types of generators.

Air-cooling is an important feature because it eliminates the legal and ecological problems of discharging heated water into natural waterways. Discharging a continuous stream of water into a sewage system raises sewer assessments and results in increased operating costs. Another important feature of the Lowther plate ozonator is its lower power requirement, compared with the other two types of commercial generators. Heat removal from both electrode surfaces is a definite design advantage. In the Otto plate and tube generators, all the heat must be removed from one electrode surface, making these units severely heat-limited. Heat from the uncooled electrode surface must pass across the relatively large discharge gap, which is filled with insulating gas, before it can be removed from the system (Rosen 1973). In the Otto plate generators, the design of the manifold and resulting gas distribution system is a drawback because operation is limited to low pressure. All factors considered, the most efficient design is the Lowther plate, followed by tube-type ozonators. The Otto plate design is the least efficient.

*Contactor Design*

Typically ozonated gas is both generated and injected into water under pressure. Four of the most popular injection methods utilize venturi action, rotary action, total injection, or diffusers at normal atmospheric pressure. All of these methods are suited for use in small aquariums in which the ozone generator is the UV type. They can also be scaled up in size and used in large aquariums in combination with silent discharge generators. Venturi and rotary devices are the least desirable because their violent mixing action accelerates ozone decomposition, which reduces disinfection efficiency. Their use also may increase the possibility of the water becoming supersaturated with oxygen (see below).

Venturi and rotary devices will not be discussed, as their use is not recommended. For descriptions, see Scott (1972) and Sander and Rosenthal (1975), respectively.

The total injection method has been used in France to disinfect large quantitites of drinking water since the early 1900s. Masschelein et al. (1975) described a small device based on the same operating principles. It can easily be adapted for ozonating aquarium water. The unit is pictured in Fig. 10-13. Ozonated gas is injected into the water at the top of the column. If the downflow velocity of the water is maintained at a minimum of 0.4 m sec$^{-1}$, the bubbles sink, a factor that greatly increases contact time and enhances disinfection. The authors recommended that ozonated gas be injected into the system at a minimum pressure of 0.5 bar. In addition, the injection point must be located 30 to 50 cm above

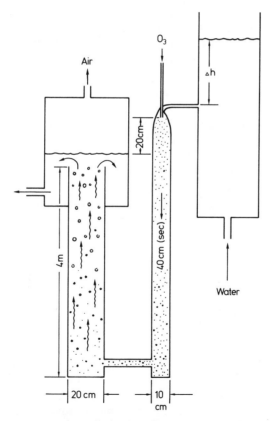

**Figure 10-13**  Pilot model of a total injection device for dispersing ozone in water. Redrawn and modified from Masschelein et al. (1975).

the level of the effluent water. The head loss, resulting from the critical downflow velocity, stays between 80 and 160 cm.

The diffuser ozonation method utilizes design principles identical to those involved in foam fractionation, except that in ozonation the contact time is more critical. Ozonated gas is injected at the base of a vertical contact column or horizontal chamber with baffles, as depicted in Fig. 10-14. After injection, movement of the gas through the contactor can be either cocurrent (with the flow of water), or countercurrent (against the flow of water), as described in Section 9.2 with foam fractionators. Cocurrent contactors are not recommended unless the sole purpose of ozonating the water is to reduce turbidity. Otherwise the short contact time will be inadequate for disinfection.

Countercurrent contactors are more effective because water moving downward restricts the velocity at which the bubbles of ozonated gas can rise. This results in a "ballasting" effect, which also occurs in the total injection method described above. In the countercurrent contact chamber depicted in Fig. 10-13, Masschelein et al. (1975) recommended that the average flow of water be a minimum of 4 to 5 cm sec$^{-1}$, and noted that additional ballasting of the bubbles could be achieved by increasing the flow to 10 to 15 cm sec$^{-1}$. An advantage of this general design is the use of the existing head of water with minimum head loss, eliminating the need for expensive pumping (Nebel et al. 1973). To be effective, such columns must retain the water for 5 to 10 min. It is doubtful whether the column depicted in Fig. 10-13 could hold water for that long without modification.

The importance of drying the feed gas to silent discharge generators cannot be overemphasized. Equipment needed to accomplish this is a key element in designing an ozonation system. Desiccators usually are preceded in series by a refrigerator for cooling the feed gas. Refrigera-

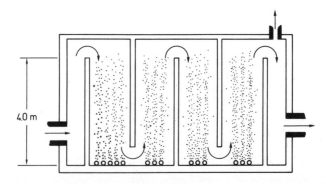

**Figure 10-14**   Diffusion method of ozonating water. From Masschelein et al. (1975).

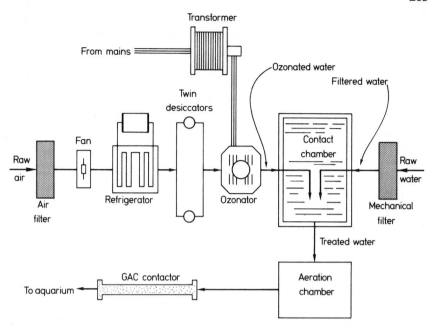

**Figure 10-15** Ozonation treatment scheme for large water systems. Redrawn and modified from O'Donovan (1965).

tion does two things: it eliminates some of the moisture in the feed gas, which makes the desiccators more efficient; and it reduces the temperature in the discharge gap, slowing down the decomposition of ozone molecules as they are produced. Water in the feed gas in amounts as low as 0.02 to 0.03 mg l$^{-1}$ will seriously impair ozone yield, although values averaging 0.03 mg l$^{-1}$ are normal in the feed gas of most wastewater treatment plant ozonators (O'Donovan 1965). An incident was reported by O'Donovan (1965) in which the moisture content of air entering an ozone generator increased from 2.313 to 4.626 mg l$^{-1}$ and caused a decrease in ozone production from 225 to 160 g hr$^{-1}$. Common desiccants are silica gel and calcium chloride. Both materials can be regenerated by passing a stream of hot air through them in the opposite direction of the normal feed gas flow. Some desiccants contain a dye that changes from blue to pink when the material is wetted (e.g., Drierite®*). When the crystals change color, it is time to dry them or throw them away. A schematic for refrigerating and drying the feed gas to a silent discharge ozonator is shown in Fig. 10-15.

* W. A. Hammond, 122 Dayton Avenue, Exenia, OH 45385.

It is imperative that the effluent from an ozone contactor be directed first to an aeration chamber where the residual $O_3$ and excess $O_2$ can be expelled. It is also a good practice to pass the water next through a GAC contactor; afterward it can be returned directly to the aquarium (Fig. 10-15). This application of GAC has been recommended before (MacLean et al. 1973, Sander and Rosenthal 1975, Stopka 1975) and probably removes most of the ozone-produced residuals that may still be present after aeration. In addition, GAC may remove toxic by-products formed from ozonation, provided they are susceptible to physical adsorption methods.

Excess or residual ozone is common in contactor effluents in which the initial $O_3$ concentration is sufficiently high to disinfect the water. Excess $O_2$ in a contactor effluent results from the decomposition of $O_3$. Both problems can be eliminated if the effluent is aerated vigorously in the aeration chamber for a minimum of 15 min. If this is not done, mortalities may occur. Roselund (1975) reported that ozone residuals of 0.01 to 0.06 mg $O_3$ $l^{-1}$ in the effluent from a contact chamber killed rainbow trout in a freshwater hatchery. The fish appeared to be irritated immediately after being subjected to treated effluent water, and some groups experienced 100% mortality within 4 hr. Pathological examination revealed gill aneurysms and gill epithelium damage. Retention of the contactor effluent for 11 min reduced the concentration of residual ozone, but did not eliminate fish mortalities, because the water had become supersaturated with oxygen as the ozone decomposed; this, too, proved to be fatal. A retention time of 11 min, in combination with aeration, alleviated the problem.

Frese (1974) observed that no gill damage occurred to fishes when aquarium seawater was ozonated directly (that is, not diverted to an aeration chamber), so long as the concentration did not exceed 0.5 mg $O_3$ $l^{-1}$ and the generator did not operate more than 6 hr $da^{-1}$. Sander and Rosenthal (1975) also recommended against continuous ozonation of aquarium water.

*Personnel Safety*

Gaseous ozone has a pungent odor that can be detected easily at low concentrations (0.02 to 0.05 mg $l^{-1}$). However olfactory fatigue develops quickly and may mask the presence of ozone at hazardous levels. Coughing is the first symptom to appear. More severe effects of ozone poisoning are depression, cyanosis, nausea, and pulmonary edema. The early signs of pulmonary edema often are delayed for several hours. The specific levels of ozone gas necessary to produce any of these effects are not known.

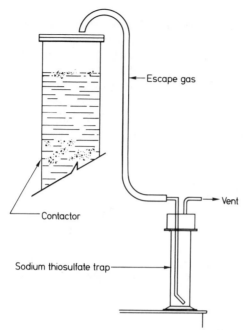

**Figure 10-16**   Ozone trap to reduce the hazard of ozone toxicity to personnel (various sources).

The U. S. government has established a limit of 0.05 mg l$^{-1}$ of ozone that can accumulate in a closed room (Fine 1974). When an amount greater than this escapes from the air vent of a contactor it should be conducted into a sodium thiosulfate trap before being vented to the atmosphere, as shown in Fig. 10-16. The room containing the contactor must be well ventilated at all times to prevent ozone from accumulating.

### Other Effects of Ozonation

Ozone is ordinarily used in aquariums for the purpose of disinfection, but ozonation affects some important nonbiological processes as well. The chemistry of ozone in freshwater is poorly understood; in seawater it is not understood at all. The conclusions presented here are based on published data in which freshwater was used in most of the experimental procedures (usually distilled water or municipal wastewater). Direct extrapolation of the results for application in seawater, as I shall do, is dangerous and certainly subject to criticism.

Some of the effects that ozone has on organic and inorganic constituents of water are documented well enough to be accepted as fact. In other cases, the processes that have been proposed are doubtful. Three processes that probably occur both in freshwater and seawater are: (1) the conversion of refractory organic compounds to substances that are biodegradable or more readily adsorbed onto activated carbon; (2) reduction of color and turbidity; and (3) enhancement of foam fractionation when ozonated gas is substituted for air at the injection point in a foam fractionator. Two processes that are unlikely to occur at reasonable dosage levels and contact times are: (1) complete oxidation of TOC to $CO_2$; and (2) conversion of ammonia in significant amounts to higher oxidation states.

*Likely Processes*

Eberhardt et al. (1975), McCreary and Snoeyink (1977), Nebel et al. (1973, 1976), and Suzuki et al. (1978) reported that refractory organic carbon could be made biodegradable by ozonation. Nebel et al. (1973, 1976) suggested that ozonation added oxygenated functional groups to the refractory compounds, producing chemical sites where biological oxidation could begin.

Adams and Spotte (1979), Guirguis et al. (1978), Meijers (1977), and Stopka (1978) demonstrated that ozonation of water increased the amount of TOC that could be adsorbed onto activated carbon. The study by Adams and Spotte was done using saline water from a dolphin pool; the other investigations were conducted in freshwater. Adams and Spotte showed that when three methods of TOC reduction were monitored (ozonation alone, GAC alone, and ozonation plus GAC), greatest TOC removal occurred when the water was ozonated and then passed through a GAC contactor. After 5 min of contact with GAC following ozonation, approximately 60% of the TOC was removed, and 78% was removed at 30 min. The results represented the average percentage of TOC removed from the mean of duplicate trials in which the initial TOC concentrations were 12.95 and 12.65 mg $l^{-1}$.

Much of the yellow color of old aquarium water is caused by the accumulation of refractory chromophoric compounds. These substances probably account for only a small portion of the TOC, but their pigmentation makes them highly visible. It is likely that ozonation removes color from aquarium water more effectively than any of the commonly used physical adsorption methods. However unlike these other processes, ozonation does not actually remove organic compounds from solution (see the next section) and cannot be considered a substitute for the use of activated carbon or foam fractionation. Ozonation probably converts chromophoric substances to nonpigmented organic compounds. Chromophoric substances in aquarium water are perhaps compounds with long chains of conjugated carbon-carbon double bonds or ring structures. Ozone is known to be effective at breaking such bonds and small doses of $O_3$ can oxidize substantial amounts of the pigmented fraction of the TOC. In addition, ozone has a high affinity for phenolic compounds and oxidizes them readily (Nebel et al. 1976). The exudates of many algae are phenols and polyphenols, which may be chromophoric under certain conditions (Section 6.1).

Foulds et al. (1971) observed foam that formed after ozonating wastewater and suggested that the increased foam stabilization was perhaps caused by the ozonation of naturally dispersed iron and manganese hydroxides. This implies that foaming with ozonated gas might be even more effective in seawater, because of the greater concentration of inorganic ions. In addition, ozonation may convert some organic compounds into materials with surfactant properties, thus enhancing the foaming process. It should be noted, however, that foam fractionation of wastewater also involves froth flotation, a process that concentrates particulate organic carbon. This, in turn, reduces the turbidity of the water. The use of ozone to remove turbidity is of questionable value, considering that mechanical filtration methods usually are cheaper and more efficient.

During turbidity reduction, ozone reacts with POC, presumably breaking it apart into smaller particles and molecules, as demonstrated by

$$POC \xrightarrow{\quad O_3 \quad} DOC \qquad (61)$$

The obvious advantage of equation 61 is improved water clarity; the drawback is that the constituents of the particles are returned to solution where they must then be removed by physical adsorption. Moreover higher turbidity levels interfere with the ability of ozone to disinfect water, as explained previously. When the POC level is high, much of the oxidizing power of the ozone is wasted on larger, nonliving materials that could be removed more easily with granular media or diatomaceous earth.

*Unlikely Processes*

It is sometimes stated that ozone removes a fraction of the TOC from water by oxidizing it. The word *removes* is misleading, because it implies that organic matter is instantly oxidized by ozone to free $CO_2$, which, if produced in amounts that exceed the concentration in the water at saturation, is then driven into the atmosphere. This rarely happens. Despite claims by Halfon et al. (1968), Huibers et al. (1969), and others that the TOC level in wastewater can be lowered significantly by ozonation, more recent research shows otherwise. As Nebel et al. (1973) noted, the first products of ozone oxidation are oxygenated compounds, also organic, that are water soluble and not highly volatile. In other words, most of the organic matter that comes into contact with ozone is oxidized to an intermediate organic state. In the study by Nebel et al. (1973), even low TOC values in the influent wastewater (approximately 10 mg TOC $l^{-1}$) could not be reduced by oxidation with 15 mg $O_3 l^{-1}$. Similar results were reported by Farooq et al. (1977a), who concluded that despite the high ozone demand in wastewater, no significant amount of TOC was converted to $CO_2$, but that intermediate organic compounds were formed instead. Elia et al. (1978) demonstrated that even very high ozone concentrations (31 mg $O_3$ $min^{-1}$) did not remove appreciable amounts of TOC from wastewater. Adams and Spotte (1979) exposed samples of saline water from a dolphin pool to ozone dosage levels of 4.13, 4.03, and 4.52 mg $O_3$ $l^{-1}$. Results of duplicate trials showed clearly that ozone had no effect on the TOC concentration after sequential contact periods of 25, 30, and 30 min (13.66 mg TOC $l^{-1}$) and 30, 30, and 30 min (12.85 mg TOC $l^{-1}$).

Hoigné and Bader (1978), Huibers et al. (1969), Singer and Zilli (1975), and others concluded that some oxidation of ammonia can occur during ozonation of freshwater, but the efficacy of the process is dependent on several factors. Some of these cannot be controlled in water systems that contain living animals and plants, or are in direct conflict with established culture theory (see below). The effect of ozonation on ammonia conversion in seawater is unknown at this time, because good kinetic studies have not been done.

It is doubtful whether ozonation of aquarium seawater results in the oxidation of significant amounts of ammonia. Two characteristics of aquarium water would appear to slow down the reaction kinetics and prolong the contact time beyond practical limits: (1) low levels of $NH_3$; and (2) the presence of other molecules and ions. Hoigné and Bader (1978) showed that ozonation had a significant effect on the ammonia concentration in freshwater only when there were relatively high levels of $NH_3$; $NH_4^+$ cannot be oxidized. The rate constant for $O_3$ depletion by reaction with $NH_3$ was $20 \pm 1$ $mole^{-1}$ $sec^{-1}$ in freshwaters of pH less than 9. The work of Hoigné and Bader was done to evaluate the efficacy of ammonia conversion by ozone in wastewater. Municipal wastewater has a total $NH_4$-N concentration of approximately 30 mg $l^{-1}$ (Singer and Zilli 1975), compared with values of about 0.1 mg total $NH_4$-$N^{-1}$ in aquariums with conditioned bacteriological filters. Moreover the hydrolysis of ammonia greatly favors $NH_4^+$ as the predominant species in natural waters. Bower and Bidwell (1978) published tables showing the percentage of the total $NH_4$-N present as $NH_3$ in seawater of varying pH, temperature, and salinity. In a typical profile of water that would be suitable for culturing marine organisms (pH = 8.2, temperature = 20°C, and $S$ = 35 o/oo), only 4.65% of the total $NH_4$-N existed as $NH_3$. This means that for a measured concentration of 0.1 mg total $NH_4$-N $l^{-1}$ at the above stated conditions, there would be $4.65 \times 10^{-3}$ mg $NH_3$ $l^{-1}$ present in solution, or probably too small an amount to be oxidized by $O_3$ at convenient dosage levels and contact times.

As the pH of water increases and shifts the $NH_3 : NH_4^+$ ratio more in favor of $NH_3$, the decomposition of $O_3$ accelerates. This results in unfavorable conditions for slow direct reactions with $O_3$ molecules. The decomposition of $O_3$ at higher pH values leads to the formation of free radicals, one of which is OH. The effect on ammonia oxidation, however, is not very different. Radiolytic and gas-phase studies have confirmed that the reaction rate constants are still slow (Hoigné and Bader 1978). The reaction kinetics could be made more attractive by increasing the percentage of $NH_3$ in solution, but such a practice would be in conflict with the work of Armstrong et al. (1978) and others who have demonstrated that $NH_3$ is more toxic to aquatic animals than $NH_4^+$ at higher pH levels.

The presence of other compounds in aquarium water has a further negative effect on the reaction kinetics of ammonia oxidation by ozone. Singer and Zilli (1975) observed that when even a fraction of the DOC present in wastewater was refractory and not subject to oxidation by $O_3$, its mere presence appeared to retard ammonia reaction kinetics.

Reports in the literature of direct oxidation of ammonia in aquarium seawater may be based on results that are more apparent than real. Honn and Chavin (1976) used ozone as an "oxidative supplement" to bacteriological filtration in a seawater aquarium of 2271 l. Filter bed effluent values for total $NH_4$-N, $NH_3$-N, and $NO_2$-N were, respectively, 0.135, 0.0074, and 0.17 mg $l^{-1}$. Ozonation (100 mg 380 $l^{-1}$ $hr^{-1}$) reduced these levels even more. Nitrate became elevated significantly during ozonation. When ozonation was stopped, the concentration of all three values rose above the levels just stated. The trend was rapidly reversed by resuming ozonation. These results are intriguing, but do not confirm that ozonation is a nitrification process, because no controls were used to eliminate interferences from microorganisms. It is possible that ozone supplied an alternate source of oxygen, which could have increased aerobic activity in the filter bed, particularly in a conditioned aquarium with a well established population of bacteria. Moreover the production of nitrite, as implied in the results, does not agree with the accepted mechanism of nitrate formation when ozone is involved. Singer and Zilli (1975) and Hoigné and Bader (1978) found that ammonia depletion by ozonation of freshwater always resulted in formation of a corresponding amount of $NO_3^-$, with no detectable buildup of $NO_2^-$. Both teams of investigators concluded that the oxidants initiate a sequence of reactions that lead only to $NO_3^-$ formation.

## 10.3  EVALUATION

UV sterilizers and ozonators are useful additions to a water system during times of severe outbreaks of epizootic disease, for routine treatment of water used to maintain organisms that are too delicate to be treated with chemotherapeutic agents, and to prevent the influx of infectious pathogens from seawater supplies. The value of disinfection rises as the density of the animal population increases, and the process is more important in hatchery and aquaculture installations than in laboratory or display aquariums, which ordinarily have a high water volume to animal mass. There are drawbacks involved with either process, but particularly with ozonation (see below).

UV irradiation of the water in a high-density fish culture operation often reduces the transmission of infectious diseases and lowers overall animal mortality. No comparable data are available for ozonation. Hoffman (1975) noted a marked reduction in both the incidence and severity of infection in rainbow trout when hatchery water infected with *Myxosoma cerebralis* was irradiated with 35,000 μw sec cm$^{-2}$ of UV. After 4.5 months, trout receiving irradiated water were 1.8 to 2.6 times heavier than the control fish and, unlike the controls, few showed gross signs of whirling disease. Sanders et al. (1972) irradiated incoming water to a salmonid hatchery with 215,000 μw sec cm$^{-2}$ of UV. When raw (nonirradiated) water was used, 20% of the juvenile rainbow trout used in the experiment died from infections caused by *Ceratomyxa shasta*. When the water was irradiated, only 1% died. In the same report, the authors stated that when a dosage level of 360,000 μw sec cm$^{-2}$ was used to treat water in which juvenile coho salmon (*Oncorhynchus kisutch*) were maintained, only 2% of the test fish became infected by *C. shasta*, compared with 60% of the controls. The control fish had been exposed to nonirradiated water throughout the experiment. Sanders and his colleagues also noted that test fish living in UV-irradiated water showed lower mortalities from the bacterial fish pathogen *Chondrococcus columnaris* than the controls. Bullock and Stuckey (1977) re-

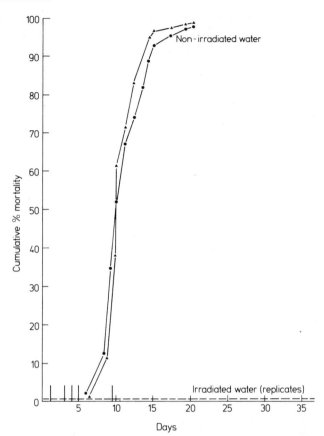

**Figure 10-17**  Efficacy of 25 $\mu$m filtration and UV irradiation (13,100 $\mu$w-sec cm$^{-2}$) of spring water (12.5°C) containing *A. salmonicida* in preventing transmission of furunculosis to fingerling Atlantic salmon. Vertical bars at the base show days that salmon were exposed to irradiated or non-irradiated water. Redrawn and modified from Bullock and Stuckey (1977).

ported that filtration through a 25 $\mu$m filter, followed by UV irradiation of clear spring water at dosages of 13,100 to 29,400 $\mu$w sec cm$^{-2}$, prevented transmission of furunculosis disease (caused by *A. salmonicida*) to Atlantic salmon (*Salmo salar*), despite the fact that the fish were exposed to irradiated water only intermittently, and the UV unit was operated at twice the recommended flow rate. The data are plotted in Fig. 10-17.

Bullock and Stuckey (1977) made an important point when they stated that the significance of percent kill of pathogenic bacteria, as reflected by their data, could not be determined because of the difficulty in predicting the number of organisms necessary to transmit disease. They wrote: "For example, a 99.99% kill of a pathogen at a density of $10^4$ ml$^{-1}$ would leave only 10 bacteria ml$^{-1}$. However, if the pathogen were virulent and with the potential amplification of the surviving bacteria in fish under intensive culture, this density of bacteria may still transmit disease." The same reasoning can be applied when ozonation is used, because its effectiveness also depends on reducing the level of free-floating pathogenic organisms to noninfectious levels. It is important to critically evaluate results obtained in the laboratory; often they cannot be applied directly in pragmatic situations. Bullock and Stuckey (1977), for example, emphasized that their work was performed on a small scale and that it would be dangerous to extrapolate the figures and apply them to a pilot operation.

It is doubtful whether the routine use of UV irradiation or ozonation is beneficial in the maintenance of seawater aquariums. From an aquarist's standpoint, neither method is an elixir that will end disease problems. Disinfection is, at best, only an aid in controlling disease. For one thing, UV does not leave a significant residual in the water to continue killing pathogens once the treated water has passed through the sterilizer, although Herald et al. (1970) suggested that UV irradiation produced peroxy compounds and other free radicals that could kill some microorganisms even if the cells had not been exposed to radiation. The percentage of cells destroyed in this way is probably low and occurs only in the immediate vicinity of the lamp. The absence of a residual of any consequence makes UV irradiation inferior to cupric sulfate, antibiotics, and even ozone. As Herald et al. (1970) pointed out, ". . . UV rays will kill the free-swimming stages of *Oodinium* as the sea water passes through the sterilizer, but will not affect the adult stages securely hidden in the gills of fishes in the display tank. Similarly, the free-swimming stages of ciliates and other organisms will be killed by contact with UV rays from the sterilizer, but the same parasites clinging safely to the host fish will not be affected. By contrast, free copper ions will usually remove these parasites from the fish."

Spanier (1978) used UV-irradiated seawater to culture larvae of the teleost *Sparus aurata* (bream). Pretreatment of the water with UV reduced the ambient population of bacteria by 99% after 11 hr, but no subsequent change in fish mortality was seen: less than 1% of the larvae survived longer than 52 days with or without pretreatment of the water with UV. Herald et al. (1970), compared fish mortalities at Steinhart Aquarium in San Francisco with and without UV irradiation of the water. The data were collected over a period of several years. When in operation, the UV sterilizer reduced the total bacterial count (which varied from 26,000 to 40,000 organisms ml$^{-1}$) by approximately 98%. Even so, the mortality rate stayed the same (about 2.5% of the fish population per month). Herald and his coauthors stated: "We are thus forced to the reluctant conclusion that aquarium fishes in good condition can live compatibly in a large water system of high bacterial content. . . . Fishes in good health in an uncrowded aquarium with proper aeration and filtration can, and do, live satisfactorily without the use of UV water sterilizers."

Ozonation of seawater often results in an oxidant residual that may persist for several hours. Mangum and McIlhenny (1975) reported that after 24 hr, 200 ml of seawater to which 6 mg of ozone had been added hourly for 5 hr showed 0.3 mg $O_3$ l$^{-1}$ (calculated as ozone), compared with an immediate value of 0.4 mg $O_3$ l$^{-1}$. It is unlikely that such determinations are actually a measure of "ozone," considering the high concentrations of oxidizable inorganic ions that normally are present in seawater. Most likely, the oxidant that can be measured after $O_3$ has dissipated is hypochlorite or hypobromite, which may be formed during the reaction of ozone with chloride or bromide ions (Blogoslawski and Rice 1975, Williams et al. 1978). Williams et al. (1978) showed that ozonation of seawater oxidized Br$^-$ to BrO$^-$. Further oxidation of BrO$^-$ to BrO$_3$, and of the formation of ClO$_2^-$, ClO$_3^-$, and ClO$_4^-$ from Cl$^-$ were considered to be thermodynamically possible, but were not investigated. Crecelius (1978), confirmed that all bromide is converted to bromate when seawater is contacted with ozone for long periods (60 min).

Overall, UV irradiation is clearly preferable to ozonation for the routine disinfection of aquarium seawater. UV sterilizers add less to the water in the way of reactive chemical species than ozonators. They are simpler in design, easier to engineer and maintain, cheaper to operate, and require a smaller capital expenditure. Perhaps most important, the dosage level of UV radiation can be controlled, whereas consistent concentrations of ozone in solution are difficult to sustain.

The level of UV radiation emitted across the surface of a lamp can be measured accurately. There is no reliable method of determining the $O_3$ concentration even in freshwater, and the problem is far more complex in seawater. Analytical methods that give a measure of the total oxidant concentration (e.g., orthotolidine, iodometry) do not work at all in saline solutions, because there is no way of knowing whether the species being measured is $O_3$, free radicals of $O_3$, or an oxidant produced as the result of reactions of $O_3$ with other inorganic ions, such as chloride and bromide. Spectrophotometric methods (e.g., Shechter 1973) are not reproducible without modification (Farooq et al. 1977a) even in freshwaters, if they are chromophoric. Direct measurement of $O_3$ spectrophotometrically at 258 nm, as described by Hoigné and Bader (1978), is effective only in pure or simple aqueous solutions. Ozone absorbs this wavelength strongly, but so do many organic compounds that are present routinely as fractions of the DOC in natural waters. With all methods, there is the ever-present difficulty of preparing reproducible standards. A general discussion on the subject of ozone determination in seawater can be found in Blogoslawski and Rice (1975).

It is possible that both UV radiation and ozone produce mutagenic effects in the larvae and gametes of marine organisms. These effects may be caused directly in the case of UV radiation, perhaps by altering the DNA components within the cells. Gruener (1978), reported that ozonated compounds were mutagenic in two strains of the bacterium *Salmonella typhimurium* (TA100 and TA98). MacLean et al. (1973) observed abnormal development of American oyster (*Crassostrea virginica*) gametes in water that had been ozonated and passed through activated carbon. They suggested that ozonation of the seawater may have produced a toxic by-product that interfered with normal development. This is not surprising if hypochlorite or hypobromite are by-products when seawater is ozonated. The problems associated with mutagenesis are more important in hatchery and aquaculture installations in which animals are reared through successive life cycles than in public aquariums and laboratories, where the breeding of seawater organisms is not the primary purpose.

Ozonation of seawater may produce toxic by-products that are not merely mutagenic but lethal. DeManche et al. (1975) demonstrated that ozonation of seawater produced a long-term residual toxicity that killed oyster larvae. Aeration did not remove the toxic substance, but passing the water through activated carbon did. The reports of DeManche et al. (1975) and MacLean et al. (1973) are disturbing because they indicate that the removal of toxic by-products of ozonation cannot always be accomplished by conventional water treatment methods.

Residual ozone is known to be dangerous to many species of marine animals and mass mortalities may result in large treated systems unless an aeration chamber is provided to aerate the water and expel excess $O_3$ (Fig. 10-15). Even then, the danger persists that oxygen may reach supersaturation, particularly in refrigerated water systems. Thus ozonation requires more careful monitoring than UV irradiation and is complicated by the absence of a reliable analytical method for $O_3$ determination. Finally no guidelines exist at present for properly sizing ozone generators to individual water systems. Contact and retention chamber design parameters are equally vague.

# CHAPTER 11
*Toxicity and Stress*

Some of the metabolic products that animals release into the water are directly toxic, whereas others become toxic through the activities of microorganisms. Still other factors in the environment are stressful and reduce an animal's chances of survival. The term "stress" has many meanings. I shall limit its use to physiological disturbances induced in aquatic animals by sudden temperature changes, by direct handling, or by brief and significant shifts in important environmental factors that occur most often during transport. My thesis will be this: brief perturbations in an aquatic animal's physiology may have effects that are long-lasting. The act of chasing and capturing a fish with a net, for example, causes it to exercise violently and culminates in exposure to the air during aquarium transfer. The procedure may take less than a minute, but the fish does not regain its normal metabolic status for several hours. Similarly, subjecting a fish to a sudden change in temperature, or to water that is low in dissolved oxygen and high in free $CO_2$, produces physiological changes so profound that death may still occur many hours or days later.

Ammonia is the toxic metabolite of most concern to aquarists and its treatment here is more detailed compared with nitrite and nitrate. Much has been published on the effects of temperature stress, so comparatively little will be said about it. The effects of handling stress are covered briefly. Interest in the subject is recent and the information available is limited. Acid-base balance, as a stress-related factor, has not yet been added to the store of aquarium knowledge, and several

275

pages have been devoted to it. Each major section of the chapter ends with a few words about management practices to put the theoretical information into proper perspective.

## 11.1  AMMONIA TOXICITY

The toxicity of ammonia to aquatic animals has been known at least since the report of McDonald (1885). Ammonia is the most lethal form of inorganic nitrogen produced in aquarium water, but the mechanisms by which it is toxic at a cellular level are controversial and poorly understood. It should be reiterated that the term "ammonia," as used here, is synonymous with total ammonia (measured at total $NH_4$-N) and is the sum of free ammonia ($NH_3$) and ammonium ion ($NH_4^+$). The hydrolysis of ammonium ion in natural waters, shown by the reaction below, has a p$K$ value of about 9, so that the percentage of $NH_4^+$ is always greater than the percentage of free ammonia.

$$NH_4^+ + H_2O \rightleftharpoons NH_3 + H_3O^+ \tag{62}$$

Reaction 62 is affected mainly by pH, temperature, and salinity, with pH exerting the greatest effect. An increase of one unit of pH causes the percentage of free ammonia to increase approximately 10-fold. Rising temperature and decreasing salinity cause much smaller increases. The temperature effect is the result of the increased hydrolysis of ammonium ions at higher temperature levels; the salinity effect is the result of the decreasing activity of free ammonia in solutions of increasing ionic strength (Hampson 1976). Thus at identical temperature and pH values, and the same amounts of total $NH_4$-N in solution, seawater contains slightly less $NH_3$ than freshwater. This is illustrated in Fig. 11-1.

### Ammonia Excretion

The movement of ammonia across membranes involves equilibrium effects, and any discussion of ammonia toxicity in aquatic animals is incomplete unless the mechanisms of ammonia excretion also are considered.

Ammonia is the main form of nitrogen released to the environment by ammonotelic animals (Section 6.3). In fishes, some ammonia is produced from precursors in the liver, transported by the blood to the gills, and eliminated into the environment (Goldstein et al. 1964, Janicki and Lingis 1970, Pequin and Serfaty 1963, Smith 1929, Wood 1958). Still

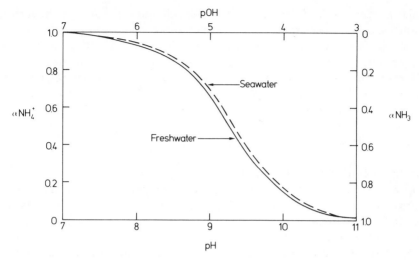

**Figure 11-1** Distribution diagram of ammonia in freshwater and seawater at 25°C. Freshwater curve from Butler (1964). Seawater curve drawn from equations in Whitfield (1974b).

another portion originates from deamination of plasma amino acids in the gill tissue (Goldstein and Forster 1961, Goldstein et al. 1964, Smith 1930). Whether the form at the moment of elimination is $NH_4^+$, $NH_3$, or both, has not been decided for certain, but experimental evidence favors $NH_4^+$ as the form excreted by both fishes and invertebrates living in either freshwater or seawater. Two possibilities exist for removal of ammonia at the gill: (1) active transport of $NH_4^+$, which takes place by ion exchange with a similarly charged species in the external environment; and (2) passive transport (diffusion) of $NH_3$. The current theories describing the mechanisms of ammonia excretion will be covered in some detail as a prelude to a discussion of ammonia's toxic effects.

The basis for the argument favoring the excretion of $NH_3$ is that free ammonia, by being electrochemically neutral, is soluble in the lipid fractions of the excretory membranes and can be passed into the external environment by passive transport along a concentration gradient. Mangum et al. (1978) pointed out, however, that in the invertebrates ammonia moves from intracellular sites of production into circulating body fluids, then into cells of the excretory epithelium, and from there into the environment. Ammonia thus passes from an intracellular to an extracellular site twice, each time moving from a fluid that has a lower pH to one in which the pH is slightly greater. At equilibrium, a molecular gradient would drive $NH_3$ into the cell and not out of it. In earlier studies (e.g., Milne et al. 1958), it was thought that the ammonium ion, because it occurs as an electrochemically charged entity, would be unable to pass through the hydrophobic linings of the excretory membranes. This supposition is no longer tenable, as shown by the work of Brierley and Stoner (1970), Guggenheim et al. (1971), and others, and it is now clear that both forms of ammonia can penetrate tissues.

### Active Transport of $NH_4^+$

It has been shown that in freshwater fishes, sodium and chloride uptake from the environment occur independently (Krogh 1937, Garcia-Romeu and Maetz 1964, Kerstetter et al. 1970). Chloride ions are usually exchanged for bicarbonate ions in the blood (Maetz and Garcia-Romeu 1964, Kerstetter and Kirschner 1972), and sodium ions in the environment are exchanged for either ammonium ions (Maetz and Garcia-Romeu 1964, Whitelaw 1973) or hydrogen ions (Kerstetter et al. 1970, Maetz 1972). The latter coupling ($Na^+/H^+$) must take place if it is assumed that the injection of $NH_4^+$ *in vivo* into a freshwater fish lowers its blood pH (Kerstetter et al. 1970). Similar ionic exchanges are known to occur in euryhaline teleosts acclimated to seawater (Evans 1973, 1975a, 1975b; Motais 1970). It has not yet been demonstrated that the same processes prevail in purely stenohaline marine species, but field observations of the many "marine" fishes living in hard freshwaters (Breder 1934, Hulet et al. 1967, Neill 1957) indicate that they do (Evans 1973).

Payan and Matty (1975), studied ammonia excretion in perfused isolated heads of rainbow trout. They referred to the earlier model of Maetz and Garcia-Romeu (1964) in which it was postulated that hydration of $CO_2$, which is accelerated by the presence of carbonic anhydrase, produces a proton that is accepted by $NH_3$. The resulting $NH_4^+$ is then available for exchange with environmental $Na^+$. Payan and Matty reasoned that by removing $CO_2$ from the perfusing fluid, the potential supply of protons would be reduced, less $NH_4^+$ could be formed, and a smaller amount of ammonium ions would be excreted. Results seemed to confirm their hypothesis. The presence of acetazolamide (an inhibitor of carbonic anhydrase) in Ringer significantly decreased the rate of ammonia excretion. At the same time, a correlation was found between sodium influx and the rate of ammonia discharge, and this offered further proof that freshwater fishes release ammonia into the environment in the form of $NH_4^+$.

Kerstetter and Keeler (1976) tested sodium uptake by perfused isolated gills of rainbow trout at pH values of 7 and 8. The concentration of free ammonia is 10 times greater at the higher pH, meaning that 10 times as much $NH_3$ should be available at any given concentration of $NH_4Cl$, compared with the amount available at pH 7. At a given concentration of $NH_4Cl$ in the external fluid, there should have been greater movement of ammonia across the membrane at the higher pH, because more of the total $NH_4$-N would have been present as $NH_3$. Furthermore if more $NH_3$ entered the membrane, additional $NH_4^+$ would have become available for $Na^+/NH_4^+$ exchange. This did not happen. There was no stimulation of the transport system at the higher pH, and the sodium influx stayed the same at both pH values. At all stages of ammonia transport, only the ionized form was considered to participate. Mangum (personal communication 1978) suggested a more probable explanation: the pH optimum of the transport enzyme is closer to 7 than to 8, and any stimulation was masked. The work of Kerstetter and Keeler contradicts an earlier model of Maetz (1971), in which it was postulated that $NH_3$ diffused across the serosal membranes, accepted a proton inside the cell, and was exchanged (as $NH_4^+$) at the border of the excretory membrane for $Na^+$.

Marine fishes drink seawater continuously, and are faced with the problem of unloading sodium to stay hyposmotic. The elimination of ammonium or hydrogen ions at the gills would necessitate the uptake of additional sodium. A process that has obvious advantages to freshwater fishes would seem to be a slight handicap to seawater species—an "ionic liability" in the words of Evans (1975a). Evans (1973) pointed out that, despite the added sodium loading, it may be a greater disadvantage to marine fishes *not* to utilize ion exchanges. He emphasized that ion exchange processes play essential roles in both nitrogen and acid-base balance, and that sodium uptake at the gill is secondary to the excretion of unwanted ions. This appears to be the case. Payan and Maetz (1973) showed that injection of either $H^+$ or $NH_4^+$ into the cat shark (*Scyliorhinus canicula*), a marine elasmobranch, stimulated the influx of $Na^+$ from seawater. Moreover injection of acetazolamide reduced $Na^+$ uptake. The mechanism of ammonia excretion at the gill thus appeared similar to that in freshwater teleosts.

The ammonium ion also appears to be a major form of ammonia excreted by marine invertebrates. Mangum et al. (1978) studied ammonium ion excretion in four invertebrates: the polychaetous annelids *Nereis succinea* and *N. virens*, the gastropod mollusk *Busycon canaliculatum* (whelk), and the lamellibranch mollusk *Rangia cuneata*. In all species, ammonium ions were excreted against a concentration gradient and excretion was slowed down by sublethal levels of a substance (ouabain) that specifically inhibits the activities of $Na^+$ and $K^+$ ATPases, enzymes thought to be important in the uptake of $Na^+$ from the water. The results of these investigators showed that the ammonium ion crosses the excretory epithelium, and that the transport mechanism is active, not passive.

*Passive Transport of $NH_3$*

Many writers (e.g., de Vooys 1969, Downing and Merkins 1955, Fromm and Gillette 1968, Goldstein et al. 1964, Hampson 1976, Kirschner 1970, Kirschner et al. 1973, Lloyd and Herbert 1960, Olson and Fromm 1971, Schrenkenbach et al. 1975), have stated that $NH_3$ is the form of ammonia excreted by ammonotelic animals, but without providing direct experimental evidence to support their claim. It seems logical that some ammonia output must be by passive transport. The pH gradient goes in the right direction in many natural waters, and the volume flow outside the gills is substantial. The question is, how much of the total $NH_4$-N is eliminated passively? Kirschner (1970) suggested that $Na^+$ uptake is involved exclusively in the excretion of $H^+$ in all freshwater animals, ammonotelic or not, and that ammonia is always released into the environment as $NH_3$. Kirschner et al. (1973), considered that ammonia excreted in the free state was converted to ammonium ion by combining with $H^+$ in the external medium.

   Fromm and Gillette (1968) exposed rainbow trout to ammonium chloride solutions containing 0, 1, 3, 5, and 8 mg total $NH_4$-N $l^{-1}$. At the end of 24 hr, the mean blood levels for total $NH_4$-N showed a direct linear correlation with ammonia in the water and ranged from 38 to 71 mg total $NH_4$-N $l^{-1}$. In terms of free ammonia, trout exposed to 0 to 1 mg $NH_3$-N $l^{-1}$ had mean blood levels within the range 0.6 to 1.3 mg $NH_3$-N $l^{-1}$. When environmental ammonia increased, there was a concurrent rise in the blood ammonia of fish exposed to it. Because blood ammonia concentration was higher in all cases than in the water in which the animals were maintained, the source of additional blood ammonia was thought to be endogenous. Thus the rate of production and release of ammonia was greater than the combined rates of excretion and metabolic detoxification. Moreover reduction of the blood-water gradient ammonia levels resulted in a decreased rate of ammonia excretion. This suggested to the authors that at all concentrations $NH_3$ was eliminated by passive transport down a concentration gradient. Maetz et al. (1976) pointed out, however, that in most experiments ammonia is excreted by the fish despite an absence of an $NH_3$ gradient, lending further support to the theory that $NH_4^+$ is actually the form excreted.

In a study of goldfish (*Carassius auratus*) in calcium-free water, Maetz (1973) attempted to verify whether $NH_3$ was the form of ammonia released. In the absence of $Ca^{2+}$, the potential across the gill of freshwater fishes is positive with respect to the external medium. The conclusion reached was that in the presence of $Na^+$ in the water, the form of ammonia eliminated to the environment was $NH_4^+$. In the absence of $Na^+$, free ammonia moved outward down a concentration gradient. Maetz postulated that in the presence of $Na^+$, but when the pH was below 7, both forms of ammonia would move across the gill.

In the brachyuran crab *Callinectes sapidus* (blue crab), which is an estuarine animal, there is an increase in blood pH when the salinity of the external medium is reduced. This is probably brought about by the ammonia produced in the catabolism of free amino acids that maintain intracellular osmolality (Weiland and Mangum 1975). It is known that $NH_3$ moves in the direction of increasing $H^+$ concentration, because the higher $H^+$ level induces more protonation and leaves less $NH_3$ (Mangum 1976). The $H^+$ gradient dictates that $NH_3$ must diffuse from blood into gill cells, but not from there into the external environment until the salinity becomes very low, paralleling the model set forth by Maetz (1973) for freshwater teleosts. Excretion of ammonia at the gill in the blue crab must occur by active transport. This is supported by the finding that ammonia is still excreted when the medium is so overloaded with $NH_4Cl$ that the $NH_3$ gradient would block molecular diffusion (Mangum et al. 1976). Mangum (1976) concluded that the role of molecular diffusion perhaps had been overemphasized in the past, but that it occurred when driven by a more acidic gradient. When a blue crab migrates from high to low salinity water, it moves from a medium that is alkaline to the blood and would block $NH_3$ excretion by diffusion, to a medium that is still alkaline but less so, and in which $NH_3$ diffusion would occur, regardless of the stage of equilibrium across the gill membrane. Some fraction of the increase in ammonia excretion at low salinity must be passive, but the percentage is probably very small because the ammonia output can be reduced substantially by ouabain, which specifically inhibits active transport.

### Toxic Effects

The idea that $NH_3$ is the only species of ammonia that is toxic to aquatic animals has been accepted unequivocally by many fish culturists. It has long been thought that (1) only $NH_3$ can penetrate tissues, and (2) $NH_3$

enters the gills of aquatic animals from the external environment. The first statement is now known to be untrue. The second, if valid, has never been demonstrated experimentally. Fromm and Gillette (1968) stated, ". . . we have no data which prove that ambient [environmental] ammonia does enter fish across the gill epithelium." This should be taken to mean ammonia of either species. Thus while it is well known that ammonotelic animals routinely excrete ammonia into the environment, the movement of either $NH_3$ or $NH_4^+$ into animals is unproved and therefore uncertain.

The conclusion often reached in the fish culture literature that $NH_3$ diffuses into the gill during periods of elevated ammonia in the environment is based largely on bioassay data. Such speculation clearly oversteps the limitations of most bioassay procedures. In no study yet published have the pH and ammonia levels of the external fluid been correlated with blood pH and ammonia. Until this is done, it is difficult to accept as fact the premise that downhill diffusion gradients exist for movement of $NH_3$ into gill tissue. Consider, for example, the possible effects of pH on ammonia transfer. Ammonium salts added to water alter the pH, particularly of freshwater. This affects membrane transfers of many types across the gill, in both directions. External ammonia, by changing the pH of the medium, may also affect the partial pressure of $NH_3$ in the blood, and consequently blood pH. This possibly occurs when increased $NH_4^+$ in the external fluid increases the concentration of $NH_3$ in proportion to the solubility, p$K$, temperature, and other factors. These shifts, in turn, change the partial pressure gradient of $NH_3$, which may then increase intracellular $NH_3$, $NH_4^+$, and pH. Armstrong et al. (1978) postulated, however, that $NH_3$ does enter the Malaysian prawn (*Macrobrachium rosenbergii*) from the environment under certain conditions. Of the total $NH_4$-N found to be toxic at a pH value of 8.4, approximately 10% would exist as $NH_3$. This concentration was four times greater than the estimated $NH_3$ concentration of the blood, and in such a situation free ammonia might diffuse inward. At a blood pH of 7.65 the free ammonia molecule would become protonated to $NH_4^+$, maintaining the $NH_3$ gradient inward. If the excess ammonia could not be expelled (or perhaps detoxified), blood ammonia would rise and toxicity would result.

Another factor to keep in mind is that the blood ammonia levels of many aquatic animals are quite high and variable. Normal values in teleosts have been measured at 0.1 to 0.4 mg% (Goldstein et al. 1964, Smith 1929), or about 10 times greater than normal values in mammalian blood (de Vooys 1969). Even higher blood ammonia levels have been reported in Amazon River fishes, which live in an environment notably low in dissolved solids (Mangum et al. 1977). The concentration gradient available for diffusion may thus be slight even in high ammonia environments.

As reviewed in the previous section, ammonia excretion seems to involve an ion exchange process, a mechanism that is much more likely to occur than the passive transport of free ammonia out of the animal. Considering that ion transport is an active process, it seems unlikely that an aquatic animal would be forced to take up ammonium ions from the water when the uptake of sodium at the gill is, in itself, secondary to the removal of unwanted ions. Moreover *in vitro* studies have shown that the excretory tissues of many different species of aquatic animals can pump ammonium ions against a concentration gradient.

The remaining possibility is that an elevated ammonia level in the external medium exerts a toxic effect indirectly. As the concentration gradient is reduced, the animal would be forced to retain metabolic ammonia, which then might reach levels that were directly toxic. The fact that in some fishes ammonia excretion slows down as the level of environmental ammonia increases seems to support this hypothesis (Fromm and Gillette 1968, Olson and Fromm 1971). At such times, metabolic ammonia "backs up" and cannot be released rapidly enough. The animal then must detoxify it or die.

Elevated blood ammonia can be detoxified in the brain of some fishes by glutamine synthesis, which may enable them to resist increasing levels of ammonia in the water. Levi et al. (1974) demonstrated that in goldfish exposed to ammonia concentrations of 12.75 mg $NH_3$ -N $l^{-1}$ for 24 to 48 hr, the concentration of cerebral glutamine increased nearly 10-fold. Free ammonia in the brain was detoxified during the conversion of glutamate to glutamine. Wilson et al. (1969) also suggested that fishes with high activities of brain glutamine synthetase might detoxify free ammonia, enabling them to tolerate higher $NH_3$ levels in the environment. According to Mehrle and Bloomfield (1974), the detoxification of ammonia in fishes occurs by the following reactions

$$\alpha\text{-oxoglutarate} + NADH + H^+ + NH_4^+$$

$$\underset{\text{dehydrogenase}}{\overset{\text{glutamate}}{\rightleftharpoons}} \text{glutamate} + NAD + H_2O \quad (63)$$

$$\text{glutamate} + ATP + NH_4^+ \underset{\text{dehydrogenase}}{\overset{\text{glutamate}}{\rightleftharpoons}} \text{glutamine}$$

$$+ ADP + \text{orthophosphate} \quad (64)$$

Both reactions take place in the brain; the first also occurs in the liver.

Olson and Fromm (1971) studied the effects of increased environmental ammonia on urea excretion in rainbow trout and goldfish. Trout showed minimal change in the overall nitrogen excretion pattern, except for decreased ammonia excretion as environmental ammonia increased. Long-term exposure to ammonia had little effect on urea excretion rates. Goldfish demonstrated a significant increase in urea excretion rates as the level of environmental ammonia increased. These rates were dependent on the external ammonia concentrations, but independent of the previous acclimation ammonia levels and the duration of acclimation. The time required for goldfish to alter urea excretion rates in response to changes in external ammonia was short. This accounts in part for the higher tolerance to ammonia in goldfish compared with trout. Thus the lack of an efficient ammonia detoxifying mechanism may reflect the inability of trout to prevent the appearance of increased blood ammonia levels as the ammonia concentration in the environment increases (Fromm and Gillette 1968). The failure of many delicate marine fishes to cope with rising ammonia levels in aquarium water may be due to the same difficulty, but this is only conjecture.

The exact mechanisms of ammonia toxicity to living cells are poorly understood and not of particular importance here. A review of the subject was written by Campbell (1973). I shall deal instead with the gross effects that exposure to sublethal levels of ammonia are known to have on aquatic animals. These effects could be due to diffusion of ammonia into the gill, the forced retention of metabolic ammonia, or both. Many reports describe histopathological changes in the gills and other organs, decreased resistance to disease, and impairment of growth. Nearly all of the published work has dealt with hatchery-reared freshwater teleosts. Presumably the effects of ammonia in marine teleosts are the same or similar.

Shreckenbach et al. (1975) observed gill necrosis in carp (*Cyprinus carpio*) after exposure to elevated levels of $NH_3$. Smart (1976) noted that the gills of rainbow trout showed some thickening of the lamellar epithelium and increased mucus production, in addition to swollen and rounded secondary lamellae. Inside the lamellae there were instances of the epithelium rupturing and of hemorrhage. Bullock (1972) noticed similar changes in gills of rainbow trout (aneurysms in the gill capillaries), and Flis (1968) saw aneurysms in carp gills. Any fusing, or "clubbing," of the lamellae reduces the surface area of the gills, which would impair respiration by interfering with the uptake of $O_2$ and the unloading of $CO_2$.

Gill hyperplasia has been described numerous times in fishes exposed to sublethal concentrations of ammonia (e.g., Burrows 1964,

Larmoyeaux and Piper 1973, Olson and Fromm 1971, Reichenbach-Klinke 1967, Robinette 1976, Smith and Piper 1975). Smith and Piper (1975) also reported that trout used in their experiments had necrotic lesions on the liver. Reichenbach-Klinke (1967) noted a swelling of the parenchyma cells of the liver in several species of European freshwater teleosts. There was also considerable congestion of the blood vessels and blood corpuscles, infiltration of blood components into liver tissue, inflammation, and degeneration of liver tissue. Similar findings were reported by Flis (1968) in the livers of carp exposed to sublethal concentrations of ammonia.

Ammonia has been implicated in such nonspecific maladies as fin and tail rot (Smart 1976), anemia (Reichenbach-Klinke 1967), dropsy or blue sac disease (Burkhalter and Kaya 1977, Wolf 1957), and bacterial gill disease (Smith and Piper 1975, Snieszko and Hoffman 1963).

Brockway (1950), Burrows (1964), Kawamoto (1961), Reichenbach-Klinke (1967), Smith and Piper (1975), Woltering et al. (1978), and Wuhrmann and Woker (1948) noted a relationship between sublethal concentrations of ammonia in hatchery water and reduced rates of growth in freshwater teleosts. Armstrong et al. (1978) reported reduced growth rate in Malaysian prawns maintained in brackish water containing sublethal concentrations of ammonia. The effects appeared to be caused more by $NH_4^+$ that $NH_3$.

Temperature, pH, and salinity may affect ammonia toxicity indirectly by controlling the hydrolysis of ammonium ion. Hypoxic conditions and the presence of high levels of free $CO_2$ in solution are thought by some investigators to enhance ammonia toxicity directly, but the mechanisms by which this is brought about have not yet been determined.

Reichenbach-Klinke (1967), noted that the oxygen content of the tissues in several species of European freshwater teleosts decreased as the tissue concentration of $NH_3$ increased, and that resistance to ammonia was lower during hypoxic conditions. Other investigators also have reported that the toxicity of $NH_3$ is magnified in waters of low oxygen tension (e.g., Downing and Merkens 1955, Larmoyeux and Piper 1973, Lloyd 1971, Lloyd and Herbert 1962, Merkens and Downing 1957, Smith and Piper 1975, Wuhrmann and Woker 1953).

According to one theory, elevated levels of ammonia in the environment in some way interfere with the ability of hemoglobin to retain oxygen. Reichenbach-Klinke (1967) noted a decrease in red blood cells in freshwater teleosts after the fishes had been maintained in water with sublethal concentrations of ammonia. Brockway (1950) reported that when ammonia in the water increased to approximately 1 mg total $NH_4$-N $l^{-1}$, the oxygen content of rainbow trout blood decreased to about 14% of its normal value, and the $CO_2$ content increased by about 15%. Fromm and Gillette (1968), however, observed that ammonia levels up to 10 mg $NH_3$-N $l^{-1}$ had no significant effect on the ability of hemoglobin to combine with oxygen when rainbow trout erythocytes were suspended in Ringer and studied *in vitro*.

Sousa and Meade (1977) used spectrophometric methods to study hemoglobin solutions from coho salmon that had been subjected to high levels of environmental ammonia. They noted a progressive shift in the absorption configuration of oxygenated hemoblobin toward deoxygenation. They postulated that prolonged exposure of the fish to elevated levels of ammonia in the water resulted in acidosis. This, in turn, interfered with the ability of hemoglobin to transport oxygen. The acidemia brought on by upsetting the internal acid-base balance caused oxygen to be released prematurely (Bohr effect). The Bohr effect is described in Section 11.6.

The most widely cited publication describing the effects of increased free $CO_2$ is the one by Lloyd and Herbert (1960), who concluded that ammonia toxicity was enhanced by high $CO_2$ levels. When the pH of the water containing ammonia was decreased from 8.2 to 7 by raising the free $CO_2$ concentration (from 3.2 to 49 mg $l^{-1}$), the 500-min $LC_{50}$ value for free ammonia decreased; the toxicity of $NH_3$, in other words, increased with a drop in pH caused by addition of $CO_2$. This is contrary to the generally accepted idea that a drop in pH decreases ammonia toxicity by reducing the percentage of the total $NH_4$-N present as $NH_3$ (e.g., Alabaster and Herbert 1954, Armstrong et al. 1978, Buckley 1978, Downing and Merkens 1955, Wuhrmann and Woker 1948). Lloyd and Herbert explained their unusual findings as follows. The $CO_2$ liberated by a fish during respiration causes a drop in pH at the surface of the gill, which is independent of the alkalinity of the water but greater when the free $CO_2$ of the water is low. At higher pH values (little free $CO_2$ present), addition of respiratory $CO_2$ causes a greater lowering of the pH and an increased conversion of $NH_3$ to $NH_4^+$; in other words, a reduction in the percentage of $NH_3$. This effect was greater than the effect that occurred when the free $CO_2$ content of the water was high (pH 7). The increased toxicity of ammonia at the lower pH was thus explained in terms of a decreased conversion of $NH_3$ to $NH_4^+$. Warren and Schenker (1962) criticized these results by pointing out that Lloyd and Herbert had not considered the effect of internal pH on the equilibrium of ammonia between the fish and the environment. If increased free $CO_2$ in the environment causes a decrease in blood pH, the concentration of $NH_3$ in the blood would then be lowered. According to Fromm and Gillette (1968), if the pH of blood containing 77 mg total $NH_4$-N $l^{-1}$

were to be lowered from pH 7.5 to 7.2, the concentration of $NH_3$ would be about 0.42 mg $NH_3$ $l^{-1}$, because at pH 7.2 only about 0.6% of the total $NH_4$-N would be present as $NH_3$. The resulting water-blood gradient (60:42) would subsequently favor diffusion of $NH_3$ into the fish. However as noted by Warren and Schenker (1962), it is still difficult to see how pH changes could cause the large differences (10-fold) in the amount of ammonia entering a fish at the different pH values, as Lloyd and Herbert proposed. That is, of course, assuming that it is possible for any ammonia to enter fishes. The effect of free $CO_2$ on ammonia toxicity is therefore uncertain. Presumably any such effects would be reduced in seawater with its large buffer capacity.

### Lethal Limits

Guidelines for the lethal limits of environmental ammonia to marine elasmobranchs and teleosts have not been set because data are lacking. Good data on marine invertebrates, particularly the osmoconformers, will be difficult to gather. In freshwater fishes, ammonia toxicity varies with such factors as species, other water quality parameters, experimental method, and the age, acclimation history, and condition of the test animals. The establishment of lethal limits at given conditions for even a single species is difficult, as proved by the varied results obtained over the years with rainbow trout. The careless procedures used in many bioassays cast doubt on the validity of much of the published work. Maetz et al. (1976) noted that despite its high solubility, ammonia is easily lost to the atmosphere during tissue perfusion studies. This may be particularly troublesome when freshwater is used and the pH is not controlled closely. In most published bioassay tests, open aquarium tanks were used and the water was aerated.

Studies that do not state the level of ammonia to which the test animals were previously acclimated are of doubtful value. Some freshwater fishes can acquire resistance to ammonia with time. Ball (1967), Lloyd and Orr (1969), and Schulze-Wiehenbrauck (1976), showed that rainbow trout acclimated to sublethal levels of ammonia later became resistant to otherwise lethal concentrations. Similar results were demonstrated by Buckley (1978), using coho salmon. Rubin and Elmaraghy (1977) studied ammonia resistance in guppy fry (*Poecilia reticulatus*). They observed that the major change in $LC_{50}$ as a function of time was evident during early exposure, whereas the 48-, 72-, and 96-hr values were about the same.

In general, lethal limits of ammonia for teleosts range from the 0.07 mg $NH_3$-N $l^{-1}$ for rainbow trout fry reported by Rice and Stokes (1975),

*Toxicity and Stress*

to 1.4 mg NH$_3$-N l$^{-1}$ for juvenile striped bass (*Morone saxatilis*), described by Hazel et al. (1971). Values of approximately 0.2 to 0.4 mg NH$_3$-N l$^{-1}$ are typically stated (Burkhalter and Kaya 1977).

The adult stages of the marine invertebrates studied to date show them to be markedly more tolerant of ammonia than fishes. The picture with respect to eggs and developing gametes is still unclear, but these evidently are more sensitive than adults. Kobayashi (1971) found that the embryonic development of the sea urchin *Anthocidaris crassispina* was retarded by addition of 1 mg NH$_4$Cl l$^{-1}$ (0.33 mg total NH$_4$-N l$^{-1}$). The larvae, however, were normal. Greenwood and Brown (1974) reported that an ammonia level equivalent to 17.5 mg total NH$_4$-N l$^{-1}$ added to the culture medium as ammonium nitrate significantly impaired fertilization of the eggs of the sea urchin *Parenchinus angulosus*, with 95% of the developing gametes failing to reach the gastrula stage. The use of ammonium nitrate in bioassay is a poor choice, because it introduces another possible toxicant (nitrate) into the procedure.

Adult stages of other invertebrates can tolerate many times more ammonia than those just cited. Brown and Currie (1973) noted that the gastropod mollusk *Bullia digitalis* (whelk) was not killed within 7 days by concentrations of ammonium nitrate of 1500 mg l$^{-1}$ (262.5 mg total NH$_4$-N l$^{-1}$), even though the animals were affected by much lower concentrations (8.75 mg total NH$_4$-N l$^{-1}$), refusing either to feed or burrow into the substratum. Epifanio and Srna (1975) found the bivalve mollusks *Crassostrea virginica* (American oyster) and *Mercenaria mercenaria* (quahog) also able to tolerate high ammonia levels. The LC$_{50}$ at 96 hr ranged from 110 to 880 mg total NH$_4$-N l$^{-1}$.

Brown (1974) monitored the effects of NH$_4$NO$_3$ on several marine invertebrates indigenous to the coast of South Africa. The species studied were the isopods *Eurydice longicornis*, *Exosphaeroma truncatitelson*, and *Pontogeloides latipes*; the mysid *Gastrosaccus psammodytes*; the nemertine worm *Cerebratulus fuscus*; and the malacostracan crustacean *Jasus lalandii* (spiny lobster). Twenty percent of the *Gastrosaccus* were dead after 1 hr at 52.5 mg total NH$_4$-N l$^{-1}$, and the survivors did not live after transfer to fresh seawater. *Cerebratulus* and *Pontogeloides* did not die in solutions of the same strength. At 87.5 mg total NH$_4$-N l$^{-1}$, all *Gastrosaccus* died or were moribund within an hour. *Eurydice* survived the hour, but 60% failed to recover in fresh seawater. All *Cerebratulus* survived an hour and recovered in fresh seawater. Only one specimen of *Exosphaeroma* failed to recover after having been in the test solution for 1.5 hr. *Pontogeloides* seemed to be completely unaffected after 1.5 hr. Specimens of *Jasus* placed in a solution equivalent to 70 mg total NH$_4$-N l$^{-1}$ were stressed, but recovered when transferred to fresh seawater after 3 hr.

**Management Practices**

Tables are available for estimating the percentage of the total $NH_4$-N that is present as $NH_3$ in seawater of stated temperature, salinity, and pH (Bower and Bidwell 1978), but the information is of doubtful practical value for two reasons. First, the factors that affect the percentage of $NH_3$ cannot be controlled directly without causing other harmful effects on the animals being maintained. Even minor changes in temperature, for example, are known to induce stress (Section 11.4). Second, there is recent evidence implicating $NH_4^+$ as also being toxic. Armstrong et al. (1978) subjected groups of Malaysian prawn larvae to equal concentrations of $NH_3$ at different pH values and compared the results. The $LC_{50}$ values for larvae exposed to 0.98 mg $NH_3$ $l^{-1}$ at pH 6.83 and 8.34 were 9 hr and 144 hr, respectively, whereas the corresponding $NH_4^+$ concentrations were 319 and 9 mg $l^{-1}$. The animals exposed to 10.2 mg $NH_3$ $l^{-1}$ survived twice as long as those exposed to 5.5 mg $NH_3$ $l^{-1}$, but the $NH_4^+$ concentration was 3.5 times higher in the latter case. Based on this experiment and others in which pH and the concentrations of $NH_3$ and $NH_4^+$ were controlled independently, Armstrong and his colleagues concluded that toxicity was caused by both $NH_3$ and $NH_4^+$. Free ammonia appeared to be the more toxic species in the higher pH ranges, with ammonium ion becoming more toxic in waters of lower pH.

It is sufficient to monitor the total $NH_4$-N concentration alone in aquarium seawater. Spotte (1979) recommended that the concentration not exceed 0.1 mg total $NH_4$-N $l^{-1}$. This is perhaps too stringent for fish hatcheries with their high animal densities, as mentioned by Smith and Piper (1975), but very low ammonia levels are easy to maintain in public aquariums where animals are kept in uncrowded conditions. Moreover many coral reef fishes seem to be much more sensitive to ammonia poisoning than rainbow trout, goldfish, and other species for which data are available. However this observation is not supported by experimental evidence.

Aquarium water must be protected from extraneous sources of gaseous ammonia. Ammoniated cleaning compounds can never be used around aquariums. It is also a poor practice to maintain laboratory aquariums near bird or rodent colonies. Hubbs et al. (1960) reported that young etheostomatine fishes and hylid tadpoles reared in a laboratory were killed by ammonia emanating from a nearby rodent colony. Sigel et al. (1972) maintained a group of nurse sharks (*Ginglymostoma cirratum*) adjacent to a room that housed chickens, mice, rats, and hamsters. The sharks failed to feed, developed large skin blisters, and eventually died. The problem was thought to have originated from atmospheric ammonia.

## 11.2  NITRITE TOXICITY

Nitrite in the blood oxidizes hemoglobin to methemoglobin, which is incapable of transporting oxygen (Jaffe 1964). Methemoglobin in fishes can be detected by the color of the blood and gills, which turn brown. It has been thought that the presence of methemoglobin could be correlated with mortality rate in aquatic animals, but this may not always be true, particularly when percent mortality in freshwater and seawater are compared using the same species of bioassay animal. Crawford and Allen (1977) showed that in chinook salmon fingerlings subjected to levels of 8.18 mg $NO_2$-N $l^{-1}$ in freshwater, 44% methemoglobin occurred with 70% mortality. Chinook salmon (*Oncorhynchus tshawytscha*) in seawater exposed to 246.97 mg $NO_2$-N $l^{-1}$ had 74% methemoglobin with only 10% mortality.

Table 11-1 summarizes some of the published values for nitrite toxicity in freshwater, brackish water, and seawater. As the results show, mortality decreases markedly with increasing salinity of the medium. Crawford and Allen (1977) attributed this to the possible protective effect of increased calcium ions, but conceded that perhaps another ion present in the medium also was involved. Perrone and Meade (1977) offered good evidence that chloride exerts a protective effect. No mortality occurred in their test animals (yearling coho salmon) in 48 hr at nitrite concentrations of 29.8 mg $NO_2$-N $l^{-1}$ and chloride levels of 261.3 mg Cl $l^{-1}$. Other salmon exposed to 3.8 mg $NO_2$-N $l^{-1}$ and 2.5 mg Cl $l^{-1}$ showed 58.3% mortality in 12 hr. No protective mechanism has been determined, but perhaps cations combine with nitrite ion and prevent its uptake from solution. Alternatively the presence of external calcium may inhibit the uptake of nitrite (assuming that toxicity takes place by assimilation). Cuthbert and Maetz (1972) demonstrated that calcium ions in solution decreased both ion and water permeability in various teleosts. A third possibility is that chloride ion could compete directly with nitrite ion, and its greater concentration in solution might inhibit the assimilation of $NO_2^-$.

### Management Practices

It is doubtful that nitrite poses a serious threat to aquarium animals maintained in brackish water or seawater aquariums, although its presence at low concentrations is definitely hazardous in freshwater. The maximum limit allowed in aquarium water of any salinity should be 0.1 mg $NO_2$-N $l^{-1}$ to be conservative (Spotte 1979). One additional factor is worth noting. Hattingh and van Pletzen (1974) reported that the methemoglobin level increased in mudfish (*Labeo umbratus*), a fresh-

**Table 11-1 Published Lethal Concentrations of NO$_2$-N in Freshwater (FW), Brackish Water (BW), and Seawater (SW)**

| Species and Size or Age | Concentration (mg NO$_2$-N l$^{-1}$) | Time (hr) | % Mortality | Medium | Source |
|---|---|---|---|---|---|
| Rainbow trout (yearling) | 0.55 | 24 | 55 | FW | Smith and Williams (1974) |
| Chinook salmon (32 g) | 0.50 | 24 | 40 | FW | Smith and Williams (1974) |
| Chinook salmon (fingerling) | 0.88 | 96 | 50 | FW | Westin (1974) |
| Rainbow trout (12 g) | 0.19 | 96 | 50 | FW | Russo et al. (1974) |
| Rainbow trout (9.1 g) | 0.23 | 96 | 50 | FW | Brown and McLeay (1975) |
| Coho salmon (yearling) | 3.80 | 12 | 58.3 | FW | Perrone and Meade (1977) |
| Chinook salmon (fingerling) | 19.00 | 48 | 50 | FW | Crawford and Allen (1977) |
| Malaysian prawn (larvae) | 8.60 | 96 | 50 | BW | Armstrong et al. (1976) |
| Chinook salmon (fingerling) | 1070.00 | 48 | 10 | SW | Crawford and Allen (1977) |
| American oyster (adult) | 658.00 | 96 | 50 | SW | Epifanio and Srna (1975) |
| American oyster (juvenile) | 798.00 | 96 | 50 | SW | Epifanio and Srna (1975) |
| Quahog (adult) | 1190.00 | 96 | 50 | SW | Epifanio and Srna (1975) |
| Quahog (juvenile) | 1133.00 | 96 | 50 | SW | Epifanio and Srna (1975) |

water teleost, when the fish were transported in tanks into which a mixed gas consisting of 95% $O_2$ and 5% $CO_2$ was bubbled. The authors suggested that the added oxygen somehow oxidized a portion of the hemoglobin in the animals to produce methemoglobin. The practice of shipping fishes in sealed plastic bags with oxygen and measurable concentrations of nitrite in solution should be investigated from this standpoint.

## 11.3  NITRATE TOXICITY

Nitrate is not acutely toxic to aquatic animals even in large concentrations, although its effects over extended periods of time have not been determined. It is possible that the pale gills seen in captive fishes after several months are the result of elevated nitrate, but this is only speculation.

Knepp and Arkin (1973) reported that nitrate levels of 400 mg $NO_3$-N $l^{-1}$ did not affect the percent mortality or growth of largemouth bass (*Micropterus salmoides*) and channel catfish (*Ictalurus punctatus*), both of which are freshwater species. Higher concentrations were not tested. Westin (1974) determined that nitrate was 2000 times less toxic than nitrite to chinook salmon and rainbow trout maintained in freshwater. Signs of trauma in chinook salmon did not occur until 5 to 8 days when the nitrate concentration was 1000 mg $NO_3$-N $l^{-1}$ or slightly less. These signs included the inability to swim upright, labored breathing, and reduced movement interspersed with erratic swimming. Some of the fishes had pale pink to dark red-brown gill filaments. Another interesting observation was that nitrate proved to be slightly more toxic when the animals were kept in brackish water ($S = 15$ o/oo). In salmon, toxicity of nitrate in brackish water was 1.14 to 1.41 times greater than in freshwater. In trout, nitrate toxicity proved to be 1.24 and 1.38 times more toxic in brackish water.

Hirayama (1966c) observed increased ventilation rates in the common octopus (*Octopus vulgaris*) maintained in seawater of low pH and alkalinity values and high nitrate concentrations. Death occurred at 7 hr when the nitrate level was 1400 mg $NO_3$-N $l^{-1}$. Kuwatani et al. (1969) concluded that nitrate concentrations up to 100 mg $NO_3$-N $l^{-1}$ had no effect on growth of the Japanese pearl oyster (*Pinctata fucada*), so long as the pH of the seawater was higher than 8.05.

Epifanio and Srna (1975) demonstrated that large amounts of sodium nitrate were not toxic to two species of bivalve mollusks kept in low salinity seawater ($S = 27$ o/oo). The 96-hr $LC_{50}$ levels of sodium nitrate were 2604 mg $NO_3$-N $l^{-1}$ for adult American oysters and 3794 mg $NO_3$-N $l^{-1}$ for juveniles. In the quahog, 50% mortality did not occur even when the $NaNO_3$ concentration reached nearly 75% of the total salinity, and the authors considered it pointless to test higher concentrations.

### Management Practices

Very high concentrations of nitrate have been reported in the seawater of several public aquariums (Section 6.3), implying that nitrate is non-toxic to marine animals. Such a premise is unacceptable until nitrate is proved to be harmless after long-germ exposure. Spotte (1979) recommended that the maximum acceptable value in routine aquarium maintenance was 20 mg $NO_3$-N $l^{-1}$.

## 11.4 TEMPERATURE STRESS

Changes in temperature exert a profound influence on aquatic ectothermic (cold-blooded) animals. Even short-term deviation from the acclimation temperature alters respiratory requirements, causes internal acid-base imbalance, and produces disturbances in fluid-electrolyte regulation (Crawshaw 1977). Animals in nature cope with sudden temperature changes in either of two ways: (1) by moving to a new location; or (2) by physiological adjustment. The first option will not be discussed because an aquarium is, by definition, a limited space. Aquarium animals have no choice but to adjust.

### Heat and Cold Stress

Heat and cold stress refer to the responses induced in ectothermic animals when the temperature is raised or lowered suddenly from ambient. The result of extreme thermal stress is *coma,* defined by Prosser (1973) as a measure of the reversible failure of function in the central nervous system. When an animal is disabled by being placed in water that is warmer than ambient (heat coma), or colder (chill coma), it is said to suffer *thermal shock.* Thermal shock in fishes is characterized by noticeable changes in behavior. If the new temperature is significantly higher than ambient, fishes often show increased activity, loss of equilibrium (including aimless fin movement and remaining in temporary but stationary positions with the tail elevated), and a general increase in ventilation rate, as measured by movements of the opercula

(Hoff and Westman 1966). If a fish is subjected to temperatures that are significantly colder than ambient, there is loss of equilibrium, increased ventilation rate, and often violent convulsions and spasms (Hoff and Westman 1966).

Prosser (1973) reviewed the general physiological changes that occur in ectothermic animals when they are exposed to temperatures above or below ambient. For reviews on how invertebrates and fishes are affected by the temperature of the environment see Kinne (1970) and Brett (1970), respectively. As body temperature is lowered, heart rate and respiration are slowed and hypoxia may result. Gill membranes become permeable and ionic gradients cannot be maintained because ion pumps stop. The liberation of energy may not be sufficient to maintain metabolic functions. The affinities of enzymes for their respective substrates are changed. Integration by the central nervous system fails and many animals enter a state of chill coma at temperatures well above the lethal limit.

Heat death is also the result of multiple causes. When the body temperature is raised, blood-oxygen transport is reduced. Lipids change in chemical state, resulting in increased permeability of cell membranes. Enzymes are inactivated. Proteins are denatured and toxic substances may be released from damaged cells.

Much has been written on the responses of aquatic ectothermic animals to heat stress. Among the maladies reported in fishes are the thermal inactivation of enzymes (Evans and Bowler 1973), increased heart rate (Stevens et al. 1972), production of toxic metabolites (Fahmy 1973, Heilbrunn et al. 1946), increased blood adrenaline (Mazeaud et al. 1977), and destablization of cell membranes (Chapman 1967, Precht et al. 1973). Heat stress also affects the quantity and state of intracellular water (Ling 1967, Precht et al. 1973), osmoregulation (Bowler et al. 1973, Garside and Chin-Yeun-Kee 1972, Heinicke and Houston 1965), and ionic balance (Maetz and Evans 1972). Rombough and Garside (1977) studied the histopathological effects of heat stress in the banded killifish (*Fundulus diaphanus*) acclimated to 25°C. The $LC_{50}$ occurred at 34.5°C. The major injuries induced by thermal stress were to the gills, which resulted in abnormal gas exchange and osmoregulation and lead to pathological changes in other tissues. The gills were characterized by subepithelial edema, congestion of the lamellar capillaries, and delamination of the respiratory epithelium from the pillar cell system. Necrotic areas were observed in part of the hypothalamus and in the liver. Damaged areas of the pancreas and adjacent blood vessels were evident, and fatty changes took place in the liver. The ovaries appeared to be extremely sensitive to high temperature and oocytes and follicular cells were injured severely after only short exposure to temperatures near the $LC_{50}$ level. Hypoxia of the central nervous system was thought to be the ultimate cause of death.

Comparatively little has been written on the physiological effects of cold stress. Woodhead and Woodhead (1965) reported that Atlantic cod (*Gadus morhua*) wintering at 2°C in the Barents Sea were unable to regulate the flux of ions. Stanley and Colby (1971) showed that cold stress in alewives (*Alosa pseudoharengus*) caused dilution of the blood components in freshwater-acclimated fish, and concentration of blood values in specimens acclimated to seawater.

**Thermal Acclimation**

Ectothermic animals vary body temperature with the environment, but compensate metabolically so that activity remains constant over a given temperature range. The metabolic compensation for adaptation to a new temperature is called *thermal acclimation*. Kinne (1964) recognized three phases in the acclimation process: (1) immediate response, which begins soon after a change in ambient temperature and is characterized by shock reactions or over- or undershoots in metabolic activity; (2) stabilization, which starts within minutes or hours after the temperature change and leads gradually to a new steady-state level; and (3) new steady state, which begins hours or weeks after attainment of near maximum adjustment.

Complete acclimation (phase 3) to higher than ambient temperatures takes a few hours to several days in most species; complete acclimation to lower temperatures takes several days or weeks. The time required to reach phase 3 (i.e., the acclimation rate) is influenced by many factors, including the dissolved oxygen concentration, salinity, season, photoperiod, age, size, sex, species, nutritional state, and composition of the diet (Precht et al. 1973). American lobsters (*Homarus americanus*) acclimated to 14.5°C and transferred to 23°C required 22 days for complete acclimation (McLeese 1956). Specimens of the brachyuran crab *Uca pugnax* (fiddler crab) kept at 22 to 27°C needed 14 days to completely acclimate to 15°C (Vernberg 1959). Doudoroff (1942) reported that when the opaleye (*Girella nigricans*), a seawater teleost, was transferred from 14 to 26°C, complete acclimation took 15 days. Specimens moved from 26 to 14°C required 25 days. The longjaw mudsucker (*Gillichthys mirabilis*), a marine teleost, took only 1 day to acclimate completely when moved from 20 to 30°C, but required 23 days when the process was reversed (Sumner and Doudoroff 1938).

### Management Practices

Newly acquired animals should be placed in water adjusted to the acclimation temperature. After observing the animals for several days, raise or lower the temperature as necessary. Most animals can acclimate faster to increases in temperature than to decreases of the same increments. If the temperature is to be raised, the maximum recommended rate is 2°C 24 hr$^{-1}$; if lowered, use 1°C 24 hr$^{-1}$.

## 11.5  HANDLING STRESS

The act of chasing a fish, netting it, and removing it from the water during aquarium transfer results in instantaneous neuroendocrine responses. This is reflected by a rapid rise in the plasma concentrations of catecholamines and corticosteroids. Adrenaline and noradrenaline increase after only a few minutes of hypoxia or struggling in cyclostomes (Mazeaud 1969a), selachians (Mazeaud 1969b), or teleosts (Mazeaud 1964, Mazeaud et al. 1977, Nakano and Tomlinson 1967). Either adrenaline or noradrenaline is more prominent, depending on the species. The results of these primary effects of stress are to induce secondary effects, such as metabolic and osmotic disturbances. It is the secondary effects that will be considered here.

Fletcher (1975) compared blood constituents in two groups of winter flounders (*Pseudopleuronectes americanus*), the first group freshly captured by scuba divers, and the second acclimated to laboratory aquariums for periods that ranged from 24 hr to 3 months. Large differences were noted. In general, newly captured flounders showed elevated values of hematocrit, mean cell volume (MCV), plasma osmolality, and the electrolytes Na$^+$ and Cl$^-$. Mean cell hemoglobin concentration (MCHC) and the concentration of one electrolyte (K$^+$) were lower in newly captured flounders. Differences in values for K$^+$ were found subsequently to be an artifact of storing the blood samples for 2 to 3 hr before analysis. Acclimated flounders that were "stressed" by being held in a net and swished back and forth in a holding tank for 15 min showed elevated levels of hematocrit, MCV, and plasma osmolality, and a significant decrease in MCHC.

In another series of experiments, flounders were stressed by being held upside down for 4 hr in small plastic buckets containing 10 to 12 l of continuously aerated seawater. The stress produced clear changes in the blood values monitored. During the first hour, hematocrit increased significantly, due in part to an increase in MCV. After 4 hr, the hematocrit and red blood cell numbers (RBC) had begun to decline, whereas the MCV continued to increase. Hematocrit, RBC, and MCV declined when the fish were returned to a holding tank, and were similar to prestress values after 24 hr.

Blood hemoglobin increased during the first 15 min of stress, whereas the mean cell hemoglobin continued to rise for the 4-hr stress period. Both factors returned to prestress values 20 hr after the stress was removed and the fish were returned to a holding tank. The MCHC dropped significantly during the stress period, but returned to prestress levels 24 hr after the start of the experiment, or 20 hr from the time the stress was removed.

The plasma protein concentration and osmolality increased during the first hour of stress. Osmolality continued to rise throughout the 4-hr period, and declined when the stress was removed. However values were still not equal to prestress levels by 24 hr. During the 4-hr period, plasma $Na^+$, $Cl^-$, and red blood $Na^+$ increased significantly. Red cell $Na^+$ returned to prestress levels within 24 hr. Plasma $Na^+$ and $Cl^-$, however, remained elevated for 2 to 3 days after the stress was removed. Plasma $K^+$ did not show a consistent change during or after stress.

The effects of handling stress in fishes are manifest clearly by elevations in blood glucose (*hyperglycemia*), which reflect a change in carbohydrate metabolism. Exposing a fish to hypoxic water or to the air is sufficient to induce increases in blood glucose. In this context, it is often referred to as "asphyxiation hyperglycemia" (McCormick and MacLeod 1925). The condition may be exacerbated by exciting the fish during netting and handling (Chavin and Young 1970), by the combined effects of elevated ammonia and low dissolved oxygen concentrations in the water (Hattingh 1977), or by raising the temperature (McCormick and MacLeod 1925).

Chavin and Young (1970) tested the effects of rapid aquarium transfer by net on goldfish, a notably hardy species. The procedure took only a few seconds. Fish were netted and moved to a nearby aquarium that was identical in all respects to the first (e.g., size, water chemistry, photoperiod, and temperature). Nevertheless the move was stressful, as shown by the hyperglycemia that persisted for 2 days. Similarly, McCormick and MacLeod (1925) and Simpson (1926) found that 4 days were required for some seawater teleosts to acclimate to new environmental conditions after capture, as determined by blood glucose levels. MacKay and Beatty (1968) noted that white suckers (*Catostomus commersoni*), which are freshwater teleosts, still did not show normal blood glucose levels a week after having been caught in a net. Fletcher (1975) reported that in newly captured winter flounders there was an immediate increase in blood glucose that did not subside for several days. Similar observations were made by Wardle (1972) in the plaice (*Pleuronectes platessa*).

## Management Practices

Ideally a fish should not be removed from the water during either capture or transfer, nor should it be chased and excited unnecessarily. Spotte (1973) recommended that fishes be captured and transferred in clear polyethylene bags whenever possible. Clear polyethylene has a refractive index similar to water, making it difficult for a fish to see and attempt to avoid. Moreover a fish captured in a bag need never leave the water and the danger of hypoxia is remote.

## 11.6  ACID-BASE IMBALANCE

Respiratory functions in man and other mammals respond quickly to changes in blood pH: ventilation rate doubles if the pH falls 0.1 unit and is halved when pH increases of 0.1 unit occur (Hoar 1975). Hyperventilation, or exaggerated heavy breathing, rapidly reduces the total $CO_2$, resulting in a rise in blood pH. Breath-holding causes the blood $CO_2$ level to rise quickly, and blood pH falls. Such instant and facile responses are impossible for aquatic ectothermic animals, and changes in ventilation rate do little to alleviate acid-base imbalance. Several factors account for this and should be considered when environmental conditions in aquarium water deteriorate to a point at which the acid-base status of the animals is affected. It is important to note that the pH of the water (pH$w$) plays no direct role in physiological acid-base regulation; rather its role is indirect by affecting the partial pressure of carbon dioxide in solution ($Pw_{CO_2}$). The factors affecting acid-base balance that will be considered here are: (1) the low solubility of oxygen versus the high solubility of carbon dioxide (28 times that of oxygen at 20°C in freshwater); (2) the high density and viscosity of water; (3) the limited physiological range of $CO_2$ in water-breathers; (4) the fact that in cold-blooded aquatic animals ventilation rate is controlled directly by the partial pressure of dissolved oxygen in the water ($Pw_{O_2}$), instead of $Pw_{CO_2}$; and (5) the effects of temperature and salinity on arterial blood pH (pH$a$) and the partial pressure of carbon dioxide in arterial blood ($Pa_{CO_2}$). See Dejours (1975) and Reeves (1977) for reviews on the subject of acid-base balance in aquatic ectotherms.

Gas exchange in water is more difficult than it is in air. Water offers greater resistance to movement by being approximately 50 times more viscous than air and 800 times denser. Water holds far less oxygen than air at saturation (5 to 10 ml $O_2$ $l^{-1}$ versus 210 ml $O_2$ $l^{-1}$). The problem is made worse by the fact that the physiological range of $CO_2$ in water breathers is probably limited to 1 to 10 mm Hg (Rahn 1966), compared with 140 mm Hg for air breathers. Aquatic animals thus are forced to function with differences in partial pressures of $CO_2$ between blood and water that often are too slight for effective unloading of $CO_2$ at the gills. If it is assumed that for each millilitre of oxygen taken up by an aquatic animal 1 ml of $CO_2$ is given off, a decrease of 1 mm Hg $O_2$ will result in an increase in the $Pw_{CO_2}$ of only 1/28 mm Hg in the gill water, even though equal volumes of oxygen and carbon dioxide are exchanged. Thus to extract the same volume of oxygen, the ventilation rate of a fish at 20°C is 28 times that of an air breather, and the $Pa_{CO_2}$ is 1/28th that of an air-breathing animal (Howell et al. 1970).

Aquatic animals—freshwater ones in particular—often encounter water in which the level of carbon dioxide is variable. The rate at which a gas diffuses through a cell membrane depends on the concentration gradient on either side of the membrane—the difference in partial pressure, in other words. Aquatic animals can unload carbon dioxide only when the partial pressure in the blood exceeds the partial pressure in the water. At such times, carbon dioxide diffuses outward down the concentration gradient. However due to the high solubility of $CO_2$, that difference is always marginal, seldom exceeding 2 to 3 mm Hg (Cameron and Randall 1972, Randall 1970). Seawater contains an inherent safety factor because it is more strongly buffered. In other words, the increase in $Pw_{CO_2}$ accompanying the fall in $Pw_{O_2}$ during respiration is much smaller than in poorly buffered waters (Dejours 1978). The reason, of course, is because of the very low concentration of $CO_2$ in seawater at pH 8.2.

Ventilation rate in fishes is a direct function of the amount of dissolved oxygen (Dejours et al. 1977) and is relatively independent of the $Pw_{CO_2}$ (Cameron 1978, Dejours 1973). This was shown by Dejours (1973) in experiments with rainbow trout in which a decrease in ventilation rate caused by *hyperoxia* (higher than normal oxygen levels) was always accompanied by an increase in $Pw_{CO_2}$ in the gill water. Ventilation rate during hyperoxia remained unchanged when the water was made *hypercapnic* (an increase in $Pw_{CO_2}$), as shown by Dejours (1973). His conclusions can be summarized as follows: (1) *hypoxia* (less than normal dissolved oxygen concentrations) increases ventilation rate; (2) hyperoxia decreases ventilation rate; (3) hypercapnia generally leads to small increases in ventilation rate (e.g., the goldfish), although in some other species, such as the rainbow trout, there may be a marked increase; and (4) altering the pH of the water but not the $Pw_{CO_2}$ results in no ventilatory response. Hypoxia induces a decrease in $Pa_{CO_2}$ in fishes, in addition to decreases in the $HCO_3^-$ and $H^+$ blood concentrations. Hyperoxia, on the other hand, leads to respiratory acidosis and increases in the above factors.

In rainbow trout, ventilation rate does not change with a change in the pH$w$ at constant $Pw_{CO_2}$. However a change in $Pw_{CO_2}$ accompanied by a pH$w$ change results in increased ventilation rates. It is probable that pH changes in seawater, if they occur slowly, do not affect ventilation rates of seawater fishes, nor ultimately acid-base balance, until the level of $Pw_{CO_2}$ increases significantly. This may not occur until the pH$w$ drops to at least 7.7, at which point the percentage molar fraction of $H_2CO_3(CO_2)$ is approximately 2 at 24°C and 2.5 at 8°C.

Consider a fish or some other marine animal forced to live in an environment with increasing $Pw_{CO_2}$ and declining pH, and assume that the animal is of a species that responds positively to a hypercapnic environment by increasing its ventilation rate. Assume further that the pH$w$ is 7.7 or lower. An air-breathing animal can adjust to the difference between the partial pressure of $CO_2$ in the air and $Pa_{CO_2}$ by changes in ventilation rate; a fish cannot. Fishes and other aquatic animals that pump water over their gills are unable to regulate internal acid-base balance by ventilation (Cameron 1978, Randall and Cameron 1973). The $Pw_{CO_2}$ in most freshwaters ordinarily is less than 5 mm Hg. In seawater the normal value is approximately 0.25 mm Hg, as shown in Fig. 11-2. As mentioned previously, this may be advantageous because the higher buffer capacity of seawater provides a larger sink for $CO_2$ elimination at the gills. In any case, the slight difference between $Pw_{CO_2}$ and $Pa_{CO_2}$ means that increases in ventilation rate have little effect either on $Pa_{CO_2}$ or pH$a$.

Even minor increases in $Pw_{CO_2}$ reduce the difference in the partial pressure of $CO_2$ between the environment and the vascular fluids, restricting still further the concentration gradient necessary for diffusion of $CO_2$ out of the gills. When equilibrium has been reached and the concentration gradient no longer exists, the internal fluids become acidic: pH$a$ declines and $Pa_{CO_2}$ continues to rise. This situation, also termed hypercapnia even though it occurs inside the animal, is not relieved easily. As the vascular fluids become acidic, some of the $CO_2$ is buffered in the blood and converted to bicarbonate ions. Bicarbonate can then be exchanged for chloride at the inner gill surface. As Hoar (1975) noted, for aquatic animals there can be no immediate pH regulation, but only long-term ion exchanges with the water.

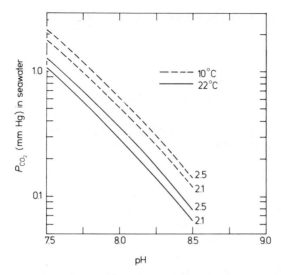

**Figure 11-2**   The partial pressure of free $CO_2$ versus pH in seawater at two temperature and alkalinity values. Drawn from equations in Takahashi et al. (1970).

The dilemma of this hypothetical fish is to find means of regulating its acid-base balance under conditions of hypercapnia. Ventilation will not help, yet the ventilation rate has increased just the same. A rise in $Pw_{CO_2}$ often causes increased ventilation in teleost fishes (Dejours 1973) and some elasmobranchs (Randall et al. 1976). A rise in $Pw_{CO_2}$ results in increases in $Pa_{CO_2}$ in fishes and a drop in pHa. Arterial pH is adjusted by increasing the bicarbonate ion concentration in rainbow trout acclimated to freshwater (Cameron and Randall 1972, Eddy et al. 1977, Haswell and Randall 1978), and spiny dogfish (*Squalus acanthias*) in seawater (Cross et al. 1969, Heisler 1978, Randall et al. 1976). Janssen and Randall (1975) concluded from their studies of rainbow trout that increased gill ventilation during hypercapnia probably was not caused by a drop in pHw, because acidification of the water with HCl instead of $CO_2$ failed to increase gill ventilation. Nor did they think the cause was a fall in pHa. The controlling factor was a rise in $Pa_{CO_2}$. In addition, the extent of the increase in gill ventilation was thought to be related to the Bohr effect, in which the oxygen bound up with hemoglobin is released prematurely to the tissues when $Pa_{CO_2}$ increases and pHa declines. Species showing little Bohr effect, such as the dogfish, do not respond so drastically to increases in $Pa_{CO_2}$.

The effect of $Pa_{CO_2}$ on blood-oxygen needs to be clarified before continuing. The usefulness of a respiratory pigment such as hemoglobin would be limited if it did not give up its stored oxygen to the tissues. This concept can be understood more clearly if reduced to the basic reaction

$$Hb + O_2 \rightleftharpoons HbO_2 \qquad (65)$$

Under conditions of adequate oxygenation of the water, hemoglobin combines with molecular oxygen from the external environment and the reaction shifts to the right. At low concentrations of $O_2$, such as would be found in oxygen-depleted tissues, the reaction shifts to the left and oxygen is released from the hemoglobin and diffuses into the tissues.

The efficiency of a respiratory pigment can be determined from its oxygen combining curve (also called oxygen equilibrium curve or oxygen dissociation curve). A typical curve is plotted by measuring the quantity of oxygen that combines with blood exposed to $O_2$ at a series of different pressures. The quantity of the gas that combines with blood at each pressure is expressed as a percentage of the amount that the blood contains when the hemoglobin is oxygen-saturated. Figure 11-3 depicts a set of oxygen combining curves from three fishes indigenous to the western North Atlantic. The middle curve shows that blood of the scup (*Stenotomus chrysops*) approaches saturation (80% $HbO_2$) at approximately 20 mm Hg of $O_2$. When followed in the opposite direction, the curve demonstrates that oxygen is released to the tissues as the partial pressure of $O_2$ diminishes, or until the blood oxygen is depleted (Hb + $O_2$). The oyster toadfish (*Opsanus tau*) has an oxygen combining curve to the left of the scup, meaning that its blood has a higher affinity for oxygen and gives up the gas to the tissues reluctantly. The opposite is true of the Atlantic mackerel (*Scomber scombrus*). Its blood has a lower affinity for oxygen than either the toadfish or scup, and its oxygen content is relinquished to the tissues readily. The oxygen combining curve of a mackerel is therefore to the right of the other two fishes.

Every organism has its own peculiar oxygen combining curve and the position and slope of the curve may be related to that organism's lifestyle and ecological adaptations. For example, a sedentary toadfish must sometimes endure inshore waters of low oxygen. During periods of hypoxia, it is more important that a toadfish's blood be able to glean all the oxygen it can from the water—have a high affinity for $O_2$, in other words. The fact that toadfish are inactive much of the time means that their oxygen requirements are relatively low and their blood need not be of a type that gives up its oxygen instantly. A mackerel, by contrast, spends its entire life in the open ocean, where dissolved oxygen is near saturation. It can afford the luxury of blood that has a lower affinity for $O_2$. On the other hand, a mackerel's furious lifestyle

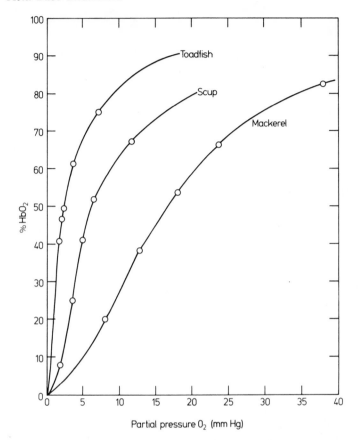

**Figure 11-3**   Oxygen combining curves for the hemoglobins of three temperate seawater fishes indigenous to the North Atlantic. Redrawn and modified from Hall and Mc-Cutcheon (1938).

means that any such oxygen bound up in the respiratory pigment must be continuously—and readily—available to supply high tissue demands.

The presence of $CO_2$ in the blood influences the shape and position of an oxygen combining curve. As $Pa_{CO_2}$ rises, the affinity of a respiratory pigment for oxygen is reduced and $O_2$ is released to the tissues more readily than it would otherwise be at comparable pressures. To say this another way, at high $Pa_{CO_2}$ the partial pressure of oxygen at which hemoglobin releases $O_2$ is higher than it is at low $Pa_{CO_2}$. The curve is shifted to the right (Bohr effect). Among cold-blooded animals, there is great variation in the Bohr effect. In some fish bloods there is a dramatic

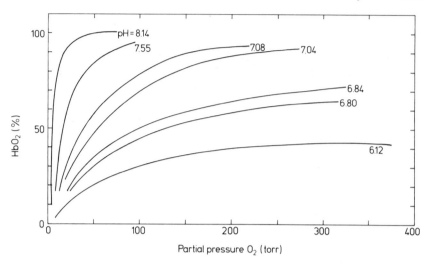

**Figure 11-4** Percent saturation of hemoglobin as a function of blood pH in the goosefish (*Lophius americanus*), a seawater teleost inhabiting the North Atlantic. The drastic shift of the oxygen combining curve to the right as blood pH declines illustrates the Root effect. The curve persists even at high $P_{O_2}$. Redrawn and modified from Green and Root (1933).

decrease in the quantity of oxygen the respiratory pigments can hold at high $Pa_{CO_2}$. This phenomenon is known as the *Root effect* (Root 1931), an example of which is shown in Fig. 11-4.

The situation of this hypothetical fish has worsened. The rise in $Pa_{CO_2}$ and subsequent fall in pH*a* have not been alleviated. The result is now *sustained* hypercapnia. The increase in $Pa_{CO_2}$ has caused an increase in ventilation rate. This has become necessary in part to obtain more oxygen from the water, even though the decreased retention time of water in the gill cavities (caused by the high pumping rate) means that a smaller percentage of oxygen is being removed per volume of water passed over the gills. Moreover the high metabolic cost of pumping water, a dense and viscous fluid, is resulting in even higher tissue oxygen demands. These undesirable conditions are worsened by the low solubility of oxygen and high solubility of carbon dioxide.

The fish has now reached a critical point. Survival may depend on species hardiness, or its evolutionary history. If it is a dogfish or some other species with blood that shows little or no Bohr effect, the respiratory pigment has a high affinity for oxygen and will not release it to the tissues readily. Under hypercapnic conditions, the fish is better off. Perhaps it is sedentary with low tissue oxygen demands, or maybe it evolved in an environment that is periodically hypoxic.

If, on the other hand, the fish is one with blood that demonstrates a high Bohr effect, its respiratory pigment has a low affinity for oxygen. As blood $CO_2$ levels increase, oxygen stored in the respiratory pigment is released quickly to the tissues. This is beneficial only in the sense that the tissues receive badly needed oxygen; otherwise the ventilation rate will remain high, fueling still heavier tissue oxygen demands. Suppose the fish is a mackerel, to take an extreme case. Mackerel blood has a notably high Bohr effect (Hall and McCutcheon 1938). Under conditions of hypercapnia a mackerel's oxygen combining curve shifts so far to the right as to be outside the useful range (Root effect). At that point $Pa_{CO_2}$, which favors unloading of oxygen at the tissues (Bohr effect), would suppress $O_2$ uptake at the gills. The mackerel suffocates, even though oxygen dissolved in the surrounding seawater may be at saturation.

Changes in temperature or salinity can make the effects of hypercapnia still worse. If, during a period of low pH$a$ and increasing $Pa_{CO_2}$, there is an increase in water temperature, the oxygen combining curve of hemoglobin is shifted to the right. A fish must then increase its arterial $HCO_3^-$ concentration so as to maintain blood pH on the basic side of neutral. Maintenance of blood pH is partly a function of temperature in ectothermic animals (Heisler 1978; Heisler et al. 1976; Howell et al. 1970, 1973; Rahn 1966, 1967; Rahn and Baumgardner 1972; Randall and Cameron 1973; Reeves 1977; Truchot 1978). The values for $K_w$ (the concentration ion product of water) at neutrality vary with temperature—the pH at which water is neutral increases by 0.6 pH units when the temperature drops from 37 to 3°C. The normal blood pH of ectothermic animals follows a similar curve and varies as an inverse function of body temperature, as seen in Fig. 11-5. To describe this phenomenon, Rahn (1967) coined the term *relative alkalinity*, defined as pH − pN, where pH is the pH of the animal's blood and pN is the pH of water at neutrality at a given temperature, indicating that the regulatory mechanism of cold-blooded animals is one of maintaining constant relative alkalinity throughout an entire range of temperatures (Rahn and Baumgardner 1972). A sudden increase in temperature causes a decline in blood pH and a general shift toward respiratory acidosis. Ectothermic animals thus differ from endothermic creatures in that body temperature varies with temperatures in the environment; blood pH alone is therefore no indication of acid-base status (Howell et al. 1970).

An increase in salinity also shifts the oxygen combining curve to the right and makes the uptake of oxygen more uncertain. There are two reasons: (1) the presence of increased solutes diminishes the solubility of oxygen; and (2) increased ions in solution may worsen the problem of

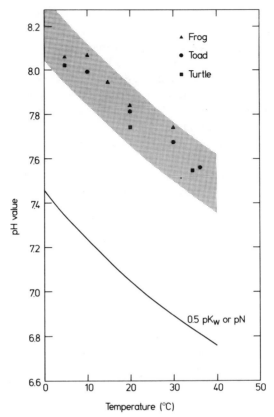

**Figure 11-5** Normal blood pH of frogs, toads, and turtles plotted against body temper-ature (mean values for 127 samples). The solid line pN or 0.5 $pK_w$, represents the pH or pOH of neutral water. The constant pH-pN difference expresses the constant relative alkalinity. Redrawn from Howell et al. (1970).

chloride loading at the gills, making the exchange of ions, and ulti-mately the release of $CO_2$, more costly in terms of energy expended.

Handling a fish or chasing it with a net, which causes it to exercise violently, results in increased lactic acid levels in the blood, depressing pH$a$ still more and increasing $Pa_{CO_2}$. The increase in blood lactic acid takes place as soon as the stress is applied and may not subside for several hours. Dominy (1971), reported a fivefold increase in blood lactic acid in the alewife after 15 min of chasing.

To summarize, an aquatic animal is handicapped severely by the high density and viscosity of water and the extreme differences in solubility of oxygen and carbon dioxide. Increased ventilation does not alleviate imbalances in acid-base status. Under conditions of hypercapnia, a fish buffers its excess arterial $CO_2$ with bicarbonate ions, which, in turn are exchanged for chloride ions in the water. Too sharp a rise in $Pa_{CO_2}$ may result in the Root effect, or the inability to take up oxygen at the gills even when sufficient dissolved oxygen is available. The Root effect can be considered an exaggerated Bohr effect. Under conditions of hypercapnia, sedentary animals that demonstrate little or no Bohr effect in their oxygen combining curves seem to survive better and recover faster once conditions in the water have returned to normal. The results of hypercapnia are more severe if declining $pHw$ values and increased $Pw_{CO_2}$ are combined with rising temperature or increased salinity.

Handling a fish or causing it to exercise violently may result in increased lactic acid levels, which acidify the vascular fluids still more and worsen the problem of acid-base balance. Peirce (1967) found, for example, that in the spiny dogfish handling was followed by metabolic acidosis that resulted from the endogenous release of lactic acid. The effect of acidosis may be to impede oxygen transport by the hemoglobin, which would cause it to be unloaded prematurely (Bohr or Root effect), resulting in suffocation. The increased sodium influx seen by Payan and Maetz (1973) in another marine elasmobranch (*Scyliorhinus canicula*) after handling may have reflected increased $H^+$ elimination at the gills, perhaps a symptom of acidosis.

Sometimes the effects of increased lactic acid are not seen for several hours, resulting in delayed mortality (Beamish 1966, Black 1958, Cailloute 1968). Beamish (1966) found that blood lactic acid was low in the haddock (*Melanogrammus aeglefinus*) before excitement, increased after handling while the fish was resting in a holding tank, and did not return to normal for 12 hr (Fig. 11-6).

The delay in the rise of blood lactic acid may be more pronounced if a fish is removed from the water. Leivestad et al. (1957) showed that when Atlantic cod struggled in air for 4 min, there was a sharp increase in muscle lactic acid. However because the circulation through the muscles had been depressed (caused by reduced heart rate), little entered the blood. When the fish were returned to the water, normal heart rate was resumed, circulation increased, and lactic acid poured into the blood.

## Management Practices

Delayed mortality is often seen in fishes that have been recently captured or transported. The reasons why it happens are not difficult to understand when the factors described in this section are considered.

*Toxicity and Stress*

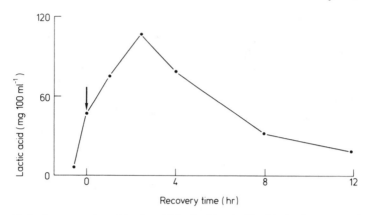

**Figure 11-6**  Concentration of lactic acid in the blood of haddock after capture by otter trawl. The arrow shows the value immediately after capture. The resting level (lowest point on the graph) was determined on fish maintained in the laboratory. Redrawn from Beamish (1966).

The act of chasing or handling a fish causes an increase in lactic acid that does not subside for several hours. During this time, the animal suffers a change in acid-base status. The condition is magnified if, during the capture procedure, the fish has been removed from the water even for a short time. Respiratory acidosis perhaps results in inadequate oxygenation of the blood through the Bohr effect. Acid-base balance is upset further if temperature or salinity are elevated in the holding container or transport box. Being ectothermic, a fish has to sustain blood pH at a level that parallels the pH of the water at neutrality; this, in turn, declines as the temperature increases.

If the water is not buffered by addition of organic buffers the $CO_2$ respired by the animal may depress the $pHw$ and elevate $Pw_{CO_2}$, resulting in a hypercapnic environment. Hypercapnia is magnified if the shipping container is filled with seawater and pure oxygen and then sealed, because the environment then becomes hyperoxic. At that point $Pa_{CO_2}$ and blood $HCO_3^-$ and $H^+$ all increase, causing respiratory acidosis. Fishes do not respond to the effects of hypercapnia when conditions in the environment are hyperoxic, and are unable to compensate for the subsequent acid-base imbalance. Increasing the $Pw_{O_2}$ with pure oxygen has little beneficial effect once $Pw_{CO_2}$ has risen to a critical level. Fishes inside the container may suffocate from the Root effect even if the water is hyperoxic.

The practice of shipping seawater fishes in sealed plastic bags in which the air directly above the water has been displaced by oxygen can result in hypercapnia and delayed mortality unless the water is buffered to prevent a rise in $Pw_{CO_2}$. Addition of inorganic buffers, such as $NaHCO_3$, is seldom adequate to maintain the buffer capacity of the water when the fish density is high (McFarland and Norris 1958). Organic buffers should be used instead. The most widely used organic buffer probably is "tris buffer," or simply tris, the chemical formula for which is 2-amino-2(hydroxymethyl)-1,3-propanediol. Tris can be purchased as preset crystals to give the desired pH upon dissolution. The correct pH for seawater is 8.2 and the recommended compound is Trisma® 8.2.* Stock solutions of tris deteriorate when left standing for several hours, and fresh solutions should be made up before use. Tris is strongly alkaline and may precipitate if added to seawater directly. Dissolve the required amount of tris crystals in distilled water. Adjust the pH, if necessary, to 8.2 with 0.01 N HCl. McFarland and Norris (1958) recommended addition of 1.3 g tris $l^{-1}$ for shipping fishes in plastic bags with oxygen and seawater. Tris was nontoxic at far higher concentrations (5.29 g tris $l^{-1}$) to the species of coral reef fishes tested by these authors.

* Sigma Chemical Co., P. O. Box 14508, St. Louis, MO 63178.

# CHAPTER 12
## Analytical Methods

B esides the usual glassware, a laboratory for the routine analysis of aquarium seawater should be equipped with a spectrophotometer (not a colorimeter), pH meter (preferably with an expanded scale), desiccator, magnetic stirrer, water still, deionization column, drying oven, analytical balance, bunsen burner, burette, and refrigerator with a freezer compartment.

The tests given here are adequate to maintain aquarium seawater in good condition. Most were taken from Spotte (1979). For complete discussions of the practical and theoretical aspects of seawater analysis see Grasshoff (1976), Riley et al. (1975), Smith and Windom (1972), and Strickland and Parsons (1972).

Turbidity will not be mentioned because it seldom is a problem in seawater aquariums after the influent water has been processed initially. See American Public Health Association et al. (1976), Lobring and Booth (1975), and Vanous (1978) for methods of turbidity measurement.

### 12.1 REACTIVE PHOSPHATE (AS TOTAL PO₄-P)

Values for inorganic or reactive phosphate in aquarium seawater ordinarily range from approximately 0.5 to 6 mg $PO_4$-P $l^{-1}$. The method described was adapted from Murphy and Riley (1962) and Martin (1972), and works well in waters of all salinities. Goulden and Brooksbank (1975) described a method for measuring total phosphorus in natural waters.

## Preparation of Glassware

1  Start with new glassware.

2  Add 8 ml of mixed reagent (see Reagents) for each 100 ml of volume and swirl to coat the walls of the glassware.

3  Allow to stand for 20 min.

4  Discard the mixed reagent and rinse each container thoroughly with triple-distilled water.

5  Store glassware in a 0.1% sulfuric acid solution (1 g concentrated $H_2SO_4$ per litre of distilled water).

6  Glassware can be used again without repeating steps 1 through 4, provided it has not been washed in detergent between tests.

## Sampling

Water samples should be collected in glass 250 ml flasks prepared by the procedure above and covered immediately with new aluminum foil. Analyze within 2 hr, if possible. Murphy and Riley (1962) reported that samples could be preserved by addition of chloroform (1 ml 150 ml$^{-1}$), although others have found the technique ineffective (see Martin 1972). Samples can be stored in polyethylene containers if they are quick-frozen. Hassen-Teufel et al. (1963) and Heron (1962) observed loss of phosphate from polyethylene containers at room temperature.

## Reagents

*Sulfuric acid solution (5 N).* Add 70 ml of concentrated $H_2SO_4$ (96%, specific gravity 1.84) to about 500 ml of triple-distilled water and dilute to one litre. *Use caution.*

*Ammonium molybdate solution.* Dissolve 40 g of reagent grade ammonium molybdate ($[NH_4]_6Mo_7O_{24} \cdot 4H_2O$) in about 900 ml of triple-distilled water and dilute to one litre. Store in a polypropylene bottle in the dark, or in an amber, phosphate-free borosilicate glass bottle (see Preparation of Glassware). (1 hr)

*Potassium antimonyl tartrate solution.* Dissolve 1.4 g of reagent grade material (tartar emetic, $K[SbO]C_4H_4O_6 \cdot 0.5H_2O$) in triple-distilled water and dilute to 500 ml. Store in a phosphate-free borosilicate glass bottle. (many months)

*L-ascorbic acid solution.* Dissolve 1.3 g of reagent grade material in 75 ml of triple-distilled water.

*Mixed reagent solution.* Add 125 ml of sulfuric acid (5 N) to a 250 ml erlenmeyer flask and add 12.5 ml potassium antimonyl tartrate solution. Mix thoroughly. Add 37.5 ml ammonium molybdate solution and mix thoroughly. Add 75 ml *L*-ascorbic acid solution and mix again. (24 hr) *Standard phosphate solution* (100 mg $PO_4$-P $l^{-1}$). Dissolve 0.439 g of reagent grade anhydrous (oven dried at 105°C for 3 hr) potassium dihydrogen phosphate ($KH_2PO_4$) in distilled water and dilute to 100 ml. Mix thoroughly. Dilute 10 ml of this solution to one litre with distilled water and add 1 ml of chloroform to retard the growth of bacteria. Store in an amber, phosphate-free borosilicate glass bottle. (many months)

### Procedure

1   Warm the sample to room temperature, then filter through a 0.45 $\mu$m membrane filter.

2   Pipette a volume of sample likely to contain 0.1 mg $PO_4$-P into a 50 ml volumetric flask, add 8 ml of mixed reagent, dilute to 50 ml with distilled water, and mix.

3   Prepare a reagent blank by adding a similar volume of sample to a 50 ml volumetric flask, dilute to 50 ml with distilled water, and mix.

4   Pipette 1 ml of standard (0.1 mg $PO_4$-P) into a 50 ml volumetric flask, add 8 ml of mixed reagent, dilute to 50 ml with distilled water, and mix.

5   Using the blank and a 2 or 5 cm cell, set the absorbance to 0.00 at 690 nm.

6   After 10 min, but before 3 hr, read and record the absorbance of the standard at the above settings.

7   Read and record the absorbance of the sample.

8   If the absorbance is greater than 1, prepare a new solution (step 2) using a smaller volume. If the absorbance is below 0.2, use a larger volume. Also prepare a new blank, but not a new standard.

9   The concentration of $PO_4$-P in milligrams per litre is given by

$$c_u = \frac{c_s V_s A_u}{V_u A_s} \qquad (66)$$

where $c_u$ is the concentration of the unknown in mg $PO_4$-P $l^{-1}$, $c_s$ is the concentration of the standard in mg $PO_4$-P $l^{-1}$, $A_u$ is the absorbance of the unknown, $A_s$ is the absorbance of the standard, $V_u$ is the volume of the unknown pipetted in litres, and $V_s$ is the volume of the standard pipetted in litres.

## 12.2   AMMONIA (AS TOTAL NH₄-N)—SPECTROPHOTOMETRIC METHOD

Ammonia is determined as total $NH_4$-N or "ammonia nitrogen." To obtain the concentration of ammonium ion ($NH_4^+$), multiply the measured value by 1.3. The percentage of free ammonia ($NH_3$) in seawater can be read from tables published by Bower and Bidwell (1978), provided that temperature, pH, and salinity measurements are made when the water sample is processed. The procedure given below was adapted from Solórzano (1969), and gives good results in waters of all salinities. Procedures that use Nesslerization do not work in saline waters without modification (Manabe 1969).

### Sampling

Water samples should be collected in clean glass 250 ml flasks and covered immediately with new aluminum foil. The samples should be analyzed within 2 hr. Degobbis (1973) reported that seawater samples could be preserved for up to 2 weeks by the addition of phenol at concentrations of $0.4$ g 100 ml$^{-1}$. The use of chloroform as a preservative proved unsuitable, as did slow and quick freezing. Storage in glass containers without preservatives resulted in a significant increase in ammonia; storage in polyethylene containers caused the ammonia level to decrease significantly.

### Reagents

*Phenol-alcohol solution.*   Dissolve 20 g of reagent grade phenol in 200 ml of 95% vol vol$^{-1}$ ethyl alcohol (USP).
*Sodium nitroferricyanide solution (0.5%).*   Dissolve 1 g of sodium nitroferricyanide in 200 ml of deionized water. Store in an amber bottle and refrigerate. (1 month)
*Alkaline solution.*   Dissolve 100 g of trisodium citrate and 5 g of sodium hydroxide in 500 ml of deionized water.
*Sodium hypochlorite solution.*   Use a commercial hypochlorite solution (e.g., Clorox®) that is at least 1.5 N.
*Oxidizing solution.*   Mix 100 ml of sodium citrate solution and 25 ml of sodium hypochlorite solution. (8 hr)
*Standard ammonia solutions.*   Dissolve 0.472 g of $(NH_4)_2SO_4$ in a litre of deionized water to obtain a 100 mg $NH_4$-N l$^{-1}$ solution. To 990 ml of deionized water, add 10 ml of the 100 mg solution to obtain a 1 mg

NH₄-N l⁻¹ solution. Use a one litre volumetric flask. To 45 ml of deionized water add 5 ml of the 1 mg solution to obtain a 0.1 mg NH₄-N l⁻¹ solution.

**Procedure**

1 Add 40 ml of sample to a 50 ml volumetric flask.
2 Add 2 ml of phenol-alcohol solution from a pipette.
3 Swirl the flask and add, in order, 2 ml of sodium nitroferricyanide solution and 5 ml of oxidizing solution. Swirl the flask after each addition. Fill to the mark with deionized water and mix well.
4 Prepare a reagent blank with 40 ml of deionized water according to steps 2 and 3.
5 Pipette in 40 ml of the standard containing 0.1 mg NH₄-N l⁻¹. Follow steps 2 and 3.
6 Cover the flask to prevent contamination by atmospheric ammonia. Let stand for 1 hr at room temperature.
7 Fill a cell of thickness greater than 1 cm with blank and set the absorbance at 0.00 for 640 nm. The turbidity blank contains 40 ml of sample diluted to 50 ml with deionized water. Use this blank if necessary.
8 Read the absorbances of the standard, unknown, and turbidity blank.
9 Calculate the concentration of total NH₄-N as follows:

$$c_u = \frac{C_s V_s (A_u - A_t)}{V_u A_s} \tag{67}$$

where $c_u$ is the concentration of the unknown in mg NH₄-N l⁻¹, $c_s$ is the concentration of the standard in mg NH₄-N l⁻¹, $V_u$ is the volume of unknown pipetted in millilitres, $V_s$ is the volume of standard pipetted in millilitres, $A_u$ is the absorbance of the unknown, $A_s$ is the absorbance of standard, and $A_t$ is the absorbance of the turbidity blank.

10 If the absorbance of the unknown is too high, a new sample solution and turbidity blank can be prepared using a smaller volume.

## 12.3 AMMONIA (AS TOTAL NH₄-N)— SPECIFIC ION ELECTRODE METHOD

Several manufacturers now produce specific ion electrodes (also called ammonia probes) for ammonia analysis in water. Those made by Orion

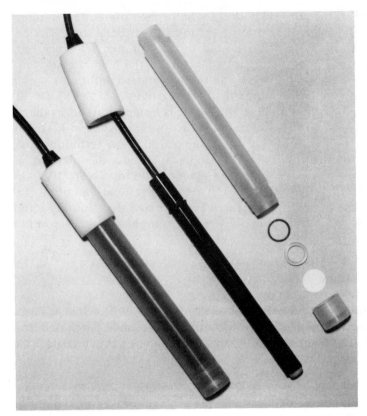

**Figure 12-1**  Specific ion electrode for ammonia (Orion Research Incorporated).

Research Incorporated* are perhaps the most widely used in aquatic animal culture (Fig. 12-1). Garside et al. (1978) described the use of these instruments for ammonia determination in seawater; the works of Gilbert and Clay (1973) and Srna et al. (1973) should be consulted for an evaluation of ammonia probes in the analysis of aquarium seawater. The second work is especially useful. The spectrophotometric method (Section 12.2) is recommended when large numbers of samples must be analyzed, because of the time saved.

Srna et al. (1973) explained how an ammonia probe works. A hydrophobic membrane separates the sample solution from the solution inside the electrode. The membrane allows small quantities of free ammonia and some amines to pass into the cell until the partial pressure

* Orion Research Incorporated, 11 Blackstone Street, Cambridge, MA 02139.

of $NH_3$ is the same on both sides of the membrane. The ammonia reacts with the internal solution to produce hydroxide ions. The change in $OH^-$ concentration is detected by the internal reference cell, which develops a potential in accordance with the Nernst equation.

The method of analysis can be by standard addition ("spiking"), or by preparation of standard solution curves. Srna et al. (1973) recommended the first method because it is faster and reduces the problems associated with loss of ammonia to the atmosphere. Klein and Hach (1977) pointed out that the standard addition technique gives more realistic values than calibration curves, because the unknown and standard are measured under the same conditions. Dean (1974) and Klein and Hach (1977) described the theory of standard addition. Tables are available from Orion Research Incorporated that simplify standard addition calculations and allow rapid computation of concentrations in unknown solutions.

### Procedure

The following procedure is from Srna et al. (1973), which is based on the instruction manual provided with each electrode purchased from Orion Research Incorporated. Analysis of a single sample takes 5 min.

1  Rinse a 50 ml pipette with the sample to be measured.
2  Pipette 50 ml of sample into a 125 ml beaker and equilibrate to 25 $\pm$ 0.05°C.
3  Add 1 ml of 10 $M$ NaOH solution.
4  Place the electrode in the solution and stir slowly using a magnetic stirrer. After 1 min, or when the potential has stabilized to $\pm 0.1$ mv, record the millivolt reading. Some ammonia can be lost to the atmosphere, depending on differences in partial pressure across the air-water interface. The beakers should be sealed with rubber stoppers with holes drilled in the centers for insertion of the electrode. Stirring should be done with a minimum of turbulence.
5  Pipette 5 ml of a standard ammonium chloride solution having about ten times the anticipated ammonia concentration of the sample. Record the second potential after the electrode has stabilized at the new sample concentration.
6  Calculate the unknown solution concentration using the value of the concentration of the known addition solution and the difference between the potential before and after standard addition.

### Electrode Drift

Drifting potentials can be caused by several factors, as summarized by Srna et al. (1973). These include inadequate temperature equilibration, improper stirring methods, membrane failure, and an unstable solution concentration. Temperature equilibration is critical and involves a stable sample temperature, in addition to stable temperature gradients in the parts of the electrode that are not immersed in the sample solution. Membrane failure ordinarily is the cause of electrode drift if temperature control is maintained and a millivolt versus time curve does not show an exponential approach to a constant $\pm 0.1$ mv value in a 0.1 $M$ NH$_4$Cl solution.

## 12.4 NITRITE (AS NO$_2$-N)

Nitrite is determined as NO$_2$-N, or "nitrite nitrogen." To obtain the concentration of nitrite ion (NO$_2^-$), multiply the measured value by 3.3. The procedure given here was adapted from Strickland and Parsons (1972), and gives reproducible results in waters of any salinity. Zafiriou and True (1977) discussed the problems of standardization.

### Sampling

Samples should be collected in clean glass 250 ml flasks and analyzed within 5 hr. Store samples in a refrigerator while awaiting analysis.

### Reagents

*Sulfanilamide solution.* Dissolve 5 g of sulfanilamide in a solution of 50 ml of concentrated HCl and about 300 ml of distilled water. Dilute to 500 ml. (several months).
*N-(1-naphthyl)-ethylenediamine dihydrochloride solution.* Dissolve 0.5g of dihydrochloride in 500 ml of distilled water. Store in the dark and discard the solution when it turns brown.
*Standard nitrite solution (10 mg NO$_2$-N l$^{-1}$).* Dry pure sodium nitrite at 110°C for several hours and store in a desiccator. Dissolve 49.3 mg of the dried material in deionized water and dilute to one litre.
*Low concentration working standard.* Dilute the standard nitrite solution by adding 10 ml to a litre of deionized water. Each millilitre contains $1 \times 10^{-3}$ mg NO$_2$-N l$^{-1}$. Make fresh each time.

**Procedure**

1   Add 2 ml each of sulfanilamide solution and $N$-(1-naphthyl)-ethylenediamine dihydrochloride solution to 40 ml of sample in a 50 ml volumetric flask. Fill to mark with deionized water.

2   Prepare standards by pipetting into 50 ml volumetric flasks 1, 2, and 5 ml of low concentration working standard and proceed as in step 1. Use deionized water to prepare a reagent blank.

3   After 10 min, but before 2 hr, read absorbance against a blank at 543 nm in a cell 1 or 2 cm thick.

4   If absorbance is above 1.5, a smaller sample should be used.

5   Plot milligrams of $NO_2$-N versus absorbance for the standard solutions. Read milligrams of $NO_2$-N of unknown from the curve and divide this value by the volume in litres to obtain the concentration in mg $NO_2$-N $l^{-1}$ (divide by 0.04 for 40 ml of sample).

## 12.5   NITRATE (AS $NO_3$-N)

Nitrate is measured as $NO_3$-N, or "nitrate nitrogen." To obtain the concentration of nitrate ion ($NO_3^-$), multiply the measured value by 4.4. The hydrazine reduction method given here works well in waters of any salinity. The original method is from Mullin and Riley (1955). A brucine method for use in saline waters was given by Kahn and Brezenski (1967).

**Sampling**

Same as in the nitrite test (Section 12.4).

**Reagents**

*Acetone.*   Reagent grade.

*Copper sulfate solution.*   Dissolve 100 mg of cupric sulfate pentahydrate in one litre of deionized water.

*Hydrazine sulfate solution.*   Dissolve 3.625 g of hydrazine sulfate in 500 ml of deionized water. (2 months)

*Phenol solution.*   Dissolve 9.072 g of phenol in 200 ml of deionized water. (2 months)

*Sodium hydroxide solution.*   Dissolve 28.35 g of sodium hydroxide in deionized water. Cool and dilute to 2 l. (6 months)

*N-(1-naphthyl)-ethylenediamine dihydrochloride solution.*   Same as in the nitrite test (Section 12.4).

*Sulfanilamide solution.*   Same as in the nitrite test (Section 12.4).

*Buffer solution.*   Mix 20 ml of sodium hydroxide solution with 20 ml of phenol solution.

*Reducer solution.*   Mix 20 ml of copper sulfate solution with 20 ml of hydrazine sulfate solution.

*Standard nitrate solution (10 mg $NO_3$-N $l^{-1}$).*   Dry reagent grade sodium nitrate at 110°C for several hours and store in a desiccator. Dissolve 60.7 mg of the dried material in a litre of deionized water. Each millilitre contains 0.01 mg $NO_3$-N.

### Procedure

1   Add 0.5 ml of sample to a 50 ml volumetric flask. Add 20 ml of deionized water, 2 ml of buffer solution, and 1 ml of reducer solution. Let stand at room temperature for 20 hr. Shield from light.

2   Prepare standards by pipetting into 50 ml volumetric flasks 0.5, 1, and 2 ml of standard nitrate solution. Proceed as in step 1. Use deionized water to prepare a reagent blank.

3   Add 2 ml of acetone and mix. Wait 2 min. Add 1 ml each of dihydrochloride solution and sulfanilamide solution and fill to mark with deionized water.

4   After 10 min, but before 2 hr, read absorbance against a reagent blank at 543 nm in a cell 1 or 2 cm thick.

5   Plot mg $NO_3$-N versus absorbance for the standard solutions, and read mg $NO_3$-N from the curve. Divide this value by the sample volume in litres (divide by 0.0005 for a 0.5 ml sample) to obtain mg $NO_3$-N $l^{-1}$.

### 12.6   ALKALINITY

Alkalinity can be defined as the number of equivalents of strong acid required to titrate one litre of water to the $CO_2$-$HCO_3^-$ endpoint. This is the same as the sum of the concentrations of the anions of carbonic and other weak acids. The procedure given here is a standard titration technique taken from Spotte (1979). More precise methods are available (e.g., Edmond 1970, Graneli and Anfalt 1977, Keir et al. 1977), but should not be necessary.

**Reagents**

*0.1 N HCl solution.*   Use commercial standard 0.1 N HCl. Add NaCl until the salinity is about equal to the salinity of the sample.
*pH 4 buffer solution.*   Prepare a pH 4 buffer solution using NBS buffer tablets or a commercial pH 4 buffer solution.

**Procedure**

1   Set up a pH meter and burette so that the pH of the sample can be measured as it is being titrated and stirred.

2   Calibrate the pH meter with pH 4 buffer solution and let the samples come to room temperature.

3   Pipette 50 ml of sample into a beaker.

4   Place the beaker on a magnetic stirrer (use low speed and a small bar). Record the starting pH. Also record the starting level of the HCl solution in the burette.

5   Titrate as rapidly as possible until the pH of the sample is reduced to 4.8. Record the difference between the starting level of HCl solution in the burette and the level after titration (total amount of titrant added to the sample).

6   Perform the above steps in triplicate for each sample and average the final values.

7   Calculate alkalinity in milliequivalants per litre by the following equation, where $A$ is the average volume of titrant and $B$ is the normality of the acid:

$$\frac{(A)(B)(1000)}{(50)} = \text{meq alkalinity } l^{-1} \tag{68}$$

## 12.7   POTENTIOMETRIC DETERMINATION OF pH

Techniques for measuring pH potentiometrically can be found in many sources and will not be repeated here. The main purpose of the discussion that follows is to show that conventional buffer standards give reproducible measurements, making it unnecessary to determine pH potentiometrically with standards that approximate the pH and ionic strength of seawater.

The pH value of aquarium seawater is usually determined potentiometrically with a "pH meter." The term needs quotation marks when first used because pH is not actually measured under ordinary circumstances. Theoretically the potential of a reversible electrochemical cell

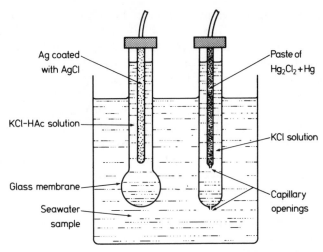

**Figure 12-2**   Measurement of pH with a glass electrode. Redrawn from Butler (1964).

can be related directly to the *activity* (effective concentration) of the ions involved in the cell reaction, rather than concentration. Activity, which is shown in braces, is a more useful concept than concentration because it takes into consideration the interionic forces involved. In the case of a pH meter, the cell consists in part of two separate glass electrodes, as shown in Fig. 12-2. Potentiometric measurement of pH is based on two emf (electromotive force) determinations made with electrodes of these configurations

$$\text{Ag}\left|\text{AgCl(s)}\right|\text{KCl, HAc}\left|\begin{array}{c}\text{glass}\\\text{membrane}\end{array}\right|\begin{array}{c}\text{unknown}\\\text{solution}\end{array}\right|$$

$$\begin{array}{c}\text{salt}\\\text{bridge}\end{array}\left|\text{KCl}\right|\text{Hg}_2\text{Cl}_2\text{(s)}\left|\text{Hg}\right.$$

The relationship

$$\text{pH} = -\log_{10}\{\text{H}^+\} \qquad (69)$$

is valid if the buffers used to standardize the electrode pair are similar in pH and ionic strength to the sample of water being tested. Ordinarily a dilute buffer solution of potassium hydrogen phthalate is used to calibrate the electrochemical cell. This buffer solution, specified by the National Bureau of Standards (NBS), has an ionic strength of 0.1 $m$, compared with 0.7 $m$ for seawater at a salinity of 35 o/oo. Moreover the pH of the NBS buffer is 7 compared with 8.2 for seawater. Because these differences are substantial, the theoretical definition of pH can be expected to correlate only roughly with the determined value. As

Hansson (1973) noted, when a cell is calibrated with a standard buffer solution of low ionic strength, such as the NBS buffer standards, "The pH-value of the sea water sample obtained by this procedure is not a measure of the concentration of $H^+$ or the activity of $H^+$. . . . It is just a value read on the pH-meter." Hansson (1973) developed a set of buffer standards that are close to the pH and ionic strength of seawater. His buffers will no doubt gain favor with chemical oceanographers once problems associated with their use have been solved—they are, for example, highly temperature sensitive (Almgren et al. 1975).

In managing aquarium seawater, the consistency and convenience by which data are acquired are more important than pinpoint accuracy. The NBS buffer standards give highly reproducible results in seawater (Hawley and Pytkowicz 1973, Pytkowicz et al. 1975) and it does not matter that the numbers fall outside the framework of thermodynamics. In determining the acid-base status of aquarium water, the value measured with a pH meter and dilute buffer standards is still "pH" for practical purposes. Further evidence that dilute buffer standards give excellent results can be found in Pytkowicz et al. (1966). They showed that pH measurements made potentiometrically with NBS standards were reproducible to $\pm 0.006$ pH units when a common reference electrode was used with different glass electrodes, and that reproducible values of $\pm 0.003$ pH units were possible with a single electrode-reference pair.

Bates (1973) recommended that pH meters be standardized at two pH values that bracket the pH range to be tested. The normal pH of seawater is considered to be 8.2, and the instrument should therefore be standardized with NBS buffers 7 and 10.

### 12.8 SALINITY (HYDROMETER METHOD)

Salinity can be measured with hydrometers (as specific gravity and converted), refractometers, or by conductivity with salinometers. Precise temperature control is essential when refractometers are used ($\pm 0.1°C$), which is not possible with hand-held models. Temperature can be controlled more easily in table models, such as the unit pictured in Fig. 12-3, but they are expensive. The durability of most conductivity salinometers is less than desirable. The conductor in the leads often breaks with extensive use, resulting in unreliable readings. The hydrometer method given here is inexpensive and accurate enough for aquarium seawater maintenance.

The conversion of specific gravity to salinity is accomplished in two steps: (*1*) determination of the actual specific gravity with a hydrometer,

**Figure 12-3**   Abbe-3L Refractometer for salinity measurement (Bausch & Lomb).

and correction of the figure obtained to the density in grams per millilitre at 15°C; and (2) conversion of density to salinity by using the value obtained in the first step.

**Procedure**

1   Fill a 500 ml graduated cylinder about two-thirds full with sample water.

2   Measure the actual specific gravity and temperature simultaneously. Estimate the specific gravity to the fourth decimal place.

3   Correct the temperature by reading from the values given in Table 12-1. For example, if the actual specific gravity is 1.022 at a temperature of 20°C, from the table 1.0220 + 11 = 1.0231.

4   From Table 12-2, read the value for salinity. In this case, the salinity is 31.2 o/oo.

Table 12-1  Differences to Convert Hydrometer Readings at Any Temperature to Density

| Observed Reading | Temperature of Water in Graduated Cylinder (°C) | | | | | | | | | | | | |
|---|---|---|---|---|---|---|---|---|---|---|---|---|---|
| | −2.0 | −1.0 | 0.0 | 1.0 | 2.0 | 3.0 | 4.0 | 5.0 | 6.0 | 7.0 | 8.0 | 9.0 | 10.0 |
| 0.9960 | | | | | | | | | | | | | |
| 0.9970 | | | | | | | | | | | | | |
| 0.9980 | | | | | | | | | | | | | |
| 0.9990 | −1 | −2 | −3 | −4 | −5 | −5 | −6 | −6 | −6 | −6 | −6 | −5 | −5 |
| 1.0000 | −2 | −3 | −4 | −5 | −5 | −6 | −6 | −6 | −6 | −6 | −6 | −5 | −5 |
| 1.0010 | −3 | −4 | −4 | −5 | −6 | −6 | −6 | −7 | −7 | −6 | −6 | −6 | −5 |
| 1.0020 | −3 | −4 | −5 | −6 | −6 | −7 | −7 | −7 | −7 | −7 | −6 | −6 | −5 |
| 1.0030 | −4 | −5 | −6 | −6 | −7 | −7 | −7 | −7 | −7 | −7 | −6 | −6 | −5 |
| 1.0040 | −4 | −5 | −6 | −7 | −7 | −7 | −8 | −8 | −7 | −7 | −7 | −6 | −6 |
| 1.0050 | −5 | −6 | −6 | −7 | −8 | −8 | −8 | −8 | −8 | −7 | −7 | −6 | −6 |
| 1.0060 | −6 | −6 | −7 | −8 | −8 | −8 | −8 | −8 | −8 | −8 | −7 | −6 | −6 |
| 1.0070 | −6 | −7 | −8 | −8 | −8 | −8 | −8 | −8 | −8 | −8 | −7 | −7 | −6 |
| 1.0080 | −7 | −8 | −8 | −9 | −9 | −9 | −9 | −9 | −8 | −8 | −7 | −7 | −6 |
| 1.0090 | −7 | −8 | −9 | −9 | −9 | −9 | −9 | −9 | −9 | −8 | −8 | −7 | −6 |

| | | | | | | | | | | | | | |
|---|---|---|---|---|---|---|---|---|---|---|---|---|---|
| 1.0100 | −6 | −7 | −8 | −8 | −9 | −9 | −10 | −10 | −10 | −10 | −9 | −9 | −8 |
| 1.0110 | −6 | −7 | −8 | −9 | −9 | −10 | −10 | −10 | −10 | −10 | −10 | −9 | −9 |
| 1.0120 | −7 | −7 | −8 | −9 | −10 | −10 | −10 | −11 | −10 | −10 | −10 | −10 | −9 |
| 1.0130 | −7 | −8 | −8 | −9 | −10 | −10 | −11 | −11 | −11 | −11 | −11 | −10 | −10 |
| 1.0140 | −7 | −8 | −9 | −10 | −10 | −11 | −11 | −11 | −11 | −11 | −11 | −11 | −10 |
| 1.0150 | −7 | −8 | −9 | −10 | −10 | −11 | −11 | −12 | −12 | −12 | −12 | −11 | −11 |
| 1.0160 | −7 | −8 | −9 | −10 | −11 | −11 | −12 | −12 | −12 | −12 | −12 | −12 | −12 |
| 1.0170 | −7 | −8 | −9 | −10 | −11 | −12 | −12 | −12 | −13 | −13 | −12 | −12 | −12 |
| 1.0180 | −7 | −8 | −9 | −10 | −11 | −12 | −12 | −13 | −13 | −13 | −13 | −13 | −13 |
| 1.0190 | −8 | −9 | −10 | −11 | −12 | −12 | −13 | −13 | −13 | −14 | −14 | −13 | −13 |
| 1.0200 | −8 | −9 | −10 | −11 | −12 | −12 | −13 | −13 | −14 | −14 | −14 | −14 | −14 |
| 1.0210 | −8 | −9 | −10 | −11 | −12 | −13 | −13 | −14 | −14 | −14 | −14 | −14 | −14 |
| 1.0220 | −8 | −9 | −10 | −11 | −12 | −13 | −14 | −14 | −15 | −15 | −15 | −15 | −15 |
| 1.0230 | −8 | −9 | −10 | −12 | −12 | −13 | −14 | −15 | −15 | −15 | −15 | −15 | −15 |
| 1.0240 | −8 | −10 | −11 | −12 | −13 | −14 | −14 | −15 | −15 | −16 | −16 | −16 | −16 |
| 1.0250 | −8 | −10 | −11 | −12 | −13 | −14 | −15 | −15 | −16 | −16 | −16 | −16 | −16 |
| 1.0260 | −8 | −10 | −11 | −12 | −13 | −14 | −15 | −16 | −16 | −16 | −17 | −17 | −17 |
| 1.0270 | −9 | −10 | −11 | −12 | −14 | −14 | −15 | −16 | −17 | −17 | −17 | −17 | −18 |
| 1.0280 | −9 | −10 | −11 | −13 | −14 | −15 | −16 | −16 | −17 | −17 | −18 | −18 | −18 |
| 1.0290 | −9 | −10 | −12 | −13 | −14 | −15 | −16 | −17 | −17 | −18 | −18 | −18 | −19 |
| 1.0300 | −9 | −10 | −12 | −13 | −14 | −15 | −16 | −17 | −18 | −18 | −19 | −19 | −19 |
| 1.0310 | −9 | −10 | −12 | −13 | −15 | −16 | −16 | −17 | −18 | −19 | −19 | −19 | −20 |

**Table 12-1  (Continued)**

| Observed Reading | Temperature of Water in Graduated Cylinder (°C) | | | | | | | | | | | |
|---|---|---|---|---|---|---|---|---|---|---|---|---|
| | 11.0 | 12.0 | 13.0 | 14.0 | 15.0 | 16.0 | 17.0 | 18.0 | 18.5 | 19.0 | 19.5 | 20.0 |
| 0.9960 | | | | | | | | | 5 | 6 | 7 | 8 |
| 0.9970 | | | | | | | | | 5 | 6 | 7 | 8 |
| 0.9980 | | | | | | | 3 | 4 | 5 | 6 | 7 | 8 |
| 0.9990 | −4 | −3 | −2 | −1 | 0 | 1 | 3 | 4 | 5 | 6 | 7 | 8 |
| 1.0000 | −4 | −3 | −2 | −1 | 0 | 1 | 3 | 4 | 5 | 6 | 7 | 8 |
| 1.0010 | −4 | −3 | −2 | −1 | 0 | 1 | 3 | 4 | 5 | 6 | 7 | 8 |
| 1.0020 | −4 | −3 | −2 | −1 | 0 | 1 | 3 | 4 | 5 | 6 | 7 | 8 |
| 1.0030 | −4 | −3 | −2 | −1 | 0 | 1 | 3 | 4 | 5 | 6 | 7 | 8 |
| 1.0040 | −5 | −4 | −3 | −1 | 0 | 2 | 3 | 5 | 6 | 6 | 7 | 8 |
| 1.0050 | −5 | −4 | −3 | −1 | 0 | 2 | 3 | 5 | 6 | 7 | 8 | 9 |
| 1.0060 | −5 | −4 | −3 | −1 | 0 | 2 | 3 | 5 | 6 | 7 | 8 | 9 |
| 1.0070 | −5 | −4 | −3 | −2 | 0 | 2 | 3 | 5 | 6 | 7 | 8 | 9 |
| 1.0080 | −5 | −4 | −3 | −2 | 0 | 2 | 3 | 5 | 6 | 7 | 8 | 9 |
| 1.0090 | −5 | −4 | −3 | −2 | 0 | 2 | 3 | 5 | 6 | 7 | 8 | 9 |
| 1.0100 | −5 | −4 | −3 | −2 | 0 | 2 | 3 | 5 | 6 | 7 | 8 | 9 |
| 1.0110 | −5 | −4 | −3 | −2 | 0 | 2 | 3 | 5 | 6 | 7 | 8 | 9 |
| 1.0120 | −6 | −4 | −3 | −2 | 0 | 2 | 3 | 5 | 6 | 7 | 8 | 9 |
| 1.0130 | −6 | −4 | −3 | −2 | 0 | 2 | 4 | 5 | 6 | 7 | 8 | 10 |
| 1.0140 | −6 | −4 | −3 | −2 | 0 | 2 | 4 | 5 | 6 | 8 | 9 | 10 |

| | | | | | | | | | | | | |
|---|---|---|---|---|---|---|---|---|---|---|---|---|
| 1.0150 | 10 | 9 | 8 | 6 | 5 | 4 | 2 | 0 | -2 | -3 | -4 | -6 |
| 1.0160 | 10 | 9 | 8 | 7 | 6 | 4 | 2 | 0 | -2 | -3 | -5 | -6 |
| 1.0170 | 10 | 9 | 8 | 7 | 6 | 4 | 2 | 0 | -2 | -3 | -5 | -6 |
| 1.0180 | 10 | 9 | 8 | 7 | 6 | 4 | 2 | 0 | -2 | -3 | -5 | -6 |
| 1.0190 | 10 | 9 | 8 | 7 | 6 | 4 | 2 | 0 | -2 | -3 | -5 | -6 |
| 1.0200 | 10 | 9 | 8 | 7 | 6 | 4 | 2 | 0 | -2 | -3 | -5 | -6 |
| 1.0210 | 10 | 9 | 8 | 7 | 6 | 4 | 2 | 0 | -2 | -3 | -5 | -6 |
| 1.0220 | 11 | 9 | 8 | 7 | 6 | 4 | 2 | 0 | -2 | -3 | -5 | -7 |
| 1.0230 | 11 | 9 | 8 | 7 | 6 | 4 | 2 | 0 | -2 | -4 | -5 | -7 |
| 1.0240 | 11 | 10 | 8 | 7 | 6 | 4 | 2 | 0 | -2 | -4 | -5 | -7 |
| 1.0250 | 11 | 10 | 8 | 7 | 6 | 4 | 2 | 0 | -2 | -4 | -5 | -7 |
| 1.0260 | 11 | 10 | 9 | 7 | 6 | 4 | 2 | 0 | -2 | -4 | -5 | -7 |
| 1.0270 | 11 | 10 | 9 | 7 | 6 | 4 | 2 | 0 | -2 | -4 | -5 | -7 |
| 1.0280 | 11 | 10 | 9 | 8 | 6 | 4 | 2 | 0 | -2 | -4 | -6 | -7 |
| 1.0290 | 11 | 10 | 9 | 8 | 6 | 4 | 2 | 0 | -2 | -4 | -6 | -7 |
| 1.0300 | 12 | 10 | 9 | 8 | 6 | 4 | 2 | 0 | -2 | -4 | -6 | -7 |
| 1.0310 |  |  |  |  |  | 4 | 2 | 0 | -2 | -4 | -6 | -8 |

**Table 12-1** (Continued)

| Observed Reading | Temperature of Water in Graduated Cylinder (°C) | | | | | | | | | | | | |
|---|---|---|---|---|---|---|---|---|---|---|---|---|---|
| | 20.5 | 21.0 | 21.5 | 22.0 | 22.5 | 23.0 | 23.5 | 24.0 | 24.5 | 25.0 | 25.5 | 26.0 | 26.5 |
| 0.9960 | | | | | | | | | | | 19 | 20 | 21 |
| 0.9970 | 9 | 10 | 10 | 11 | 12 | 14 | 15 | 16 | 17 | 18 | 19 | 20 | 22 |
| 0.9980 | 9 | 10 | 11 | 12 | 13 | 14 | 15 | 16 | 17 | 18 | 19 | 21 | 22 |
| 0.9990 | 9 | 10 | 11 | 12 | 13 | 14 | 15 | 16 | 17 | 18 | 20 | 21 | 22 |
| 1.0000 | 9 | 10 | 11 | 12 | 13 | 14 | 15 | 16 | 17 | 19 | 20 | 21 | 22 |
| 1.0010 | 9 | 10 | 11 | 12 | 13 | 14 | 15 | 17 | 18 | 19 | 20 | 21 | 23 |
| 1.0020 | 9 | 10 | 11 | 12 | 13 | 14 | 16 | 17 | 18 | 19 | 20 | 22 | 23 |
| 1.0030 | 9 | 10 | 11 | 12 | 13 | 15 | 16 | 17 | 18 | 19 | 21 | 22 | 23 |
| 1.0040 | 9 | 10 | 11 | 12 | 14 | 15 | 16 | 17 | 18 | 20 | 21 | 22 | 23 |
| 1.0050 | 10 | 11 | 12 | 13 | 14 | 15 | 16 | 17 | 19 | 20 | 21 | 22 | 24 |
| 1.0060 | 10 | 11 | 12 | 13 | 14 | 15 | 16 | 18 | 19 | 20 | 21 | 23 | 24 |
| 1.0070 | 10 | 11 | 12 | 13 | 14 | 15 | 17 | 18 | 19 | 20 | 21 | 23 | 24 |
| 1.0080 | 10 | 11 | 12 | 13 | 14 | 16 | 17 | 18 | 19 | 20 | 22 | 23 | 24 |
| 1.0090 | 10 | 11 | 12 | 13 | 15 | 16 | 17 | 18 | 19 | 21 | 22 | 23 | 25 |

| | | | | | | | | | | | | | |
|---|---|---|---|---|---|---|---|---|---|---|---|---|---|
| 1.0100 | 10 | 11 | 12 | 14 | 15 | 16 | 17 | 18 | 20 | 21 | 22 | 24 | 25 |
| 1.0110 | 10 | 12 | 13 | 14 | 15 | 16 | 17 | 19 | 20 | 21 | 22 | 24 | 25 |
| 1.0120 | 10 | 12 | 13 | 14 | 15 | 16 | 18 | 19 | 20 | 21 | 23 | 24 | 25 |
| 1.0130 | 11 | 12 | 13 | 14 | 15 | 16 | 18 | 19 | 20 | 22 | 23 | 24 | 26 |
| 1.0140 | 11 | 12 | 13 | 14 | 15 | 17 | 18 | 19 | 20 | 22 | 23 | 24 | 26 |
| 1.0150 | 11 | 12 | 13 | 14 | 16 | 17 | 18 | 20 | 21 | 22 | 23 | 25 | 26 |
| 1.0160 | 11 | 12 | 13 | 14 | 16 | 17 | 18 | 20 | 21 | 22 | 24 | 25 | 26 |
| 1.0170 | 11 | 12 | 13 | 15 | 16 | 17 | 18 | 20 | 21 | 22 | 24 | 25 | 27 |
| 1.0180 | 11 | 12 | 14 | 15 | 16 | 17 | 19 | 20 | 21 | 23 | 24 | 25 | 27 |
| 1.0190 | 11 | 12 | 14 | 15 | 16 | 18 | 19 | 20 | 21 | 23 | 24 | 26 | 27 |
| 1.0200 | 11 | 13 | 14 | 15 | 16 | 18 | 19 | 20 | 22 | 23 | 24 | 26 | 27 |
| 1.0210 | 12 | 13 | 14 | 15 | 17 | 18 | 19 | 21 | 22 | 23 | 25 | 26 | 27 |
| 1.0220 | 12 | 13 | 14 | 15 | 17 | 18 | 19 | 21 | 22 | 23 | 25 | 26 | 28 |
| 1.0230 | 12 | 13 | 14 | 16 | 17 | 18 | 20 | 21 | 22 | 24 | 25 | 26 | 28 |
| 1.0240 | 12 | 13 | 14 | 16 | 17 | 18 | 20 | 21 | 22 | 24 | 25 | 27 | 28 |
| 1.0250 | 12 | 13 | 15 | 16 | 17 | 18 | 20 | 21 | 23 | 24 | 25 | 27 | 28 |
| 1.0260 | 12 | 13 | 15 | 16 | 17 | 19 | 20 | 22 | 23 | 24 | 26 | 27 | 29 |
| 1.0270 | 12 | 14 | 15 | 16 | 17 | 19 | 20 | 22 | 23 | 24 | 26 | 27 | 29 |
| 1.0280 | 12 | 14 | 15 | 16 | 18 | 19 | 20 | 22 | 23 | 25 | 26 | 28 | 29 |
| 1.0290 | 13 | 14 | 15 | 16 | 18 | 19 | 21 | 22 | 23 | | | | |
| 1.0300 | 13 | 14 | 15 | 16 | 18 | | | | | | | | |
| 1.0310 | | | | | | | | | | | | | |

**Table 12-1** (Continued)

| Observed Reading | Temperature of Water in Graduated Cylinder (°C) | | | | | | | | | | | | |
|---|---|---|---|---|---|---|---|---|---|---|---|---|---|
| | 27.0 | 27.5 | 28.0 | 28.5 | 29.0 | 29.5 | 30.0 | 30.5 | 31.0 | 31.5 | 32.0 | 32.5 | 33.0 |
| 0.9960 | 23 | 24 | 25 | 27 | 28 | 29 | 31 | 32 | 34 | 35 | 37 | 38 | 40 |
| 0.9970 | 23 | 24 | 26 | 27 | 28 | 30 | 31 | 33 | 34 | 36 | 37 | 39 | 40 |
| 0.9980 | 23 | 25 | 26 | 27 | 29 | 30 | 31 | 33 | 34 | 36 | 38 | 39 | 41 |
| 0.9990 | 24 | 25 | 26 | 28 | 29 | 30 | 32 | 33 | 35 | 36 | 38 | 39 | 41 |
| 1.0000 | 24 | 25 | 26 | 28 | 29 | 31 | 32 | 34 | 35 | 37 | 38 | 40 | 41 |
| 1.0010 | 24 | 25 | 27 | 28 | 30 | 31 | 32 | 34 | 35 | 37 | 39 | 40 | 42 |
| 1.0020 | 24 | 26 | 27 | 28 | 30 | 31 | 33 | 34 | 36 | 37 | 39 | 41 | 42 |
| 1.0030 | 25 | 26 | 27 | 29 | 30 | 32 | 33 | 35 | 36 | 38 | 39 | 41 | 42 |
| 1.0040 | 25 | 26 | 28 | 29 | 30 | 32 | 33 | 35 | 36 | 38 | 40 | 41 | 43 |
| 1.0050 | 25 | 26 | 28 | 29 | 31 | 32 | 34 | 35 | 37 | 38 | 40 | 42 | 43 |
| 1.0060 | 25 | 27 | 28 | 30 | 31 | 32 | 34 | 36 | 37 | 39 | 40 | 42 | 44 |
| 1.0070 | 26 | 27 | 28 | 30 | 31 | 33 | 34 | 36 | 38 | 39 | 41 | 42 | 44 |
| 1.0080 | 26 | 27 | 29 | 30 | 32 | 33 | 35 | 36 | 38 | 39 | 41 | 43 | 44 |
| 1.0090 | 26 | 28 | 29 | 30 | 32 | 33 | 35 | 36 | 38 | 40 | 41 | 43 | 45 |

| | | | | | | | | | | | | | |
|---|---|---|---|---|---|---|---|---|---|---|---|---|---|
| 1.0100 | 26 | 28 | 29 | 31 | 32 | 34 | 35 | 37 | 38 | 40 | 42 | 43 | 45 |
| 1.0110 | 27 | 28 | 30 | 31 | 32 | 34 | 36 | 37 | 39 | 40 | 42 | 44 | 45 |
| 1.0120 | 27 | 28 | 30 | 31 | 33 | 34 | 36 | 37 | 39 | 41 | 42 | 44 | 46 |
| 1.0130 | 27 | 29 | 30 | 32 | 33 | 35 | 36 | 38 | 39 | 41 | 43 | 44 | 46 |
| 1.0140 | 27 | 29 | 30 | 32 | 33 | 35 | 36 | 38 | 40 | 41 | 43 | 45 | 46 |
| 1.0150 | 28 | 29 | 31 | 32 | 34 | 35 | 37 | 38 | 40 | 42 | 43 | 45 | 47 |
| 1.0160 | 28 | 29 | 31 | 32 | 34 | 35 | 37 | 39 | 40 | 42 | 44 | 45 | 47 |
| 1.0170 | 28 | 30 | 31 | 33 | 34 | 36 | 37 | 39 | 40 | 42 | 44 | 46 | 47 |
| 1.0180 | 28 | 30 | 31 | 33 | 34 | 36 | 38 | 39 | 41 | 42 | 44 | 46 | 48 |
| 1.0190 | 29 | 30 | 32 | 33 | 35 | 36 | 38 | 39 | 41 | 43 | 44 | 46 | 48 |
| 1.0200 | 29 | 30 | 32 | 33 | 35 | 37 | 38 | 40 | 41 | 43 | 45 | 47 | 48 |
| 1.0210 | 29 | 31 | 32 | 34 | 35 | 37 | 38 | 40 | 42 | 43 | 45 | 47 | 49 |
| 1.0220 | 29 | 31 | 32 | 34 | 36 | 37 | 39 | 40 | 42 | 44 | 45 | 47 | 49 |
| 1.0230 | 30 | 31 | 33 | 34 | 36 | 37 | 39 | 41 | 42 | 44 | 46 | 47 | 49 |
| 1.0240 | 30 | 31 | 33 | 34 | 36 | 37 | 39 | 41 | 42 | 44 | 46 | 48 | 49 |
| 1.0250 | 30 | 31 | 33 | 35 | 36 | 38 | 39 | 41 | 43 | 44 | 46 | 48 | 50 |
| 1.0260 | 30 | 32 | 33 | 35 | 37 | 38 | 40 | 41 | 43 | 45 | 46 | 48 | 50 |
| 1.0270 | 30 | 32 | 34 | 35 | 37 | 38 | 40 | | | | | | |
| 1.0280 | 31 | 32 | | | | | | | | | | | |
| 1.0290 | | | | | | | | | | | | | |
| 1.0300 | | | | | | | | | | | | | |
| 1.0310 | | | | | | | | | | | | | |

Source: Zerbe and Taylor (1953).

**Table 12-2  Corresponding Densities and Salinities***

| Density | Salinity | Density | Salinity | Density | Salinity | Density | Salinity |
|---|---|---|---|---|---|---|---|
| 0.9991 | 0.0 | 1.0036 | 5.8 | 1.0081 | 11.6 | 1.0126 | 17.5 |
| 0.9992 | 0.0 | 1.0037 | 5.9 | 1.0082 | 11.8 | 1.0127 | 17.7 |
| 0.9993 | 0.2 | 1.0038 | 6.0 | 1.0083 | 11.9 | 1.0128 | 17.8 |
| 0.9994 | 0.3 | 1.0039 | 6.2 | 1.0084 | 12.0 | 1.0129 | 17.9 |
| 0.9995 | 0.4 | 1.0040 | 6.3 | 1.0085 | 12.2 | 1.0130 | 18.0 |
| 0.9996 | 0.6 | 1.0041 | 6.4 | 1.0086 | 12.3 | 1.0131 | 18.2 |
| 0.9997 | 0.7 | 1.0042 | 6.6 | 1.0087 | 12.4 | 1.0132 | 18.3 |
| 0.9998 | 0.8 | 1.0043 | 6.7 | 1.0088 | 12.6 | 1.0133 | 18.4 |
| 0.9999 | 0.9 | 1.0044 | 6.8 | 1.0089 | 12.7 | 1.0134 | 18.6 |
| 1.0000 | 1.1 | 1.0045 | 6.9 | 1.0090 | 12.8 | 1.0135 | 18.7 |
| 1.0001 | 1.2 | 1.0046 | 7.1 | 1.0091 | 12.9 | 1.0136 | 18.8 |
| 1.0002 | 1.3 | 1.0047 | 7.2 | 1.0092 | 13.1 | 1.0137 | 19.0 |
| 1.0003 | 1.5 | 1.0048 | 7.3 | 1.0093 | 13.2 | 1.0138 | 19.1 |
| 1.0004 | 1.6 | 1.0049 | 7.5 | 1.0094 | 13.3 | 1.0139 | 19.2 |
| 1.0005 | 1.7 | 1.0050 | 7.6 | 1.0095 | 13.5 | 1.0140 | 19.3 |
| 1.0006 | 1.9 | 1.0051 | 7.7 | 1.0096 | 13.6 | 1.0141 | 19.5 |
| 1.0007 | 2.0 | 1.0052 | 7.9 | 1.0097 | 13.7 | 1.0142 | 19.6 |
| 1.0008 | 2.1 | 1.0053 | 8.0 | 1.0098 | 13.9 | 1.0143 | 19.7 |
| 1.0009 | 2.2 | 1.0054 | 8.1 | 1.0099 | 14.0 | 1.0144 | 19.9 |
| 1.0010 | 2.4 | 1.0055 | 8.2 | 1.0100 | 14.1 | 1.0145 | 20.0 |
| 1.0011 | 2.5 | 1.0056 | 8.4 | 1.0101 | 14.2 | 1.0146 | 20.1 |
| 1.0012 | 2.6 | 1.0057 | 8.5 | 1.0102 | 14.4 | 1.0147 | 20.3 |
| 1.0013 | 2.8 | 1.0058 | 8.6 | 1.0103 | 14.5 | 1.0148 | 20.4 |
| 1.0014 | 2.9 | 1.0059 | 8.8 | 1.0104 | 14.6 | 1.0149 | 20.5 |
| 1.0015 | 3.0 | 1.0060 | 8.9 | 1.0105 | 14.8 | 1.0150 | 20.6 |

| | | | | | | | |
|---|---|---|---|---|---|---|---|
| 1.0016 | 3.2 | 1.0061 | 9.0 | 1.0106 | 14.9 | 1.0151 | 20.8 |
| 1.0017 | 3.3 | 1.0062 | 9.2 | 1.0107 | 15.0 | 1.0152 | 20.9 |
| 1.0018 | 3.4 | 1.0063 | 9.3 | 1.0108 | 15.2 | 1.0153 | 21.0 |
| 1.0019 | 3.5 | 1.0064 | 9.4 | 1.0109 | 15.3 | 1.0154 | 21.2 |
| 1.0020 | 3.7 | 1.0065 | 9.6 | 1.0110 | 15.4 | 1.0155 | 21.3 |
| 1.0021 | 3.8 | 1.0066 | 9.7 | 1.0111 | 15.6 | 1.0156 | 21.4 |
| 1.0022 | 3.9 | 1.0067 | 9.8 | 1.0112 | 15.7 | 1.0157 | 21.6 |
| 1.0023 | 4.1 | 1.0068 | 9.9 | 1.0113 | 15.8 | 1.0158 | 21.7 |
| 1.0024 | 4.2 | 1.0069 | 10.1 | 1.0114 | 16.0 | 1.0159 | 21.8 |
| 1.0025 | 4.3 | 1.0070 | 10.2 | 1.0115 | 16.1 | 1.0160 | 22.0 |
| 1.0026 | 4.5 | 1.0071 | 10.3 | 1.0116 | 16.2 | 1.0161 | 22.1 |
| 1.0027 | 4.6 | 1.0072 | 10.5 | 1.0117 | 16.3 | 1.0162 | 22.2 |
| 1.0028 | 4.7 | 1.0073 | 10.6 | 1.0118 | 16.5 | 1.0163 | 22.4 |
| 1.0029 | 4.8 | 1.0074 | 10.7 | 1.0119 | 16.6 | 1.0164 | 22.5 |
| 1.0030 | 5.0 | 1.0075 | 10.8 | 1.0120 | 16.7 | 1.0165 | 22.6 |
| 1.0031 | 5.1 | 1.0076 | 11.0 | 1.0121 | 16.9 | 1.0166 | 22.7 |
| 1.0032 | 5.2 | 1.0077 | 11.1 | 1.0122 | 17.0 | 1.0167 | 22.9 |
| 1.0033 | 5.4 | 1.0078 | 11.2 | 1.0123 | 17.1 | 1.0168 | 23.0 |
| 1.0034 | 5.5 | 1.0079 | 11.4 | 1.0124 | 17.3 | 1.0169 | 23.1 |
| 1.0035 | 5.6 | 1.0080 | 11.5 | 1.0125 | 17.4 | 1.0170 | 23.3 |
| 1.0171 | 23.4 | 1.0211 | 28.6 | 1.0251 | 33.8 | 1.0291 | 39.0 |
| 1.0172 | 23.5 | 1.0212 | 28.8 | 1.0252 | 34.0 | 1.0292 | 39.2 |
| 1.0173 | 23.7 | 1.0213 | 28.9 | 1.0253 | 34.1 | 1.0293 | 39.3 |
| 1.0174 | 23.8 | 1.0214 | 29.0 | 1.0254 | 34.2 | 1.0294 | 39.4 |
| 1.0175 | 23.9 | 1.0215 | 29.1 | 1.0255 | 34.4 | 1.0295 | 39.6 |

**Table 12-2** (Continued)

| Density | Salinity | Density | Salinity | Density | Salinity | Density | Salinity |
|---|---|---|---|---|---|---|---|
| 1.0176 | 24.1 | 1.0216 | 29.3 | 1.0256 | 34.5 | 1.0296 | 39.7 |
| 1.0177 | 24.2 | 1.0217 | 29.4 | 1.0257 | 34.6 | 1.0297 | 39.8 |
| 1.0178 | 24.3 | 1.0218 | 29.5 | 1.0258 | 34.8 | 1.0298 | 39.9 |
| 1.0179 | 24.4 | 1.0219 | 29.7 | 1.0259 | 34.9 | 1.0299 | 40.1 |
| 1.0180 | 24.6 | 1.0220 | 29.8 | 1.0260 | 35.0 | 1.0300 | 40.2 |
| 1.0181 | 24.7 | 1.0221 | 29.9 | 1.0261 | 35.1 | 1.0301 | 40.3 |
| 1.0182 | 24.8 | 1.0222 | 30.1 | 1.0262 | 35.3 | 1.0302 | 40.4 |
| 1.0183 | 25.0 | 1.0223 | 30.2 | 1.0263 | 35.4 | 1.0303 | 40.6 |
| 1.0184 | 25.1 | 1.0224 | 30.3 | 1.0264 | 35.5 | 1.0304 | 40.7 |
| 1.0185 | 25.2 | 1.0225 | 30.4 | 1.0265 | 35.7 | 1.0305 | 40.8 |
| 1.0186 | 25.4 | 1.0226 | 30.6 | 1.0266 | 35.8 | 1.0306 | 41.0 |
| 1.0187 | 25.5 | 1.0227 | 30.7 | 1.0267 | 35.9 | 1.0307 | 41.1 |
| 1.0188 | 25.6 | 1.0228 | 30.8 | 1.0268 | 36.0 | 1.0308 | 41.2 |
| 1.0189 | 25.8 | 1.0229 | 31.0 | 1.0269 | 36.2 | 1.0309 | 41.4 |
| 1.0190 | 25.9 | 1.0230 | 31.1 | 1.0270 | 36.3 | 1.0310 | 41.5 |

| Density | Salinity | Density | Salinity | Density | Salinity | Density | Salinity |
|---|---|---|---|---|---|---|---|
| 1.0191 | 26.0 | 1.0231 | 31.2 | 1.0271 | 36.4 | 1.0311 | 41.6 |
| 1.0192 | 26.1 | 1.0232 | 31.4 | 1.0272 | 36.6 | 1.0312 | 41.7 |
| 1.0193 | 26.3 | 1.0233 | 31.5 | 1.0273 | 36.7 | 1.0313 | 41.9 |
| 1.0194 | 26.4 | 1.0234 | 31.6 | 1.0274 | 36.8 | 1.0314 | 42.0 |
| 1.0195 | 26.5 | 1.0235 | 31.8 | 1.0275 | 37.0 | 1.0315 | 42.1 |
| 1.0196 | 26.7 | 1.0236 | 31.9 | 1.0276 | 37.1 | 1.0316 | 42.3 |
| 1.0197 | 26.8 | 1.0237 | 32.0 | 1.0277 | 37.2 | 1.0317 | 42.4 |
| 1.0198 | 26.9 | 1.0238 | 32.1 | 1.0278 | 37.3 | 1.0318 | 42.5 |
| 1.0199 | 27.1 | 1.0239 | 32.3 | 1.0279 | 37.5 | 1.0319 | 42.7 |
| 1.0200 | 27.2 | 1.0240 | 32.4 | 1.0280 | 37.6 | 1.0320 | 42.8 |
| 1.0201 | 27.3 | 1.0241 | 32.5 | 1.0281 | 37.7 | | |
| 1.0202 | 27.5 | 1.0242 | 32.7 | 1.0282 | 37.9 | | |
| 1.0203 | 27.6 | 1.0243 | 32.8 | 1.0283 | 38.0 | | |
| 1.0204 | 27.7 | 1.0244 | 32.9 | 1.0284 | 38.1 | | |
| 1.0205 | 27.8 | 1.0245 | 33.1 | 1.0285 | 38.2 | | |
| 1.0206 | 28.0 | 1.0246 | 33.2 | 1.0286 | 38.4 | | |
| 1.0207 | 28.1 | 1.0247 | 33.3 | 1.0287 | 38.5 | | |
| 1.0208 | 28.2 | 1.0248 | 33.5 | 1.0288 | 38.6 | | |
| 1.0209 | 28.4 | 1.0249 | 33.6 | 1.0289 | 38.8 | | |
| 1.0210 | 28.5 | 1.0250 | 33.7 | 1.0290 | 38.9 | | |

Source: Zerbe and Taylor (1953).
* Density at 15°C. Salinity in parts per thousand.

## 12.9  DISSOLVED OXYGEN (TITRATION METHOD)

The procedure given here is a titration method for dissolved oxygen adapted from American Public Health Association et al. (1976). Duval et al. (1974) gave a method for the spectrophotometric measurement of oxygen in natural waters. Dissolved oxygen meters are available from several manufacturers, and are reliable to various degrees. The remote stirrers tend to fail on some units; the stirrer blades on others corrode after several weeks of use with seawater. The National Oceanographic Instrumentation Center* has evaluated several commercially available dissolved oxygen meters and will mail the published results on request.

### Sampling

Collect samples in 300 ml glass-stoppered bottles. Siphon water into the bottles with a length of airline tubing, keeping the discharge end of the siphon tube completely submerged. Allow water from the aquarium to overflow the bottle 3 to 4 times its volume. Insert the stopper without trapping air. Analyze within 2 hr.

### Reagents

*Manganous sulfate solution.*    Dissolve any of the following manganous sulfates (hydrous) in a little distilled water, then filter and dilute to 100 ml: 48 g $MnSO_4 \cdot 4H_2O$, 40 g $MnSO_4 \cdot 2H_2O$, or 36.4 g $MnSO_4 \cdot H_2O$.

*Alkali-iodide-azide solution.*    Dissolve 50 g of NaOH (or 70 g of KOH) and 15 g of KI in distilled water and dilute to 100 ml. Add 1 g of $NaN_3$ dissolved in 4 ml of distilled water.

*Starch solution.*    Blend 0.5 to 0.6 g of soluble starch in a beaker with a little distilled water. Add to a beaker containing 100 ml of boiling water and continue boiling for a few minutes. Add a few drops of chloroform to preserve.

*Sodium thiosulfate stock solution.*    Dissolve 2.48 g of $Na_2S_2O_3 \cdot 5H_2O$ in boiled and cooled distilled water. Dilute to 100 ml with distilled water and add 0.5 ml of chloroform to preserve.

*Standard sodium thiosulfate titrant (0.025 N).*    Dilute 25 ml of sodium thiosulfate stock solution to 100 ml with distilled water. Add 0.5 ml of chloroform to preserve. 1 ml of titrant $= 0.2$ mg $O_2$ ml$^{-1}$.

*Sulfuric acid.*    Concentrated (36 N).

* National Oceanographic Instrumentation Center, National Ocean Survey, NOAA, Rockville, MD 20852.

*Potassium dichromate stock solution (0.025 N).* Dry some $K_2Cr_2O_7$ for 2 hr in a desiccator at 103°C. Weigh out 0.0225 g and dissolve in 100 ml of distilled water in a volumetric flask.

### Standardization

1 Dissolve 2 g of KI in 100 to 150 ml of distilled water. Add 10 ml of a solution containing 1 part sulfuric acid and 9 parts distilled water.

**Table 12-3  Dissolved Oxygen (mg $O_2$ $l^{-1}$) at Saturation in Freshwater, Brackish Water, and Seawater at Different Temperatures**

| Temperature (°C) | Chlorinity (‰) | | | | | | | | | | |
|---|---|---|---|---|---|---|---|---|---|---|---|
| | 0 | 2 | 4 | 6 | 8 | 10 | 12 | 14 | 16 | 18 | 20 |
| 1 | 14.24 | 13.87 | 13.54 | 13.22 | 12.91 | 12.59 | 12.29 | 11.99 | 11.70 | 11.42 | 11.15 |
| 2 | 13.84 | 13.50 | 13.18 | 12.88 | 12.56 | 12.26 | 11.98 | 11.69 | 11.40 | 11.13 | 10.86 |
| 3 | 13.45 | 13.14 | 12.84 | 12.55 | 12.25 | 11.96 | 11.68 | 11.39 | 11.12 | 10.85 | 10.59 |
| 4 | 13.09 | 12.79 | 12.51 | 12.22 | 11.93 | 11.65 | 11.38 | 11.10 | 10.83 | 10.59 | 10.34 |
| 5 | 12.75 | 12.45 | 12.18 | 11.91 | 11.63 | 11.36 | 11.09 | 10.83 | 10.57 | 10.33 | 10.10 |
| 6 | 12.44 | 12.15 | 11.86 | 11.60 | 11.33 | 11.07 | 10.82 | 10.56 | 10.32 | 10.09 | 9.86 |
| 7 | 12.13 | 11.85 | 11.58 | 11.32 | 11.06 | 10.82 | 10.56 | 10.32 | 10.07 | 9.84 | 9.63 |
| 8 | 11.85 | 11.56 | 11.29 | 11.05 | 10.80 | 10.56 | 10.32 | 10.07 | 9.84 | 9.61 | 9.40 |
| 9 | 11.56 | 11.29 | 11.02 | 10.77 | 10.54 | 10.30 | 10.07 | 9.84 | 9.61 | 9.40 | 9.20 |
| 10 | 11.29 | 11.03 | 10.77 | 10.53 | 10.30 | 10.07 | 9.84 | 9.61 | 9.40 | 9.20 | 9.00 |
| 11 | 11.05 | 10.77 | 10.53 | 10.29 | 10.07 | 9.84 | 9.63 | 9.41 | 9.20 | 9.00 | 8.80 |
| 12 | 10.80 | 10.53 | 10.29 | 10.06 | 9.84 | 9.63 | 9.41 | 9.21 | 9.00 | 8.80 | 8.61 |
| 13 | 10.56 | 10.30 | 10.07 | 9.84 | 9.63 | 9.41 | 9.21 | 9.01 | 8.81 | 8.61 | 8.42 |
| 14 | 10.33 | 10.07 | 9.86 | 9.63 | 9.41 | 9.21 | 9.01 | 8.81 | 8.62 | 8.44 | 8.25 |
| 15 | 10.10 | 9.86 | 9.64 | 9.43 | 9.23 | 9.03 | 8.83 | 8.64 | 8.44 | 8.27 | 8.09 |
| 16 | 9.89 | 9.66 | 9.44 | 9.24 | 9.03 | 8.84 | 8.64 | 8.47 | 8.28 | 8.11 | 7.94 |
| 17 | 9.67 | 9.46 | 9.26 | 9.05 | 8.85 | 8.65 | 8.47 | 8.30 | 8.11 | 7.94 | 7.78 |
| 18 | 9.47 | 9.27 | 9.07 | 8.87 | 8.67 | 8.48 | 8.31 | 8.14 | 7.97 | 7.79 | 7.64 |
| 19 | 9.28 | 9.08 | 8.88 | 8.68 | 8.50 | 8.31 | 8.15 | 7.98 | 7.08 | 7.65 | 7.49 |
| 20 | 9.11 | 8.90 | 8.70 | 8.51 | 8.32 | 8.15 | 7.99 | 7.84 | 7.66 | 7.51 | 7.36 |
| 21 | 8.93 | 8.72 | 8.54 | 8.35 | 8.17 | 7.99 | 7.84 | 7.69 | 7.52 | 7.38 | 7.23 |
| 22 | 8.75 | 8.55 | 8.38 | 8.19 | 8.02 | 7.85 | 7.69 | 7.54 | 7.39 | 7.25 | 7.11 |
| 23 | 8.60 | 8.40 | 8.22 | 8.04 | 7.87 | 7.71 | 7.55 | 7.41 | 7.26 | 7.12 | 6.99 |
| 24 | 8.44 | 8.25 | 8.07 | 7.89 | 7.72 | 7.56 | 7.42 | 7.28 | 7.13 | 6.99 | 6.86 |
| 25 | 8.27 | 8.09 | 7.92 | 7.75 | 7.58 | 7.44 | 7.29 | 7.15 | 7.01 | 6.88 | 6.75 |
| 26 | 8.12 | 7.94 | 7.78 | 7.62 | 7.45 | 7.31 | 7.16 | 7.03 | 6.89 | 6.76 | 6.63 |
| 27 | 7.98 | 7.79 | 7.64 | 7.49 | 7.32 | 7.18 | 7.03 | 6.91 | 6.78 | 6.65 | 6.52 |
| 28 | 7.84 | 7.65 | 7.51 | 7.36 | 7.19 | 7.06 | 6.92 | 6.79 | 6.66 | 6.53 | 6.40 |
| 29 | 7.69 | 7.52 | 7.38 | 7.23 | 7.08 | 6.95 | 6.82 | 6.68 | 6.55 | 6.42 | 6.29 |
| 30 | 7.56 | 7.39 | 7.25 | 7.12 | 6.96 | 6.83 | 6.70 | 6.58 | 6.45 | 6.32 | 6.19 |

Source:  Spotte (1979) from data in Murray and Riley (1969).

2   Add 20 ml of potassium dichromate stock solution.

3   Dilute to 400 ml with distilled water and titrate with the thiosulfate titrant. Add starch solution (1 to 2 ml) near the end point of the titration when a pale yellow color is reached. 20 ml of titrant are required when the standard sodium thiosulfate titrant is exactly 0.025 N.

### Procedure

1   Add 2 ml of manganous sulfate solution, followed by 2 ml of alkali-iodide-azide solution. Keep the end of the pipette submerged in the water sample.

2   Replace the stopper without trapping air. Invert the bottle several times, allowing the precipitate to settle halfway each time before inverting again.

NOTE: In brackish water and seawater samples, wait 10 min before proceeding to the next step.

3   Add 2 ml of sulfuric acid to the sample by letting it run out of the pipette down the inside of the bottle neck. Restopper and invert gently several times until the precipitate dissolves.

4   Pour 200 ml of sample into a beaker. Titrate with sodium thiosulfate titrant to a pale yellow color. Add 1 to 2 ml of starch solution and continue titration until the pale blue color disappears. After the starch has been added, avoid going past the endpoint by adding the titrant a drop at a time and gently swirling the beaker after each drop. 1 ml of titrant = 1 mg $O_2$ $l^{-1}$.

NOTE: If the amount of titrant used during standardization is not exactly 20 ml (step 2), at the end of the test procedure the amount of dissolved oxygen in the sample can be determined by

$$\text{mg } O_2 \, l^{-1} = \frac{\text{ml of test titrant} \times 10}{\text{actual ml of standardization titrant}} \qquad (70)$$

5   Compare the measured value with the concentration of dissolved oxygen at saturation (Table 12-3) at the proper temperature and salinity.

# Literature Cited

Adams, G. and S. Spotte. 1979. Effects of tertiary methods on TOC reduction in saline marine mammal pools. In preparation.

Alabaster, J. S. and D. W. M. Herbert. 1954. Influence of carbon dioxide on the toxicity of ammonia. Nature **174:** 404.

Alderson, R. and B. R. Howell. 1973. The effect of algae on the water conditions in fish rearing tanks in relation to the growth of juvenile sole, *Solea solea* (L.) Aquaculture **2:** 281–288.

Allison, F. E., J. H. Doetsch, and E. M. Roller. 1953b. Availability of fixed ammonium in soils containing different clay minerals. Soil Sci. **75:** 373–381.

Allison, F. E., J. H. Doetsch, and E. M. Roller. 1951. Ammonium fixation and availability in Harpster clay loam. Soil Sci. **72:** 187–200.

Allison, F. E., M. Kefauver, and E. M. Roller. 1953c. Ammonium fixation in soils. Proc. Soil Sci. Soc. Amer. **17:** 107–110.

Allison, F. E., E. M. Roller, and J. H. Doetsch. 1953a. Ammonium fixation and availability in vermiculite. Soil Sci. **75:** 173–180.

Almgren, T., D. Dyrssen, and M. Strandberg. 1975. Determination of pH on the moles per kg seawater scale ($M_w$). Deep-Sea Res. **22:** 635–646.

American Public Health Association, American Water Works Association, and Water Pollution Control Federation. 1976. Standard methods for the examination of water and wastewater, 14th ed. Amer. Pub. Health Assoc., Washington, DC, 1193 pp.

Anikouchine, W. A. and R. W. Sternberg. 1973. The world ocean: an introduction to oceanography. Prentice-Hall, Englewood Cliffs, NJ, 338 pp.

Anonymous. 1971. Starting with sea water. II. Aeration and filtration. Petfish Mon. **6:** 21–22.

Anthonisen, A. C., R. C. Loehr, T. B. S. Prakasam, and E. G. Srinath. 1976. Inhibition of nitrification by ammonia and nitrous acid. J. Wat. Pollut. Contr. Fed. **48:** 835–852.

Armstrong, D. A., D. Chippendale, A. W. Knight, and J. E. Colt. 1978. Interaction of ionized and un-ionized ammonia on short-term survival and growth of prawn larvae, *Macrobrachium rosenbergii*. Biol. Bull. **154:** 15–31.

Armstrong, D. A., M. J. Stephenson, and A. W. Knight. 1976. Acute toxicity of nitrite to larvae of the giant Malaysian prawn, *Macrobrachium rosenbergii*. Aquaculture **9:** 39–46.

Arnon, D. I. and G. Wessel. 1953. Vanadium as an essential element for green plants. Nature **172:** 1039–1040.

Atz, J. W. 1964. Some principles and practices of water management for marine aquariums. *In* Sea-water systems for experimental aquariums: a collection of papers, J. R. Clark and R. L. Clark (eds). Res. Rpt. 63, Bur. Sport Fish. Wildl., Washington, DC, pp. 3–16.

Balderston, W. L. and J. M. Sieburth. 1976. Nitrate removal in closed-system aquaculture by columnar denitrification. Appl. Environ. Microbiol. **32:** 808–818.

Ball, I. R. 1967. The relative susceptibilities of some species of freshwater fish to poisons—I. Ammonia. Wat. Res. **1:** 767–776.

Barber, R. T. 1966. Interaction of bubbles and bacteria in the formation of organic aggregates in sea-water. Nature **211:** 257–258.

Barcelona, M. J. and D. K. Atwood. 1978. Gypsum-organic interactions in natural seawater: effect of organics on precipitation and crystal morphology. Mar. Chem. **6:** 99–115.

Barcelona, M. J., T. R. Tosteson, and D. K. Atwood. 1976. Study of organic-calcium interactions: gypsum precipitation in tropical surface waters. Mar. Chem. **4:** 89–92.

Barnabe, G. 1974. Some heating devices for sea water aquaculture. Aquaculture **4:** 305–306.

Bates, R. G. 1973. Determination of pH: theory and practice, 2nd ed. Wiley, New York, 479 pp.

Batoosingh, E., G. A. Riley, and B. Keshwar. 1969. An analysis of experimental methods for producing particulate organic matter in sea water by bubbling. Deep-Sea Res. **16:** 213–219.

Baxendale, J. H. 1964. Effects of oxygen and pH in the radiation chemistry of aqueous solutions Rad. Res. Suppl. **4:** 114–135.

Baylor, E. R., W. H. Sutcliffe, and D. S. Hirshfield. 1962. Adsorption of phosphate onto bubbles. Deep-Sea Res. **2:** 120–124.

Beamish, F. W. H. 1966. Muscular fatigue and mortality in haddock, *Melanogrammus aeglefinus*, caught by otter trawl. J. Fish. Res. Board Can. **23:** 1507–1521.

Berner, R. A. 1966. Diagenesis of carbonate sediments: interaction of magnesium in sea water with mineral grains. Science **153:** 188–191.

Berner, R. W. 1975. The role of magnesium in the crystal growth of calcite and aragonite from sea water. Geochim. Cosmochim. Acta **39:** 489–504.

Bienfang, P. K. 1975. Steady state analysis of nitrate-ammonium assimilation by plankton. Limnol. Oceanogr. **20:** 402–411.

Billen, D., G. Hellerman, and L. Carreira. 1972. Gene frequency analysis of chromosomal initiation sites in *Bacillus subtilis* after ultraviolet light or x-ray exposure. J. Bacteriol. **109:** 379–384.

Bischoff, J. L. 1968. Kinetics of calcite nucleation: magnesium ion inhibition and ionic strength catalysis. J. Geophys. Res. **73:** 3315–3322.

Bishop, D. F., J. A. Heidman, and J. B. Stamberg. 1976. Single-stage nitrification-denitrification. J. Wat. Pollut. Contr. Fed. **48:** 520–532.

Black, E. C. 1958. Hyperactivity as a lethal factor in fish. J. Fish. Res. Board Can. **15:** 573–586.

Blinks, L. R. 1963. The effect of pH upon the photosynthesis of littoral marine algae. Protoplasma **57**: 126–136.

Blogoslawski, W. J. and R. G. Rice. 1975. Aquatic applications of ozone. Internat. Ozone Inst., Cleveland, 226 pp.

Bonner, J. and A. W. Galston. 1952. Principles of plant physiology. W. H. Freeman, San Francisco, 499 pp.

Bowen, H. J. M. 1966. Trace elements in biochemistry. Academic Press, London, 241 pp.

Bower, C. E. and J. P. Bidwell. 1978. Ionization of ammonia in seawater: effects of temperature, pH, and salinity. J. Fish. Res. Board Can. **35**: 1012–1016.

Bowler, K., C. J. Duncan, R. T. Gladwell, and T. F. Davison. 1973. Cellular heat injury. Comp. Biochem. Physiol. **45A**: 441–450.

Braren, R. and J. W. Zahradnik. 1974. The design and evaluation of an inexpensive sea water heater. Publ. No. 007-1-74, Univ. Mass. Aquacult. Engr. Lab., Wareham, 28 pp.

Breder, C. M. Jr. 1934. Ecology of an oceanic fresh-water lake, Andros Island, Bahamas, with special reference to its fishes. Zoologica **18**: 57–88.

Breder, C. M. Jr. and H. W. Smith. 1932. On use of sodium bicarbonate and calcium in the rectification of sea-water in aquaria. J. Mar. Biol. Assoc. N. S. **18**: 199–200.

Brett, J. R. 1970. Temperature (3.3 Animals, 3.32 Fishes). *In* Marine ecology: a comprehensive, integrated treatise on life in oceans and coastal waters, Vol. 1, Part 1, O. Kinne (ed.). Wiley, London, pp. 515–560.

Brewer, P. G. 1975. Minor elements in sea water. *In* Chemical oceanography, Vol. 1, 2nd ed., J. P. Riley and G. Skirrow (eds). Academic Press, London, pp. 415–496.

Brewer, P. G. and J. C. Goldman. 1976. Alkalinity changes generated by phytoplankton growth. Limnol. Oceanogr. **21**: 108–117.

Brierley, G. P. and C. D. Stoner. 1970. Swelling and contraction of heart mitochondria suspended in ammonium chloride. Biochemistry **9**: 708–713.

Broadwater, W. T., R. C. Hoehn, and P. H. King. 1973. Sensitivity of three selected bacterial species to ozone. Appl. Microbiol. **26**: 391–393.

Brock, T. D. 1970. Biology of microorganisms. Prentice Hall, Englewood Cliffs, NJ, 737 pp.

Brockway, D. R. 1950. Metabolic products and their effects. Prog. Fish-Cult. **12**: 127–129.

Brown, A. C. 1974. Observations on the effect of ammonium nitrate solutions on some common marine animals from Table Bay. Trans. Roy. Soc. S. Afr. **41**: 217–223.

Brown, A. C. and A. B. Currie. 1973. Tolerance of *Bullia digitalis* (Prosobranchiata) to solutions of ammonium nitrate in natural sea water. S. Afr. J. Sci. **69**: 219–220.

Brown, D. A. and D. J. McLeay. 1975. Effect of nitrite on methemoglobin and total hemoglobin of juvenile rainbow trout. Prog. Fish-Cult. **37**: 36–38.

Brylinsky, M. 1977. Release of dissolved organic matter by some marine macrophytes. Mar. Biol. **39**: 213–220.

Buckley, J. A. 1978. Acute toxicity of un-ionized ammonia to fingerling coho salmon. Prog. Fish-Cult. **40**: 30–32.

Bullock, G. L. 1972. Studies on selected myxobacteria pathogenic for fishes and on bacterial gill disease in hatchery-reared salmonids. Tech. Pap. 60, Bur. Sport Fish. Wildl., Washington, DC, 30 pp.

Bullock, G. L. and H. M. Stuckey. 1977. Ultraviolet treatment of water for destruction of five gram-negative bacteria pathogenic to fishes. J. Fish. Res. Board Can. **34:** 1244–1249.

Burkhalter, D. E. and C. M. Kaya. 1977. Effects of prolonged exposure to ammonia on fertilized eggs and sac fry of rainbow trout (*Salmo gairdneri*). Trans. Amer. Fish. Soc. **106:** 470–475.

Burleson, G. R., T. M. Murray, and M. Pollard. 1975. Inactivation of viruses and bacteria by ozone, with and without sonication. Appl. Microbiol. **29:** 340–344.

Burns, R. L. and A. C. Mathieson. 1972. Ecological studies of economic red algae. II. Culture studies of *Chondrus crispus* Stackhouse and *Gigartina stellata* (Stackhouse) Batters. J. Exp. Mar. Biol. Ecol. **8:** 1–6.

Burns, R. M. and W. W. Bradley. 1967. Protective coatings for metals, 3rd ed. Reinhold, New York, 735 pp.

Burrows, R. E. 1964. Effects of accumulated excretory products on hatchery-reared salmonids. Res. Rpt. 66, Bur. Sport Fish. Wildl., Washington, DC, 12 pp.

Buswell, A. M., T. Shiota, N. Lawrence, and I. V. van Meter. 1954. Laboratory studies on the kinetics of the growth of *Nitrosomonas* with relation to the nitrification phase of the B.O.D. test. Appl. Microbiol. **2:** 21–25.

Butler, J. N. 1964. Ionic equilibrium: a mathematical approach. Addison-Wesley, Reading, MA, 547 pp.

Caillouet, C. W. Jr. 1968. Lactate acidosis in channel catfish. J. Fish. Res. Board Can. **25:** 15–23.

Cameron, J. N. 1978. Regulation of blood pH in teleost fish. Respir. Physiol. **33:** 129–144.

Cameron, J. N. and D. J. Randall. 1972. The effect of increased ambient $CO_2$ on arterial $CO_2$ tension, $CO_2$ content and pH in rainbow trout. J. Exp. Biol. **57:** 673–680.

Campbell, J. W. 1973. Nitrogen excretion. *In* Comparative animal physiology, 3rd. ed., C. L. Prosser (ed.). W. B. Saunders, Philadelphia, pp. 279–316.

Carey, C. 1938. The occurrence of nitrifying bacteria in the sea. J. Mar. Res. **1:** 291–304.

Carlucci, A. F. and P. M. McNally. 1969. Nitrification by marine bacteria in low concentrations of substrate and oxygen. Limnol. Oceanogr. **14:** 736–739.

Carlucci, A. F. and J. D. H. Strickland. 1968. The isolation, purification and some kinetic studies of marine nitrifying bacteria. J. Exp. Mar. Biol. Ecol. **2:** 156–166.

Castro, W. E., P. B. Zielinski, and P. A. Sandifer. 1975. Performance characteristics of air lift pumps of short length and small diameter. Proc. 6th Ann. Meet. World Maricult. Soc., J. W. Avault Jr. and R. Miller (eds.). World Maricult. Soc., La. State Univ., Baton Rouge, pp. 451–461.

Chang, J. P. and J. E. Morris. 1962. Studies on the utilization of nitrate by *Micrococcus denitrificans*. J. Gen. Microbiol. **29:** 301–310.

Chapman, A. R. C. 1973. Methods for macroscopic algae. *In* Handbook of phycological methods, J. R. Stein (ed.). Cambridge Univ. Press, Cambridge, pp. 87–104.

Chapman, A. R. O. and E. M. Burrows. 1970. Experimental investigations into the controlling effects of light conditions on the development and growth of *Desmarestia aculeata* (L.) Lamour. Phycologia **9:** 103–108.

Chapman, D. 1967. The effect of heat on membrane constituents. *In* Thermobiology, A. H. Rose (ed.). Academic Press, London, pp. 123–146.

Chapman, V. J. 1962. The algae. St. Martin's Press, London, 472 pp.

Chave, K. E. 1965. Carbonates: association with organic matter in surface seawater. Science **148:** 1723–1724.

Chave, K. E., K. S. Deffeyes, P. K. Weyl, R. M. Garrels, and M. E. Thompson. 1962. Observations on the solubility of skeletal carbonates in aqueous solutions. Science **137:** 33–34.

Chave, K. E. and E. Suess. 1967. Suspended minerals in seawater. Trans. N. Y. Acad. Sci. **29:** 991–1000.

Chave, K. E. and E. Suess. 1970. Calcium carbonate saturation in seawater: effects of dissolved organic matter. Limnol. Oceanogr. **15:** 633–637.

Chavin, W. and J. E. Young. 1970. Factors in the determination of normal serum glucose levels of goldfish, *Carassius auratus* L. Comp. Biochem. Physiol. **33:** 629–653.

Chow, D. K. and M. M. David. 1977. Compounds resistant to carbon adsorption in municipal wastewater treatment. J. Amer. Wat. Wks. Assoc. **69:** 555–561.

Clark, C. and E. L. Schmidt. 1967a. Growth response of *Nitrosomonas europaea* to amino acids. J. Bacteriol. **93:** 1302–1308.

Clark, C. and E. L. Schmidt. 1967b. Uptake and utilization of amino acids by resting cells of *Nitrosomonas europaea.* J. Bacteriol. **93:** 1309–1315.

Clark, J. R. and R. L. Clark (eds.). 1964. Sea-water systems for experimental aquariums: a collection of papers. Res. Rpt. 63, Bur. Sport Fish. Wildl., Washington, DC, 192 pp.

Clark, J. R. and R. Eisler. 1964. Sea water from ground sources. *In* Sea-water systems for experimental aquariums: a collection of papers, J. R. Clark and R. L. Clark (eds.). Res. Rpt. 63, Bur. Sport Fish. Wildl., Washington, DC, pp. 173–184.

Cleasby, J. L. and C. F. Woods. 1975. Intermixing of dual media and multimedia granular filters. J. Amer. Wat. Wks. Assoc. **67:** 197–203.

Colberg, P. J. and A. J. Lingg. 1978. Effect of ozonation on microbial fish pathogens, ammonia, nitrate, nitrite, and BOD in simulated reuse hatchery water. J. Fish. Res. Board Can. **35:** 1290–1296.

Colinvaux, L. H., K. M. Wilbur, and N. Watabe. 1965. Tropical marine algae: growth in laboratory culture. J. Phycol. **1:** 69–78.

Collins, M. T., J. B. Gratzek, D. L. Dawe, and T. G. Nemetz. 1975. Effects of parasiticides on nitrification. J. Fish. Res. Board Can. **32:** 2033–2037.

Collins, M. T., J. B. Gratzek, D. L. Dawe, and T. G. Nemetz. 1976. Effects of antibacterial agents on nitrification in an aquatic recirculating system. J. Fish. Res. Board Can. **33:** 215–218.

Conrad, J. F., R. A. Holt, and T. D. Kreps. 1975. Ozone disinfection of flowing water. Prog. Fish-Cult. **37:** 134–135.

Conover, J. T. and J. M. Sieburth. 1966. Effect of tannins excreted from Phaeophyta on planktonic animal survival in tide pools. *In* Proc. Fifth Internat. Seaweed Symp., E. G. Young and J. L. McLachlan (eds.). Pergamon Press, Oxford, pp. 99–100.

Cooper, L. H. N. 1932. On the effect of long continued additions of lime to aquarium sea-water. J. Mar. Biol. Assoc. U. K. **18:** 201–202.

Corpe, W. A. 1970. An acid polysaccharide produced by a primary film forming marine bacterium. Develop. Indus. Microbiol. **11:** 402–412.

Corpe, W. A. 1974. Periphytic marine bacteria and the formation of microbial films on solid surfaces. *In* Effect of the ocean environment on microbial activities, R. R. Colwell and R. Y. Morita (eds.). Univ. Park Press, Baltimore, pp. 397–417.

Cox, R. A., M. J. McCartney, and F. Culkin. 1968. Pure water for relative density standard. Deep-Sea Res. **15:** 319–325.

Craft, T. F. 1966. Review of rapid sand filtration theory. J. Amer. Wat. Wks. Assoc. **58:** 428–439.

Craigie, J. S. and J. McLachlan. 1964. Excretion of colored ultraviolet absorbing substances by marine algae. Can. J. Bot. **42:** 23–33.

Craigie, J. S., J. McLachlan, W. Majak, R. C. Ackman, and C. S. Tocher. 1966. Photosynthesis in algae. II. Green algae with special reference to *Dunaliella* spp. and *Tetraselmis* spp. Can J. Bot. **44:** 1247–1254.

Crawford, R. E. and G. H. Allen. 1977. Seawater inhibition of nitrite toxicity to chinook salmon. Trans. Amer. Fish. Soc. **106:** 105–109.

Crawshaw, L. I. 1977. Physiological and behavioral reactions of fishes to temperature change. J. Fish. Res. Board Can. **34:** 730–734.

Crecelius, E. A. 1978. Measurement of oxidants in ozonizated seawater and some biological reactions. Pap. pres. 2nd Workshop Mar. Freshw. Ozone Appl., Internat. Ozone Assoc., Orlando, FL., Dec. 1975 (Abst.)

Cross, C. E., B. S. Packer, J. M. Linta, H. V. Murdaugh Jr., and E. D. Robin. 1969. $H^+$ buffering and excretion in response to acute hypercapnia in the dogfish *Squalus acanthias*. Amer. J. Physiol. **216:** 440–452.

Culkin, F. 1965. The major constituents of sea water. *In* Chemical oceanography, Vol. 1, J. P. Riley and G. Skirrow (eds.). Academic Press, London, pp. 121–161.

Culp, R. L. 1977. Direct filtration. J. Amer. Wat. Wks. Assoc. **69:** 375–378.

Culp, R. L. and G. L. Culp. 1971. Advanced wastewater treatment. Van Nostrand Reinhold, New York, 310 pp.

Culp, R. L., G. M. Wesner, and G. L. Culp. 1978. Handbook of advanced wastewater treatment, 2nd ed. Van Nostrand Reinhold, New York, 632 pp.

Cuthbert, A. W. and J. Maetz. 1972. The effects of calcium and magnesium on sodium fluxes through the gills of *Carassius auratus* L. J. Physiol., Lond. **221:** 633–643.

Cutler, D. W. and L. M. Crump. 1933. Some aspects of the physiology of certain nitrite-forming bacteria. Ann. Appl. Biol. **20:** 291–296.

Davies, T. R. and D. F. Toerien. 1971. Population description of a denitrifying microbial system. Wat. Res. **5:** 553–564.

Davis, I. 1961. Microbiologic studies with ozone. Quantitative lethality of ozone for *Escherichia coli*. Rpt. 61-54, U.S.A.F. School Aerospace Med., pp. 1–16.

Dawes, C. J., J. W. LaClaire, and R. E. Moon. 1976. Culture studies on *Eucheuma nudum* J. Agardh, a carrageen producing red alga from Florida. Aquaculture 7: 1–9.

Dawson, E. Y. 1956. How to know the seaweeds. Wm. C. Brown, Dubuque, IA, 197 pp.

Dawson, R. N. and K. L. Murphy. 1972. The temperature dependency of biological dentrification. Wat. Res. **6:** 71–83.

Dawson, V. K., L. L. Marking, and T. D. Bills. 1976. Removal of toxic chemicals from water with activated carbon. Trans. Amer. Fish. Soc. **105:** 119–123.

Dean, W. M. 1974. Instrumental methods of analysis, 5th ed. D. Van Nostrand, New York, 860 pp.

Deering, R. A. 1962. Ultraviolet radiation and nucleic acid. Sci. Amer. **207(6):** 135–144.

Deffeyes, K. S., F. J. Lucia, and P. K. Weyl. 1964. Dolomitization: observation on the island of Bonaire, Netherlands Antilles. Science **143:** 678–679.

Deffeyes, K. S., F. J. Lucia, and P. K. Weyl. 1965. Dolomitization and limestone diagenesis. Spec. Publ. 13, SEPM, L. Pray and R. C. Murray (eds.). Soc. Econ. Paleontol. Mineral., Tulsa, pp. 71–88.

Degobbis, D. 1973. On the storage of seawater samples for ammonia determination. Limnol. Oceanogr. **18:** 146–150.

DeGroot, K. and E. M. Duyvis. 1966. Crystal form of precipitated calcium carbonate as influenced by adsorbed magnesium ions. Nature **212:** 183–184.

Dejours, P. 1973. Problems of control of breathing in fishes. *In* Comparative physiology, L. Bolis, K. Schmidt-Nielsen, and S. H. P. Maddrell (eds.). North-Holland, Amsterdam, pp. 117–132.

Dejours, P. 1975. Principles of comparative respiratory physiology. North-Holland, Amsterdam, 253 pp.

Dejours, P. 1978. Carbon dioxide in water- and air-breathers. Respir. Physiol. **33:** 121–128.

Dejours, P. and H. Beekenkamp. 1977. Crayfish respiration as a function of water oxygenation. Respir. Physiol. **30:** 241–251.

Dejours, P., W. F. Garey, and H. Rahn. 1970. Comparison of ventilatory and circulatory flow rates between animals in various physiological conditions. Respir. Physiol. **9:** 108–117.

Dejours, P., A. Toulmond, and J. P. Truchot. 1977. The effect of hyperoxia on the breathing of marine fishes. Comp. Biochem. Physiol. **58A:** 409–411.

DeLong, D. C., J. E. Halver, and E. T. Mertz. 1958. Nutrition of salmonid fishes. VI. Protein requirements of chinook salmon at two water temperatures. J. Nutrit. **65:** 589–600.

DeManche, J. M., P. L. Donaghay, W. P. Breese, and L. F. Small. 1975. Residual toxicity of ozonized seawater to oyster larvae. Publ. No. ORESU-T-75-003, Oregon State Univ., School Oceanogr., Corvallis, 7 pp.

Delwiche, C. C. 1956. Denitrification. *In* Symposium on inorganic nitrogen metabolism, W. D. McElroy and B. Glass (eds.). Johns Hopkins Press, Baltimore, pp. 233–256.

Delwiche, C. C. and B. A. Bryan. 1976. Denitrification. Ann. Rev. Microbiol. **30:** 241–262.

Delwiche, C. C. and M. S. Finstein. 1965. Carbon and energy sources for the nitrifying autotroph *Nitrobacter*. J. Bacteriol. 102–107.

de Vooys, C. G. N. 1969. Formation and excretion of ammonia in Teleostei. II. Occurrence and transport of ammonia in the blood. Arch. Internat. Physiol. Biochim. **77:** 112–118.

Dodd, D. J. R. and D. H. Bone. 1975. Nitrate reduction by denitrifying bacteria in single and two stage continuous flow reactors. Wat. Res. **9:** 323–328.

Dominy, C. L. 1971. Changes in blood lactic acid concentrations in alewives (*Alosa pseudoharengus*) during passage through a pool and weir fishway. J. Fish. Res. Board Can. **28:** 1215–1217.

Doudoroff, P. 1942. The resistance and acclimation of marine fishes to temperature changes. 1. Experiments with *Girella nigricans* (Ayeres). Biol. Bull. **83:** 219–244.

Downing A. L. and G. A. Truesdale. 1955. Some factors affecting the rate of solution of $O_2$ in water. J. Appl. Chem. **5:** 570–581.

Downing, K. M. and J. C. Merkens. 1955. The influence of dissolved-oxygen concentration on the toxicity of un-ionized ammonia to rainbow trout (*Salmo gairdneri* Richardson). Ann. Appl. Biol. **43:** 243–246.

Doxtader, K. G. and M. Alexander. 1966. Nitrification by heterotrophic soil micro-organisms. Proc. Soil Sci. Soc. Amer. **30:** 351–355.

Droop, M. R. 1969. Algae. *In* Methods in microbiology 3B, J. R. Norris and D. W. Ribbons (eds.). Academic Press, New York, pp. 269–313.

Dugdale, R. C. and J. J. Goering. 1967. Uptake of new and regenerated forms of nitrogen in primary productivity. Limnol. Oceanogr. **12:** 196–206.

Duursma, E. K. and W. Sevenhuysen. 1966. Note on chelation and solubility of certain metals in sea water at different pH values. Nethl. J. Sea Res. **3:** 95–106.

Duval, W. S., P. J. Brockington, M. S. von Melville, and G. H. Green. 1974. Spec-trophotometric determination of dissolved oxygen concentration in water. J. Fish. Res. Board Can. **31:** 1529–1530.

Eberhardt, M., S. Madsen, and H. Sontheimer. 1975. Untersuchungen zur Verwendung Biologisch Arbeitender Akivkohlefilter bei der Tinkwasseraufbereitung. Gas Was-serfach Wass./Abwass. **116:** 245–247.

Eddy, F. B., J. P. Lomholt, R. E. Weber, and K. Johansen. Blood respiratory properties of rainbow trout (*Salmo gairdneri*) kept in water of high $CO_2$ tension. J. Exp. Biol. **67:** 37–47.

Edmond, J. M. 1970. High precision determination of titration alkalinity and total carbon dioxide content of seawater by potentiometric titration. Deep-Sea Res. **17:** 737–750.

Elia, V. J., C. S. Clark, K. T. McGinnis, T. E. Cody, and R. N. Kinman. 1978. Ozonation in a wastewater reuse system: examination of products formed. J. Wat. Pollut. Contr. Fed. **50:** 1727–1732.

Epifanio, C. E. and R. F. Srna. 1975. Toxicity of ammonia, nitrite ion, nitrate ion, and orthophosphate to *Mercenaria mercenaria* and *Crassostrea virginica*. Mar. Biol. **33:** 241–246.

Eppley, R. W. and J. N. Rogers. 1970. Inorganic nitrogen assimilation of *Ditylum brightwellii*, a marine planktonic diatom. J. Phycol. **6:** 344–351.

Eppley, R. W., J. N. Rogers, J. J. McCarthy, and A. Sournia. 1971. Light/dark periodicity in nitrogen assimilation of the marine phytoplankters *Skeletonema costatum* and *Coccolithus huxleyi* in N-limited chemostat culture. J. Phycol. **7:** 150–154.

Evans, D. H. 1973. Sodium uptake by the sailfin molly, *Poecilia latipinna*: kinetic analysis of a carrier system present in both freshwater-acclimated and seawater-acclimated individuals. Comp. Biochem. Physiol. **45A:** 843–850.

Evans, D. H. 1975a. The effects of various external cations and sodium transport in-hibitors on sodium uptake by the sailfin molly, *Poecilia latipinna*, acclimated to sea water. J. Comp. Physiol. **96B:** 111–115.

Evans, D. H. 1975b. Ionic exchange mechanism in fish gills. Comp. Biochem. Physiol. **51A:** 491–496.

Evans, P. R. and K. Bowler. 1973. The thermal death and denaturation of proteins. Sub-Cell. Biochem. **2:** 91–95.

Fahmy, F. K. 1973. Effects of partial exposure to lethal temperature on heterogeneously acclimated fish. Can. J. Zool. **5:** 1249–1255.

Fair, G. M. and J. C. Geyer. 1958. Elements of water supply and waste-water disposal. Wiley, New York, 615 pp.

Falkowski, P. G. 1975. Nitrate uptake in marine phytoplankton: comparison of half-saturation constants from seven species. Limnol. Oceanogr. **20:** 412–417.

Farooq, S., E. S. K. Chian, and R. S. Engelbrecht. 1977a. Basic concepts in disinfection with ozone. J. Wat. Pollut. Contr. Fed. **49:** 1818–1831.

Farooq, S., R. S. Engelbrecht, and E. S. K. Chian. 1977b. Influence of temperature and U. V. light on disinfection with ozone. Wat. Res. **11:** 737–741.

Feder, W. A. and F. Sullivan. 1969. Ozone-depression of frond multiplication and floral production in duckweed. Science **165:** 1373–1374.

Feldhoff, P. W., J. L. Sullivan, and A. G. DeBusk. 1973. Increased viability of a strain of *Neurospora crassa* after treatments with ultraviolet radiation or other agents. J. Bacteriol. **113:** 1509–1511.

Fetner, R. H. 1958. Chromosome breakage in *Vicia faba* by ozone. Nature **181:** 504–505.

Fetner, R. H. 1962. Ozone-induced chromosome breakage in human cell cultures. Nature **194:** 793–794.

Fetner, R. H. and R. S. Ingols. 1956. A comparison of the bactericidal activity of ozone and chlorine against *Escherichia coli* at 1°. J. Gen. Microbiol. **15:** 381–385.

Fine, S. D. 1974. Ozone generators and other devices generating ozone. Fed. Reg. **39:** 13773–13774.

Finstein, M. S. and C. C. Delwiche. 1965. Molybdenum as a micronutrient for *Nitrobacter*. J. Bacteriol. **89:** 123–128.

Fletcher, G. L. 1975. The effects of capture, "stress," and storage of whole blood on the red blood cells, plasma proteins, glucose, and electrolytes of the winter flounder (*Pseudopleuronectes americanus*). Can. J. Zool. **53:** 197–206.

Flis, J. 1968. Anatomicohistopathological changes induced in carp (*Cyprinus carpio* L.) by ammonia water. Part I. Effects of toxic concentrations. Acta Hydrobiol. **10:** 205–224.

Fogg, G. E. 1968. Photosynthesis. English Univ. Press, London, 116 pp.

Fogg, G. E. and G. T. Boalch. 1958. Extracellular products in pure cultures of a brown alga. Nature **181:** 789–790.

Fogg, G. E., C. Nalewajko, and W. D. Watt. 1965. Extracellular products of phytoplankton photosynthesis. Proc. Royal Soc. **162B:** 517–534.

Folk, R. L. 1974. The natural history of crystalline calcium carbonate: Effect of magnesium content and salinity. J. Sed. Petrol. **44:** 40–53.

Forster, J. R. M. 1974. Studies on nitrification in marine biological filters. Aquaculture **4:** 387–397.

Foulds, J. M., D. B. Wilson, and J. W. Clark. 1971. Ozone generated froth for sewage treatment. Wat. Sew. Wks. **118(3):** 80–83.

Frese, R. 1974. Ozonisierung odor biologische Filterung. Eine Vergleichende Studie mit Einbeziehung der Erfahrungen am Kieler Aquarium. Diplomarbeit Christian Albrecht, Univ. Kiel, 58 pp.

Fromm, P. O., and J. R. Gillette. 1968. Effect of ambient ammonia on blood ammonia and nitrogen excretion of rainbow trout (*Salmo gairdneri*). Comp. Biochem. Physiol. **26:** 887–896.

Gallagher, J. L. 1967. An economical cooling system for aquaria. Amer. Biol. Teach. **29:** 535–536.

Garcia-Romeu, F. and J. Maetz. 1964. The mechanism of sodium and chloride uptake by the gills of a fresh-water fish, *Carassius auratus*. I. Evidence for an independent uptake of sodium and chloride ions. J. Gen. Physiol. **47:** 1195–1207.

Garrels, R. M. and M. E. Thompson. 1962. A chemical model for sea water at 25°C and one atmosphere total pressure. Amer. J. Sci. **260**: 53–67.

Garside, C., G. Hull, and S. Murray. 1978. Determination of submicromolar concentrations of ammonia in natural waters by a standard addition method using a gas-sensing electrode. Limnol. Oceanogr. **23**: 1073–1076.

Garside, E. T. and Z. K. Chin-Yeun-Kee. 1972. Influence of osmotic stress on upper lethal temperatures in the cyprinodontid fish, *Fundulus heteroclitus* (L.). Can. J. Zool. **50**: 787–791.

Gevaudan, P., G. Bossy, C. Gulian, and Z. Sanchey. 1971. Action of ozone on the poliomyelitis virus in water. Terres Eaux **67**: 25–28, 31–34 (Fr.). Chem. Abst. **75**: 112769n (1971).

Giese, A. C. and E. Christensen. 1954. Effects of ozone on organisms. Physiol. Zool. **27**: 101–115.

Gilbert, T. R. and A. M. Clay. 1973. Determination of ammonia in aquaria and in sea water using the ammonia electrode. Anal. Chem. **45**: 1758–1759.

Goering, J. J., D. D. Wallen, and R. A. Naumann. 1970. Nitrogen uptake by phytoplankton in the discontinuity layer of the eastern subtropical Pacific Ocean. Limnol. Oceanogr. **15**: 789–796.

Goldizen, V. C. 1970. Laboratory culture of marine organisms. *In* Food-drugs from the sea, Proc. Mar. Tech. Soc. 1969, H. W. Youngken Jr. (ed.). Mar. Tech. Soc., Washington, DC, pp. 113–117.

Goldman, J. C. 1976. Identification of nitrogen as a growth-limiting nutrient in wastewaters and coastal marine waters through continuous algal assays. Wat. Res. **10**: 97–104.

Goldman, J. C., W. J. Oswald, and D. Jenkins. 1974. The kinetics of inorganic carbon limited algal growth. J. Wat. Pollut. Contr. Fed. **46**: 554–574.

Goldman, J. C., D. B. Porcella, E. J. Middlebroods, and D. F. Toerien. 1972. The effect of carbon on algal growth—its relationship to eutrophication. Wat. Res. **6**: 637–679.

Goldstein, L. and R. P. Forster. 1961. Source of ammonia excreted by the gills of the marine teleost, *Myoxocephalus scorpius*. Amer. J. Physiol. **200**: 1116–1118.

Goldstein, L., R. P. Forster, and G. M. Fanelli Jr. 1964. Gill blood flow and ammonia excretion in the marine teleost, *Myoxocephalus scorpius*. Comp. Biochem. Physiol. **12**: 489–499.

Goulden, P. D. and P. Brooksbank. 1975. The determination of total phosphate in natural waters. Anal. Chim. Acta **80**: 183–187.

Govindjee and B. Z. Braun. 1974. Light absorption, emission and photosynthesis. *In* Algal physiology and biochemistry, Bot. Monogr. Vol. 10, W. D. P. Stewart (ed.). Univ. Calif. Press, Berkeley, pp. 346–390.

Graneli, A. and T. Anfält. 1977. A simple automatic phototitrator for the determination of total carbonate and total alkalinity of sea water. Anal. Chim. Acta **91**: 175–180.

Grasshoff, K. (ed.). 1976. Methods of seawater analysis. Verlag Chemie, Weinheim, 327 pp.

Green, A. A. and R. W. Root. 1933. The equilibrium between hemoglobin and oxygen in the blood of certain fishes. Biol. Bull. **64**: 383–404.

Greenwood, P. J. and A. C. Brown. 1974. Effect of ammonium nitrate solutions on fertilization and development of the sea urchin, *Parachinus angulosus*. Zool. Afr. **9**: 205–209.

Greve, W. 1970. Cultivation experiments on North Sea ctenophores. Helgoländer Wiss. Meeresunters **20:** 304–317.

Gruener, N. 1978. Mutagenicity of ozonated recycled water. Bull. Environ. Contam. Toxicol. **20:** 522–526.

Guggenheim, S. J., J. Bourgoignie, and S. Klahr. 1971. Inhibition by ammonium of sodium transport across isolated toad bladder. Amer. J. Physiol. **220:** 1651–1659.

Guillard, R. R. L. 1975. Culture of phytoplankton for feeding marine invertebrates. *In* Culture of marine invertebrate animals, W. L. Smith and M. H. Chanley (eds.). Plenum, New York, pp. 29–60.

Guillard, R. R. L. and J. H. Ryther. 1962. Studies of marine planktonic diatoms. I. *Cyclotella nana* Hustedt and *Detonula confervacea* (Cleve) Gran. Can. J. Microbiol. **8:** 229–239.

Guirguis, W., T. Cooper, J. Harris, and A. Ungar. 1978. Improved performance of activated carbon by pre-ozonation. J. Wat. Pollut. Contr. Fed. **50:** 308–320.

Gundersen, K. 1955. Effects of B-vitamins and amino-acids on nitrification. Physiol. Plantar. **8:** 136–141.

Gundersen, K. 1966. The growth and respiration of *Nitrosocystis oceanus* at different partial pressures of oxygen. J. Gen. Microbiol. **42:** 387–396.

Gundersen, K. and C. W. Mountain. 1973. Oxygen utilization and pH change in the ocean resulting from biological nitrate formation. Deep-Sea Res. **20:** 1083–1091.

Halfon, A., D. T. Huibers, and R. McNabney. 1968. Organic residue removal from waste waters by oxidation with ozone. Amer. Chem. Soc., Div. Wat. Air Waste Chem., Gen. Pap. **8:** 32–43. Chem. Abst. **72:** 12486q (1970).

Hall, F. G. and F. H. McCutcheon. 1938. The affinity of hemoglobin for oxygen in marine fishes. J. Cell. Comp. Physiol. **11:** 205–212.

Hamelin, C. and Y. S. Chung. 1974. Optimal conditions for mutagenesis by ozone in *Escherichia coli* K12. Mutat. Res. **24:** 271–279.

Hamelin, C. and Y. S. Chung. 1976. Rapid test for assay of ozone sensitivity in *Escherichia coli*. Mol. Gen. Genet. **145:** 191–194.

Hamelin, C., F. Sarhan, and Y. S. Chung. 1977. DNA degradation caused by ozone in mucoid mutants of *Escherichia coli* K12. FEMS Microbiol. Let. **2:** 149–152.

Hampson, B. L. 1976. Ammonia concentration in relation to ammonia toxicity during a rainbow trout rearing experiment in a closed freshwater-seawater system. Aquaculture **9:** 61–70.

Hansson, I. 1973. A new set of pH-scales and standard buffers for sea water. Deep-Sea Res. **20:** 479–491.

Harris, G. P., and J. N. A. Lott. 1973. Light intensity and photosynthetic rates in phytoplankton. J. Fish. Res. Board Can. **30:** 1771–1778.

Harvey, H. W. 1940. Nitrogen and phosphorus required for the growth of phytoplankton. J. Mar. Biol. Assoc. U. K. **24:** 115–123.

Harvey, H. W. 1941. On changes taking place in sea water during storage. J. Mar. Biol. Assoc. U. K. **25:** 225–233.

Hasan, M. and J. B. Hall. 1977. Dissimilatory nitrate reduction in *Clostridium tertium*. Z. Alleg. Mikrobiol. **17:** 501–506.

Hassen-Teufel, W., R. Jagitsch, and F. F. Koczy. 1963. Impregnation of glass surface against sorption of phosphate traces. Limnol. Oceanogr. **8:** 152–156.

Haswell, M. S. and D. J. Randall. 1978. The pattern of carbon dioxide excretion in the rainbow trout *Salmo gairdneri*. J. Exp. Biol. **72:** 17–24.

Hattingh, J. 1977. Blood sugar as an indicator of stress in the freshwater fish *Labeo capensis* (Smith). J. Fish Biol. **10:** 191–195.

Hattingh, J. and A. J. J. van Pletzen. 1974. The influence of capture and transportation of some blood parameters of fresh water fish. Comp. Biochem. Physiol. **49A:** 607–609.

Hawley, J. E. and R. M. Pytkowicz. 1973. Interpretation of pH measurements in concentrated electrolyte solutions. Mar. Chem. **1:** 245–250.

Hazel, C. R., W. Thomsen, and S. J. Meith. 1971. Sensitivity of striped bass and stickleback to ammonia in relation to temperature and salinity. Calif. Fish and Game **57:** 138–153.

Heilbrunn, L. V., D. L. Harris, P. G. LeFevre, W. L. Wilson, and A. A. Woodward. 1946. Heat death, heat injury and toxic factor. Physiol. Zool. **19:** 404–429.

Heinicke, E. A. and A. H. Houston. 1965. A note on water balance in the goldfish, *Carassius auratus* L., during lethal heat shock. Can. J. Zool. **43:** 847–852.

Heisler, N. 1978. Bicarbonate exchange between body compartments after changes of temperature in the larger spotted dogfish *(Scyliorhinus stellaris)*. Respir. Physiol. **33:** 145–160.

Heisler, N., H. Weitz, and A. M. Weitz. 1976. Extracellular and intracellular pH with changes of temperature in the dogfish *Scyliorhinus stellaris*. Respir. Physiol. **26:** 249–263.

Hellebust, J. A. 1965. Excretion of some organic compounds by marine phytoplankton. Limnol. Oceanogr. **10:** 192–206.

Hellebust, J. A. 1974. Extracellular products. *In* Algal physiology and biochemistry, Bot. Monogr. Vol. 10, W. D. P. Steward (ed.). Univ. Calif. Press, Berkeley, pp. 838–863.

Henrici, A. T. and D. E. Johnson. 1935. Studies on fresh-water bacteria. II. Stalked bacteria, a new order of the Schizomycetes. J. Bacteriol. **30:** 61–93.

Herald, E. S., R. P. Dempster, and M. Hunt. 1970. Ultraviolet sterilization of aquarium water. Spec. Ed., Drum and Croaker, W. Hagen (ed.). U. S. Dept. Inter., Washington, DC, pp. 57–71.

Herald, E. S., R. P. Dempster, C. Walters, and M. Hunt. 1962. Filtration and ultraviolet sterilization of seawater in large closed and semi-closed aquarium systems. Bull. Inst. Oceanogr. Monaco, No. Spec. IB: 49–61.

Heron, J. 1962. Determination of phosphate in water after storage in polyethylene. Limnol. Oceanogr. **7:** 316–321.

Heukelekian, H. and E. S. Crosby. 1956a. Slime formation in polluted waters. Sew. Indus. Wastes **28:** 78–92.

Heukelekian, H. and E. S. Crosby. 1956b. Slime formation in sewage. Sew. Indus. Wastes **28:** 206–210.

Heukelekian, H. and A. Heller. 1940. Relation between food concentration and surface for bacterial growth. J. Bacteriol. **40:** 547–558.

Hewes, C. G. and R. R. Davison. 1973. Renovation of waste water by ozonation. AIChE Symp. Ser. **69:** 71–80. Chem. Abstr. **79:** 34866h (1973).

Higbie, R. 1935. The rate of absorption of a pure gas into a still liquid during short periods of exposure. Trans. Amer. Inst. Chem. Engr. **31:** 365–389.

Hill, R. F. 1965. Ultraviolet-induced lethality and revision of phototrophy in *Escherichia coli* strains with normal and reduced repair ability. Photochem. Photobiol. **4:** 563–568.

Hill, W. F. Jr., F. E. Hamblet, and E. W. Atkin. 1967. Survival of poliovirus in flowing turbid seawater treated with ultraviolet light. Appl. Microbiol. **15:** 533–536.

Hirayama, K. 1966a. Studies on water control by filtration through sand bed in a marine aquarium with closed circulating system. III. Relation of grain size of filter sand to purification of breeding water. Bull. Jap. Soc. Sci. Fish. **32:** 11–19.

Hirayama, K. 1966b. Studies on water control by filtration through sand bed in a marine aquarium with closed circulating system. IV. Rate of pollution of water by fish, and the possible number and weight of fish kept in an aquarium. Bull. Jap. Soc. Sci. Fish. **32:** 20–26.

Hirayama, K. 1966c. Influence of nitrate accumulated in culturing water on *Octopus vulgaris*. Bull. Jap. Soc. Sci. Fish. **32:** 105–111.

Hirayama, K. 1970. Studies of water control by filtration through sand bed in a marine aquarium with closed circulating system. VI. Acidification of aquarium water. Bull. Jap. Soc. Sci. Fish. **36:** 26–34 (misnumbered at publication; should have been V).

Hirayama, K. 1974. Water control by filtration in closed systems. Aquaculture **4:** 369–385.

Hoar, W. S. 1975. General and comparative physiology, 2nd ed. Prentice-Hall, Englewood Cliffs, NJ, 848 pp.

Hoehn, R. C. and A. D. Ray. 1973. Effects of thickness on bacterial film. J. Wat. Pollut. Contr. Fed. **45:** 2302–2320.

Hoff, J. G. and J. R. Westman. 1966. The temperature tolerances of three species of marine fishes. J. Mar. Res. **24:** 131–140.

Hoffman, G. L. 1970. Intercontinental and transcontinental dissemination and transfaunation of fish parasites with emphasis on whirling disease (*Myxosoma cerebralis*). In A symposium on diseases of fishes and shellfishes, S. F. Snieszko (ed.). Spec. Pub. No. 5, Amer. Fish. Soc., Washington, DC, pp. 69–81.

Hoffman, G. L. 1974. Disinfection of contaminated water by ultraviolet irradiation, with emphasis on whirling disease (*Myxosoma cerebralis*) and its effect on fish. Trans. Amer. Fish. Soc. **103:** 541–550.

Hoffman, G. L. 1975. Whirling disease (*Myxosoma cerebralis*): control with ultraviolet irradiation and effect on fish. J. Wildl. Dis. **11:** 505–507.

Hoigné, J. and H. Bader. 1976. The role of hydroxyl radical reactions in ozonation processes in aqueous solutions. Wat. Res. **10:** 377–386.

Hoigné, J. and H. Bader. 1978. Ozonation of water: kinetics of oxidation of ammonia by ozone and hydroxyl radicals. Environ. Sci. Tech. **12:** 79–84.

Honig, C. 1934. Nitrates in aquarium water. J. Mar. Biol. Assoc. U. K. **19:** 723–725.

Honn, K. V. and W. Chavin. 1976. Utility of ozone treatment in the maintenance of water quality in a closed marine system. Mar. Biol. **34:** 201–209.

Howell, B. J., F. W. Baumgardner, K. Bondi, and H. Rahn. 1970. Acid-balance in poikilotherms as a function of body temperature. Amer. J. Physiol. **218:** 600–606.

Howell, B. J., H. Rahn, D. Goodfellow, and C. Herreid. 1973. Acid-base regulation and temperature in selected invertebrates as a function of temperature. Amer. Zool. **13:** 557–563.

Hubbs, C., M. J. Littlejohn, and P. Littlejohn. 1960. Reduced survival of young etheostomatine fishes and hylid tadpoles due to ammonia fumes produced by a rodent colony. Copeia **1960:** 68–69.

Huff, C. G., H. F. Smith, W. D. Boring, and N. A. Clarke. 1965. Study of ultraviolet disinfection of water and factors in treatment efficiency. Pub. Health Rpt. **80:** 695–704.

Huguenin, J. E. 1976. Heat exchangers for use in the culturing of marine organisms. Ches. Sci. **17:** 61–64.

Huibers, D. T. A., R. McNabney, and A. Halfon. 1969. Ozone treatment of secondary effluents from waste-water treatment plants. Rpt. No. TWRC-4, Fed. Water Pollut. Contr. Adm., Cincinnati, 62 pp.

Hulet, W., S. J. Masel, L. H. Jodrey, and R. G. Wehr. 1967. The role of calcium in survival of marine teleosts in dilute sea water. Bull. Mar. Sci. **17:** 677–685.

Ingols, R. S. and R. H. Fetner. 1957. Ozone for use in water treatment. Proc. Soc. Wat. Treat. Exam. **6:** 1, 8.

Jackson, G. A. and J. J. Morgan. 1978. Trace metal-chelator interactions and phyto-plankton growth in seawater media: theoretical analysis and comparison with reported observations. Limnol. Oceanogr. **23:** 268–282.

Jaffe, E. R. 1964. Metabolic processes involved in the formation and reduction of methemoglobin in human erythrocytes. *In* The red blood cell, C. Bishop and D. Surgenor (eds.). Academic Press, New York, pp. 397–422.

Janicki, R. and J. Lingis. 1970. Mechanism of ammonia production from asparate in teleost liver. Comp. Biochem. Physiol. **37:** 101–105.

Janssen, R. G. and D. J. Randall. 1975. The effects of changes in pH and $P_{CO_2}$ in blood and water on breathing in rainbow trout, *Salmo gairdneri*. Respir. Physiol. **25:** 235–245.

Jensen, H. L. and K. Gundersen. 1955. Biological decomposition of nitro-compounds. Nature **175:** 341.

Jeris, J. S. and R. W. Owens. 1975. Pilot-scale, high-rate biological denitrification. J. Wat. Pollut. Contr. Fed. **47:** 2043–2057.

Johnson, B. D. 1976. Nonliving organic particle formation from bubble dissolution. Limnol. Oceanogr. **21:** 444–446.

Johnson, P. W. and J. M. Sieburth. 1976. *In situ* morphology of nitrifying-like bacteria in aquaculture systems. Appl. Environ. Microbiol. **31:** 423–432.

Johnson, R. L., F. J. Lowes Jr., R. M. Smith, and T. J. Powers. 1964. Evaluation of the use of activated carbons and chemical regenerants in treatment of wastewaters. PHS Publ. No. 999-WP-13, Pub. Health Serv., Cincinnati, 48 pp.

Jolliffe, E. A. and E. B. Tregunna. 1970. Studies on $HCO_3^-$ ion uptake during photo-synthesis in benthetic marine algae. Phycologia **9:** 293–303.

Jones, A. C. 1970. *Chlorella* for rearing of marine fish larvae. FAO Fish Cult. Bull. **2:** 3.

Jones, R. F. 1962. Extracellular mucilage of the red alga *Porphyridium cruentum*. J. Cell. Comp. Physiol. **60:** 61–64.

Joyce, R. S. and V. A. Sukenik. 1964. Feasibility of granular activated-carbon adsorption for waste-water renovation. PHS Publ. No. 999-WP-12, Pub. Health Serv., Cincin-nati, 32 pp.

Kahn, L. and F. T. Brezenski. 1967. Determination of nitrate in estuarine waters: compari-son of a hydrazine reduction and a brucine procedure and modification of a brucine procedure. Environ. Sci. Tech. **1:** 488–491.

Kain, J. M. 1966. The role of light in the ecology of *Laminaria hyperborea. In* Light as an ecological factor, R. Bainbridge, C. G. Evans, and O. Rackman (eds.). Oxford Univ. Press, Oxford, pp. 109–130.

Kalle, K. 1937. Meereskundliche chemische Untersuchen mit Hilfe des Zeisschen Pulfrich Photometers. Ann. Hydrog. Berl. **65:** 276–282.

Kalle, K. 1966. The problem of the Gelbstoff in the sea. Oceanogr. Mar. Biol. Ann. Rev. **4:** 91–104.

Kanwisher, J. 1963. On the exchange of gases between the atmosphere and the sea. Deep-Sea Res. **10:** 195–207.

Katz, A. 1973. The interaction of magnesium with calcite during crystal growth at 25°C–90°C and one atmosphere. Geochim. Cosmochim. Acta **37:** 1563–1586.

Kawai, A., Y. Yoshida, and M. Kimata. 1964. Biochemical studies on the bacteria in aquarium with circulating system. I. Changes of the qualities of breeding water and bacterial population of the aquarium during fish cultivation. Bull. Jap. Soc. Sci. Fish. **30:** 55–62.

Kawai, A., Y. Yoshida, and M. Kimata. 1965. Biochemical studies on the bacteria in aquarium with circulating system. II. Nitrifying activity of the filter sand. Bull. Jap. Soc. Sci. Fish. **31:** 65–71.

Kawai, A., M. Sugiyama, R. Shiozaki, and I. Sugahara. 1971. Microbiological studies on the nitrogen cycle in aquatic environments. I. Effects of oxygen tension on the microflora and the balance of nitrogenous compounds in the experimental aquarium. Mem. Res. Inst. Food Sci., Kyoto Univ. **32:** 7–15.

Kawamoto, N. Y. 1961. The influence of excretory substances of fishes on their own growth. Prog. Fish-Cult. **23:** 70–75.

Kawamura, S. 1975a. Design and operation of high-rate filters—part 1. J. Amer. Wat. Wks. Assoc. **67:** 535–544.

Kawamura, S. 1976b. Design and operation of high-rate filters—part 2. J. Amer. Wat. Wks. Assoc. **67:** 653–662.

Keenan, J. D. and D. A. Hegemann. 1978. Chlorination and ozonation in water and wastewater treatment. Chemosphere **1:** 9–28.

Keir, R. S., S. P. Kounaves, and A. Zirino. 1977. Rapid determination of the "titration alkalinity" of sea water by equilibration with $CO_2$. Anal. Chim. Acta **91:** 181–187.

Kelly, C. B. 1961. Disinfection of seawater by ultraviolet radiation. Amer. J. Pub. Health **51:** 1670–1680.

Kerfoot, W. B. and R. F. Vaccaro. 1973. Adsorptive extraction for analysis of copper in seawater. Limnol. Oceanogr. **18:** 689–693.

Kerstetter, T. H. and M. Keeler. 1976. On the interaction of $NH_4^+$ and $Na^+$ fluxes in the isolated trout gill. J. Exp. Biol. **64:** 517–527.

Kerstetter, T. H. and L. B. Kirschner. 1972. Active chloride transport by the gills of rainbow trout *(Salmo gairdneri).* J. Exp. Biol. **56:** 263–272.

Kerstetter, T. H., L. B. Kirschner, and D. D. Rafuse. 1970. On the mechanisms of sodium ion transport by the irrigated gills of rainbow trout *(Salmo gairdneri).* J. Gen. Physiol. **56:** 342–359.

Kester, D. R. 1975. Dissolved gases other than $CO_2$. *In* Chemical oceanography. Vol. 1, 2nd ed., J. P. Riley and G. Skirrow (eds.). Academic Press, London, pp. 497–556.

Kester, D. R. and R. M. Pytkowicz. 1967. Determination of the apparent dissociation constants of phosphoric acid in seawater. Limnol. Oceanogr. **12**: 243–252.

Kester, D. R. and R. M. Pytkowicz. 1970. Effect of temperature and pressure on sulfate ion association in sea water. Geochim. Cosmochim. Acta **34**: 1039–1051.

Khailov, K. M. 1963. Some unknown organic substances in seawater. Dokl. Acad. Nauk SSSR **147**: 1355–1357. (Transl.)

Khailov, K. M. and Z. P. Burkalova. 1969. Release of dissolved organic matter by marine seaweeds and distribution of their total organic products to inshore communities. Limnol. Oceanogr. **14**: 521–527.

Khailov, K. M. and Z. Z. Fineko. 1970. Organic macromolecular compounds dissolved in sea-water and their inclusion into food chains. *In* Marine food chains, J. H. Steele (ed.). Oliver and Boyd, Edinburgh, pp. 6–18.

Kholdebarin, B. and J. J. Oertli. 1977. Effect of suspended particles and their sizes on nitrification in surface water. J. Wat. Pollut. Contr. Fed. **49**: 1693–1697.

Kils, U. 1976/1977. The salinity effect on aeration in mariculture. Meersforsch. **25**: 201–206.

Kimata, M., A. Kawai, and Y. Yoshida. 1961. Studies on marine nitrifying bacteria. I. On the method of cultivation and distribution. Bull. Jap. Soc. Sci. Fish. **27**: 593–597.

Kimura, T., M. Yoshimizu, K. Tajima, Y. Ezura, and M. Sakai. 1976. Disinfection of hatchery supply water by ultra-violet (U.V.) irradiation. I. Susceptibility of some fish-pathogenic bacterium and microorganisms inhabiting pond waters. Bull. Jap. Soc. Sci. Fish. **42**: 207–211. (Japanese)

King, J. M. and S. Spotte. 1974. Marine aquariums in the research laboratory. Aquarium Systems, Inc., Eastlake, OH, 38 pp.

Kinman, R. N. 1972. Ozone in water disinfection. *In* Ozone in water and wastewater treatment, F. L. Evans (ed.). Ann Arbor Sci., Ann Arbor, MI, pp. 123–143.

Kinne, O. 1964. Animals in aquatic environments: crustaceans. *In* Handbook of physiology, Sect. 4, D. B. Dill, E. F. Adolph, and C. G. Wilber (eds.). Amer. Physiol. Soc., Washington, DC, pp. 669–682.

Kinne, O. 1970. Temperature (3.3 Animals, 3.31 Invetebrates). *In* Marine ecology: a comprehensive, integrated treatise on life in oceans and coastal waters, Vol. 1, Part 1, O. Kinne (ed.). Wiley, London, pp. 407–514.

Kinne, O. 1976. Cultivation of marine organisms: water-quality management and technology. *In* Marine ecology: a comprehensive, integrated treatise of life in oceans and coastal waters, Vol. III, Part 1, O. Kinne (ed.). Wiley, London, pp. 19–300.

Kirschner, L. B. 1970. The study of NaCl transport in aquatic animals. Amer. Zool. **10**: 365–376.

Kirschner, L. B., L. Greenwald, and T. H. Kerstetter. 1973. Effect of amiloride on sodium transport across body surfaces of freshwater animals. Amer. J. Physiol. **224**: 832–837.

Kitano, Y. 1962. The behavior of various inorganic ions in the separation of calcium carbonate from a bicarbonate solution. Bull. Chem. Soc. Jap. **35**: 1973–1980.

Klein, R. Jr. and C. Hach. 1977. Standard additions: uses and limitations in spectrophotometric analysis. Amer. Lab. **9(7)**: 21–27.

Knepp, G. L. and G. F. Arkin. 1973. Ammonia toxicity levels and nitrate tolerance of channel catfish. Prog. Fish-Cult. **35**: 221–224.

Knowles, G., A. L. Downing, and M. J. Barrett. 1965. Determination of kinetic constants for nitrifying bacteria in mixed culture, with the aid of an electronic computer. J. Gen. Microbiol. **38:** 263–278.

Kobayashi, N. 1971. Fertilized sea urchin eggs as an indicatory material for marine pollution bioassay: preliminary experiments. Publ. Seto Mar. Biol. Lab. **18:** 379–406.

Kroes, H. W. 1970. Excretion of mucilage and yellow-brown substances by some brown algae from the intertidal zone. Bot. Mar. **13:** 107–110.

Krogh, A. 1937. Osmotic regulation in freshwater fishes by active adsorption of chloride ions. Z. Vergl. Physiol. **24:** 656–666.

Kuwatani, Y., T. Nishii, and F. Isogai. 1969. Effects of nitrate in culture water on the growth of the Japanese pearl oyster. Bull Natl. Pearl Res. Lab. **14:** 1735–1747. (Japanese)

Lackey, J. B. 1956. Some visibility problems in large aquaria. I. Plankton problems at Marineland. Quart. J. Fla. Acad. Sci. **19:** 259–273.

Lam, Y. and D. J. D. Nicholas. 1969. Aerobic and anaerobic respiration in *Micrococcus denitrificans*. Biochim. Biophys. Acta **172:** 450–457.

Larmoyeux, J. D. and R. G. Piper. 1973. Effects of water reuse on rainbow trout in hatcheries. Prog. Fish-Cult. **35:** 2–8.

Lees, H. 1952. The biochemistry of the nitrifying organisms. 1. The ammonia-oxidizing systems of *Nitrosomonas*. Biochem. J. **52:** 134–139.

Lees, H. and J. H. Quastel. 1946a. Biochemistry of nitrification in soil. 2. The site of soil nitrification. Biochem. J. **40:** 815–823.

Lees, H. and J. H. Quastel. 1946b. Biochemistry of nitrification in soil. 3. Nitrification of various organic nitrogen compounds. Biochem. J. **40:** 824–828.

Leiguarda, R. H., O. A. Peso, and A. Z. R. Palazzola. 1949. Bactericidal action of ozone. Ann. Assoc. Quim. Argent. **37:** 165–176. Wat. Pollut. Abst. **22:** 1432 (1949).

Leivestad, H., H. Andersen, and P. F. Schlonder. 1957. Physiological response to air exposure in codfish. Science **126:** 505.

Lemlich, R. 1972. Adsubble processes: foam fractionation and bubble fractionation. J. Geophys. Res. **77:** 5204–5210.

Levi, G., G. Morisi, A. Coletti, and R. Catanzaro. 1974. Free amino acids in fish brain: normal levels and changes upon exposure to high ammonia concentrations *in vivo*, and upon incubation of brain slices. Comp. Biochem. Physiol. **49A:** 623–636.

Levine, G. and T. L. Meade. 1976. The effects of disease treatment on nitrification in closed system aquaculture. Proc. 7th Ann. Meet. World Maricult. Soc., J. W. Avault Jr. (ed.). World Maricult. Soc., La. State Univ., Baton Rouge, pp. 483–493.

Lewin, J. C. 1955. Silicon metabolism in diatoms. II. Sources of silicon for growth of *Navicula pelliculosa*. Plant Physiol. **30:** 129–134.

Lewin, J. C. 1965. The boron requirements of a marine diatom. Naturwiss. **52(3):** 70.

Lewin, J. C. 1966. Physiological studies of the boron requirement of the diatom, *Cylindrica fusiformis* Reimann and Lewin. J. Exp. Bot. **17:** 473–479.

Liebermann, L. 1957. Air bubbles in water. J. Appl. Phys. **28:** 205–211.

Ling, G. N. 1967. Effects of temperature on the state of water in the living cell. *In* Thermobiology, A. H. Rose (ed.). Academic Press, London, pp. 5–24.

Lippmann, F. 1960. Versuche zur Aufklarung der Bildungsbedingungen von Calcit und Aragonit. Fortschr. Mineral. **38:** 156–161.

Lippmann, F. 1973. Sedimentary carbonate minerals. Springer-Verlag, New York, 228 pp.

Lloyd, R. 1961. The toxicity of ammonia to rainbow trout (*Salmo gairdneri*). Waste Wat. Treat. J. **8:** 278–279.

Lloyd, R. and D. W. M. Herbert. 1960. The influence of carbon dioxide on the toxicity of un-ionized ammonia to rainbow trout (*Salmo gairdnerii* Richardson). Ann. Appl. Biol. **48:** 399–404.

Lloyd, R. and D. W. M. Herbert. 1962. The effect of the environment on the toxicity of poisons to fish. Pap. Pres. Meet. Inst. Pub. Health Engrs., Westminster, London, Jan. 1962, 13 pp.

Lloyd, R. and L. D. Orr, 1969. The diuretic response by rainbow trout to sub-lethal concentrations of ammonia. Wat. Res. **3:** 335–344.

Lobring, L. G. and R. L. Booth. 1975. Understanding turbidity measurements. Proc. Amer. Wat. Wks. Assoc. Tech. Conf., Atlanta, Dec. 1975, 6 pp.

Lui, N. S. T. and O. A. Roels. 1970. Nitrogen metabolism of aquatic organisms. I. The assimilation and formation of urea in *Ochromonas malhamensis*. Arch. Biochem. Biophys. **139:** 269–277.

Lüning, K. 1971. Seasonal growth of *Laminaria hyperborea* under recorded underwater light conditions near Helgoland. *In* Proc. 4th European Mar. Biol. Symp., D. J. Crisp (ed.). Cambridge Univ. Press, Cambridge, pp. 347–361.

Lyman, J. 1956. Buffer mechanism of seawater. Ph.D. thesis, Univ. Calif., Los Angeles, 196 pp.

MacIsaac, J. J. and R. C. Dugdale. 1972. Interaction of light and inorganic nitrogen in controlling nitrogen uptake in the sea. Deep-Sea Res. **19:** 209–232.

MacKay, W. C. and D. D. Beatty. 1968. Plasma glucose levels of the white sucker, *Catostomus commersonii*, and the northern pike, *Esox lucius*. Can. J. Zool. **46:** 797–803.

MacLean, S. A., A. C. Longwell, and W. J. Blogoslawski. 1973. Effects of ozone-treated seawater on the spawned, fertilized, meiotic, and cleaving eggs of the commercial American oyster. Mutat. Res. **2:** 282–285.

Maetz, J. 1971. Fish gills: mechanisms of salt transfer in fresh water and sea water. Philos. Trans. Roy. Soc. Lond. **262B:** 209–249.

Maetz, J. 1972. Branchial sodium exchange and ammonia excretion in the goldfish *Carassius auratus*. Effects of ammonia-loading and temperature changes. J. Exp. Biol. **56:** 601–620.

Maetz, J. 1973. Na$^+$/NH$_4^+$ exchanges and NH$_3$ movement across the gill of *Carassius auratus*. J. Exp. Biol. **58:** 255–275.

Maetz, J. and D. H. Evans. 1972. Effects of temperature on branchial sodium exchange and extrusion mechanisms in the seawater-adapted flounder, *Platichthys flesus* L. J. Exp. Biol. **56:** 565–585.

Maetz, J. and F. Garcia-Romeu. 1964. The mechanism of sodium and chloride uptake by the gills of a fresh-water fish, *Carassius auratus*. II. Evidence for NH$_4^+$/Na$^+$ and HCO$_3^-$/Cl$^-$ exchanges. J. Gen. Physiol. **47:** 1209–1227.

Maetz, J., P. Payan, and G. de Renzis. 1976. Controversial aspects of ionic uptake in freshwater animals. *In* Perspectives in experimental biology, Vol. 1, P. S. Davis (ed.). Pergamon Press, Oxford, pp. 77–92.

Majak, W., J. S. Craigie, and J. McLachlan. 1966. Photosynthesis in algae. I. Accumulation products in the Rhodophyceae. Can. J. Bot. **44:** 541–549.

Malone, P. G., and K. M. Towe. 1970. Microbial carbonate and phosphate precipitates from sea water cultures. Mar. Geol. **9**: 301–309.

Malone, T. C., C. Garside, K. C. Haines, and O. A. Roels. 1975. Nitrate uptake and growth of *Chaetoceros sp.* in large outdoor continuous cultures. Limnol. Oceanogr. **20**: 9–19.

Mamrelli, E. S. (chmn.). 1975. AWWA standard for polyvinyl chloride (PVC) pressure pipe, 4 in. through 12 in., for water. AWWA C900-75, Amer. Wat. Wks. Assoc., Denver, 17 pp.

Manabe, T. 1969. New modification of Lubrochinsky's indophenol method for direct microanalysis of ammonia-N in sea water. Bull. Jap. Soc. Sci. Fish. **35**: 897–906. (Japanese)

Mangum, C. P. 1976. The function of respiratory pigments in estuarine animals. *In* Estuarine processes, Vol. 1, M. L. Wiley (ed.). Academic Press, New York, pp. 356–380.

Magnum, C. P., J. A. Dykens, R. P. Henry, and G. Polites. 1978. The excretion of $NH_4^+$ and its ouabain sensitivity in aquatic annelids and molluscs. J. Exp. Zool. **203**: 151–157.

Mangum, C. P., M. S. Haswell, and K. Johansen. 1977. Low salt and high pH in the blood of Amazon fishes. J. Exp. Zool. **200**: 163–168.

Mangum, C. P., S. U. Silverthorn, J. L. Harris, D. W. Towle, and A. R. Krall. 1976. The relationship between blood pH, ammonia excretion and adaptation to low salinity in the blue crab *Callinectes sapidus*. J. Exp. Zool. **195**: 129–136.

Mangum, D. C. and W. F. McIlhenny. 1975. Control of marine fouling in intake systems—a comparison of ozone and chlorine. *In* Aquatic applications of ozone, W. J. Blogoslawski and R. G. Rice (eds.). Internat. Ozone Inst., Cleveland, pp. 138–153.

Maqsood, R. and A. Benedek. 1977. Low-temperature organic removal and denitrification in activated carbon columns. J. Wat. Pollut. Contr. Fed. **49**: 2107–2117.

Martin, D. M. 1972. Marine chemistry, Vol. 1, 2nd ed. Marcel-Dekker, New York, 389 pp.

Masschelein, W., G. Fransolet, and J. Genot. 1975. Techniques for dispersing and dissolving ozone in water. Part 1. Wat. Sew. Wks. **122(12)**: 57–60.

Matulewich, V. A., P. F. Strom, and M. S. Finstein. 1975. Length of incubation for enumerating nitrifying bacteria present in various environments. Appl. Microbiol. **29**: 265–268.

Mautner, H. G. 1954. The chemistry of brown algae. Econ. Bot. **8**: 174–192.

Mazeaud, F. 1964. Vitesse de production de l'hyperglycémie adrénalique en fonction de la température chez la carpe. Intensité de la résponse en fonction de la dose d'hormone. C. R. Soc. Biol. **158**: 36–40.

Mazeaud, M. 1969a. Adrenalinemie et noradrenalinemie chez la lamproie marine (*Petromyzon marinus* L.). C. R. Soc. Biol. **163**: 349–352.

Mazeaud, M. 1969b. Influence du stress sur les teneurs en catécholamines du plasma et des corps axillaires chez un sélecien *Scyliorhinus canicula* L. C. R. Soc. Biol. **163**: 2262–2266.

Mazeaud, M. M., F. Mazeaud, and E. M. Donaldson. 1977. Primary and secondary effects of stress in fish: some new data with a general review. Trans. Amer. Fish. Soc. **106**: 201–212.

McCarthy, J. J. 1971. The role of urea in marine phytoplankton ecology. Ph.D. thesis, Scripps Inst. Oceanogr., La Jolla, CA, 165 pp.

McCarthy, J. J. 1972a. The uptake of urea by marine phytoplankton. J. Phycol. **8(Suppl.):** 216–222.

McCarthy, J. J. 1972b. The uptake of urea by natural populations of marine phytoplankton. Limnol. Oceanogr. **17:** 738–748.

McCarthy, J. J. and R. W. Eppley. 1972. A comparison of chemical, isotopic, and enzymatic methods for measuring nitrogen assimilation of marine phytoplankton. Limnol. Oceanogr. **17:** 371–382.

McCarthy, J. J. and D. Kamykowski. 1972. Urea and other nitrogenous nutrients in La Jolla Bay during February, March and April 1970. Fish. Bull. (NOAA) **70:** 1261–1274.

McCarthy, J. J. and C. H. Smith. 1974. A review of ozone and its application to domestic wastewater treatment. J. Amer. Wat. Wks. Assoc. **66:** 718–725.

McCauley, W. J. 1971. Vertebrate physiology. W. B. Saunders, Philadelphia, 422 pp.

McCormick, N. A. and J. J. R. MacLeod. 1925. The effect on the blood sugar of fish of various conditions including removal of the principal islets (isletectomy). Proc. Roy. Soc. **98B:** 1–29.

McCreary, J. J. and V. L. Snoeyink. 1977. Granular activated carbon in water treatment. J. Amer. Wat. Wks. Assoc. **69:** 437–444.

McDonald, M. 1885. Effect of waste products from Page's ammoniacal works upon young shad fry. Bull. U. S. Fish Comm. **5:** 313–314.

McFarland, W. N., and K. S. Norris. 1958. The control of pH by buffers in fish transport. Calif. Fish and Game **44:** 291–310.

McGregor, D. 1973. An inexpensive cooled recirculating system for the maintenance of marine flat fish. Lab. Anim. **7(1):** 13–17.

McLachlan, J. 1973. Growth media—marine. *In* Handbook of phycological methods, J. R. Stein (ed.). Cambridge Univ. Press, Cambridge, pp. 25–51.

McLachlan, J. 1964. Some considerations of the growth of marine algae in artificial media. Can. J. Microbiol. **10:** 769–782.

McLeese, D. W. 1956. Effects of temperature, salinity and oxygen on the survival of the American lobster. J. Fish. Res. Board Can. **13:** 247–272.

McMahon, B. R. and J. L. Wilkens. 1975. Respiratory and circulatory responses to hypoxia in the lobster *Homarus americanus*. J. Exp. Biol. **62:** 637–655.

Meade, T. L. 1974. The technology of closed system culture of salmonids. Tech. Rpt. 30, Anim. Sci./NOAA Sea Grant, Univ. R. I., Kingston, 30 pp.

Meddows-Taylor, J. 1947. Some characteristics of ozone in relation to water treatment. J. Inst. Wat. Engrs. **1:** 187–201.

Mehrle, P. M. and R. A. Bloomfield. 1974. Ammonia detoxifying mechanisms of rainbow trout altered by dietary dieldrin. Toxicol. Appl. Pharmacol. **27:** 355–365.

Meijers, A. P. 1977. Quality aspects of ozonisation. Wat. Res. **11:** 647–652.

Meiklejohn, J. 1954. Some aspects of the physiology of the nitrifying bacteria. *In* Symposium on autotrophic microorganisms (Fourth Symp., Soc. Gen. Microbiol.), B. A. Fry and J. L. Peel (eds.). Cambridge Univ. Press, Cambridge, pp. 68–83.

Menzel, D. W. 1966. Bubbling of sea water and the production of organic particles: a re-evaluation. Deep-Sea Res. **13:** 963–966.

Merkens, J. C. and K. M. Downing. 1957. The effect of tension of dissolved oxygen on the toxicity of un-ionized ammonia to several species of fish. Ann. Appl. Biol. **45:** 521–527.

Meyers, P. A., and J. G. Quinn. 1971. Interaction between fatty acids and calcite in seawater. Limnol. Oceanogr. **16**: 992–997.

Milne, M. D., B. H. Schribner, and M. A. Crawford. 1958. Non-ionic diffusion and excretion of weak acids and bases. Amer. J. Med. **24**: 709–729.

Moebus, J. 1972. The influence of storage on antibacterial activity of sea water. I. Experiments with sea water stored at 18°C. Mar. Biol. **13**: 346–351.

Mohsen, A. F., A. F. Khaleata, M. A. Hashem, and A. Metwalli. 1974. Effect of different nitrogen sources on growth, reproduction, amino acid, fat and sugar contents in *Ulva fasciata* Delile. Bot. Mar. **17**: 218–222.

Mohsen, A. F., A. H. Nasr, and A. M. Metwalli. 1973. Effect of different light intensities on growth, reproduction, amino acid synthesis, fat and sugar contents in *Ulva fasciata* Delile. Hydrobiologia **43**: 125–235.

Morel, A. 1966. Etude experimentale de la diffusion de la lumiere par l'eau, les solutions de chlorure de sodium et l'eau de mer optiquement pures. J. Chim. Phys. **10**: 1359–1366.

Morel, F., R. E. McDuff, and J. J. Morgan. 1976. Theory of interaction intensities, buffer capacities, and pH stability in aqueous systems, with application to the pH of seawater and a heterogeneous model ocean system. Mar. Chem. **4**: 1–28.

Morris, J. C. and W. J. Weber Jr. 1964. Adsorption of biochemically resistant materials from solution. 1. PHS Publ. No. 999-WP-11, Pub. Health Serv., Cincinnati, 74 pp.

Motais, R. 1970. Effect of actinomycin D on the branchial Na-K dependent ATPase activity in relation to sodium balance of the eel. Comp. Biochem. Physiol. **34**: 497–501.

Mulbarger, M. C. 1971. Nitrification and denitrification in activated sludge systems. J. Wat. Pollut. Contr. Fed. **43**: 2059–2070.

Mullin, J. D. and J. P. Riley. 1955. The spectrophotometric determination of nitrate in natural waters, with particular reference to sea-water. Anal. Chim. Acta **12**: 464–480.

Munro, A. L. S. and T. D. Brock. 1968. Distinction between bacterial and algal utilization of soluble substances in the sea. J. Gen. Microbiol. **51**: 35–42.

Murray, C. N. and J. P. Riley. 1971. The solubility of gases in distilled water and in seawater. 4. Carbon dioxide. Deep-Sea Res. **18**: 533–541.

Murray, S. N. and P. S. Dixon. 1973. The effect of light intensity and light period on the development of thallus form in the marine red alga *Pleononsporium squarrulosum* (Harvey) Abbott (Rhotophyta: Ceramiales). I. Apical cell division—main axes. J. Exp. Mar. Biol. Ecol. **13**: 15–27.

Murray, S. N. and P. S. Dixon. 1975. The effects of light intensity and light period on the development of thallus form in the marine red alga *Pleononsporium squarrulosum* (Harvey) Abbott (Rhodophyta: Ceramiales). II. Cell enlargement. J. Exp. Mar. Biol. Ecol. **19**: 165–176.

Murphy, J. and J. P. Riley. 1962. A modified single solution method for the determination of phosphate in natural waters. Anal. Chim. Acta **27**: 31–36.

Musani-Marazović, L. and Z. Pučar. 1977. Interaction of $^{54}$Mn and $^{55(59)}$Fe with EDTA in seawater and 0.55 M NaCl solutions. Mar. Chem. **5**: 229–242.

Nagy, R. 1964. Application and measurement of ultraviolet radiation. Amer. Indus. Hyg. Assoc. J. **25**: 274–281.

Nakano, T. and N. Tomlinson. 1967. Catecholamine and carbohydrate concentrations in rainbow trout (*Salmo gairdneri*) in relation to physical disturbance. J. Fish. Res. Board Can. **24**: 1701–1715.

National Academy of Sciences. 1973. Nutrient requirements of domestic animals, No. 11: Nutrient requirements of trout, salmon, and catfish. Nat. Acad. Sci., Washington, DC, 57 pp.

Nebel, C., R. D. Gottschling, R. L. Hutchison, T. J. McBride, D. M. Taylor, J. L. Pavoni, M. E. Tittlebaum, H. E. Spencer, and M. Fleischman. 1973. Ozone disinfection of industrial-municipal secondary effluents. J. Wat. Pollut. Contr. Fed. **45**: 2493–2507.

Nebel, C., R. D. Gottschling, P. C. Unangst, H. J. O'Neill, and G. V. Zintel. 1976. Ozone provides alternative for secondary effluent disinfection. I. Wat. Sew. Wks. **123(4):** 76–78.

Neill, W. T. 1957. Historical biogeography of present-day Florida. Bull. Fla. State Mus. **2:** 175–220.

Német, A. G. 1961. Flow of gas-liquid mixtures in vertical tubes. Indus. Engr. Chem. **53:** 151–154.

Newburn, L. H. (ed.). 1975. ISCOTABLES: a handbook of data for biological and physical scientists, 6th ed. Instrumentation Specialities Co., Lincoln, NE., 48 pp.

Neyfert, A. V. 1969. A refrigeration unit for aquariums with running water. *Hydrobiol. J.* **5:** 68–71.

Nicol, J. A. C. 1967. The biology of marine animals, 2nd ed. Sir Isaac Pitman and Sons, London, 699 pp.

Nigrelli, R. F. 1936. Life-history of *Oodinium ocellatum*. Zoologica **21:** 129–164 + 9 pl.

Nigrelli, R. F. and G. D. Ruggieri. 1966. Enzootics in the New York Aquarium caused by *Cryptocaryon irritans* Brown, 1951 (=*Ichthyophthirius marinus* Sikama, 1961), a histophagous ciliate in the skin, eyes and gills of marine fishes. Zoologica **51:** 97–102 + 7 pl.

Ng, K. S. and J. C. Mueller. 1975. Foam separation—a technique for water pollution abatement. Wat. Sew. Wks. **122(6):** 48–55.

Nowak, S. H. 1974. A solid state temperature controller with heating and cooling control. Tech. Rpt. No. 495, Environ. Can., Fish. Mar. Serv., 16 pp.

O'Donovan, D. C. 1965. Treatment with ozone. J. Amer. Wat. Wks. Assoc. **57:** 1167–1194.

O'Kelley, J. C. 1974. Inorganic nutrients. *In* Algal physiology and biochemistry, Bot. Monogr. Vol. 10, W. D. P. Stewart (ed.). Univ. Calif. Press, Berkeley, pp. 610–635.

Oliver, J. H. 1957. The chemical composition of sea water in the aquarium. Proc. Zool. Soc. Lond. **129:** 137–145.

Olson, K. R. and P. O. Fromm. 1971. Excretion of urea by two teleosts exposed to different concentrations of ambient ammonia. Comp. Biochem. Physiol. **40A:** 999–1007.

O'Melia, C. R. and W. Stumm. 1967. Theory of water filtration. J. Amer. Wat. Wks. Assoc. **59:** 1393–1412.

O'Neill, R. V. 1968. A simple marine aquarium system. Turtox News, **46:** 166–168.

Owens, O. v. H. and W. E. Esaias. 1976. Physiological responses of phytoplankton to major environmental factors. Ann. Rev. Plant Physiol. **27:** 461–483.

Ozretich, R. J. 1977. An investigation of the transition from aerobic to nitrate respiration in marine bacteria in continuous culture. Diss. Abst. Internat. **38:** 1002-B.

Pace, D. M., P. A. Landolt, and B. T. Alftonomos. 1969. Effects of ozone on cells *in vitro*. Arch. Environ. Health **18:** 165–170.

Painter, H. A. 1970. A review of literature on inorganic nitrogen metabolism in microorganisms. Wat. Res. **4:** 393–450.

Park, P. K. 1969. Oceanic $CO_2$ system: an evaluation of ten methods of investigation. Limnol. Oceanogr. **14:** 179–186.

Parkhurst, J. D., F. D. Dryden, G. N. McDermott, and J. English. 1967. Pomona activated carbon pilot plant. J. Wat. Pollut. Contr. Fed. **39:** R70–R81.

Payan, P. and J. Maetz. 1973. Branchial sodium transport mechanisms in *Scyliorhinus canicula:* evidence for $Na^+/NH_4^+$ $Na^+$ $H^+$ exchanges and for a role of carbonic anhydrase. J. Exp. Biol. **58:** 487–502.

Payan, P. and A. J. Matty. 1975. The characteristics of ammonia excretion by a perfused isolated head of trout (*Salmo gairdneri*): effect of temperature and $CO_2$-free Ringer. J. Comp. Physiol. **96:** 167–184.

Peirce, E. C. II. 1967. Acid-base relationships in blood of *Squalus acanthias:* preliminary nomogram. Bull. Mt. Desert Isl. Biol. Lab. **7:** 36–37.

Peleg, M. 1976. Review paper: the chemistry of ozone in the treatment of water. Wat. Res. **10:** 361–365.

Pequin, L. and A. Serfaty. 1963. L'excretion ammoniacale chez un teleosteen dulcicole: *Cyprinus carpio* L. Comp. Biochem. Physiol. **10:** 315–324.

Perrone, S. J. and T. L. Meade. 1977. Protective effect of chloride on nitrite toxicity to coho salmon (*Oncorhynchus kisutch*). J. Fish. Res. Board Can. **34:** 486–492.

Phillips, G. B. and E. Hanel Jr. 1960. Use of ultraviolet radiation in microbiological laboratories. Tech. Rpt. BL 28 (Revis. Spec. Rpt. 211), U. S. Army Chem. Corps., Biol. Lab., Ft. Detrick, MD, 295 pp.

Plummer, L. N. and F. T. Mackenzie. 1974. Predicting mineral solubility from rate data: application to the dissolution of magnesian calcites. Amer. J. Sci. **274:** 61–83.

Poddar, R. K. and R. L. Sinsheimer. 1971. Nature of the complementary strands synthesized in vitro upon the single-stranded circular DNA of bacteriophage ØX174 after ultraviolet irradiation. Biophys. J. **11:** 355–369.

Prat, R., C. Nofre, and A. Cier. 1968. Effets de l'hypochlorite de sodium de l'ozone et des radiations ionisantes sur les constituants phyrimidiques d'*Escherichia coli*. Ann. Inst. Pasteur **114:** 595–607.

Precht, H., H. Laudien, and B. Havsteen. 1973. The normal temperature range. *In* Temperature and life, H. Precht (ed.). Springer-Verlag, New York, pp. 302–352.

Presnell, M. W. and J. M. Cummins. 1972. Effectiveness of ultra-violet radiation units in the bactericidal treatment of seawater. Wat. Res. **6:** 1203–1212.

Prince, J. S. 1974. Nutrient assimilation and growth of some seaweeds in mixtures of sea water and secondary sewage treatment effluents. Aquaculture **4:** 69–79.

Prosser, C. L. 1973. Temperature. *In* Comparative animal physiology, 3rd ed., C. L. Prosser (ed.). W. B. Saunders, Philadelphia, pp. 362–428.

Provasoli, L. 1964. Growing marine seaweeds. *In* Proc. Fourth Internat. Seaweed Symp., D. DeVirville and J. Feldman (eds.). Pergamon Press, Oxford, pp. 9–17.

Provasoli, L. and A. F. Carlucci. 1974. Vitamins and growth regulators. *In* Algal physiology and biochemistry, Bot. Monogr. Vol. 10, W. D. P. Stewart (ed.). Univ. Calif. Press, Berkeley, pp. 741–787.

Pytkowicz, R. M. 1972. The chemical stability of the oceans and the $CO_2$ system. *In* The changing chemistry of the oceans, D. Dryssen and D. Jagner (eds.). Almqvist and Wiksell, Stockholm, pp. 147–152.

Pytkowicz, R. M. and E. Atlas. 1975. Buffer intensity of seawater. Limnol. Oceanogr. **20:** 222–229.

Pytkowicz, R. M., E. Atlas, and C. H. Culberson. 1975. Chemical equilibrium in seawater. *In* Marine chemistry in the coastal environment, ACS Symp. Ser. No. 18, T. M. Church (ed.). Amer. Chem. Soc., Washington, DC, pp. 1–24.

Pytkowicz, R. M. and J. W. Hawley. 1974. Bicarbonate and carbonate ion-pairs and a model of seawater at 25°C. Limnol. Oceanogr. **19:** 223–234.

Pytkowicz, R. M., D. R. Kester, and R. C. Burgener. 1966. Reproducibility of pH measurements in seawater. Limnol. Oceanogr. **11:** 417–419.

Quastel, J. H., P. G. Scholefield, and J. W. Stevenson. 1950. Oxidation of pyruvic–oxime by soil organisms. Nature **166:** 940–942.

Rahn, H. 1966. Aquatic gas exchange theory. Respir. Physiol. **1:** 1–12.

Rahn, H. 1967. Gas transport from the external environment to the cell. *In* Development of the lung, Ciba Found. Symp., A. V. S. DeReuck and R. Porter (eds.). Little, Brown, Boston, pp. 3–29.

Rahn, H. and F. W. Baumgardner. 1972. Temperature and acid-base regulation in fish. Respir. Physiol. **14:** 171–182.

Randall, D. J. 1970. Gas exchange in fish. *In* Fish physiology, Vol. 4, W. S. Hoar and D. J. Randall (eds.). Academic Press, London, pp. 253–292.

Randall, D. J. and J. N. Cameron. 1973. Respiratory control of arterial pH as temperature changes in rainbow trout *Salmo gairdneri*. Amer. J. Physiol. **225:** 997–1002.

Randall, D. J., N. Heisler, and F. Drees. 1976. Ventilatory response to hypercapnia in the larger spotted dogfish *Scyliorhinus stellaris*. Amer. J. Physiol. **230:** 590–594.

Reeves, R. B. 1977. The interaction of body temperature and acid-base balance in ectothermic vertebrates. Ann. Rev. Physiol. **39:** 559–586.

Reichenbach-Klinke, von H.-H. 1967. Untersuchungen über die Einwirkung des Ammoniakgehalts auf den Fischorganismus. Arch. Fischereiwiss. **17:** 122–132.

Rice, S. D. and R. M. Stokes. 1975. Acute toxicity of ammonia to several developmental stages of rainbow trout, *Salmo gairdneri*. Fish. Bull. (NOAA) **73:** 207–211.

Riley, G. A. 1963. Organic aggregates in sea water and the dynamics of their formation and utilization. Limnol. Oceanogr. **8:** 372–381.

Riley, G. A., D. van Hemert, and P. J. Wangersky. 1965. Organic aggregates in surface and deep waters of the Sargasso Sea. Limnol. Oceanogr. **10:** 354–363.

Riley, J. P. and R. Chester. 1971. Introduction to marine chemistry. Academic Press, London, 465 pp.

Riley, J. P., D. E. Roberton, J. W. R. Dutton, N. T. Mitchell, and P. J. LeB. Williams. 1975. Analytical chemistry of sea water. *In* Chemical oceanography, Vol. 3, 2nd ed., J. P. Riley and G. Skorrow (eds.). Academic Press, London, pp. 193–514.

Riley, J. P. and I. Roth. 1971. The distribution of trace elements in some species of phytoplankton grown in culture. J. Mar. Biol. Assoc. U. K. **51:** 63–72.

Robinette, H. R. 1976. Effect of selected sublethal levels of ammonia on the growth of channel catfish (*Ictalurus punctatus*). Prog. Fish-Cult. **38:** 26–29.

Robinson, F. W., J. C. Tash, and S. H. Holanov. 1978. Cooling discontinuous waters with a single refrigeration unit. Prog. Fish-Cult., **40:** 15.

Robinson, J. H. (chmn.). 1972. AWWA standard for filtering material. AWWA B100-72, Amer. Wat. Wks. Assoc., Denver, 11 pp.

Rombough, P. J. and E. T. Garside. 1977. Hypoxial death inferred from thermally induced injuries at upper lethal temperatures, in the banded killifish, *Fundulus diaphanus* (LeSueur). Can. J. Zool. **55:** 1705–1719.

Root, R. 1931. The respiratory function of the blood of marine fishes. Biol. Bull. **61:** 427–456.

Rosen, H. M. 1973. Use of ozone and oxygen in advanced wastewater treatment. J. Wat. Pollut. Contr. Fed. **45:** 2521–2536.

Rosenlund, B. D. 1975. Disinfection of hatchery influent by ozonation and the effects of ozonated water on rainbow trout. *In* Aquatic applications of ozone, W. J. Blogoslawski and R. G. Rice (eds.). Internat. Ozone Inst., Cleveland, pp. 59–69.

Rubin, A. J. and G. A. Elmaraghy. 1977. Studies on the toxicity of ammonia, nitrate and their mixtures to guppy fry. Wat. Res. **11:** 927–935.

Russo, R. C., C. E. Smith, and R. V. Thurston. 1974. Acute toxicity of nitrite to rainbow trout (*Salmo gairdneri*). J. Fish. Res. Board Can. **31:** 1653–1655.

Saeki, A. 1958. Studies on fish culture in filtered closed-circulation aquaria. I. Fundamental theory and system design standards. Bull. Jap. Soc. Sci. Fish. **23:** 684–695. Transl. from Jap. by E. R. Hope, Dir. Sci. Info. Serv., Def. Res. Board Can., issued Jan. 1964.

Saeki, A. 1962. The composition and some chemical control of the sea water of the closed circulating aquarium. Bull. Mar. Biol. Sta. Asamushi **11:** 99–104.

Sander, E. 1967. Skimmers in the marine aquarium. Petfish Mon. **2:** 48–51.

Sander, E. and H. Rosenthal. 1975. Application of ozone in water treatment for home aquaria, public aquaria and for aquaculture purposes. *In* Aquatic applications of ozone, W. J. Blogoslawski and R. G. Rice (eds.). Internat. Ozone Inst., Cleveland, pp. 138–153.

Sanders, J.E., J. L. Fryer, D. A. Leith, and K. D. Moore. 1972. Control of the infectious protozoan *Ceratomyxa shasta* by treating hatchery water supplies. Prog. Fish-Cult. **34:** 13–17.

Schlesner, H. and G. Rheinheimer. 1974. Auswirkungen einer Ozonisierungsanlage auf den Bakteriengehalt des Wassers eines Schauaquariums. Kieler Meeresforsuch. **30:** 117–129.

Schmidt-Nielsen, K. 1975. Animal physiology: adaptation and environment. Cambridge Univ. Press, Cambridge, 699 pp.

Schreckenbach, K., R. Spangenberg, and S. Krug. 1975. Cause of gill necrosis. Z. Binnenfisch. DDR **22:** 257–288. (German)

Schreiber, E. 1927. Die Reinkultur von marinem Phytoplankton und deren Bedeutung für die Erforschung der Produktionsfähigkeit des Meerwassers. Wiss. Meeresunters. N. S. **16:** 1–34.

Schulze-Wiehenbrauck, H. 1976. Effects of sublethal ammonia concentrations on metabolism in juvenile rainbow trout (*Salmo gairdneri* Richardson). Ber. Dtsch. Wiss. Komm. Meeresforsch. **24:** 234–250.

Scott, D. B. M. and E. C. Lesher. 1963. Effect of ozone on survival and permeability of *Escherichia coli*. J. Bacteriol. **85:** 567–576.

Scott, K. R. 1972. Comparison of the effiency of various aeration devices for oxygenation of water in aquaria. J. Fish. Res. Board Can. **29:** 1641–1643.

Scott, K. R. and D. C. Gillespie. 1972. A compact recirculation unit for rearing and maintenance of fish. J. Fish. Res. Board Can. **29:** 1071–1074.

Sebba, F. 1962. Ion flotation. Elsevier, Amsterdam, 154 pp.

Segedi, R. and W. E. Kelley. 1964. A new formula for artificial sea water. *In* Sea-water systems for experimental aquariums: a collection of papers, J. R. Clark and R. L. Clark (eds.). Res. Rpt. 63, Bur. Sport Fish. Wildl., Washington, DC, pp. 17–19.

Selmeczi, J. G. 1971. Capture mechanisms in deep-bed filtration. Indus. Wat. Engr. **8(6):** 25–28.

Setlow, R. B., P. A. Swenson, and W. L. Carrier. 1963. Thymine dimers and inhibition of DNA synthesis by ultraviolet irradiation of cells. Science **142:** 1464–1466.

Sharma, B. and R. C. Ahlert. 1977. Nitrification and nitrogen removal. Wat. Res. **11:** 897–925.

Shelbourne, J. E. 1964. Sea-water systens for rearing fish larvae. *In* Sea-water systems for experimental aquariums: a collection of papers, J. R. Clark and R. L. Clark (eds.). Res. Rpt. 63, Bur. Sport Fish. Wildl., Washington, DC, pp. 81–93.

Shechter, H. 1973. Spectrophotometric method for determination of ozone in aqueous solutions. Wat. Res. **7:** 729–739.

Sheldon, R. W., T. P. T. Evelyn, and T. R. Parsons. 1967. On the occurrence and formation of small particles in seawater. Limnol. Oceanogr. **12:** 367–375.

Siddall, S. E. 1974. Studies of closed marine culture systems. Prog. Fish-Cult. **36:** 8–15.

Sidwell, V. D., P. R. Foncannon, N. S. Moore, and J. C. Bonnet. 1974. Composition of the edible portion of raw (fresh or frozen) crustaceans, finfish, and mollusks. I. Protein, fat, moisture, ash, carbohydrate, energy value, and cholesterol. Mar. Fish. Rev. **36(3):** 21–35.

Sieburth, J. M. 1969. Studies on algal substances in the sea. III. The production of extracellular organic matter by littoral marine algae. J. Exp. Mar. Biol. Ecol. **3:** 290–309.

Sieburth, J. M. and A. Jensen. 1968. Studies on algal substances in the sea. I. Gelbstoff (humic material) in terrestrial and marine waters. J. Exp. Mar. Biol. Ecol. **2:** 174–189.

Sieburth, J. M. and A. Jensen. 1969. Studies on algal substances in the sea. II. The formation of gelbstoff (humic material) by exudates of Phaeophyta. J. Exp. Mar. Biol. Ecol. **3:** 275–289.

Sieburth, J. M. and A. Jensen. 1970. Production and transformation of extracellular organic matter from littoral marine algae: a resume. *In* Symposium on organic matter in natural waters, D. W. Hood (ed.). Univ. Alaska, Fairbanks, pp. 203–223.

Sigel, M. M., G. Ortiz-Muniz, and R. B. Shouger. 1972. Toxic effect of ammonia dissolved in sea water. Comp. Biochem. Physiol. **42A:** 261–262.

Simkiss, K. 1964. The inhibitory effects of some metabolites on the precipitation of calcium carbonate from artificial and natural sea water. J. Conseil Internat. Explor. Mer **19:** 6–18.

Simon, G. and C. H. Oppenheimer. 1968. Bacterial changes in sea water samples, due to storage and volume. Z. Alleg. Mikrobiol. **8:** 209–214.

Simpson, W. W. 1926. The effects of asphyxia and isletectomy on the blood sugar of *Myoxocephalus and Ameiurus.* Amer. J. Physiol. **77:** 409–418.

Singer, P. C. and W. B. Zilli. 1975. Ozonation of ammonia in wastewater. Wat. Res. **9:** 127–134.

Skerman, V. B. D. and I. C. MacRay. 1957. The influence of oxygen in the reduction of nitrate by adapted cells of *Pseudomonas denitrificans.* Can. J. Microbiol. **3:** 215–230.

Skirrow, G. 1975. The dissolved gases—carbon dioxide. *In* Chemical oceanography, Vol. 2, 2nd ed., J. P. Riley and G. Skirrow (eds.). Academic Press, London, pp. 1–192.

Smart, G. 1976. The effect of ammonia exposure on gill structure of the rainbow trout (*Salmo gairdneri*). J. Fish Biol. **8:** 471–475.

Smith, A. J. and D. S. Hoare. 1968. Acetate assimilation by *Nitrobacter agilis* in relation to its obligate autotrophy. J. Bacteriol. **95:** 844–855.

Smith, C. E. and R. G. Piper. 1975. Lesions associated with chronic exposure to ammonia. *In* The pathology of fishes, W. E. Ribelin and G. Migaki (eds.). Univ. Wis. Press, Madison, pp. 497–514.

Smith, C. E. and W. G. Williams. 1974. Experimental nitrite toxicity in rainbow trout and chinook salmon. Trans. Amer. Fish. Soc. **103:** 389–390.

Smith, H. W. 1929. The excretion of ammonia and urea by the gills of fish. J. Biol. Chem. **81:** 727–742.

Smith, H. W. 1930. Metabolism of the lung-fish, *Protopterus aethiopicus*. J. Biol. Chem. **88:** 97–130.

Smith, R. G. Jr. and H. L. Windom. 1972. Analytical handbook for the determination of arsenic, cadmium, cobalt, copper, iron, lead, manganese, mercury, nickel, silver and zinc in the marine and estuarine environments. Tech. Rpt. Ser. 72–6, Ga. Mar. Sci. Cen., Univ. Ga., Savannah, 62 pp.

Smith, W. W. and C. E. ZoBell. 1937. Direct microscopic evidence of an autochthonous bacterial flora in Great Salt Lake. Ecology **18:** 453–458.

Snieszko, S. F. and G. L. Hoffman. 1970. Control of fish diseases. Lab. Anim. Care **13:** 197–206.

Solórzano, L. 1969. Determination of ammonia in natural waters by the phenolhypochlorite method. Limnol. Oceanogr. **14:** 799–801.

Sontheimer, H. 1974. Use of activated carbon in water treatment practice and its regeneration. Spec. Subj. 3, Lehrstuhl für Wasserchimie der Universität Karlruhe, West Germany, 6 pp.

Sousa, R. J. and T. L. Meade. 1977. The influence of ammonia on the oxygen delivery system of coho salmon hemoglobin. Comp. Biochem. Physiol. **58A:** 23–28.

Spanier, E. 1978. Preliminary trials with an ultraviolet liquid sterilizer. Aquaculture **14:** 75–84.

Spencer, C. P. 1966. Theoretical aspects of the control of pH in natural seawater and synthetic culture media for marine algae. Bot. Mar. **9:** 81–89.

Spencer, C. P. 1975. The micronutrient elements. *In* Chemical oceanography, Vol. 2, 2nd ed., J. P. Riley and G. Skirrow (eds.). Academic Press, London, pp. 245–300.

Spotte, S. 1973. Marine aquarium keeping: the science, animals, and art. Wiley, New York, 173 pp.

Spotte, S. 1974. Aquarium techniques: closed-system marine aquariums. *In* Experimental marine biology, R. N. Mariscal (ed.). Academic Press, New York pp. 1–19.

Spotte, S. 1979. Fish and invertebrate culture: water management in closed systems, 2nd ed. Wiley, New York, 179 pp.

Sprague, J. B. 1966. Filtration of seawater for marine biological laboratories. Mss. Rpt. Ser. (Biol.) No. 851, Fish. Res. Board Can., 22 pp.

Srna, R. F. and A. Baggaley. 1975. Kinetic response and perturbed marine nitrification systems. J. Wat. Pollut. Contr. Fed. **47:** 472–486.

Srna, R. F., C. Epifanio, M. Hartman, G. Pruder, and A. Stubbs. 1973. The use of ion specific electrodes for chemical monitoring of marine systems. I. The ammonia electrode as a sensitive water quality indicator probe for recirculating mariculture systems. DEL-SG-73, Coll. Mar. Stud., Univ. Del., Newark, 20 pp.

St. Amant, P. P. and P. L. McCarty. 1969. Treatment of high nitrate waters. J. Amer. Wat. Wks. Assoc. **61:** 659–622.

Stanley, J. G. and P. J. Colby. 1971. Effects of temperature on electrolyte balance and osmoregulation in the alewife (*Alosa pseudoharengus*) in fresh and sea water. Trans. Amer. Fish. Soc. **100:** 624–638.

Stark, W. H., J. Stadler, and E. McCoy. 1938. Some factors affecting the bacterial population of fresh water lakes. J. Bacteriol. **36:** 653–654.

Starr, R. C. 1973. Apparatus and maintenance. *In* Handbook of phycological methods, J. R. Stein (ed.). Cambridge Univ. Press, Cambridge, pp. 171–179.

Steinmüller, W. and B. Bock. 1977. Enzymatic studies on autotrophically, mixotrophically and heterotrophically grown *Nitrobacter agilis* with special reference to nitrite oxidase. Arch. Microbiol. **115:** 51–54.

Stevens, E. D., G. R. Beenion, D. J. Randall, and G. Shelton. 1972. Factors affecting arterial pressures and blood flow from the heart in intact, unrestrained lingcod, *Ophiodon elongatus*. Comp. Biochem. Physiol. **43A:** 681–695.

Stopka, K. 1975. European and Canadian experiences with ozone in controlled closed circuit fresh and salt water systems. *In* Aquatic applications of ozone, W. J. Blogoslawski and R. G. Rice (eds.). Internat. Ozone Inst., Cleveland, pp. 170–176.

Stopka, K. 1978. Ozone-activated carbon can remove organics. Wat. Sew. Wks. **125(5):** 88.

Strickland, J. D. H., O. Holm-Hansen, R. W. Eppley, and R. J. Linn. 1969. The use of a deep tank in plankton ecology. I. Studies of the growth and composition of phytoplankton crops at low nutrient levels. Limnol. Oceanogr. **14:** 23–34.

Strickland, J. D. H. and T. R. Parsons. 1972. A practical handbook of seawater analysis, 2nd ed. Bull. 167, Fish. Res. Board Can., Ottawa, 310 pp.

Stumm, W. 1954. Der Zerfall von Ozon in wasseriger Losung. Helv. Chim. Acta **37:** 773–778.

Suess, E. 1970. Interaction of organic compounds with calcium carbonate. I. Association phenomena and geochemical implications. Geochim. Cosmochim. Acta **34:** 157–168.

Sumner, F. B. and P. Doudoroff. 1938. Some experiments on temperature acclimatization and respiratory metabolism in fishes. Biol. Bull. **74:** 403–429.

Sutcliffe, W. H., E. R. Baylor, and D. W. Menzel. 1963. Sea surface chemistry and Langmuir circulation. Deep-Sea Res. **10:** 233–243.

Suzuki, J., K. Hukushima, and S. Suzuki. 1978. Effect of ozone treatment upon biodegradability of water-soluble polymers. Environ. Sci. Tech. **12:** 1180–1183.

Swenson, P. A., J. M. Boyle, and R. L. Schenley. 1974. Thermal reactivation of ultraviolet-irradiated *Escherichia coli*: relationship to respiration. Photochem. Photobiol. **19A:** 1–7.

Swenson, P. A. and R. B. Setlow. 1966. Effects of ultraviolet radiation on macromolecular synthesis in *Escherichia coli*. J. Mol. Biol. **15:** 201–219.

Sylvia, A. E., D. A. Bancroft, and J. D. Miller. 1977. A method for evaluating granular activated carbon efficiency. J. Amer. Wat. Wks. Assoc. **69:** 99–102.

Takahashi, T., R. F. Weiss, C. H. Culberson, J. M. Edmond, D. E. Hammond, C. S. Wong, Y-H. Li, and A. E. Bainbridge. 1970. A carbonate chemistry profile at the 1969

Geosecs intercalibration station in the eastern Pacific Ocean. J. Geophys. Res. **75:** 7648–7666.

Taylor, A. C. 1976. The respiratory responses of *Carcinus maenas* to declining oxygen tension. J. Exp. Biol. **65:** 309–322.

Tate, R. L. 1977. Nitrification in histosols: a potential role for the heterotrophic nitrifier. Appl. Environ. Microbiol. **33:** 911–914.

Tchobanoglous, G. 1970. Filtration techniques in tertiary treatment. J. Wat. Pollut. Contra. Fed. **42:** 604–623.

Tchobanoglous, G. (ed.). 1972. Wastewater engineering: collection, treatment, disposal. McGraw-Hill, New York, 782 pp.

Tenore, K. R. and J. E. Huguenin. 1973. A flowing experimental system with filtered and temperature-regulated seawater. Ches. Sci. **14:** 280–282.

Tomlinson, T. G., A. G. Boon, and C. N. A. Trotman. 1966. Inhibition of nitrification in the activated sludge process of sewage disposal. J. Appl. Bacteriol. **29:** 266–291.

Topinka, J. A. and J. V. Robbins. 1976. Effects of nitrate and ammonium enrichment on growth and nitrogen physiology in *Fucus spiralis*. Limnol. Oceanogr. **21:** 659–664.

Truchot, J-P. 1978. Mechanisms of extracellular acid-base regulation as temperature changes in decapod crustaceans. Respir. Physiol. **33:** 161–176.

Uhlig, H. H. 1971. Corrosion and corrosion control, 2nd ed. Wiley, New York, 419 pp.

Van den Driessche, T. and S. Bonotto. 1972. *In vivo* activity of the chloroplasts of *Acetabularia* in continuous light and in light dark cycles. Arch. Biol. **83:** 89–104.

Vanous, R. D. 1978. Understanding nephelometric instrumentation. Amer. Lab. **10(7):** 67–79.

Vernberg, F. J. 1959. Studies on the physiological variation between tropical and temperate zone fiddler crabs of the genus *Uca*. 3. The influence of temperature acclimation on oxygen consumption of whole organisms. Biol. Bull. **117:** 582–593.

Vlasenko, M. I. 1969. Ultraviolet rays as a method for the control of diseases of fish eggs and young fishes. J. (Prob.) Ichthyol. **9:** 697–705.

Waaland, J. R. 1973. Experimental studies on the marine algae *Iridaea* and *Gigartina*. J. Exp. Mar. Biol. Ecol. **11:** 71–80.

Wace, P. F. and D. L. Banfield. 1966. Foam separation. Rpt. AERE-R5189, U. K. At. Ener. Res. Estab., Harwell, Berkshire, England, 24 pp.

Waite, T. and R. Mitchell. 1972. The effect of nutrient fertilization on the benthic alga *Ulva lactuca*. Bot. Mar. **15:** 151–156.

Wallace, G. T. Jr. and R. A. Duce. 1975. Concentration of particulate trace metals and particulate organic carbon in marine surface waters by a bubble flotation mechanism. Mar. Chem. **3:** 157–181.

Wallace, G. T. Jr. and D. F. Wilson. 1969. Foam separation as a tool in chemical oceanography. Rpt. 6958, U. S. Naval Res. Lab., Washington, DC, 17 pp.

Wallace, W., S. E. Knowles, and D. J. D. Nicholas. 1970. Intermediary metabolism of carbon compounds by nitrifying bacteria. Arch. Mikrobiol. **70:** 26–42.

Wangersky, P. J. and D. C. Gordon. 1965. Particulate carbonate, organic carbon and $Mn^{++}$ in the open ocean. Limnol. Oceanogr. **10:** 544–550.

Wardle, C. S. 1972. The changes in blood glucose in *Pleuronectes platessa* following capture from the wild: a stress reaction. J. Mar. Biol. Assoc. U. K. **52:** 635–651.

Warren, K. W. and S. Schenker. 1962. Differential effect of fixed acid and carbon dioxide on ammonia toxicity. Amer. J. Physiol. **203**: 903–906.

Wattenberg, H. and E. Timmerman. 1936. Über die Sattigung des Seewassers an $CaCO_3$ und die anorganogene Bildung von Kalksedimenten. Ann. Hydrog. Mar. Met. **24**: 23–31.

Watson, S. W. 1965. Characteristics of a marine nitrifying bacterium, *Nitrosocystis oceanus* sp. N. Limnol. Oceanogr. **10(Suppl.)**: R274–R289.

Weber, W. J. and W. Stumm. 1963. Buffer systems of natural fresh waters. J. Chem. Engr. Data **8**: 464–468.

Wedemeyer, G. A. and N. C. Nelson. 1977. Survival of two bacterial fish pathogens (*Aeromonas salmonicida* and the enteric redmouth bacterium) in ozonated, chlorinated, and untreated waters. J. Fish. Res. Board Can. **34**: 429–432.

Weiland, A. L. and C. P. Mangum. 1975. The influence of environmental salinity on hemocyanin in the blue crab *Callinectes sapidus*. J. Exp. Zool. **193**: 265–274.

Weiss, J. 1935. Investigations on the radical $HO_2$ in solution. Trans. Faraday Soc. **31**: 668–681.

West, J. A. 1967. *Pilayella littoralis* F. *rupincola* from Washington: the life history in culture. J. Phycol. **3**: 150–153.

West, J. A. 1974. Controlling *Rhodochorton* production. Carolina Tips **37(1)**: 1–2.

Westin, D. T. 1974. Nitrate and nitrite toxicity to salmonid fishes. Prog. Fish-Cult. **36**: 86–89.

Weyl, P. K. 1967. The solution behavior of carbonate materials in sea water. Stud. Trop. Oceanogr., Miami **5**: 178–228.

Weyl, P. K. 1970. Oceanography: an introduction to the marine environment. Wiley, New York, 535 pp.

Wheaton, F. W. 1977. Aquacultural engineering. Wiley, New York. 708 pp.

Whitelaw, D. A. 1973. Sodium uptake and ammonium excretion in the gill of the goldfish *C. auratus*. S. Afr. J. Sci. **69**: 217–219.

Whitfield, M. 1974a. The ion-associated model and the buffer capacity of the carbon dioxide system in seawater at 25°C and 1 atmosphere total pressure. Limnol. Oceanogr. **19**: 235–248.

Whitfield, M. 1974b. The hydrolysis of ammonium ions in sea water—a theoretical study. J. Mar. Biol. Assoc. U. K. **54**: 565–580.

Williams, J. 1962. Oceanography. Little, Brown, Boston, 242 pp.

Williams, P. J. LeB. 1975. Biological and chemical aspects of dissolved organic material in sea water. *In* Chemical oceanography, Vol. 2, 2nd ed., J. P. Riley and G. Skirrow (eds.). Academic Press, London, pp. 301–363.

Williams, P. M., R. V. Baldwin, and K. J. Robertson. 1978. Ozonation of seawater: preliminary observation on the oxidation of bromide, chloride and organic carbon. Wat. Res. **12**: 385–388.

Williamson, K. and P. L. McCarty. 1976. A model of substrate utilization by bacterial films. J. Wat. Pollut. Contr. Fed. **48**: 9–24.

Wilson, T. R. S. 1975. Salinity and the major elements of sea water. *In* Chemical oceanography, Vol. 1, 2nd ed., J. P. Riley and G. Skirrow (eds.). Academic Press, London, pp. 365–413.

Wilson, R. P., R. O. Anderson, and R. A. Bloomfield. 1969. Ammonia toxicity in selected fishes. Comp. Biochem. Physiol. **28:** 107–118.

Witkin, E. M. 1966. Radiation-induced mutations and their repair. Science **152:** 1345–1353.

Witkin, E. M. 1971. Ultraviolet mutagenesis in strains of *E. coli* deficient in DNA polymerase. Nature New Biol. **229:** 81–82.

Wolf, K. 1957. Blue-sac disease investigations: microbiology and laboratory induction. Prog. Fish-Cult. **19:** 14–18.

Woltering, D. M., J. L. Hedtke, and L. J. Weber. 1978. Predator-prey interactions of fishes under the influence of ammonia. Trans. Amer. Fish. Soc. **107:** 500–504.

Wood, J. D. 1958. Nitrogen excretion in some marine teleosts. Can. J. Biochem. Physiol. **36:** 1237–1242.

Woodhead, P. M. J. and A. D. Woodhead. 1965. Seasonal changes in the physiology of the Barents Sea cod (*Gadus morhua* L.) in relation to its environment. 2. Physiological reactions to low temperatures. ICNAF Environ. Symp., Spec. Publ. Internat. Comm. NW Atlan. Fish. **6:** 717–734.

Wooster, W.S., A. J. Lee, and D. Deitrich. 1969. Redefinition of salinity. J. Mar. Res. **27:** 358–360.

Wuhrmann, K. and K. Mechsner. 1965. Über den influss von Sauerstoffspannung und Wasserstoffionen Konzentration des Mileus auf die mikrobielle Denitrification. Pathol. Microbiol. **28:** 199–206.

Wuhrmann, K. and H. Woker. 1948. Beiträge zur Toxikologie der Fische. II. Experimentelle Untersuchungen über die Ammoniak- und Blausäurevergiftung. Schweiz. Z. Hydrol. **11:** 210–244.

Wuhrmann, K. and H. Woker. 1953. Beiträge zur Toxikologie der Fische. VIII. Über die Giftwirkungen von Ammoniak- und Zyanidlösungen mit verschiedener Sauerstoffspannung und Temperatur auf Fische. Schweiz. Z. Hydrol. **15:** 235–259.

Wyman, J. Jr., P. F. Scholander, G. A. Edwards, and L. Irving. 1952. On the stability of gas bubbles in sea water. J. Mar. Res. **11:** 47–62.

Yao, K. M., M. T. Habibian, and C. R. O'Melia. 1971. Water and waste water filtration: concepts and applications. Environ. Sci. Tech. **5:** 1105–1112.

Yoshida, Y. 1967. Studies on the marine nitrifying bacteria, with special reference to characteristics and nitrite formation of marine nitrite formers. Bull. Misaki Mar. Biol. Inst., Kyoto Univ., No. 11, 58 pp.

Yoshida, Y., A. Kawai, and M. Kimata. 1967. Studies on marine nitrifying bacteria (nitrite formers and nitrate formers)—V. Effects of environmental factors on the nitrite formation of cell free extracts of a marine nitrifying bacterium. Bull. Jap. Soc. Sci. Fish. **33:** 421–425.

Yoshida, Y. and M. Kimata. 1967. Studies on marine nitrifying bacteria (nitrite formers and nitrate formers)—VII. Distribution of marine nitrifying bacteria in the offshore regions. Bull. Jap. Soc. Sci. Fish. **33:** 578–585.

Zafiriou, O. C. and M. B. True. 1977. The determination of nitrite in sea waters—a revision concerning standardization. Anal. Chim. Acta **92:** 223–225.

Zelac, R. E., H. L. Cromroy, W. E. Bolch, B. G. Dunavant, and H. A. Bevis. 1971. Inhaled ozone as a mutagen. II. Effects on the frequency of chromosome aberrations observed in irradiated Chinese hamsters. Environ. Res. **4:** 325–342.

Zerbe, W. B. and C. B. Taylor. 1953. Sea water temperature and density reduction tables. Spec. Publ. 198, U. S. Coast Geodetic Surv., 21 pp.

ZoBell, C. E. 1970. Substratum as an environmental factor for aquatic bacteria, fungi and blue-green algae. *In* Marine ecology: a comprehensive treatise on life in oceans and coastal waters, Vol. 1, Part 3, O. Kinne (ed.). Wiley, London, pp. 1251–1270.

ZoBell, C. E. and D. Q. Anderson. 1936. Observations on the multiplication of bacteria in different volumes of stored seawater. Biol. Bull. **71:** 324–342.

# Index

Absorbance:
  in ammonia test, 314
  in nitrate test, 319
  in nitrite test, 318
  in reactive phosphate test, 312
Acclimation temperature, 129, 293
*Acetabularia*, 13, 17
Acetate:
  excretion by algae, 91
  synthesis by nitrifiers of, 123
  use in dissimilation, 143
  utilization by nitrifiers of, 122
Acetazolamide, 278, 279
*Achromobacter*, 139
Acid-base balance:
  effect of ammonia, 286
  handling and, 307, 308
  maintenance by ion exchanges, 279
  regulation of, 298-309
  salinity effect on, 298, 305, 307
  as stress-related factor, 275
  temperature effect on, 293, 298, 305, 307
  ventilation rate and, 298-301, 304-306
Acidosis:
  from ammonia, 286
  from Bohr effect, 307, 308
  hyperoxia and, 300, 308
  relative alkalinity and, 305
Acids:
  buffer capacity and, 74, 78
  production by oxidation, 74
  *see also* Organic acids

Activated carbon:
  DOC adsorption by, 217
  manufacture of, 217
  ozonation and, 266, 274
  physical adsorption by, 209
  removal of organics by, 266
  sizes of, 217, 218
  *see also* Granular activated carbon
Activated sludge:
  denitrification in, 140, 142
  heavy metal toxicity in, 128, 129
  toxicants in, 123
Active transport:
  of ammonium ion, 277-283
  concentration of elements by, 33
  definition of, 27, 28
Activity:
  definition in thermodynamics, 320
  of hydrogen ion, 321
Admirality bronze, 183
Adrenaline:
  handling stress and, 296
  heat stress and, 294
Adsorbate:
  activated carbon pore size and, 217
  definition of, 209
  removal by GAC, 218-220
Adsorbent:
  definition of, 209
  GAC as, 218, 219
Adsorption isotherm:
  definition of, 218

**371**

*Anthocidaris,* 288
Anthracite:
  effective size, 173
  as granular medium, 165, 190
  in high-rate filters, 168, 172
  loss during backwash, 176
  specific gravity of, 174
  terminal settling velocity of, 176
  uniformity coefficient of, 173
  *see also* Coal
*Anthrobacter,* 121
Antibacterial agents, 127
Antibiotics:
  compared with UV, 272
  versus disinfection, 228
Antirachitic range, 229
Aquarium of Niagara Falls, 47, 159, 194
Aquarium Systems, Inc., 43, 64
Aquarium tanks:
  heat flow in, 1, 5-9
  as mixing containers, 43
Aragonite, 81, 83
Argon gas, 234, 235
Arthropods, 223
Artificial seawater:
  aeration of, 43
  buffer capacity of, 77
  characterization of, 42
  contamination of, 43
  as culture medium, 26
  description of, 41-54
  mixing of, 43-54
  prepackaged mixes, 42, 43
  reagent grade components in, 43
  technical grade components in, 43
  trace element addition to, 33, 34
ASARCO Diamond Line[R] Zinc Anode
  Ribbon, 188
*Ascophyllum:*
  DOC release by, 102
  effect on pH, 91
  exudates of, 208
  nitrogen release by, 122
Asparate, 123
Asphyxiation hyperglycemia, 297
Assimilation:
  of animal metabolites, 144
  of nitrate, 139
  in nitrogen conversion, 117
Atlantic cod, *see Gadus*
Atlantic mackerel, *see Scomber*

Atlantic salmon, *see Salmo Salar*
Atmosphere:
  buffer system and, 73
  free ammonia contamination from, 314
  gas exchange with, 56-58, 61, 90, 102, 112
  loss of carbon dioxide to, 267
  loss of DIP to, 110
  loss of free ammonia to, 287, 316
  loss of nitrogen to, 117, 139, 144
  venting of ozone to, 265
  wastewater treatment and, 135
Atomic weight silver, 38
Autoclaving:
  of enriched seawaters, 40, 41
  of seawater, 204
Autotrophic bacteria:
  attachment to gravel grains, 118
  dissimilation by, 139
  distribution in filter beds, 158
  nitrate production by, 88
  nitrification and, 121, 122
  as periphytes, 135
  in stored seawater, 204
  time lags and, 151
  uptake of organics by, 152
  utilization of inorganics by, 118, 121-123
  *see also* Nitrifying bacteria

Bacillus, 139, 230
Backwash:
  of DE filters, 192, 196, 198, 201, 202
  description of, 174
  factors affecting, 172
  filter media depth and, 177
  flow rate for, 172, 175, 176
  fluidization and, 173, 176
  gravel shape for, 178
  of high-rate filters, 172
  intermixing of filter media, 173, 174, 183
  optimum conditions for, 176
  of rapid sand filters, 171, 172
  of slow sand filters, 171
  underdrain systems and, 180, 181, 183
Bacteria:
  aggregate formation and, 71
  biological filtration and, 117, 118
  buffer system and, 73, 81, 90
  contaminant removal by, 170
  on GAC, 217, 221
  MLD of UV for, 233
  mutability of, 231